MILLENNIAL GLORY VII

MW01630425

UNITED WE STAND!

A Novel About The Earth's Last Days.

WENDIE L. EDWARDS

Cover design

Braun Edwards © 2008

Published by Seventh Seal Publishing, Inc.

Cedar Hills, Utah

Copyright © 2008 Wendie L. Edwards

All rights reserved. No part of this book may be reproduced in any form or by any means without permission in writing from the publisher, Seventh Seal Publishing, Inc.

This is a work of fiction. The characters, names, incidents, places, and dialogue are products of the author's imagination, and are to be construed theoretical.

Library of Congress Catalog Card Number: 2008902652

ISBN-10: 0-9712228-8-6

ISBN-13: 978-0-9712228-8-5

First Printing 2008

First Edition

Printed in the United States of America

The Millennial Glory Series

Hidden Light,
Millennial Glory I

A strange plague breaks out among a rebellious segment of society. The sickness is related to a mysterious man who claims that he is the resurrected Savior of the world. His intent is to hide the light of the truth as he stands in its stead. His words are hypnotic. His message is deadly. Corrynne Rogers is an Intensive Care nurse who cares for those clinging to life. Through her hospital association she uncovers a destructive plan to implant computer chips under the skin of any who worships the false Christ in an effort to control them. Some followers are killed by flesh-eating bacteria as they turn away from the religious leader. Eventually, Corrynne exposes the deadly plan but not in time to protect one of her own from the lethal chip. The Zulu countdown has begun. Fire is prophesied to rain from heaven to punish those who refuse to accept the false Christ. But will it? Time will tell.

Wars of Light,
Millennial Glory II

Bo, the father of the Rogers family, learns that he and his eldest son, Braun, share a gift of dreams and are able to see mysterious things that often tell of the future. Through his dreams Bo realizes that two of his children will soon fall prey to the mysterious Antichrist that is growing in power. Bo is painfully admonished by the Spirit not to interfere but to allow his children to face the evil man alone in fulfillment of agreements they made before their life on earth. How can he do this? Through his trials he learns that an unseen war comprising all of God's children, both good and evil, continues in the world from when it began in heaven. Bo comes to understand that there are greater powers than his own in charge of his life. He is expected to exercise true faith in God's power and not to lean on his own understanding. Can he be brave enough to sit back and trust in Heavenly Father's promises to save his children? It's a request almost too hard to bear.

Apocalypse, the Unveiling, Millennial Glory III

Chaos hits Utah as a large earthquake rips the land apart. The Rogers family must

escape its fury. It's their struggle to see God's wisdom in the trial of the Saints. Dane Rogers lies in a coma induced by the deadly bacteria unleashed in his hand by the chip. In his deep sleep he is introduced to the Spirit World and the reality of God's existence is unveiled. In the world of light he learns of the eternal nature of God, the importance of the plan of salvation, and preparations of the world by both the living and the dead for the Second Coming of Christ. He also learns that this life is only a moment in time but it is in that moment that we define ourselves and our futures. Through the Rogers family's difficulties they become stronger, realizing their true blessings on earth lie in each other.

The Ascension, Millennial Glory IV

Braun, the eldest son of the Rogers family, is directed by the Spirit to fulfill an

internship as an aide to the Secretary General of the United Nations. Through his dreams and visions of beasts and monsters he is able to act as Daniel of old to Secretary Klump to warn him of things to come. Together they uncover an ancient secret design as it unfolds. The man who is one of the richest on the earth plots to take control of the world through manipulating its leaders. Braun feels a great responsibility to stop his ascension to total and complete power, but what can he, a lowly aide, do? Conrad, the second oldest in the Rogers family, is on a mission in Israel. At first, he has limited success among the Jews, but as time moves on the Spirit of truth rests heavily upon him. He is able to be instrumental in the conversion of a group of Rabbis who in turn bring other Jews to the church in droves as they begin to believe in Christ.

Hanging by a Thread,
Millennial Glory V

Braun Rogers travels to America and takes a position at the White House in an effort to warn the President of the danger that awaits the nation. He finds the country in political disarray as the constitution hangs by a thread. Through his visions, he sees the outcome of the present chaos as it spirals toward destruction. The country must return to the values that inspired its beginnings if it hopes to be protected from the secret combinations that are designing its downfall. Brea Rogers, the eldest sister of the family, discovers that she is trapped in an unholy web of deceit as she unravels the truth about her husband, Matt, and his family. The facts are too horrible to believe and too deadly to ignore. She must make some difficult decisions to protect her unborn children. Just what will that do to her love for Matt and the marriage they share? Elder Conrad Rogers becomes a hostage in Israel but his burden is made light through participating in prophecy. The long-awaited Jewish temple rises. The Jews know their Messiah is coming. Do you?

Justice of Affliction,
Millennial Glory VI

Braun is protectively catapulted to the deadliest, northernmost region of the world to hide from the mastermind behind America's destruction. At the same time, Dane, now a soldier in the National Police is caught on the East Coast of America. The nation begins a melt-down that has been carefully planned and executed by that same mastermind and his secret, international associates. Dane must use all his resources and knowledge if he's going to avoid the violent and hungry mobs that rampage over the land. His goal is to make it home alive! Brea is condemned to a life of loneliness in her last term of pregnancy as Matt divorces her to appease his father. Young Carea is ripped from the ones she loves and taken to a prison camp in response to the violence around the nation. She is targeted as a high-risk to the nation's security because of the chip that remains in her forehead. Bo's heart is ripped from his chest in mourning as Corrynne tries to comfort him. His family is falling apart! Did God forget them? Is he forsaking them? Life is full of affliction! Where is their justice?

United We Stand,
Millennial Glory VII

Reeling from the sudden collapse of the American government, the Rogers' family struggles to gain control of their world. Eventually, the UN sends food and financial relief to Utah, but requires each person to give up their American rights and submit to international laws in return for support. A computer chip is implanted in each new international citizen and each receives entrance into a new global economy. The LDS community is surprised as the Prophet sends a message by ham radio to every stake advising all to refuse the computer chip and instead, to look to each other for their needs. Now each must make a choice: do they listen to the Prophet and lose the privileges of economy but maintain their identity and faith, or do they submit to the UN and give up every freedom America ever stood for? Each citizen makes their own choice and communities are fractured, but the righteous are rewarded with spiritual gifts and power as independent tent cities rise all over America under the glorious banner of the flag. They enjoy miracles and blessings beyond their expectations! For country, for liberty, for freedom—for GOD! *United We Stand!*

IT IS THE END OF DAYS AND ALL IS IN COMMOTION!

CHARACTERS

ROGERS FAMILY

Bo Andrew Rogers	46	Father
Corrynne Rochelle Rogers	43	Mother
Braun Joseph Rogers	22	First Son
Conrad Ryan Rogers	21	Second Son
Brea Nicole Rogers	20	First Daughter
Dane Russell Rogers	19	Third Son
Carea Lorrell Rogers	18	Second Daughter
Jax William Rogers	12	Fourth Son
Ry Benjamin Rogers	10	Fifth Son
Rocwell Joshua Rogers	8	Sixth Son
Striynna Chandelle Rogers	2	Third Daughter
		First Twin
Strykker Adam Rogers	2	Seventh Son
		Second Twin

TABLE OF CONTENTS

REVIEW: JUSTICE OF AFFLICTION

Finally realizing their love for each other, Braun and Chenille hide from MD in the deadliest, northernmost region of the world. While trying to survive in the sub-zero terrain, they are rescued by John the Apostle and the three Nephite disciples written of in the Book of Mormon. Braun and Chenille see the words of the scriptures fulfilled as they realize that the four prophets have acquired translated bodies at the hand of Jesus Christ. Translated bodies are unable to age, be injured, or die, thus these men who seem young are over two thousand years old! Both Braun and Chenille are surprised and honored to join the prophets to teach and lead a lost people to their inheritance among the children of Israel. But what will that mean for them? Their future is yet to be made.

Conrad continues to serve the people of Israel in building the Jewish temple, as the two apostles preach the good news to those who will listen.

Brea is condemned to a life of loneliness in her last term of pregnancy. She must go into hiding if she's going to protect her unborn children. What is going to happen to them?

Matt divorces Brea to appease his father. He is taught the ways of world domination and control; however, there is a price—loss of *everything* he values. Can he endure the pain and ignore his heart so he might turn the tables on his father? He doesn't know. It's a big gamble, one he can't afford to lose.

Dane, now a soldier in the National Police, is caught on the East Coast of the United States as the nation begins a carefully planned and prophesied melt-down. In his struggle to stay alive, he discovers Nebraska, a trapped and suddenly orphaned, five-year-old girl. Dane is vigilant as he protects Nebraska in their escape from New York City. When the way home seems impossible, Dane and Nebraska meet Louise, a middle-aged, well-to-do professor, who holds the key to their safe passage. From there, their situation becomes very bizarre.

Carea, because of the chip in her forehead, is deemed a security risk to the nation and is sent to a prison camp in Alaska run by prisoners. Now, among violent strangers, it's her challenge to make the best of things. Since there's nothing else to lose, she develops a cunning and brave plan to assure her survival. Soon, *she* will be their leader.

Bo's heart is ripped from his chest in mourning as Corrynne tries to comfort him. His family is falling apart! His oldest five children are missing! Are they alive? Did God forget them? Where is their justice? Only God knows.

PREVIOUSLY...

Last Moments

Provo, Utah

Bo settled on the only channel that seemed to work. It was a broadcast out of Europe.

The British reporter spoke rapidly, "...Tragedy continues in the United States as internal strife mounts due to a seized economy."

There was no money in America. All of it had been sucked out of every bank to pay the nation's international debts. Bo had been told his Credit Union still had some, but not much. He had a feeling it wouldn't be long until all the money was completely gone. It was good that Corrynne still worked at the hospital. Bo figured the health care system would be the last to fail.

"...A large death toll claims the East Coast in cities such as New York, Baltimore, Washington, D.C., and Miami," continued the reporter.

Bo's eyes moved from image to image as they flashed on the screen. He was thankful it was still relatively peaceful in Provo—at least around his home. Community emergency supplies had staved off panic. He hoped it would stay that way.

"The dead go unburied as the nation turns its attention to finding food and water. Security systems are failing as the military struggles to control looting. From Mexico, people are flowing into America by the hundreds of thousands on foot. The UN has set up over one hundred relief stations throughout the more populated areas of the United States to distribute food and water, but it isn't enough for the struggling nation."

Bo reviewed in his mind his supply of food and water. He was lucky to have saved enough food for his family for two years. They would have to purify any water that might come out of the tap because he heard the purification systems were down, but that was OK. It was the least of his problems. At least they'd have water.

"...Gasoline is unavailable in America so no relief aid is obtainable outside the UN-facilitated relief zones. The death of millions seems inevitable..."

This news was painful. Bo closed his eyes and rubbed his face hard with his hands. Things were going to get tough in the other parts of the nation. He was glad he didn't have to watch America dissolve. Just knowing it was happening was bad enough.

Orem, Utah

"Dane!" said Louise as the car began to sputter. "The engine light is on. It's overheating!"

Dane sat forward and looked at the dashboard. Right then, the car jerked and hissed, dying in the middle of the street. Smoke streamed out from under the hood.

Retrieving his gun, Dane slipped it into his waistband. "I'll go out and see what's going on. You guys stay in the car."

"Fine," said Louise.

"OK," whined Nebraska, who was staring out the window at a closed McDonalds. She was hungry for french fries.

Dane stepped out of the car, closed the door and then crawled under the front to see if there was an oil leak. He knew that a crack in the pan was probably the reason the engine had overheated. The bottom of the car had scraped the asphalt after they had taken air from a bump in the road a ways back. They had been speeding to escape road pirates.

"Is there a problem?" asked a deep voice from the street.

Dane noticed shiny black shoes and dark pants from his vantage point. Most likely it was a police officer. Slowly, he crawled out from under the car as he was told.

Suddenly, there was a scurry of feet. "He's got a weapon! He's got a weapon!" said a different voice.

"Hands up! Don't reach for your gun! We have you surrounded. Keep your hands up!"

Dane did as he was told but then his wrists were jerked down and pulled behind his back. He was handcuffed as his gun was pulled from his waist.

"What are you doing out here, soldier?" asked the first policeman as he tightened the cuffs.

"Did you defect? Are you a deserter?" asked a second.

"No! I'm not a deserter!" Dane exclaimed.

"What military are you from?" asked the first again.

"The National Police."

"I found more weapons in here," called out a third officer, rifling through the back seat of the car while Nebraska and Louise huddled in the front.

"Hey!" yelled Dane. "I need my gear. That's federal property!"

"Shut up!" said the first officer putting an elbow in Dane's back. "Only speak when we ask you a question."

"Hey! What's that?" asked another officer with a strange tone to his voice.

"What?" asked a third.

"*I've been bit*!" the second said, batting something out of the air.

Dane looked up in time to see a swarm of bugs attacking the four officers. The first officer released his grip on Dane as he too fought off the stinging insects.

Dane ducked and then half crawled, half wiggled under the car again. There wouldn't be any bugs under there, since it was so hot. He watched a few minutes of yelling and running from underneath the car, and then together, all four officers fell onto the pavement. Something *strange* was going on.

"Dane?" called Louise.

"Dane?" mimicked Nebraska as she looked under the car. "Come out."

Dane crawled from under the car. "What happened out here?" he asked, looking from one unconscious officer to another, then back to Louise as she unlocked his cuffs.

"Louise got those guys with her bugs," said Nebraska.

Louise maintained an innocent look and ignored Dane's question as well as Nebraska's comment. "Let's go. Which way to your house?"

"...Who *are* you?" asked Dane.

Louise stared back with cool gray eyes. She looked like she was considering her words carefully. Finally, she said, "You don't want to know who I am. Now just show us which way to go and be thankful you're not in jail."

Denali Federal Prison Camp
Denali National Park, Alaska

"Everyone out!" yelled the prison guard.

After the girls had exited the bus, blankets and packs were tossed on the ground. The doors of the bus slammed with a bang and the bus drove away.

Suddenly, a swarm of people dressed in black fur rushed the girls and stole the gear off the ground.

Quickly, Carea ran after the group. She was fast enough to snatch one bag from a boy's grasp. "That's my blanket and bag, *thank you*!" she said with triumph.

Turning she walked back to the girls, but then she froze as she felt something sharp and cold at her neck.

"Yeah, that's right. Stop right there!" said the boy in a gritty, angry tone. "Those bags and supplies are *ours,*" he said as he reached over Carea's shoulder and pulled the bags from her arms, throwing her to the ground.

Carea looked behind her to see the man-sized boy disappear into a thicket of trees.

"No!" Carea exclaimed. She would not accept defeat! She would get back those bags! With the speed of lightning, she too, disappeared into the woods.

Provo, Utah

"What does the text message say?" asked Bo.

"It says, 'Third to come, three in one, third to leave, but first in your heart, and last to leave again'," said Corrynne, shaking her head. "See? It's a joke. Who would send a message like that?"

Bo studied his wife's face as he seemed to think about the riddle. "I don't know, but I think we should think about this. Who's third in our family, three in one, and third to leave?"

Corrynne contemplated Bo's words. "I'm assuming the third to come means, third to be born. If that's the case, it would be Brea."

"And isn't she three people in one?"

"Do you think it's really her?" asked Corrynne, afraid to hope. "Matt said there couldn't be any communication between us."

There was a swishing sound as a person in a floor-length, hooded brown cloak came around the corner. The hood fell down and exposed the beautiful face of Brea.

"It *is* you!" she exclaimed. It was true! Corrynne burst into tears as she wrapped her arms around her deeply missed first-born daughter.

After a moment of crying and hugging, Corrynne wiped her face. She looked back at Bo and he winked. Then it dawned on her; he had known about this. Somehow he had arranged it. She held out an arm to him and he and Strykker joined the group. Together they all stood in each other's arms. The joy was beyond words. They had been blessed!

Frankfurt, Germany

Men in black robes and hoods poured into the library from an unknown door. "What's this?" Matt asked his father. "Wait!"

MD stood and pulled up his waistband. "It will be easier if you don't fight us."

"What will be easier? ...Dad! I did everything you asked! *Wait!*" he stood and faced the hooded men. *"What are you doing?"*

"What I should have done a long time ago," said MD as Matt's hands were tied behind his back. "Take him," said MD in a frightening voice that wasn't his own. The evil in the room was overwhelming.

Matt stared at his father in disbelief. Then he understood...playing games with the devil wouldn't be without its price. He closed his eyes in excruciating inner turmoil as he was led away down a winding stone staircase into his father's secret ceremonial chamber.

PROLOGUE

PAIN WROUGHT BY FEAR

"...I will go and do the things which the Lord hath commanded, for I know that the Lord giveth no commandments unto the children of men, save he shall prepare a way for them that they may accomplish the thing which he commandeth them" (1 Nephi 3:7).

Monday, September 22nd

Go, Preach, Save

In the confines of the mind
In a space with no time

Bo feasted on his dreams.[1] Many entered and exited his mind. After what felt like a busy lunch hour at a fast food restaurant, Bo was engorged with thoughts. After his meal, the acrid taste of one particular unsavory dream played on, capturing his mind.

The voice of God, communicating through the power of the Holy Ghost,[2] spoke difficult words.[3] In a profound and metered voice Bo was told, *"The path you walk will not be easy. It will be filled with frustrations—and little satisfaction."*

Bo's gut ached with acknowledgement. "Little satisfaction." Those words echoed in his mind. Why did God have to tell him that? Now he knew another trial was coming. That was not good news.

"My people you serve will hear thee indeed," continued the voice, *"but some will understand not; and seeing—perceive not."*[4]

Bo was alarmed. What? *His* people? Who was that? His ward members? After thinking, he decided it had to be. The baptized were those symbolically in God's kingdom on earth,[5] or in his church[6] and called *His*.

"...Why?" asked Bo.

Bo's mind scampered from thought to thought like a frightened rodent. Suddenly, he felt mentally and emotionally exhausted. How could what God was telling him, be true? It couldn't be, he rationalized. He was *sure* he didn't understand what he was hearing. But then, a feeling rose within him that told him—it was true.[7]

"No, Father. Don't let this happen. Not now. There's too much coming at me at one time with money and our jobs disappearing and..."

Before Bo could complete his sentence, a sharp clarification entered his mind. Hardship, even more than already pressed his neighborhood, was coming.[8] It would test the righteous.[9] Some of those he loved among his friends and ward members would rise[10] while others would fall.[11]

"What am I to do?" asked Bo, feeling weak.

Without words, Bo was encouraged to listen carefully to the Holy Ghost in hopes of buoying up those that might have difficulty. He would be told what to say. He was assured that he was a powerful person, blessed with the ability to sway with his words and he was to use his influence through the coming trials for good.[12]

"No, I can't do this!" gasped Bo, feeling completely overwhelmed. He imagined watching helplessly as some of his friends became bitter and angry in their trials, and then abandoning that which they had professed to be true. The consequences of such would mean they could lose everything eternal! As a Bishop, could he just stand by and watch it all happen? Could his heart stand it? Where was the strength of the Saints? Trials normally pulled people together! What was different this time?

There was a pause, then in response God spoke. *"Great wonders will occur in the sight of men,[13] and if possible, even the elect will be deceived."[14]*

With those words, Bo panicked. God was quoting scriptures pointing to an antichrist organization in the last days. Had that time come? If that was true, then the trials that were approaching were *way* over his head! He had dealt with Imam Mahdi, and now his daughter was gone because of it! That was enough! No more! *It was someone else's turn to be Bishop!*

"No, Father…!" Bo said with effort, meaning to argue—politely, but then the voice in his dream began again, shaking him to his core and causing him to lose his voice. He was meant to listen, not talk.

"For the heart of some of my people has waxed gross, and their ears are dull of hearing…"

"No, no, no…" whispered Bo, more to himself than anyone. This was such bad news. Bo had a sudden strong urge to run or maybe hide from God, but where could one hide from an omniscient being? It was a fleeting, foolish thought, but Bo had to admit he had been tempted.

The voice of God continued in his mind. *"…and their eyes have they closed; lest they should see with their eyes, and hear with their ears…"*

"Why, Heavenly Father?" Bo asked in urgency, gaining some of his strength back and hoping to get a direct answer.

The Spirit, carrying the voice of God, whispered to Bo, *"Men love the things of the world more than me."*

Bo was astonished. Love of the world? The world was gone! Hadn't everything worldly just collapsed along with the banks? How could anyone be worldly without money? Something didn't make sense. Would money be restored? What did an Antichrist, money, and worldliness have in common?

The answer didn't come. Instead a familiar admonishment was given. *"Sanctify yourself. Yea, purify your heart, and cleanse your hands and your feet before me, that I may make you without blemish."*

Bo was speechless. He had come full circle. He bowed his head in humility.

"Then, I say unto you, feed my sheep." He was reminded of all his previous dreams where the same theme played out. He was to purify himself and obey without question, searching for opportunities to support the Saints. Hopefully complete understanding of what he would be up against in the future would come in time.

Taking a deep breath he said, "OK, I'll do my best."

Then with a deep, full voice, filled with emotion, God said, *"Through your witness, thou will bind up the law and seal up the testimony..."*

Bo's mind stopped, caught in surprise. His heart was touched by the sound of God's voice. It wasn't so much what God said that affected him; it was *how* it was said. It sounded to Bo as if God was—*sad* as he spoke.

"This will prepare the Saints for the hour of judgment which is to come," continued the voice, *"that their souls may escape the desolation of abomination which awaits the wicked."*

As Bo listened, he realized that although God was all powerful, he wasn't immune to devastation. Through the Spirit, Bo knew that Heavenly Father mourned his lost ones.

Suddenly, Bo understood something he hadn't before. God was just like him! God had emotions and he was trying just as Bo was trying, to save his children. He yearned after every one, and was willing to do whatever it took to prick their hearts to remember him, even if it inconvenienced Bo. Even if it inconvenienced his people...because *judgment would fall upon those in the gospel as well as upon the wicked...In that day, God would not remember them if they turned from him.*

There it was; the source of God's sadness. Bo understood now. A law had been given, mercy held out, but because the mercy would go unclaimed, even by those who claimed to know the truth, justice had to be applied. In the end, when time ran out, there could be no more mercy. In justice even God could not hold back the laws.[15] The symbolically blind and deaf, even among his own people, would be destroyed.[16]

Bo thought about God's words. He thought about his part in teaching those words to his ward members, and anyone else who would listen. He imagined trying to head off Satan as he moved with his anti-God plans. There would be more hard times, and Bo had to be strong through them.

"Father, how long shall I warn thy people?"

"Until the cities be wasted without inhabitant..."

This answer was hard for Bo. He winced and shook his head. Would it really get that bad? In response to his thought, a vision opened up to Bo, and he saw empty streets, and knew at this moment, it was already beginning.[17]

"...And the houses without man and the land be utterly desolate,"[18] continued the voice of God in Bo's dream.

Eventually, desolation would cover the earth. All that would be left of modern man and his accomplishments would be the skeletons of his buildings and the criss-crossings of empty streets.

"But be comforted..." continued the voice in a soothing tone.

Bo was hoping for some comfort.

*"Those who wish to be mine—**will** hear my voice..."*

Bo bowed his head in thankfulness, before his Father even finished his sentence.

"...And they will be lifted up in the last day."[19]

There, God said it. The righteous would be rewarded. It would all be worth it! If he could just get people to hear that part, he would be successful.

"Behold, I stand at the door and knock..."[20] said the deep, heavenly voice.

Yes, there was hope, thought Bo. There was still more time. People could change their paths. He could make a difference.

"Behold, I stand at the door and knock ..." repeated the voice again.

This was his job, to preach unfailingly through hard times, through times of persecution, through times of devastation.[21]

"Behold...I stand at the door... and knock," God repeated for the third time.

Now Bo was committed. He was to preach[22] to reach those that would listen, to save them, to help them be lifted up and protected from all that was coming on earth.[23] And why would he do this? Because...God was knocking, calling to his children, and as long as God was calling, Bo would be preaching. Why? Because that's what he had been called to do!

Notes to "Prologue"

Go, Preach, Save

[1] Dream: "One way that God reveals his will to men and women on earth. Not all dreams are revelations, however. Inspired dreams are the fruit of faith." Examples of inspired dreams from the scriptures: "He dreamed, and behold a ladder reached to heaven..." (Genesis 28:12). "Joseph dreamed a dream..." (Genesis 37:5). "The Lord will speak to him in a dream..." (Numbers 12:6). "Nebuchadnezzar dreamed dreams..." (Dan. 2:1-3). "Old men shall dream dreams..." (Joel 2:28 and Acts 2:17). "The angel of the Lord appeared to him in a dream..." (Matt. 1:20 and Matt. 2:19). "Lehi wrote many things he had seen in dreams..." (1 Nephi 1:16). "Lehi dreamed a dream..." (1 Nephi 8). (See *Guide to the Scriptures*, "Dreams," www.scriptures.lds.org).

[2] Prayer, or any communication with God the Father is powered by the Holy Ghost, and ratified in the name of Jesus Christ. For an example of the voice of God answering a simple man's prayer, like Bo, see Enos 1: 4-6.

"And my soul hungered; and I kneeled down before my Maker, and I cried unto him in mighty prayer and supplication for mine own soul; and all the day long did I cry unto him; yea, and when the night came I did still raise my voice high that it reached the heavens. And there came a voice unto me, saying: Enos, thy sins are forgiven thee, and thou shalt be blessed. And I, Enos, knew that God could not lie; wherefore, my guilt was swept away."

[3] The Lord doesn't always speak peace to our souls. Sometimes, he asks us to do difficult things that we wish to either ignore or hide from. See the story of Jonah: "Now the word of the LORD came unto Jonah the son of Amittai, saying, Arise, go to Nineveh, that great city, and cry against it; for their wickedness is come up before me. But Jonah rose up to flee unto Tarshish from the presence of the LORD" (Jonah 1:1-2).

[4] "And upon my house shall it begin, and from my house shall it go forth, saith the Lord; First among those among you, saith the Lord, who have professed to know my name and have not known me, and have blasphemed against me in the midst of my house, saith the Lord" (D&C 112:25-26).

[5] "Verily, verily, I say unto thee, Except a man be born of water and of the Spirit, he cannot enter into the kingdom of God" (John 3:5).

[6] "And again, by way of commandment to the church concerning the manner of baptism—All those who humble themselves before God, and desire to be baptized, and come forth with broken hearts and contrite spirits, and witness before the church that they have truly repented of all their sins, and are willing to take upon them the name of Jesus Christ, having a determination to serve him to the end, and truly manifest by their works that they have received of the Spirit of Christ unto the remission of their sins, shall be received by baptism into his church" (D&C 20:37).

[7] "It is evident that the members of the Church who are not observing the commandments of the Lord in this day will likewise experience the wrath of God. This chastening will serve as a valuable purpose in helping the Church prepare the world for the coming of the Lord. Many great tasks await the Lord's people if the world is to be ready for the return of the Savior. These chastening judgments will tend to weed out the wicked and unfaithful membership of the Church so that the Lord will have a people who will carry out his will in all things. Many of the prophets have testified that the judgments of God would come upon the Church because some of its members do not keep their covenants. Joseph F. Smith, who later became sixth president of the Church of Jesus Christ of Latter-day Saints, bore witness to this fact in a general conference address in 1880. '...I further testify, that unless the Latter-day Saints will live their religion, keep their covenants with God and their brethren, honor the Priesthood which they bear, and try faithfully to bring themselves into subjection to the laws of God, they will be the first to fall beneath the judgments of the Almighty, for his judgment will begin at his own house'" (Gerald N. Lund, *The Coming of the Lord*, pg. 71).

[8] "After a while the gentiles will gather by the thousands to this place, and Salt Lake City will be classed among the wicked cities of the world. A spirit of speculation and extravagance will take possession of the Saints, and the results will be financial bondage. Persecution comes next and all true Latter-day Saints will be tested to the limit. Many will apostatize and others will be still not knowing what to do. ...Before that day comes, however, the Saints will be put to tests that will try the integrity of the best of them. The pressure will become so great that the more righteous among them will cry unto the Lord day and night until deliverance comes" (Heber C. Kimball, May 23 1931, *Deseret News*, pg. 3).

[9] "But we believe that these severe, natural calamities are visited upon men by the Lord for the good of his children, to quicken their devotion to others, and to bring out their better natures, that they may love and serve him. We believe, further that they are the heralds and tokens of his final judgment, and the schoolmasters to teach the people to prepare themselves, by righteous living, for the coming of the Savior to reign upon the earth, when every knee shall bow and every tongue confess that Jesus is the Christ" (Joseph F. Smith, *The Improvement Era*, June, 1906, pg. 654).

[10] "Zion is not going to be moved out of her place. The Lord will plead with her strong ones, and if she sins he will chastise her until she is purified before the Lord. I do not pretend to tell how much sorrow you or I are going to meet with before the coming of the Son of Man. That will depend upon our conduct" (Wilford Woodruff, 1889, *Millennial Star*, Vol. 51, pg. 547).

[11] "If the Latter-day Saints do not desist from running after the things of this world, and begin to reform and do the work the Father has given them to do, they will be found wanting, and they, too, will be swept away and counted as unprofitable servants" (Brigham Young, *Journal of Discourses,* October 8, 1876, Vol. 18, pg. 262).

[12] "It matters not what the minds and feelings of men are, the Lord is determined to raise up a people that will worship him; and if he has to whip and scourge, and drive us through a whole generation, he will chastise us until we are willing to submit to righteousness and truth, or until we are like clay in the hands of the potter. The chastisements we have had from time to time have been for our good, and are essential to learn wisdom, and carry us through a school of experience we never could have passed through without. I hope, then, that we may learn from the experience we have had to be faithful and humble, and be passive in the hands of God, and do his commandments..." (Wilford Woodruff, *Journal of Discourses*, February 25, 1855, Vol. 2, pg. 198).

[13] "And I beheld another beast coming up out of the earth; and he had two horns like a lamb, and he spake as a dragon...and he doeth great wonders, so that he maketh fire come down from heaven on the

earth in the sight of men, And deceiveth them that dwell on the earth by the means of those miracles which he had power to do in the sight of the beast..." (Revelation 13:11, 13-14).

[14] "For there shall arise false Christs, and false prophets, and shall shew great signs and wonders; insomuch that, if it were possible, they shall deceive the very elect" (Matthew 24:24).

[15] "But there is a law given, and a punishment affixed, and a repentance granted; which repentance, mercy claimeth; otherwise, justice claimeth the creature and executeth the law, and the law inflicteth the punishment; if not so, the works of justice would be destroyed, and God would cease to be God. But God ceaseth not to be God, and mercy claimeth the penitent, and mercy cometh because of the atonement; and the atonement bringeth to pass the resurrection of the dead; and the resurrection of the dead bringeth back men into the presence of God; and thus they are restored into his presence, to be judged according to their works, according to the law and justice. For behold, justice exerciseth all his demands, and also mercy claimeth all which is her own; and thus, none but the truly penitent are saved. What, do ye suppose that mercy can rob justice? I say unto you, Nay; not one whit. If so, God would cease to be God. And thus God bringeth about his great and eternal purposes, which were prepared from the foundation of the world. And thus cometh about the salvation and the redemption of men, and also their destruction and misery" (Alma 42:22-26).

[16] "And thus we see that except the Lord doth chasten his people with many afflictions, yea, except he doth visit them with death and with terror, and with famine and with all manner of pestilence, they will not remember him" (Helaman 12:3).

[17] "And thus, with the sword and by bloodshed the inhabitants of the earth shall mourn; and with famine, and plague, and earthquake, and the thunder of heaven, and the fierce and vivid lightning also, shall the inhabitants of the earth be made to feel the wrath, and indignation, and chastening hand of an Almighty God, until the consumption decreed hath made a full end of all nations" (D&C 87:6).

[18] This section was inspired by counsel the Lord gave Isaiah that parallels our day. "And he said, Go, and tell this people, Hear ye indeed, but understand not; and see ye indeed, but perceive not. Make the heart of this people fat, and make their ears heavy, and shut their eyes; lest they see with their eyes, and hear with their ears, and understand with their heart, and convert, and be healed. Then said I, Lord, how long? And he answered, until the cities be wasted without inhabitant, and the houses without man, and the land be utterly desolate" (Isaiah 6:9-11).

[19] "Hear my words and learn of me; for I do know that whosoever shall put their trust in God shall be supported in their trials, and their troubles, and their afflictions, and shall be lifted up at the last day" (Alma 36:3).

[20] "Behold, I stand at the door, and knock: if any man hear my voice, and open the door, I will come in to him, and will sup with him, and he with me" (Revelation 20:3).

[21] "Lift up your voices and spare not. Call upon the nations to repent, both old and young, both bond and free, saying: Prepare yourselves for the great day of the Lord For if I, who am a man, do lift up my voice and call upon you to repent, and ye hate me, what will ye say when the day cometh when the thunders shall utter their voices from the ends of the earth, speaking to the ears of all that live, saying—Repent, and prepare for the great day of the Lord? Yea, and again, when the lightnings shall streak forth from the east unto the west, and shall utter forth their voices unto all that live, and make the ears of all tingle that hear, saying these words—Repent ye, for the great day of the Lord is come?" (D&C 43: 20-22).

[22] "Wherefore, labor ye, labor ye in my vineyard for the last time—for the last time call upon the inhabitants of the earth. For in mine own due time will I come upon the earth in judgment, and my people shall be redeemed and shall reign with me on earth" (D&C 43:28-29).

[23] "And again, the Lord shall utter his voice out of heaven, saying: Hearken, O ye nations of the earth, and hear the words of that God who made you. O, ye nations of the earth, how often would I have gathered you together as a hen gathereth her chickens under her wings, but ye would not! How oft have I called upon you by the mouth of my servants, and by the ministering of angels, and by mine own voice, and by the voice of thunderings, and by the voice of lightnings, and by the voice of

tempests, and by the voice of earthquakes, and great hailstorms, and by the voice of famines and pestilences of every kind, and by the great sound of a trump, and by the voice of judgment, and by the voice of mercy all the day long, and by the voice of glory and honor and the riches of eternal life, and would have saved you with an everlasting salvation, but ye would not! Behold, the day has come, when the cup of the wrath of mine indignation is full" (D&C 43:23-26).

CHAPTER ONE

THE POWERS THAT BE

"And they who are in the north countries shall come in remembrance before the Lord; and their prophets shall hear his voice, and shall no longer stay themselves; and they shall smite the rocks, and the ice shall flow down at their presence. And a highway shall be cast up in the midst of the great deep" (D&C 133:26-27).

00:03:08, 05:45:22, Zulu
Monday, September 22nd

The Genesis of a Second Exodus

Yamal Peninsula, Russia
9:15 p.m.

After Braun and Chenille's wedding ceremony, John called an emergency meeting with his brethren. Land had risen from the depths of the Pacific Ocean and now, it was time for the tribes to start their collective journeys. Kneeling, John scanned a crude, native drawing of the Arctic Circle. It lay flat on the tent floor as he and his three Nephite companions studied travel routes.

The companions crouched similarly, knees folded against their chests, their long black hair falling forward over their shoulders as they balanced comfortably on the soles of their feet. Two of them were to John's right, the third to his left.

"Are the tribes in the west ready to move?" John asked the three, gesturing to the map.

"Yes," said the one nearest his right. "All the tribes west of the Laptev Sea will begin their trek tonight."

John studied his map. The west border of the Laptev Sea marked the approximate half-way point between the east and west boundaries of Siberia. "Good," he said. "The tribes should travel in small groups for safety. Warn them, however, to keep a distance from those from other tribes that travel ahead of them."

"What purpose does the distance serve?" asked the companion to his left, as he too studied the map.

"The Russians have eyes in the sky and can see our people move. We are unimportant right now but that will change if too many tribes congregate."

"Ahh, we need to be invisible," said the companion to his left, nodding.

"The Russians are intelligent," continued John. "If their armies realize we are veering from our migratory routes they will attempt to stop our exodus. We cannot alert them in any way. We must stay dispersed, and invisible, at least for now. Eventually we'll have to gather at the coast before we cross, but by then the Russians will be helpless to stop us."

The two companions to John's right nodded in understanding as the one to the left said, "We'll counsel the tribes as you say."

Changing the subject, John asked, "Have you seen the land bridge that has risen from the depths of the sea?"

The three glanced at each other, and then back to John. Each shook his head.

"We have looked, but all we see is water. It is unchanged," said the one to John's farthest right.

"The Chukchi people who live along the coast grow uneasy," said the one on the left. "Their faith is tested because the water's border continues as it always has."

"The land is there," said John nodding. "Assure them of that fact. The water that remains is shallow and will recede when God wills it to. Encourage the people to be patient. Bolster their faith. Remind them that it is prophesied that they will walk across on a highway thrust up from the deep just as their ancestors, the Israelites, did many years ago.[1] All will be rewarded for their patience."

"OK," said the two on the right.

"Direct the Chukchi to live life as usual as others travel to them. It will be a while until we are all together and can cross."

"We'll do that," said the first.

"The journey of those in the west will be difficult. It will take them at least three months by reindeer to travel to the coastal tribes."

"We understand," said the first on the right as the other two nodded in agreement.

"Any other concerns?" asked John.

The second companion to the right said, "Yes. There is something important we need to discuss."

"What is it?" asked John.

"The Russians have been sending people to tag the tribes."

"'*Tag*' the tribes?" asked John.

"Yes, 'tag.' That is what they call it."

"What is 'tag'?" asked John, his eyes squinted.

"We do not know," said the companion on the left, as he checked with his brethren who nodded in agreement.

"We feel uneasy about it," added the first on the right.

"What do the Russians say it is?" asked John.

"They say the tag will help the people eat without herding. It will give them money and passage into the cities. The people seem anxious to try it," answered the first again. "They are promised doctors and medicine to help the young and the sick."

John shook his head. "This tag is not good. It will reveal our numbers to the Russians. Tell the people to refuse it. We must stay hidden a little longer. We don't need anything from the Russians. The Lord will provide for us. We'll have enough."

"Very good," said the second to the right.

"Now go. Encourage the people. Continue to have them serve each other. Find those who do not know the truth yet about their identity and continue to teach."

"We will," said two of the three.

"Good, thank you," said John,

Then one by one each Nephite bowed his head and disappeared; swept back to the areas of the arctic where they had been serving.

John stood, rolled his map and exited his tent. There was work to do.

Illumination

Orem, Utah
12:05 p.m.

Dane walked with determination. He maintained a slight lead, ahead of Louise and Nebraska. With every step he promised himself he would *not* be bullied into leading Louise Anderson, the wealthy, middle-aged, mysterious woman he had met in Maryland, to his home and family without *knowing* who she was and *if* she was safe! Dane reviewed in his mind what had happened back at the car. It wasn't logical that she could have power over flying insects—and if she did, then Louise definitely wasn't what she pretended to be! The thought made Dane very uncomfortable.

Dane glanced over his shoulder then he turned back. Who was she? Now that he thought about it, Louise looked familiar, but from where? A magazine? Television? Dane had told Louise he didn't care who she was, but now things were different. Way different.

A memory of grown men hollering, police officers being bit by flying bugs echoed again in his mind. It replayed over and over. Dane shook his head. He was stumped. What had happened? What *bugs* bit the police? Could there be some sort of technology that controlled insects?

Dane looked back again briefly, but this time, he was caught. Louise met his look with a restrained but satisfied stare. He could tell she knew he was wondering about her. What should he do now? Right then and there he decided. It was time for this charade to be over. Dane slowed his pace so Louise and Nebraska could catch up. When Louise was near, in a low voice he said, "We have to talk before we go any farther."

"Dane, I'm hungry," said Nebraska, looking up at him with hopeful eyes. "Do you have anything to eat?"

"Why?" asked Louise, ignoring Nebraska, looking at Dane like she knew full well what was about to transpire.

"Isn't it obvious?" asked Dane feeling a little irritated.

Nebraska put her hands in Dane's vest pocket, oblivious to the conversation happening over her head. "Do you have raisins left?"

"No," Dane answered Nebraska, pulling her hands out of his pockets but at the same time, reaching into an inside vest where he pulled his very last package of dehydrated fruit and nuts.

"Yeeeeah!" she said as her eyes lit up. "Is that chocolate?"

"No," said Dane. "But you'll like it," he said as he ripped the package open. After giving the food to Nebraska, he returned his attention to Louise. Continuing in a low voice, and with a finger pointing at the ground, he said, "You need to come clean with me. *Now*."

Louise gazed at something off in the distance and shook her head. With a look of obvious deceit, she said, "I don't know what you're talking about."

Dane called her bluff. "Yes, you do. You're very intelligent. You aren't just anyone. You're someone important, aren't you?"

Louise nodded slowly as if she was considering what to say.

"If you want my help," continued Dane, "don't lie to me." Looking at Nebraska, then back to Louise, Dane didn't know if he should continue in front of the little girl. He was about to get brutally honest.

Louise must have had the same thought because she leaned down to Nebraska. "Do you want to go play on that playground?" asked Louise, pointing to a nearby schoolyard.

"What playground?" asked Nebraska looking around, her interest perked as her package of food was nearly gone.

"That one, right over there," said Louise bending down and pointing at Nebraska's eye level.

Nebraska's eyes lit up and she jumped up and down. "I want to go to the playground! There's a twisty slide! I can see it!" she cried, pointing. "Can I go there? *Please, please?*"

Louise looked at Dane as if to get a confirmation. She was going to allow him to make the decision.

"Sure, go play. Louise and I are going to talk while you play," said Dane.

"OK!" said Nebraska as she ran towards the playground with renewed energy.

"Now, what were you going to say?" asked Louise as they both followed Nebraska slowly.

Dane scratched his head and said, "I'm sure you understand I have to be cautious."

"Of course. We all do," said Louise, nodding.

"Well, where my family's involved, I have to make sure I'm not leading someone dangerous to them."

Louise gave Dane a patronizing smile. "What makes you think I would harm *anyone* in your family?"

Dane sighed and smiled back, almost in amusement. "Louise, now that I've seen the bad side of the world I've realized there was a lot I didn't know before. I was too trusting. But now I'm different. I'm smarter. I've realized there are few people who deserve to be trusted."

"I understand. I have to say, I agree," said Louise, coolly.

"Good, then you won't be offended, when I tell you you're *not* one of them."

Louise studied Dane for a moment, as if testing his resolve.

Dane hoped his stance and his cold stare said it all. He wanted Louise to know he wasn't backing down.

Finally, Louise nodded. She seemed to concede. To what, Dane wondered.

"I can understand your reservation," said Louise.

Dane nodded, but decided her answer was more political than genuine.

Louise took a deep breath and then with a thoughtful look said, "Let me ask you a question."

"Go ahead," said Dane, bracing for the mind games.

"Have I ever threatened you or Nebraska, or given you reason to think I might be an enemy?"

Dane thought for a moment. She hadn't. But that could have been just a strategic move. "No," he said, "but that doesn't mean you aren't an enemy. The reality of this situation is that I don't know you, your motives, or what's important to you. For all I know, you could decide to attack me or the people I love if I didn't do what you wanted. I'm telling you right now, I won't be controlled that way."

"Of course not!" said Louise with a look of shock. "Look, judge me by my actions. Believe me, if I wanted to get rid of you, I would have let those policemen cart you away, but I didn't."

"I know," said Dane. She had a point.

"In fact, I did the opposite," continued Louise. "I found a way to *stop* the policemen. I *protected* you, despite the fact that I knew by doing so I would reveal too much about myself."

Dane nodded slowly.

"I didn't have to do *anything* in your defense if I didn't want to, and it probably would have been better for our relationship if I hadn't," finished Louise, looking a little flushed.

"Yes, but surely, there's a reason you did put everything on the line," said Dane. "There's something you want from me, isn't there? And it must be more valuable than maintaining your façade. Maybe you wanted to put me in your debt."

Louise raised her eyebrows. "In my debt?" asked Louise taking on an air of amusement. "I hadn't thought of that, but now that you mention it…"

Dane smirked and wagged his finger at her. "No, no, no. Don't play that game with me. Don't change the direction of our conversation."

Louise gave a nod and wiped the smile from her face. "No, seriously. Think about it. Dane, we've helped each other survive equally. When you needed a car, I handed mine over."

"As I did my gas."

"Right, and working *together* we've overcome heavy odds."

"Sure," said Dane, realizing she was right. Without her bug trick, Dane would be behind bars right now. Without his gas and planning, she would still be back in Maryland. All of them were better off because of their teamwork.

"So why would I jeopardize that relationship?" asked Louise. "I consider you a valuable contact. I trust you and that means a lot to me. Like you, there's not many I believe deserve my trust, but I've seen you in many situations and I know you are worthy of the title of Private in the National Police and I feel lucky to have known you, officer."

Dane didn't offer anything. To tell the truth, her speech impressed him. She seemed very comfortable in their debate. Was this who she truly was?

Louise continued, "I'll tell you right now, I'm on your side, Private Rogers. It's in both of our interest to be on *each other's side.*"

Dane kicked a rock out of his path. "OK, Louise, you can stop with the pep talk. I want to be honest with you and tell you how I'm seeing things."

"Please," encouraged Louise.

"I'd really like to take you at your word. It would make me happier and things would be simpler."

"Right," said Louise.

"But to do that, you have to level with me."

"How?"

"Tell me who you really are. I have to have full disclosure so I can weigh things out in my mind."

A pained look came across Louise's face. She seemed like she was struggling. "I ah…ah…"

"Yes?" asked Dane. "I'm listening."

"Ah," said Louise again as she looked around. "Can we sit down? I can see this is going to take longer than a moment."

There was a bench along the playground and both Dane and Louise saw it at the same time.

"Let's go over there," said Dane motioning to the seat.

"Great," said Louise, seeming slightly relieved.

They walked to the bench in charged silence.

Dane was amazed by the heaviness in the air. What could possibly be Louise's secret? It was obviously a big one. He waited with baited breath, and braced himself.

Trek

Yamal Peninsula, Russia
10:15 p.m.

With a cloud of breath, Braun hefted the last few furs from the inside of their tent onto a reindeer-drawn sleigh. The furs had made the bed and flooring of the tent and had been a generous wedding present given to them that day. Chenille joined him with her own load of dried moss that served as soft bedding and insulation from the cold frozen ground of the Arctic.

"I still don't understand why we have to leave *now*, on our wedding night," said Chenille. "Why can't we just leave in the morning?" she asked as she put an armful of moss down and then quickly stole a hug from her new husband. "Shouldn't we have a honeymoon?"

Braun gave Chenille a short, soft kiss and gazed into her eyes. Tucking some stray hair behind her ear he said, "John says our trip will be long and we have to start right away. Don't worry, Chenille. We'll have a honeymoon. A *three month* honeymoon on our journey."

"What kind of honeymoon is that?" asked Chenille with a puzzled look.

"The perfect one," said Braun, smiling. "That's why we were married tonight in the first place, remember? We want to be *married* on our journey," he said with a glint in his eye. "That's much better than *not* being married, if you know what I mean. There's going to be many cold nights and I'd rather spend them under the furs with you, than without you."

Chenille smirked and then said, "But what difference will just one night make?" asked Chenille. "I mean, even if the others take off without us, couldn't we just catch up?"

Braun shook his head. "I don't think so. Don't you remember how lost we were when we were on our own?"

"Sure, but..."

"The snow makes north, south, east and west, all mesh into one. You know navigation isn't one of my strong suits."

"That's true," said Chenille with a laugh.

"I know it's true!" said Braun laughing too. "I normally can't tell which way we're going most times. We can't risk getting lost."

Chenille leaned forward until her forehead rested on Braun's chest and in a disappointed voice she said, "OK, OK, I give in. I see what you're saying."

Braun lifted Chenille's chin gently so she was looking at him. With a smile he softly kissed her. It was lingering and promising. Then with an intense stare he pleaded, "Don't be sad."

Chenille shrugged and smiled back. "I'm not sad, I'm just disappointed. It'll be fine."

"You know, we really aren't different from most people back home."

"How's that?" asked Chenille.

"Most people travel for their honeymoons."

"Yes, to *get away* from people, not rush to stay *with* them!"

"Does it matter?" asked Braun.

"Sure! Everyone will be watching us out of the corner of their eyes, tittering about the newlyweds, all imagining things about us. I hate that."

"Why?" asked Braun, teasing Chenille a little.

"Because it's none of their business!"

"What do we care?" asked Braun. "Let them wonder," he said hugging Chenille close.

"You're right," said Chenille with a resigned smile and a sigh.

Braun slowly swung Chenille back and forth. "Ahh my sweet, sweet love, did you know you're absolutely beautiful?"

"You're changing the subject," said Chenille with a wry smile.

Braun nodded and kissed her again. "I know I am, but I can't help myself. You're overwhelming my brain." With a last hug he continued, "Let's get going. I understand our group is behind schedule."

"We have a schedule?" asked Chenille with surprise. "Since when do these people have schedules?"

"Well, all I know is that we need to be across this continent by the end of December. That's over 3,000 miles."

"Can we do that?" asked Chenille with worried eyes.

"Sure. I hear these reindeer are pretty fast on the snow."

"How fast do you think?"

Braun shrugged. "I don't know, Chenille. I've never clocked a reindeer."

"So then how do you know we're behind schedule, or even if we can make it in such a short period of time?"

Braun shook his head. "Are you trying to be a pain, or just delay our trip?"

Chenille laughed and shook her head. "Both. You know me."

"Yeah, I know you," said Braun with a chuckle as he released Chenille and began to tuck the brown, dried peat moss under the furs on the sleigh. "All I know is that John is in charge. He knows what he's talking about. I just do what he asks...." Then Braun turned and playfully dipped Chenille and nibbled on her ear.

Chenille let out a little squeal. "Braun! No fair! Don't bite my ear! That's cheating!"

"All's fair in love and war," Braun whispered near her ear. Allowing Chenille up, he twirled her out of the dip.

Chenille laughed again and hugged Braun with her head to his chest. "I love you, Braun Rogers."

"I love you too—Chenille *Rogers*," he returned with another squeeze. "Woo. Chenille *Rogers*, that sounds soooo gooood," he added with a smirk.

"I kind of like it," said Chenille wiping her ear dry.

Turning from Chenille, Braun cleared his throat. Then in the most business-like tone, he said, "Now, let's get this tent taken down. You're distracting me. Time is ticking."

Both Chenille and Braun turned to face their tent.

"How do we take that thing down?" asked Chenille.

"Got me," said Braun, scratching his head under his fur hat. "I'm still figuring that part out."

Chenille shook her head and laughed. "We're so hopeless!"

"No, I'll figure it out," he said as he circled the tent. "It shouldn't be hard—but if you have any ideas, feel free to contribute."

Chenille eyed the tent and the center post inside. She bet she could start there. "Wasn't it generous of these people to give us our own tent and skins?" she asked through the walls as she wiggled the support rod.

"Hey!" called Braun. "Get out of there! I'm taking the tent down in a few seconds. It's going to topple and I don't want you caught in it."

"Ooops, sorry. Where do you want me to start?" she asked stepping back out of the tent.

"Around here."

"OK," said Chenille rounding the tent where Braun had figured out how to unwrap the skins from the wood skeleton. As they started to remove the skins it became unstable. Then suddenly, the whole thing fell over with a thump.

"Is that how you do it?" asked Chenille.

"I don't know," said Braun. "It's the way I'm doing it because I don't know any better," he said as he untangled the skins from the wood frame. "I'm sure there's a science to this task, but I don't know it."

"We'll figure it out," said Chenille.

"Maybe," said Braun attempting to lift his load but obviously finding it too large. He began dragging it, instead.

"Wow, how many reindeer skins do you think this tent is made out of?" Chenille asked watching her husband struggle.

"Probably around fifteen," said Braun, his voice strained as he dragged the freed skins to the sleigh. "Including those used as bedding and the flooring."

"That's so many!" said Chenille as she pitched in and tried to lift some pelts to help. "And they're heavy!"

"Ahh, yeah!" said Braun red-faced as he forced them onto the sleigh. "Be careful. Don't hurt yourself."

"Don't *you* hurt yourself," said Chenille.

"I won't," said Braun, throwing the last bit on top of the pile. After roughly piling the skins on the sleigh in a semi-smooth lump and smashing it down, Braun asked in astonishment, "How do these people put up and take down these tents so easily when they migrate?"

"I don't know," said Chenille shaking her head but hiding a laugh behind her hand.

"What's so funny?" asked Braun.

"You!" said Chenille, now laughing out loud.

"Me?" asked Braun as he stood up with a confused look on his face.

"This!" she said gesturing to the sleigh. "Who'd believe what we're doing here in the North Pole?"

Braun stepped off the sleigh and shook his head. "Not me."

The reindeer that was hooked to the sleigh snorted and clawed the ground. "What's wrong, bud?" asked Braun as he patted the buck. "Tired of standing around?"

A horn sounded off in the distance.

"What was that?" asked Chenille looking across the tundra.

"The signal to take off. We have to go," said Braun looking determined. "Help me get this wood on the sleigh."

Both Braun and Chenille worked together to lay the poles, side by side on top of the sleigh, moss and the skins.

"Are you sure those poles are supposed to ride on top?" asked Chenille after they were finished. "Don't you think they might roll off?"

Braun looked at her in frustration, "I don't know. I hope not." Picking up several lengths of leather rope, he threw Chenille one end. "Here, help me lash those poles down so they're secure."

Chenille looked at the rope helplessly. "I don't know how to do that. Aren't there special knots you use?"

"No. Just tie any old knots right now," said Braun down behind the sleigh. "We've got to hurry."

"OK," said Chenille. She squatted down and tied the ropes the best she could as Braun threw them to her.

Finally, when everything was secure, Braun took his place in the driver's seat. "Ready?"

Chenille mounted and sat next to him. "Ready."

"OK, let's go," said Braun. "Yeehha!" he yelled as he shook the reigns.

The reindeer looked back at Braun with a bored expression.

"I don't think you're doing it right," said Chenille, stifling a snicker.

Braun looked at Chenille with frustration. "Thanks."

"You're welcome," she said.

"Yeehha!" he yelled again, slapping the reindeer's back even harder this time with the reigns.

The reindeer blew air through its nose and tugged back on the reigns.

"Here, I'll help you," said Chenille as she dismounted the sleigh and took the reigns.

"What are you doing?" asked Braun.

"Come on, baby," she coaxed sweetly, pulling forward on the straps.

The reindeer bellowed and snorted as he took steps to pull the sleigh.

Chenille smiled back over her shoulder at Braun as the sleigh began to move. "He just needed a woman's touch," she said, beginning to walk faster next to the sleigh.

"I can understand that!" laughed Braun. Then to the reindeer he yelled, "We're more alike than you know! But remember, *she's mine*!"

Chenille laughed as she hopped onto the slowly moving sleigh.

"Yeeehhah!" yelled Braun. This time it worked and urged the deer forward.

Now they were on their way, accelerating by the light of the moon.

The New Deal

Orem, Utah
12:45 p.m.

"So tell me," started Dane, "I think I deserve to know who you are…" he stalled as he studied Louise. She looked stressed by his question. He didn't want the conversation to be so serious, so he changed his angle. "I mean, don't tell me you're some secret FBI agent!" joked Dane, trying to lighten the mood, "Or worse, a *Russian* agent!"

Louise smiled and then shook her head.

"Tell me you're American, at least," requested Dane, still waiting for a response.

Louise became serious again. "Of course I'm American. I'm as American as they come, but as far as being a secret agent, I regret that I can't tell you everything in that arena."

"So you're saying I was *right*? You're a *secret agent*?" asked Dane, astonished.

"No," said Louise shaking her head and holding up one hand. "No, no, no, Dane."

"But you didn't deny it," said Dane, pointing an incriminating finger.

"Yes, I'm denying it now. I'm not a secret agent, but my identity must remain secret as if I were."

Dane frowned. "Now I'm really confused."

Louise nodded and shrugged slightly, "I know this is hard to understand, but my identity must remain classified. My protection depends on it."

"Classified?" asked Dane. That was a strange word to use.

"Yes," said Louise abruptly, shaking a hand as if back-tracking. She looked worried that she had revealed too much. "Please don't expect me to divulge everything. I just can't, especially now that our government has broken down. There are those who would rejoice if my blood was spilt."

"Why?" Dane asked, trying figure out who would want this woman dead.

"I can't tell you that," said Louise with an anxiety-filled voice.

"OK, then..." said Dane, not quite knowing where to go with this conversation.

"All I want is to remain anonymous and continue under your protection," said Louise.

Dane smiled and looked down at the ground. This discussion was getting strange. "So, let me understand this. You're saying you want me to trust you and protect you—even though I don't know who you are."

"Yes, I am," said Louise nodding. "I know that request might be outside what you are willing to offer, but I'm hoping it's not."

Dane nodded slowly as he considered what Louise was asking. Could he afford the risk?

"In truth," continued Louise. "I'm quite vulnerable right now. If you were to decide to leave me here, I'd understand, but know that I have no skills for survival. I have no connections, no resources, no money and if certain people were to find out who I truly was, I'd be dead within the day."

Dane watched Louise. She seemed very anxious. His heart went out to her and for some reason he knew she was telling the absolute truth. She needed him to survive.

"There's only one thing I can offer you that might make you feel more comfortable. I can offer you a promise," said Louise as she held up her right hand as if taking an oath. "I promise you that I'll never be dishonest, threatening, or selfish in relationship to you or your family. I might tell you I can't divulge sensitive information, but know beyond that, I am 100% trustworthy."

Dane thought about Louise's pledge for a moment. Was her word good enough? Did he feel good about leading this stranger home? If Louise was a normal middle-aged woman, would he offer his home to her? He knew he would. Looking deep inside himself, he decided he felt comfortable with Louise, even if she couldn't reveal all that he asked. Then he had an idea.

"OK, Louise. Let's start over again and just decide right now that you are truly Louise Anderson, the college professor."

"I'd like that," said Louise nodding.

"And as far as I'm concerned, everyone has the right to their history, privacy, and their name..."

"Thank you, thank you," said Louise, beginning to get emotional.

"...And I also believe everyone deserves a second chance,"[2] he continued. "What would the laws of Christianity be without repentance and an opportunity to start over?"[3]

Louise's eyes became moist as she looked down before they filled and spilled over. With shaking hands she dabbed her face, getting rid of the tears as soon as they appeared.

There were a few moments of quiet as Dane allowed Louise to compose herself. He watched Nebraska playing on the playground while he waited. There were a couple of other kids playing too. She caught his gaze and waved at him from the top of the monkey bars. Smiling, Dane waved back.

When Louise seemed more comfortable, Dane asked, "So, back to our conversation, are you saying you're in danger, even now?"

"Yes," Louise said with a sniff.

"Even here, in Utah?"

"Yes. I will be in danger until the day I die."

"OK then, tell me what I can do."

"I need a vow of protection."

"But you can defend yourself," said Dane with a smile, referring to the police and the mysterious bugs.

"Only so many times. Soon, my tools will be obsolete."

"I see," said Dane. "Well, soon, mine will too."

"I know, but you have more than just a gun. You have morals, standards, and a sixth sense about you that's unique. I've found you to be very unusual and I feel I can trust you. I'd like to surround myself with people just like you."[4]

"Thank you."

"Also, you have a home and a family…"

"Ahhh," said Dane understanding deeper and connecting the dots. "I see where you're going with this. You want to disappear into a family. You want a network already in place. You think you can hide better that way."

"Well, I wouldn't be so bold…"

"No, I think my family would love to have you join us and I think both you and Nebraska would like my family. Also, I could protect you better that way. You know, I come from a home with seven sons."

Louise stared at Dane for a moment. "Seven sons? Are you serious?"

"Yes, that's crazy, huh?"

"No, that's wonderful! Are they all like you?" Louise asked.

"Some are better—at least in my opinion."

Louise shook her head. "How would it be to be a part of something like that?"

Dane was confused. "Don't you have a family?"

Louise shook her head and took a deep breath, looking out at some distant point she said, "Nope."

"What about your daughter and your home in Las Vegas?"

"I don't have a daughter."

"But I thought…"

"…My daughter died twenty years ago. Her grave is in Las Vegas."

"I'm so sorry," said Dane, now feeling embarrassed for bringing up a sad topic. "But you're married, right? You're wearing a wedding ring."

"My husband died a few years ago, too. I'm all alone."

"No extended family—brothers, sisters?"

"I was an only child. My parents were quite wealthy and loved to travel."

"Where are they now?"

"My father died of heart disease and my mother died of a stroke."

"Wow," said Dane, astonished. He couldn't imagine not having a family. "You must be very lonely."

"I haven't been. My job was my life. I was protected there, but now that it's gone, as well as all the perks that went with it. I have nothing. My world has been replaced by fear."

"Why?"

"One, because I have many enemies. And two, I don't know how to live without room service, butlers, and security."

"I see," said Dane, "you mean it's been a while since you've been normal—a normal citizen."

"No, I've never been normal," said Louise. "I'm quite crippled if you want to know the honest truth. I know nothing of practical living. I'll need someone to teach me."

"Like my family."

"If they'll have me."

"They'll have you," said Dane with determination. "You can bet on that. How about becoming Aunt Louise to our bunch?"

Louise brushed her shoulder-length silver hair to the side and nodded. "Sure, that has a nice ring to it."

"Then it's decided. You'll be Aunt Louise."

"That will be wonderful," said Louise as she put her hand in her pocket. "I have an idea."

"What?" asked Dane.

"How about, as a token of my good faith, in appreciation of you helping me to keep my identity secret, I give you the last valuable thing I have in this world. I give you total control over the assassin bugs."

"Is that what those bugs are called?" asked Dane, very interested.

"Yes. I trust you to use them however you see fit. How's that for trust?"

Dane's eyes lit up but he couldn't tempt himself. With both hands he waved as he refused. "No, I couldn't…that's your…"

"No, I insist," said Louise pulling a metal container from her pocket. "As a token of my appreciation and my good will, I want to give you this weapon. I want you to know that I am holding nothing back."

"Except your true identity," quipped Dane, with a laugh.

Louise smiled. "OK, you have me there. But otherwise, I'm delivering everything to you."

Dane was taken back by Louise's intensity. "You don't have to do this."

"I want to," said Louise, with pleading eyes. "Who better to be a steward over these miraculous machines than the one person I trust with my protection?" She held the metal container out with both hands. "Take it."

"But I don't even know how to use it."

"I'll teach you. It's not hard."

Dane thought a moment. Studying Louise, he saw her desire and her pain displayed at the same time. He could tell there was no other acceptable choice for him but to do as she asked. With a simple nod, Dane put his hands out. "If you want me to have them, I'll take them."

"I do," said Louise placing a thin, gold-colored metal container in his palm.

"Open it," she coaxed.

Carefully, Dane opened the lid. Inside were approximately twenty tiny insect-looking machines.

"Those are flying machines filled with hypnotic medications in an extremely concentrated form."

Dane shook his head. "These are amazing."

"Each bug can sting over a hundred times before the drug is completely deployed."

"A hundred?"

"Yes, and these particular machines have only been used once, so they have many more potential uses."

"On the policemen."

"Right."

Dane studied the scientific wonders. "Where did you get these?" he asked in awe.

Louise smiled and shook her head. "I could lie, or I could tell you I can't tell you."

"Oh, got it," said Dane. "Never mind. Tell me instead what these bugs are normally used for."

"The name tells it all. They are secret machines created initially to fly behind the enemy line in war and assassinate particular targets with pinpoint accuracy. Through these bugs, collateral deaths could be eliminated."

"The military created them then," said Dane, not expecting an answer.

"Originally, yes, but since then, the use of the bugs have evolved to other uses."[5]

"Do they normally carry poison?"

"Yes, but these don't. They carry a drug that just puts people to sleep. I was given these to help defend myself in case I was separated from my normal modes of security. I have no interest in killing people, only in survival. This drug causes the target to be confused with one sting, or faint with multiple stings for approximately fifteen minutes."

"Hmmm," said Dane touching one of the delicate mechanical creatures. "These things are so amazing. How do you control them?"

Louise smiled and said, "There are many ways. You can program a physical satellite address, a chip resonance, if the target carries a chip, or you can use these," said Louise as she took dark glasses from another pocket. "If the target is within sight by the human eye, these glasses read the angle of your vision and are able to pinpoint the target from the eye."

"That's remarkable!" Dane was completely enthralled with the technology. "How do the bugs know how much drug to deliver with each bite, or sting—whatever it does?"

"The glasses have a voice-activated control panel. I simply have to verbalize the appropriate command and the bugs estimate the body surface area of the target and deliver the amount to obtain the desired effect."

"So one sting causes—confusion…?" started Dane.

"Yes, and that's the word you use too. The command is 'confusion'."

"And the second level?"

"The second state is a condition of delirium. So the command would be 'delirium'."

"Got it. And the third?"

"Sleep."

"So sleep is the third command," said Dane.

"Right."

"These bugs cause fainting, is that what you said?"

"Yes, essentially."

"What drug is in these bugs?" asked Dane.

Louise shook her head. "I was told once, but I don't know enough about pharmacology to remember. It was a long word. It was some sort of sedation that's known as a 'hypnotic.' It definitely wasn't a medication I was familiar with."

Dane shrugged. "I guess it doesn't matter."

"It really doesn't," said Louise. "It's used for defense. It's a good choice when faced with the decision to kill, versus temporarily incapacitating your enemy."

Dane carefully took the metal container in his hands and poked at each inactive machine. With a whistle, he shook his head.

Louise watched him and said, "So does this mean you feel good about what we've talked about?"

Dane didn't look up. Weighing everything in his head and then checking it out with his heart, he remembered he had been instructed by Spirit[6] to give Louise his gas. It was true that she had never done anything threatening to him, and it was also true that she defended him when he needed it the most. Dane had to admit that these machines in addition to Louise's obvious vast knowledge might be extremely helpful in desperate times.

With a nod, Dane replaced the lid on the metal container and slipped the glasses into his breast pocket.

"I feel fabulous," Dane said with a smile. "You have yourself a bodyguard for the foreseeable future. I'll protect you as one of my family."

Louise closed her eyes and let out a relieved sigh. Looking up into the sky she nodded. "Thank you. I'm very relieved."

Dane stood up. "I think my family will love to meet you," he said. "Let's get going."

Raw

Frankfurt, Germany
9:10 p.m.

"How's he doing?" a woman's voice asked in a whisper.

"He's doing just fine," said another with a heavy German accent. "His vital signs are stable."

"How are his—wounds?" asked the first.

"They look good; only a little blood on the dressings now. Every day they should heal further."

"No infection?" asked the first.

"No. Everything looks good."

Matt opened his eyes a sliver. He could see the light on. His mother was talking to a woman he didn't know. What were they talking about? ...Were they talking about him?

Matt struggled to wake up, but he couldn't open his eyes long enough. What was wrong with his eyes? They refused to stay open—too heavy. ...What happened? Was he drugged? He felt drugged. He bet....

Matt struggled to remember what had happened to him. Could he remember? Then images, particles of memories, washed over him in waves. Cold stone...Black robes...steel blades...a loud bang...blood, then the sound of laughing. Was this a dream?

Waves of darkness came at him like an unforgiving ocean, drowning him in their truth. He couldn't breathe! Evil...evil was everywhere...there was nowhere it didn't lurk...he was caught...tied...bound...he couldn't get away—"Help! Help!" he whispered.

No one heard. No one delivered him.

Wave after wave continued to come. "...Brea! ...Brea!" Matt called into the darkness. No answer from his beloved. Where was she? Where was his wife? "...Brea!" ...No answer. Had she left him? Was he alone? That thought threatened to snuff out his life.

"Ahhh!" He screamed in terror. Could he live one second more?

Zzzzzzap!

A stinging filled his forehead. Drowsily, he wondered what had happened. It sounded like the chip injector—who was getting a chip?

His body was being pushed into the bed.

"Matthew!"

Someone was calling his name.

"You're dreaming again! Wake up!" the voice, a woman's voice, said again.

Matt's shoulder was being pushed.

He opened his eyes. "What's..." he asked with parched lips. His tongue felt like cotton. "What happened to me?" he managed to whisper, finally freed from the prison of his nightmares.

"There was an accident," said the woman, who looked like a nurse. "But you're OK."

"What happened?" asked Matt as he tried to swallow.

"Your hands were severed, and you lost a lot of blood, but we saved you."

Matt frowned as he struggled to understand. "My hands...?" he asked, now waking up more fully. "What's wrong with my hands?" Matt commanded his arms to rise so he could see his hands.

"You have bandages on, so you can't see your wounds. But I assure you, you will be fine," said the German nurse, patting his arm, as if that would make everything OK.

Matt searched for his hands. He could only raise his arms so far. Something held them down. He struggled to look down with his head. Slowly, he was able to coordinate his limbs, eyes, and head enough that they came into view. Two stubs of fluff on the end of his wrists met his foggy gaze. But wait...his arms were too short! What...

Suddenly, Matt knew, his nightmares were—*TRUE! There hadn't been an accident!* ***His father had done this!***

"*AHHHHHHHHHH*!" he yelled, as he began to thrash about. He could feel restraints on his wrists and ankles.

"Oh," said the nurse's voice in a patronizing tone. "I thought we'd be able to wake you up this time. Nope, no waking for you. Go back to sleep," she said. "We'll try again later."

A numbing feeling flowed over Matt. He realized he had just been given more drugs. He was being put to sleep. No! *He would fight it!* He would....

Notes to "The Powers that Be"

The Genesis of a Second Exodus

[1] "And an highway shall be cast up in the midst of the great deep" (D&C 133:27).

"The 'great deep' means the ocean or a body of water (see Genesis 7:11; Isaiah 51:10). The scriptures do not explain how a highway will be cast up in the midst of the deep for the ten lost tribes to come to Zion. But the language of this prophecy is related to the account of how Moses parted the Red Sea. With Pharaoh and his army at their backs and the Red Sea in front of them, Israel had come to an impasse. Then a miracle took place: a highway was cast up in the midst of the deep, and Israel crossed over on dry ground (See Exodus 14; Isaiah 11:15-16)" (*Doctrine and Covenants Student Manual, Religion 324 and 325*, pg. 341).

The New Deal

[2] "[Christ] set up a new code for living—to love one another, even one's enemies. He enjoined us to judge not, to forgive, and to give all men a second chance. Think what a change this would make in the world today if we as individuals and the nations of the earth could live up to this code. We have often heard people say, 'Well, I will forgive, but I won't forget,' which, of course, means they do not forgive. In Doctrine and Covenants 64:8–11 the Lord tells us that it is our duty to forgive one another, and that he who does not forgive his brother stands condemned and is the *greater sinner of the two"* (O. Leslie Stone, "Commandments to Live By," *Ensign*, Nov 1979, 72).

[3] "Yea, and as often as my people repent will I forgive them their trespasses against me. And ye shall also forgive one another your trespasses; for verily I say unto you, he that forgiveth not his neighbor's trespasses when he says that he repents, the same hath brought himself under condemnation" (Mosiah 26:30-31).

[4] "'A city that is set on an hill cannot be hid. Neither do men light a candle, and put it under a bushel, but on a candlestick; and it giveth light unto all that are in the house. Let *your* light so shine before men, that they may see your good works, and glorify your Father which is in heaven'(Matthew 5:14-16 emphasis added). ...The world expects something better of us. It is not always easy to live in the world and not be a part of it. We have a responsibility to take our places in the world. We can be gracious. We can be inoffensive. We can avoid any spirit or attitude of self-righteousness. But we can maintain our standards. As we observe standards taught by the Church, many in the world will respect us and find strength to follow that which they too know is right" (Gordon B. Hinckley, "Come Listen to a Prophet's Voice: Set upon a Hill," *Ensign*, July 1990, pgs. 2–5).

[5] Mechanical bugs are factual. They have many covert uses and are in the process of scientific evolution towards fulfilling the functions described in the text.

"'I'd never seen anything like it in my life,' the Washington lawyer said. 'They were large for dragonflies. I thought, 'Is that mechanical, or is that alive?' That is just one of the questions hovering over a handful of similar sightings at political events in Washington and New York. Some suspect the insect-like drones are high-tech surveillance tools, perhaps deployed by the Department of Homeland Security. Others think they are, well, dragonflies—an ancient order of insects that even biologists concede look about as robotic as a living creature can look. No agency admits to having deployed insect-size spy drones. But a number of U.S. government and private entities acknowledge they are trying. Some federally funded teams are even growing live insects with computer chips in them, with the goal of mounting spyware on their bodies and controlling their flight muscles remotely. The robobugs could follow suspects, guide missiles to targets or navigate the crannies of collapsed buildings to find survivors. The technical challenges of creating robotic insects are daunting, and most experts doubt that fully working models exist yet. 'If you find something, let me know,' said Gary Anderson of the Defense Department's Rapid Reaction Technology Office. But the CIA secretly developed a simple dragonfly snooper as long ago as the 1970s. And given recent advances, even skeptics say there is always a chance that some agency has quietly managed to make something operational" (Rick Weiss, "Dragonfly or Insect Spy? Scientists at Work on Robobugs" *Washingtonpost.com,* October 9, 2007,;http://www.washingtonpost.com/wp-yn/content/article/2007/10/08/AR2007100801434_pf.html).

[6] "There is a knowledge that our Father in Heaven wants each of us to have, and that is a personal knowledge that he hears and answers our prayers. ...We each have so much need for his help as we seek to learn gospel truths and then live them, as we seek his help in the major decisions of our lives...Our list of needs is long and real and deeply felt. ...But is prayer only one-way communication? No! One of the reasons 'prayer is the soul's sincere desire' (*Hymns,* no. 220) is because prayer is such a privilege—not only to speak to our Father in Heaven, but also to receive love and inspiration from him. ...*'You must study it out in your mind; then you must ask me if it be right, and if it is right I will cause that your bosom shall burn within you; therefore, you shall feel that it is right. But if it be not right you shall have no such feelings, but you shall have a stupor of thought.' (D&C 9:8–9.)* Learning the language of prayer is a joyous, lifetime experience. Sometimes ideas flood our mind as we listen after our prayers. Sometimes feelings press upon us. A spirit of calmness assures us that all will be well. But always, if we have been honest and earnest, we will experience a good feeling—feeling of warmth for our Father in Heaven and a sense of his love for us. ...And since our Father in Heaven loves us with more love than we have even for ourselves, it means that we can trust in his goodness, we can trust in him; it means that if we continue praying and living as we should, our Father's hand will guide and bless us" (Spencer W. Kimball, "'Pray Always'," *Tambuli*, March 1982, pg. 1).

CHAPTER TWO

ON ALERT

"Ye shall walk after the LORD your God, and fear him, and keep his commandments, and obey his voice, and ye shall serve him, and cleave unto him" (Deuteronomy 13:4).

00:03:08, 01:50:22, Zulu
Monday, September 22nd

Emergency Meeting

Provo, Utah
3:10 p.m.

Bo held up his hands, to quiet his friends and neighbors. "Shh, let me have your attention." There were approximately 200 people at this meeting. That represented two-thirds of his neighborhood. He wondered where the rest were. He had sent out the deacons to knock on all the doors of the ward but maybe they didn't get to everyone.

Bo took a seat up on the stage of the cultural hall, placing himself just slightly above his neighbors' heads so he could see everyone. "Let me have your attention," he said again.

The worried faces of those he knew and loved quieted and looked at Bo. He felt the weight of their expectations for him to make everything better. Bo had no idea what he was going to do or say in this difficult situation. People were worried about loved ones they couldn't contact, how they would get to work, and where their next meal was going to come from. He prayed for inspiration. Forcing his thoughts to focus from his worry to the first things that needed to be done, he began.

"First of all, does everyone have what they need? Food, water?" he asked looking around the room.

"Sure, right now we do," said Brother Jensen, a middle aged, man with a large family. "But that won't last long."

Bo was confused. Didn't his ward have emergency supplies? "Now, it has been the practice of our church to prepare for days like this,"[1] he said, looking from person to person. "Who feels like they're prepared right now, with the adequate needs of living?"

Only a fraction of the two hundred raised their hands.

A feeling of worry entered Bo's stomach. How could that be true? "OK. Let's start from the beginning. Who's good for the next 72 hours?"

Everyone in the group raised their hands.

"Good, that's a start," said Bo. "Who'd be OK, food-wise, for a few months?"[2]

There were nods as they looked at one another and raised their hands. Almost all of the people present felt they could last a few months. That was good news.

"Six months?" asked Bo.

Three-fourths of the people kept their hands raised.

"Alright. Now, how about a year?"[3]

Approximately half of his people kept their hands up.[4]

"I've got some things that would last for a year, but not others," said Sister Carver. "I have food, but I don't have things like toilet paper or shampoo."

Bo nodded. "I understand, but you have what you need to survive?"

Sister Carver nodded. "If eating wheat sprouts counts."

"It does," said Bo, nodding. "It does. Might not be what we're used to, but if you have wheat you can sprout for salads, cook for breakfast and grind for bread, you're doing very well."

"Is that healthy—to eat from only one food group?" asked Sister Carver. "I know my digestive system won't tolerate it."

Bo nodded. "Right now, Sister Carver, we're worrying about staying alive. We don't have the convenience of eating from all the food groups at every meal even though, I agree, it's a healthy practice normally. There's no gas, money, or food in the stores. What we have in our homes is it. Yes, I would say, eating from one food source for the next little while or so should be fine," said Bo. Turning to Corrynne he asked, "Don't you think, Corrynne?"

Corrynne nodded. "Anything's doable for a short period."

"Right," said Bo. "My plan is to create a list of what we have as a ward, or maybe even as a Stake, so that we can trade and help each other out through these hard times. If we shoulder each other's burdens, then they won't be so heavy."[5]

Turning to Sister Smith, Bo asked, "How are the elderly doing in our ward? How's your mother?"

"We brought her into our home," said Sister Smith. "She has her own room."

"Excellent. Thank you for doing that."

"It was the least I could do. She raised me and my seven brothers and sisters."

"I love that attitude," said Bo. "Let's make sure all of our elderly and fragile members are being watched over by loved ones. Family is the first choice to be caregivers to those that can't provide for themselves."[6]

Brother Wright, a stout gentleman who was new to the ward, raised his hand sheepishly.

"Brother Wright?" called Bo.

"Ah, I need insulin."

Bo looked at Brother Wright. He didn't look good. "You don't even have a short term supply?" he asked looking at Corrynne for help.

Corrynne shrugged indicating she didn't have access to insulin.

Brother Wright shook his head. "I was getting low and was planning to get out this week and replace it."

"How's your blood sugar right now?" asked Bo.

"I haven't checked it today, but I can tell it's high," he said as he wiped his brow with his handkerchief.

"Anyone else out of some medicine they need to stay alive?"[7]

"I need my selenium," said Sister Carver, with manicured, arched eyebrows lifted as high as Bo had ever seen on anyone.

"Selenium?" asked Bo. "What's that used for?" he asked looking at Corrynne.

Corrynne smiled "That's a trace mineral taken for its antioxidant properties."

"It helps me with my cardiovascular health," said Sister Carver with a hand on her heart. "Heart attacks run in my family. There'll be trouble without it!"

"Yes, but it's available in foods, like wheat, for example," said Corrynne, rescuing Bo.

There were a couple of people in the group that laughed quietly at that.

Sister Carver didn't seem to get the ironic nature of her request, since wheat was all she claimed to have.

"So, I understand, if Sister Carver eats the wheat in her storage, she'll get her selenium? Is that right?"

"Yes," said Corrynne. "She might not get the same dose, but she'll get enough."

"There you go," said Bo, feeling happy Sister Carver's problem wasn't more difficult to solve.

Sister Hodges raised her hand. "I have some extra insulin that Brother Wright can have. My son's diabetic, but he doesn't live with me any more. I just keep it around for emergencies. I don't think it's expired."

"Excellent, Sister Hodges! Now *that's* what I'm talking about!" said Bo in an excited tone. "You made my next point perfectly! Individually, we probably don't have all that we need, but together, I bet you we have more to draw on. That's the most basic essence of the Law of Consecration."[8]

"Yes, but, we aren't living that law, Bishop,"[9] said Brother Wilcox, a historically bitter old man, living in the neighborhood. "And you shouldn't ask us to. The authority hasn't been given to you."

"First of all," said Bo. "I'm not asking you to give up all you have, I'm just asking that we be more aware of the needs of our neighbors and help out, if necessary. And second of all, we should be living the Law of Consecration in our hearts through our tithes and offerings, gifts of time, and our service to God and each other anyway.[10] Remember, everything we have belongs to the Lord, Brother Wilcox. It's only ours because the Lord wishes it to be."[11]

"I understand that," said Brother Wilcox with a sneer. "However, I have a say over *my* things."

"Yes, you do," said Bo.

"And I'd appreciate you not addressing us as if we're children."

Bo shot a look at Corrynne. This was harder with people like Brother Wilcox.

Corrynne smiled reassuringly and gave Bo a nod.

Bo shook his head and rubbed his brow. "I hope you don't feel like I'm talking to you, my close friends, as children. I believe, however, if we're called on to provide the necessities to our brothers and sisters, after everything they can do themselves, of course, that request should not be difficult for us if we are square in our hearts and true to our covenants."[12]

"That may be, but I stored what my family needed, as I was instructed by the Brethren and if I give it away, I wouldn't be providing for my own, now would I?"

"Brother Wilcox, your children are grown and gone..." offered Corrynne in a shocked tone.

"That makes no difference!" interrupted Brother Wilcox angrily. "If they need what I have, it's theirs. I stored it for them and if they come around, I want to give it to them. So don't be expecting me to give up my extra. It's not extra to me!"

Brother Wilcox's statement was punctuated by silence.

Bo nodded. "OK, Brother Wilcox. No one will ask you for your food. It's yours and you decide what happens to it."

"Thank you!" said Brother Wilcox, and with that he turned and left the gym.

After an uncomfortable minute, Sister Johnson raised her hand.

"Yes?" asked Bo, trying to release his tension. He could feel his hands shaking a little.

"Have you heard how long this banking crisis is expected to go on?"

Bo shook his head. "I know what you know. My television is quiet except for a single international channel. I do know that the city has emergency broadcasting stations on KBYU 89.1 FM, KSL 102.7 FM and KSL 1160 AM. You might try tuning in to those channels to find news."

"Does anyone have a portable radio?" asked Sister Johnson. "The only one I have is in my car, and I'm out of gas."

"I have one," said Sister Wilcox.

"So do I," said Sister Coteter, an unselfish mother of six.

"Wonderful," said Sister Johnson. "Have either of you heard anything new?"

Sister Coteter shook her head. "I've been listening and nothing new has been reported."

Sister Johnson nodded, with disappointment. "OK, thanks."

Bo took a deep breath and said, "I expect this situation to go on for a while. According to that international channel, I understand our main government is not functioning and there's widespread looting and violence everywhere else."

"Yeah, whole cities are dead," said Brother Wright, bluntly.

Bo cringed inside. That wasn't exactly what he wanted said at this meeting.

"Is that true?" asked Sister Carver, looking a little shocked.

Bo found himself nodding. "Yes, I do believe it's true."

"What cities?"

"Large ones," said Bo.

"Like Los Angeles?" asked Sister Carver, now looking like she might faint. "My daughter's family is in Los Angeles."

Bo shook his head. "I haven't heard anything about Los Angeles."

"How do we contact our families out of state?" asked Brother Staples. "Does the church have radios that can communicate to other states? I heard they do."[13]

Bo nodded. "Yes, they do, but those are saved for emergency communications. The only way that I know of to talk to people in other states is to have your own ham radio."

"I've been doing that," said Sister Kamp, a woman with three daughters. "My oldest daughter and I have been talking back and forth because we both have radios. It's great. I feel much better knowing she's OK."

"Where does your daughter live?" asked Brother Staples.

"She lives in Jordan Valley."

"Utah?" asked Brother Staples with a tinge of sarcasm in his voice.

Sister Kamp nodded. "Yes, but you're welcome to come over and try and call someone else, if you wish."

"Thank you, Sister Kamp," said Bo, eyeing Brother Staples. "You're very generous."

"What about gas?" asked Brother Cosgrave. "I need to get to work. I work for the city's emergency disaster department, and I have to get there to do my job."

Bo looked around the room. "Does anyone have gas?"

No one offered.

"You could ride a bicycle," suggested Bo.

Brother Cosgrave shook his head in frustration. "I guess I could try that."

"Let's focus on our ward's immediate needs right now," said Bo. "Let's take care of each other, then maybe eventually, things will smooth out and we can go back to business as usual."

"Yes, but you said yourself, you don't expect this situation to get better any time soon."

"Yes, that's what I said. I don't. But that's why we're meeting today and that's why I'm going to ask each of you to inventory what you have in your homes. I want to know everything you have, down to the last salt shaker. Then your home teachers will come around and gather that information. Finally, we'll tally the lists, figure out who needs what and match up families that complement each other's needs. Does that sound like a plan?" asked Bo, feeling good about his ideas.

The response from the crowd was positive, but less than stellar.

"I thought the Church had all this food stored somewhere for times like these," said Brother Krane.

Bo looked at Brother Krane, the eternal college student in his thirties.

"The Church is *us*, Brother. *We* do have food stored up somewhere for times like this, in our basements and pantries. *We* support each other. *We* are each other's help. *We* can dig deep and serve the needs of each and every person here, as well as our non-member neighbors. I know we can. We just need to put a plan into place and no one needs to suffer. There is the Bishop's storehouse food that theoretically is partially allotted to us, but without gas, it's not going to be available any time soon."

"Bishop?" asked Sister Carver.

"Yes?"

"I think we're all just so anxious not knowing what comes next."

"I understand that," said Bo. "I know it doesn't help to tell you that there's no need to be anxious about what's happening, but think about it, anxiety doesn't change a thing. Our environment will be as it is regardless of our outlook."

"That's true," she said with a thoughtful nod.

"Instead, let's be filled with thankfulness for our perception of what lies ahead. Pray for a feeling of well-being and peace and as long as you are doing all that you can to help yourself and others, it will come."[14]

"OK," said Sister Carver. "I'll try that."

"Let's value our independence as a people and feel good that we are prepared to the degree we enjoy.[15] Look at it this way. It could be worse." Bo looked from face to face.

Many were thoughtful, some were smiling, others looked unsure.

"OK?" he asked, trying to conjure up more support out of the air.

"OK," said a few as others nodded their heads.

"Remember," said Bo, trying to have a positive tone to his voice. "Remember the promises the Lord has given us concerning these days. He has said that he will have power over us, his saints, and shall reign in our midst.[16] He has also told us that, his divine intervention would attend us in the midst of tribulation. This means that his church, meaning *us*, will be able to stand independent and be delivered in the last days when we will become rulers in many kingdoms.[17] Do you know what this means?" asked Bo.

The group looked at Bo with blank stares.

"It means we're going to be successful through these times! We're going to make it! The Lord has given us a vision of the future and it's beautiful!"

"I'll be happier, Bishop, once everything's sorted out," said Brother Simonson.

"I understand," said Bo nodding and pointing, gaining energy as he spoke. "Most likely everyone will be." Bo stood up on the stage and with a grand sweeping gesture said, "But *know,* we'll be fine. Whatever needs to happen to give us success, we'll have it. *I know it*," he said confidently. And inside, the crazy thing was, he knew it was true. He was saying it as it was, and that was so—*fantastic*!

"Will we be getting directions from Salt Lake?" asked Sister Wilcox in a very quiet voice.

"Yes!" said Bo, overly excited now. "Umm, Sister Wilcox asked a good question. Did the rest of you hear her?"

Some people shook their heads.

"She asked," began Bo with enthusiasm and a bright smile, "'Will we be receiving directions from Salt Lake?' and the answer is yes! Absolutely! We'll be getting direction through the ham radios that the Stake owns."

"Good," said Sister Wilcox. Then she smiled.

Bo felt great. That smile told it all. He was getting through. "So go home..." he began.

"Wait!" said Sister Wilcox.

"What?" asked Bo.

"Remind everyone to boil their water."

"Oh, yes. Sister Wilcox, you've got things under control. People, please, we don't know if our water from the tap is clean, so everyone be sure to put eight drops of bleach per gallon of water you use, or boil it for fifteen minutes before you use it. And now..." Bo looked around in case anyone else wanted to interject anything more. "I think we're done."

Bo felt like hitting a gavel or something, since he didn't have one, he jumped off the stage and kissed his wife. It was almost as effective!

True Identity

Provo, Utah
8:10 p.m.

Dane carried Nebraska's limp, sleeping body in his arms. Her hands and legs hung down and swung in cadence with his walk. They were making slow time, but now that had to be OK. All of them were exhausted. They needed rest.

Dane was toying with the idea of finding a place to lie down for a while. This trek was taking much longer than it should have. Earlier, when they were only five miles from his home, he had led Louise in the opposite direction thinking he was protecting his family. By the time he found out she wasn't a threat, they had traveled about five miles, making them ten miles from his house. Now, despite walking all day, they still had at least four to go. That was frustrating. Oh, well, no use being pessimistic. It wouldn't help anything.

Louise was limping, but still trying to keep up with Dane. The Achilles tendon area of each ankle was crusted over with old blood from being rubbed raw from her business shoes. She was walking barefoot now. The shoes had been thrown in a trash bin a couple miles back. Good thing it wasn't raining or too cold.

Dane's arms were getting tired from Nebraska's weight, so he adjusted her onto his shoulder. Nebraska continued to sleep as if nothing was different. She was a heavy sleeper.

"How much further?" asked Louise as she tiptoed through some broken glass on the sidewalk. "I thought your neighborhood was closer than this."

Dane shook his head in response to her question, but he wasn't really listening. Instead, he was listening for a different sound, a new sound. He held up a hand as he listened.

"What's wrong?" asked Louise.

"I hear something."

"Like what?" asked Louise, beginning to look around.

"A grinding noise, like wheels rolling slowly on the pavement."

"What?" asked Louise, looking behind.

A feeling of danger came over Dane. Someone important enough to still have gas was following them! *"Trees!"* whispered Dane urgently. *"Run, Louise!"*

As if hit with a hot poker, Louise seemed to forget about the pain in her feet and ran as Dane followed.

Wheels peeled, an engine gunned as bright spotlights fired up. Whoever they were, once discovered, they didn't hesitate to show their strength. A black, large car was almost upon them!

Diving behind a neat row of fir trees, Louise's voice was filled with fear. "It's them, Dane! They can't find me!"

"Who?" asked Dane.

"They're going to kill me!"

"No they're not," said Dane.

The car skidded to a stop, spinning the back end so that its bright lights shone into the trees.

"Who's that?" asked Dane. "Looks like someone important."

Louise was terrified and shaking. She opened her mouth, but she couldn't answer.

Two men dressed in black suits stepped out of the car. Both of them had a handgun. "Madam President?" called one of them as both of them pointed their pistols at Louise. "We can see you. Come out. There's no use hiding."

Dane looked at Louise with shock. *"Madam President?"*

Louise, pale faced and shaking, hid behind the thick fir trunk.

"Come out, Madam President," said the second man again now moving slowly to the side. "You can't run any further. It's time to take accountability for the country."

Country? thought Dane. Was this man talking about *his* country? Suddenly, he saw Louise through whole new eyes. *That's* where he had seen Louise! *On TV!* This was *Grace MacEntire*!

"Madam President?" questioned Dane, with astonishment.

Louise looked at Dane with apologetic eyes.

"Well, why didn't you say so in the first place?" said Dane, with a smile. "Here," he said, handing the still sleeping Nebraska to Louise. "I have *work* to do!"

"No, Dane, you can't win," said Louise in a whisper. "I should surrender."

"No! You shouldn't *surrender*!" said Dane, pulling out his weapon and taking off the safety. With a great feeling of pride, he said, "We're not beaten, and I can guarantee we're not going down without a fight! We're *true* Americans!"

Dane fell to his stomach and in two shots had ripped the guns from the men's hands. Both the men screamed out in pain as they fell to their knees. One gun spun on the sidewalk, the other had landed in the grass.

"Yeah!" said Dane nodding and congratulating himself.

"That won't stop them for long," said Louise shaking her head. "They're killers. You've got to be a killer too. Shoot to kill!"

Dane paused. He didn't want to kill anyone if he didn't have to. He'd never killed anyone before, but he wouldn't argue.

Both injured men retreated, attempting to get back to their car for cover. As one of the men slowed to pick up his gun, Dane shot him in the leg. The man screamed again and rolled on the ground in agony.

Just then three more cars peeled around a corner over the hill.

Now Dane knew they were in trouble! Two men per car, making eight to one—bad odds.

"The assassin bugs, Dane!" coaxed Louise as Nebraska woke up and started to cry. Holding the little girl to her chest she said, "Use them!"

Recognition hit Dane. "Oh, yeah!" He had those bugs! Dane got to his knees and ripped the metal container from his pocket, eager to use the secret weapon before the other men could get any advantage.

"Remember, put on the glasses to lock on the target!"

"How many bugs should I use?" asked Dane, releasing the mechanical insects, one by one by dialing a rotating button.

"One per man. Release eight!"

Dane counted eight and then said, "Run, Louise! I'll take it from here. Get Nebraska out of here!"

"How will you find us?" asked Louise over Nebraska's wail.

Dane waved her off. "I'll just find you! Run!" he said as he slipped the container back in one pocket and pulled the glasses out of his other pocket. Sliding them on, he edged around the side of the group of trees. From this vantage point he'd have a clear view of the men.

The bugs rose and flew out towards the man on the ground. Dane was impressed! The glasses worked perfectly! Wherever he looked the bugs would fly in a swarm, looking for a target, waiting for the command.

The three new cars, identical to the one already parked, slid into place with screeches and their doors flew open. Men dove out of their cars and used their doors as shields.

"Who ever you are, there's more of us than you!" yelled one man. "Put down your weapon and come out with your hands up!"

Dane smiled. Now was the perfect time to strike! The men *thought* they were safe, but he could get to them! The bugs would attack them from the backside...But then, his mind went blank! He couldn't remember the stupid words to cause bugs to strike! *What were they?*

"Faint!" Dane said, emphatically, trying to remember.

An explosion rang through the air, bouncing off the mountains. A bullet spun by Dane's ear. He was being shot at!

"Darn! They saw me!" he said under his breath as he ducked behind the tree trunk. Dane waited a moment and then looked around the trunk to see if the bugs were attacking. They weren't.

Dane blinked hard, hoping it would help him remember the command words. Taking out his gun, he held it in the air.

Another shot rang out and Dane could feel the tree where he was hiding shudder. It had been hit. These men knew exactly where he was.

"Come out now. More back up is coming!" yelled another man. "Then we'll surround you."

"Yeah right," said Dane, shooting his gun over the men's heads, just to give a little back.

All the men ducked behind their doors as the injured man dragged himself to safety.

"Ahh, Louise said there were three settings—" Dane rehearsed. "They cause...dizziness? No, that's not it." Then it came to him, ***"Confusion!"*** he nearly yelled out.

The bugs immediately responded.

"Yes!" said Dane very relieved. He had guessed one of the words!

All the men he could see were attacked as fast as he could look at them. In response, the men flung themselves wildly on the ground as they tried to bat the bugs away.

"Yes!" said Dane excitedly. He felt like doing a little dance!

"Take cover!" yelled the hidden injured man who had crawled into his car. "She's using the assassin bugs!"

"Oops!" Dane had forgotten that guy! "*Confusion!*" he said looking to where the man was probably hiding, feeling a little like he should be holding a wand or something—this was magic! But then he wondered, would the bug find the target if the man wasn't in his line of sight? Dane waited. No voices. No shots fired.

"Come on pantywaists! Give me what 'cha got!" he yelled, feeling invincible.

Again, no response.

Good, thought Dane. The bugs had worked as expected! *"Wahoo!"* he yelped, in an unrestrained war whoop.

Dane poked his head around the fir tree trunk and watched the slow, drugged chaos. Three men were stumbling around near their cars, unaware, like bumbling idiots. Four others were sitting, dazed on the ground and.... Where was the last man? There were eight! Oh, yes, the injured man. He still couldn't see him. He was probably still sitting in his car. Let him stay there!

Dane's defenses relaxed. He tested the waters by stepping away from the tree in plain view. He kept his gun drawn, just in case.

The men didn't respond to him.

Dane wondered if he could take their weapons. Wouldn't it be great to show up at home with an arsenal of protection?

Dane carefully approached the men and their cars. Slowly, he took each gun without resistance, making a pile on the grass. He found ten guns in all because some of the men had more than one weapon! Jack pot!

Holstering his own revolver, Dane was feeling very happy with himself. He became a little more daring. He studied the cars. All of them were running.... Dane wondered.... With his thoughts churning, he stepped through the open door of one of the cars. Maybe he could *drive* Nebraska and Louise home in style! What would his family think when he arrived in a sleek, black—what were these cars? He saw the insignia on the hood of each. They were Cadillacs! Yes! That would be *sweet*! But the moment he entered the car, he was scanned by some laser-like thing. Then he knew he was in trouble. These were armed cars! If he wanted to live he'd better—get...

A series of bullets rang out from somewhere inside the car. Luckily Dane hit the pavement and rolled out of the car.

Dane looked back at the car. That's what he got for being too greedy. There must have been a secret compartment he hadn't seen. He'd better stay away from the inside of the cars.

A strong hand reached out and grabbed his ankle in a vice grip.

"What?" exclaimed Dane, having the heebie-jeebies scared out of him!

The man growled at him through gritted teeth. The drugs were wearing off. Dane struggled to get free. Frantically he tried to think of other command words.

Dane kicked and squirmed, but the suited man wouldn't let go. "Let go, you freak!" he yelled, watching the bugs circle above. "Pass out!" he yelled as he finally kicked the man's hand off his ankle. No, the word started with a "D," he realized. "D—d—d," he was trying to remember what it was. Louise had said it earlier. Once again the man grabbed his foot. *What was wrong with his brain?*

Another man stood up from where he had been sitting and was walking towards him zombie-like, with heavy steps and wobbly legs. There was a moment where he felt like he was living one of his video games as each began to close in. *Surreal!*

Dane shook his head to clear his thoughts as he peeled the man's hand off his shoe. It was time to get out of there! Dane stood and rushed back to the safety of the fir trees.

Turning back, Dane saw all the men standing and beginning to come after him. Well, if he wanted to shoot to kill, now would be the time! Not one of them had any cover! They were walking targets. Stupid!

"Talk about stupid! The gun pile!" he exclaimed, feeling foolish. In his arrogance he had left the guns unprotected. Dane drew his own gun and while rehearsing all the D words he knew, he hoped to shake his memory. Dane ran out onto the grass and picked the guns up.

"Dumb, deltoid, dog, doo-doo, dufus, deli—deli—*delirium*!" he exclaimed standing and looking at the men. "Delirium!" he repeated. That was it!

Suddenly, the bugs attacked again.

Dane hooted in excitement as each man went down. Yes! Dane waited a couple of moments to see if he had missed anyone. He hadn't and all of them stayed down this time. Dane decided the combination of the "Confusion" and the "Delirium" commands had put them out. Now they were sleeping like babies.

Dane blew out a lung full of air in relief. "That was close!" he said to himself as he shook his head. "Too close."

After securing each gun in a pocket of his vest, he took out the metal tin again. He looked at the tin in puzzlement. Now, how was he supposed to get the bugs back in the can?

Dane held out the tin for the bugs to fly in. Instead they just continued to circle above the heads of the men. Louise had forgotten to tell him this part, so he guessed. "If I look at the tin, maybe they'll come." Dane looked at the tin and whispered, "Come on," more out of desire than in command, but he was rewarded. "Come" must have been the appropriate command and the bugs flew straight into the hole of the tin. It was a miracle!

Dane smiled and closed his eyes. This was a great moment. "Thank you, Father, for letting me experience this day," he said, feeling a tad guilty for just how much he had enjoyed this battle, but not enough to stop him from smiling or enjoying the victory.

For fun, Dane blew on the tin, as if it was his six-iron and put it in his right zipper pocket. Next, he took off his glasses, slipped them casually into his chest pocket where it felt like they belonged and sauntered off, imagining himself disappearing into the darkness and the credits rolling. The thought made him laugh.

Dane blinked twice as he looked around. He had to refocus. Now, to find Nebraska and Louise. Dane took off, walking across the grass the way he had seen the two run. Studying the ground, he noticed a clear path across the long grass. Good thing those men in the suits weren't following them! They would have been sitting ducks! He followed the grass trail until he came to a back door of an old brick house. Gently, Dane knocked.

Louise answered. "Did it work?" she asked, looking cautious and peering past him.

"Of course it worked," said Dane, smiling ear to ear. "I just had to remember the commands."

Louise's eyes widened. "Oh no! You forgot them?"

Dane nodded. "Well, yes, but I remembered our conversation and I figured them out."

"Good," said Louise.

"After almost getting shot," said Dane.

"After almost getting shot?" she asked with a wince.

"Yep, but as you can see, 'almost,' isn't 'quite.' I'm whole," Dane said, as he held his arms out wide for inspection.

"Well, good," said Louise. "Come in."

Dane walked through the doorway and looked around the house.

"So, what did you think? Impressive technology?" asked Louise.

"It was a riot. And to top it all off, I got the job done," said Dane, with a single, self-satisfied nod.

"That's all that's important," said Louise.

Dane nodded in agreement as he sighed in relief. "How'd you get in here? Is this house empty?" he asked, looking down a hall.

"Yes, it's empty. I had to break a window in the basement to get in," said Louise. "I was lucky there wasn't a security alarm, but this is an inexpensive home. I didn't think it would."

"How did you know no one was home?" asked Dane.

"There were a couple of newspapers on the porch and lots of mail."

"Hmmm," said Dane looking around.

"It looks like it's been empty for a little over a week, at least. I doubt the owners are still alive."

"Why do you say that?" asked Dane running his hand along the kitchen counter.

"Because on one of the cork boards in the bedrooms, there were Broadway play brochures with dates circled and a calendar next to it with red marks crossing the days off."

"Yes?" said Dane, waiting for the rest of the story.

"That would mean whoever lived in this house flew out to New York to attend those plays. Since whoever did that is not here..."

"Oh," said Dane, his stomach twisting a little. The poor people who lived here had been caught in New York like Nebraska's family had. "OK, I get it. No one will be coming home tonight."

"Right," said Louise. "That's good for us. I think we should stay here for the night. There're great beds in the back bedrooms."

"Alright," said Dane, looking around. "How many bedrooms does this place have?" he asked.

"Three."

"Where's Nebraska?" Dane asked.

"Asleep in one of the beds."

"Perfect," said Dane, completely enticed by the thought of a good night's sleep on a real bed. But he had to keep his wits about him. "What's going to happen when those guys wake up out there?" asked Dane, holding off this time on the celebrating. "Will it be safe to sleep here tonight?"

"Sure," said Louise. "Those guys will wake up and go back to where they came from. They won't remember a thing—as long as they were dosed with enough drug."

"Oh, they were dosed alright," said Dane, nodding.

"Well, good then. There's nothing to worry about," said Louise.

"So they won't remember they found us, right?" asked Dane.

"No," said Louise. "Complete amnesia. No reports, no trail, no memory. That's the beauty of drugs."

"Then, to bed it is," said Dane, swaggering down the hall, towards what he thought was a bedroom. "Good night, *Madam President*," he said in a slight sarcastic tone over his shoulder, and then he laughed.

"Don't be smart!" she called after him.

Dane chuckled. "Obviously I'm not *that* smart, because I didn't even suspect the truth!" Growing serious he said, "Oh, by the way, it's very good to meet you!" he said with a bow as he entered the room backwards.

Dane glanced up just enough to see Louise smile. And that was good. She needed some kudos!

Dane was still amazed at all the things that had happened to him in the last week, and now, to top it all off, he was protecting the President of the United States! *The Commander-in-Chief!* Wow! he thought, as he threw himself on the empty bed.

What a trip! Too bad no one else could know.

Notes to "On Alert"

Emergency Meeting

[1] "...It is essential that we plan for our future. I believe it is time, and perhaps with some urgency, to review the counsel we have received in dealing with our personal and family preparedness. We want to be found with oil in our lamps sufficient to endure to the end. President Spencer W. Kimball admonished us: 'In reviewing the Lord's counsel to us on the importance of preparedness, I am impressed with the plainness of the message. The Savior made it clear that we cannot place sufficient oil in our preparedness lamps by simply avoiding evil. We must also be anxiously engaged in a positive program of preparation.' He also said: 'The Lord will not translate one's good hopes and desires and intentions into works. Each of us must do that for himself' (*The Miracle of Forgiveness*, 1969, pg. 8). On a daily basis we witness widely fluctuating inflation; wars; interpersonal conflicts; national disasters; variances in weather conditions; innumerable forces of immorality, crime, and violence; attacks and pressures on the family and individuals; technological advances that make occupations obsolete; and so on. The need for preparation is abundantly clear. The great blessing of being prepared gives us freedom from fear, as guaranteed to us by the Lord in the Doctrine and Covenants: 'If ye are prepared ye shall not fear' (D&C 38:30). Just as it is important to prepare ourselves spiritually, we must also prepare ourselves for our temporal needs. Each of us needs to take the time to ask ourselves, What preparation should I make to care for my needs and the needs of my family? ...Acquire and store a reserve of food and supplies that will sustain life. Obtain clothing and build a savings account on a sensible, well-planned basis that can serve well in times of emergency. As long as I can remember, we have been taught to prepare for the future and to obtain a year's supply of necessities. I would guess that the years of plenty have almost universally caused us to set aside this counsel. I believe the time to disregard this counsel is over. With events in the world today, it must be considered with all seriousness." (L. Tom Perry, "'If Ye Are Prepared Ye Shall Not Fear'," *Ensign*, Nov. 1995, pg. 35).

[2] "Build a small supply of food that is part of your normal, daily diet. One way to do this is to purchase a few extra items each week to build a one-week supply of food. Then you can gradually increase your supply until it is sufficient for three months. These items should be rotated regularly to avoid spoilage" ("Three Month Supply," *providentliving.org*, http://www.providentliving.org/content/list/0,11664,7445-1,00.html).

[3] "Recent surveys of Church members have shown a serious erosion in the number of families who have a year's supply of life's necessities. Most members plan to do it. Too few have begun. We must sense again the spirit of the persistent instruction given by Elder Harold B. Lee as he spoke to the

members in 1943: 'Again there came counsel in 1942. ... "We renew our counsel, said the leaders of the Church, and repeat our instruction: Let every Latter-day Saint that has land, produce some valuable essential foodstuff thereon and then preserve it." ... Let me ask you leaders who are here today: In 1937 did you store in your own basements and in your own private storehouses and granaries sufficient for a year's supply? You city dwellers, did you in 1942 heed what was said from this stand?' (*Conference Report*, April 1943, pg. 127). Undergirding this pointed call is the stirring appeal from our own living prophet, President Ezra Taft Benson, wherein he has given specific suggestions for putting these teachings into action: 'From the standpoint of food production, storage, handling, and the Lord's counsel, wheat should have high priority. ... Water, of course, is essential. Other basics could include honey or sugar, legumes, milk products or substitutes, and salt or its equivalent. The revelation to produce and store food may be as essential to our temporal welfare today as boarding the ark was to the people in the days of Noah (*Ensign*, Nov. 1980, pg. 33)" (Thomas S. Monson, "Guiding Principles of Personal and Family Welfare," *Ensign*, Sep. 1986, pg. 3).

[4] "While we are powerless to alter the fact of the Second Coming and unable to know its exact time, we can accelerate our own preparation and try to influence the preparation of those around us. A parable that contains an important and challenging teaching on this subject is the parable of the ten virgins. Of this parable, the Lord said, 'And at that day, when I shall come in my glory, shall the parable be fulfilled which I spake concerning the ten virgins' (D&C 45:56). Given in the 25th chapter of Matthew, this parable contrasts the circumstances of the five foolish and the five wise virgins. All ten were invited to the wedding feast, but only half of them were prepared with oil in their lamps when the bridegroom came. The five who were prepared went into the marriage feast, and the door was shut. The five who had delayed their preparations came late. The door had been closed, and the Lord denied them entrance, saying, 'I know you not' (Matt. 25:12). 'Watch therefore,' the Savior concluded, 'for ye know neither the day nor the hour wherein the Son of man cometh' (Matt. 25:13). The arithmetic of this parable is chilling. The ten virgins obviously represent members of Christ's Church, for all were invited to the wedding feast and all knew what was required to be admitted when the bridegroom came. But only half were ready when he came" (Dallin H. Oaks, "Preparation for the Second Coming," *Ensign*, May 2004, pg. 7).

[5] "Bear ye one another's burdens and so fulfill the law of Christ" (Galatians 6:2).

[6] "Too frequently, the emotional, social, and, in some instances, even the material essentials are not provided by children for their aged parents. This is displeasing to the Lord. It is difficult to understand how one mother can take care of seven children more easily than seven children can take care of one mother. President J. Reuben Clark, Jr., gave clear direction on this matter: 'The prime responsibility for supporting an aged parent rests upon [the] family, not upon society. ... The family which refuses to keep its own is not meeting its duty.' (*Conference Report*, April 1938, pg. 107). President Stephen L. Richards gave an inspired appeal as he rallied members with these sentiments: "How can sons and daughters who owe everything they have—their education, their ideals of life, their capacity to acquire independent living and their characters—to parents who have worked, sacrificed, prayed, wept, and striven for them to the exhaustion of their bodies and their energies be parties to a scheme which would make their fathers and mothers the objects of charity and cast the burden of their support on the community and stigmatize them with the loss of independence and self-respect. '...I think my food would choke me if I knew that while I could procure bread my aged father or mother or near kin were on public relief' (*Conference Report*, Oct. 1944, pg. 138)" (Thomas S. Monson, "Guiding Principles of Personal and Family Welfare," *Ensign*, September 1986, pg. 3).

[7] The first thing mentioned on an emergency supply list is prescriptive medications necessary to support the health of the individual during an emergency. See http://www.providentliving.org/content/display/0,11666,5653-1-2808-1,00.html .

[8] "The intent of the law of consecration was that every man is to be 'equal according to his family, according to his circumstances and his wants and needs' (D&C 51:3). Under it, every man, including the poor, was to receive a 'portion' ... such as would make him equal to others according to his circumstances, his family, his wants and needs" (Marion G. Romney, "Living the Principles of the Law of Consecration," *Ensign*, Feb. 1979, pg. 3).

[9] "Behold, I say unto you, were it not for the transgressions of my people, speaking concerning the church and not individuals, they might have been redeemed even now. But behold, they have not learned to be obedient to the things which I required at their hands, but are full of all manner of evil, and do not impart of their substance, as becometh saints, to the poor and afflicted among them; And are not united according to the union required by the law of the celestial kingdom; And Zion cannot be built up unless it is by the principles of the law of the celestial kingdom; otherwise I cannot receive her unto myself" (D&C 105:2-5).

[10] "When we discuss the subject of consecration, the first thing that often comes to mind is the consecration of our temporal means. What is currently required in this regard is to pay our tithes and offerings as a preparatory step in learning to return to the Father a portion of what He has given us. But the law of consecration goes beyond the mere payment of tithes and offerings or the consecration of monies and properties to the Lord. 'The law of consecration,' said Elder Bruce R. McConkie (1915–85) of the Quorum of the Twelve Apostles, 'is that we consecrate our time, our talents, and our money and property to the cause of the Church; such are to be available to the extent they are needed to further the Lord's interests on earth' (Obedience, Consecration, and Sacrifice," *Ensign,* May 1975, pg. 50)" (Stephen B. Oveson and Dixie Randall Oveson, "Personal Consecration," *Ensign,* Sep. 2005, pgs. 42–46).

[11] "I, the Lord, stretched out the heavens, and built the earth, my very handiwork; and all things therein are mine. And it is my purpose to provide for my saints, for all things are mine. But it must needs be done in mine own way; and behold this is the way that I, the Lord, have decreed to provide for my saints, that the poor shall be exalted, in that the rich are made low. For the earth is full, and there is enough and to spare; yea, I prepared all things, and have given unto the children of men to be agents unto themselves. ...And again, a commandment I give unto you concerning your stewardship which I have appointed unto you. Behold, all these properties are mine, or else your faith is vain, and ye are found hypocrites, and the covenants which ye have made unto me are broken; and if the properties are mine, then ye are stewards; otherwise ye are no stewards. But, verily I say unto you, I have appointed unto you to be stewards over mine house, even stewards indeed" (D&C 104:14-17, 54-57).

[12] "In the 1820s, *consecrate* was defined as 'to make or declare to be sacred, by certain ceremonies or rites; to appropriate to sacred uses; to set apart, dedicate, or devote, to the service and worship of God' (*Noah Webster's First Edition of an American Dictionary of the English Language*, 'Consecrate'). Members of the Church today, in living the law of consecration, are expected 'to appropriate [themselves] to sacred uses.' Doing so requires them to dedicate their time, talents, and possessions to The Church of Jesus Christ of Latter-day Saints and its purposes. Perhaps we may never be asked to give all, but our willingness to put everything on the altar is a sign between us and God that we submit to His will in all things" (Stephen B. Oveson and Dixie Randall Oveson, "Personal Consecration," *Ensign,* September 2005, pgs. 42–46).

[13] "The Church [Church of Jesus Christ of Latter-day Saints] supports programs to help members become Amateur Radio operators, to provide communications between Church facilities during disasters. High Frequency ham radio equipment enables logistics needs to be met worldwide, while VHF operations link local leaders. In areas with high expectation of needing such services (such as quake-prone Southern California), license classes and exams are periodically held in local chapels, and open to all, regardless of age or religious preference" (*Wikipedia*, "Culture of The Church of Jesus Christ of Latter-day Saints," http://en.wikipedia.org/wiki/Culture_of_The_Church_of_Jesus_Christ_of_Latter-day_Saints).

[14] "Occasionally discouragement may darken our pathway; frustration may be a constant companion. In our ears there may sound the sophistry of Satan as he whispers, 'You cannot save the world; your small efforts are meaningless. You haven't time to be concerned for others.' Trusting in the Lord, let us turn our heads from such falsehoods and make certain our feet are firmly planted in the path of service and our hearts and souls dedicated to follow the example of the Lord. In moments when the light of resolution dims and when the heart grows faint, we can take comfort from His promise: 'Be not weary in well-doing. ... Out of small things proceedeth that which is great. Behold, the Lord requireth the heart and a willing mind' (D&C 63:33-34)" (Thomas S. Monson, "Finding Peace," *Ensign*, March 2004, pgs. 2–7).

[15] "And I will also ease the burdens which are put upon your shoulders, that even you cannot feel them upon your backs, even while you are in bondage; and this will I do that ye may stand as witnesses for me hereafter, and that ye may know of a surety that I, the Lord God, do visit my people in their afflictions" (Mosiah 24:14).

[16] See D&C 1:36.

[17] "...through my providence, notwithstanding the tribulation which shall descend upon you, that the church may stand independent above all other creatures beneath the celestial world; That you may come up unto the crown prepared for you, and be made rulers over many kingdoms" (D&C 78:14-15).

CHAPTER THREE

CONTROL

"...The powers of heaven cannot be controlled nor handled only upon the principles of righteousness" (D&C 121:36).

00:03:07, 08:30:16, Zulu
Tuesday, September 23rd

Daunting Numbers

Provo, Utah
8:30 a.m.

"How's the ward doing, Brother Jensen?" asked Bo, talking to his Elders' Quorum President in his den. He was anxious to wrap his mind around the amounts of food storage and supplies in the ward[1] so he and his counselors could head off potential suffering and fill deficits before they became problems.[2] Without other resources available from the city or the Church, he knew chances were good that people would be knocking on his door soon expecting assistance[3] and he wanted to be prepared.

"Did the home teachers finish their survey?" Bo asked. "We have to be on top of things. No time to waste."

"Well, half the ward is surveyed," said Brother Jensen.

"What about the other half?"

"Their home teachers haven't reached them yet."

"Why not? We can't afford a delay."

"I'm not sure. Why do we ever have problems with home teaching?" asked Brother Jenson, looking apologetic and stressed. "But we'll get the numbers, even if my counselors and I have to go out ourselves."

"No, Brother Jensen," said Bo shaking his head. "Let the brothers serve the families they are assigned. They'll go out, just encourage them."

"We'll try," said Brother Jensen with a nod.

"You can't do it all yourself, even though I know you want to. That's a lesson I've learned."[4]

Brother Jensen smiled. "You're right, Bishop. As long as you know I'm putting forth effort."

"Absolutely," said Bo, with a smile. "You're doing great. Sorry to press you. That was my fault and a reflection of my insecurities, not your performance. Forgive me."

"No problem, Bishop," said Brother Jensen.

"Thank you," said Bo. "OK, let's talk about the half we know about. How does it look?"

Brother Jensen flipped his computer screen around so Bo could see his numbers. "I've broken down food by families and then I've compiled a list that calculates the needs of every person in our ward and what it would take to feed all of them."

"That's great, Brother Jensen. Coming through for me again," said Bo feeling pleased. "What'd you find?"

"Twenty percent of the families we surveyed hold sixty percent of the food in the ward."[5]

"Sixty percent?" repeated Bo. "That's surprising."

"Yep, that's what it looks like."

"What's that? Three families?"

"Out of the ones we surveyed, more around five."

"Oh, that's disappointing. That means, if we are to survive adequately, all conditions remaining as they are now, without gas or jobs, there's going to have to be some significant sharing, isn't there?"

Brother Jensen nodded. "That's how I see it."

Bo was worried. Coming from the emergency meeting, he knew there were some people who were very possessive about their food. How was he going to encourage them to share? How was he going to make this work? Bo shook his head. "I'm feeling a little overwhelmed at the moment," he said with a forced smile.

Brother Jensen nodded. "I think we all are, Bishop. Wouldn't want to be in your position."[6]

Bo took a deep breath and said, "Well, then, let's say we were successful in encouraging people to share their food. Would we have enough for everyone?"

Brother Jensen nodded. "I think so. We'd have enough for people to survive for a couple of years just on the wheat. We'd have to ration, but we could do it."

"So getting through the winter won't be a problem."

"No," said Brother Jensen, shaking his head. "If you can get people to share, that is."

"Right," said Bo. "What about gardens and fruit trees? Did you take into account those resources?"

"No, I didn't, but you have a great point. If each family has a garden, and if those families with fruit trees would allow others to harvest fruit too, that would increase the quality of everyone's diet and stretch out our supply of wheat."

"OK," said Bo. "So between now and then, we have other canned food to add variety to the wheat, right?"

"Right, if you pool the resources," said Brother Jensen.

Bo whistled thoughtfully through his teeth, as he considered all this information. "That's good to know," he said after a few moments. "I'm feeling a little better."

"Sure," said Brother Jensen, nodding. "The potential is there. There's just limits to reality. You, as the Bishop can only do what you can do."[7]

"I know," said Bo, feeling very heavy. "And by myself that's not much. I don't have access to the storehouse food anymore." He shook his head. "I hope it doesn't get to the point where I'm begging for people to help each other. I'm not very good at begging."

"Is anyone?" Brother Jensen asked with a smile.

Bo shook his head. "I don't think so. I'm hoping people will see the need of their neighbors and spontaneously share. If not, we're in trouble, and we aren't even discussing the non-members in our neighborhood. I'm sure they have needs too."

"I know," said Brother Jensen, nodding. "This problem just continues to get bigger and bigger, doesn't it?"

"Yes," said Bo. "But I know there are answers, we just have to find them."

"I agree," said Brother Jensen.

"How about you?" asked Bo. "Would you be willing to share your family's food? I know your supply is healthy."

Brother Jensen nodded slowly. "Yes, I'd be willing to share, but I have to assure my own family has what they need."

"Of course," said Bo. "That's the first and foremost priority in this situation. We must all provide for our own. Your wife and six children are definitely your first priority, no question about it, and that's the way it should be."[8]

"Thanks for understanding, Bishop."

"Sure, I have a big crew to take care of too."

"Yes, you do," said Brother Jensen. "But, I have another concern, too."

"What is it?"

"We also don't want to be taken advantage of, either," Brother Jensen said with a nod. "If you know what I mean. Nice people often get abused and taken to the cleaners."

Bo looked down at his hands and then rubbed them together. "To the cleaners, huh?"

"Right."

"Tell me what you're getting at."

Brother Jensen took a deep breath and said, "Just because I was prepared, doesn't mean I'm the only one giving my food away. I think if we are to share, we should work something out so that if people need something, then we trade, barter, or serve each other in some way."

"I agree. No one should receive something for nothing."[9]

"Another idea is to wait," offered Brother Jensen.

"What do you mean?" asked Bo.

"Wait for people to run out of food. Don't force this thing. Maybe through home teaching and visiting teaching, people will spontaneously see each other's needs[10] and the Spirit will do your work for you."

Something clicked inside Bo. Brother Jensen was on to something. "Yes, you're right! That's the best idea yet! Sharing needs to be voluntary. No one should feel coerced."[11]

"That's what I think," said Brother Jensen. "It's kind of like the wind and the sun scenario. If the wind blows hard, people hang on to their coats, but if you warm them up, they take their coats off freely."

Bo nodded. "Oh, if it were that easy—encouraging people to feel that sunshine will be the difficult part. The sun is always shining, but some people just don't feel it. They have hearts of ice."

"Don't be so pessimistic, Bishop."

Bo nodded. "You're right. I shouldn't. I should put my shoulder to the wheel and go to work. Something is bound to work out."

"Yes! That's the spirit," said Brother Jensen.

Bo pointed to Brother Jensen, "But, you know, I think you're on to something. The Spirit always needs to be involved in every particle of our lives. Maybe this hardship will drive people closer to humility and then sunshine won't be so hard to feel."[12]

"Yes, maybe." said Brother Jensen.

"I'm going to talk with my counselors about our course of action, but in the mean time, I think it would be good if you were to follow up on the ward survey. After you get the results, look at the home teaching companionships as well as the families they teach. Pray about them. Reassign them as the Spirit dictates."

"Sure. I'll get right on it."

"We'll talk about the home teaching list on Sunday, in welfare meeting."

"Alright, Bishop," said Brother Jensen standing. "Thank you," he said as he put out his hand.

"No, thank you," said Bo as he shook Brother Jensen's hand and escorted him out of his home office and then out the front door. "Have a great day," he said with a wave.

"You too, Bishop," said Brother Jensen, as he walked down the porch stairs.

Bo watched his friend leave. The feeling of being overwhelmed eased as the Spirit reassured him that the Lord's work would be done.

Strategic Pursuit

Denali National Park, Alaska
9:50 a.m.

Carea rushed after the man-sized, masked boy with lightning speed. He had ripped away her supplies and threatened her with a weapon—and that was the wrong move. Waking the sleeping giant within her that despised abuse of power, she vowed he wouldn't get away with this!

Assessing her body as she ran, Carea was pleased with how strong she felt. Her muscles, well trained, responded to the terrain as her thick mountain blood delivered oxygen to her body. Good thing she had been training hard in the high elevation of Utah for her martial arts competitions. It had increased her stamina. She knew she was prepared for this match. Soon, the boy wouldn't know what hit him.

Carea watched carefully as her attacker ran in front of her. He darted to the right and then rolled under a broken branch.

Carea did the same.

Jumping over a stump and then dashing left, he slid between two rock walls as he turned to see if she was following. Exhaustion was beginning to show in his eyes already. That was good. The boy was losing strength and beginning to grasp the fact that he couldn't shake her. That made her happy. Carea still had more in her, especially after the long bus ride. This activity was exactly what her body yearned for.

With an internal chuckle she allowed herself to enjoy this cat-and-mouse game. She wanted the boy to wonder about her. She wanted him to talk her up to his buddies. It would only help psyche out her opponents in the future.

The boy glanced back at Carea again, his breath billowing out in a frosty cloud. Now Carea could see that there was more than worry in his eyes, there was—*fear.* This triggered her to slow down. She didn't want him to be afraid, because fear led to desperation and he'd most likely lash out like a caged tiger. That could be dangerous. She'd back off a little, and let him think he was gaining some advantage. If they engaged in combat, she wanted a fair fight.

Suddenly, the boy threw the supplies that he had been carrying down in Carea's path and took off at a quicker pace. He was trying to bait her into stopping, but it wouldn't work. She jumped over the heap and kept running, tailing the boy. Why settle for a little when there was more? She decided she wanted all the stolen blankets and supplies. After all, it belonged to her and the girls. She'd continue to follow him to his lair.

...But...then her thoughts changed...the fact that he gave up his booty so easily, probably meant they were close to his hideout and didn't have much further to run. It was a desperate move. He wanted her to stop chasing him badly enough that he surrendered. Hmmm, thought Carea. OK...an alternate plan emerged. Maybe it was time to let the boy *think* he had lost her so she could sneak around and find his hideout without the threat of a fight. It would be better to investigate the opponent and discover their strengths and weaknesses rather than rush headlong into something that might be too much for her to handle alone. She knew she could handle this boy in hand-to-hand combat, but not a group of armed men.

Carea stopped and hid behind a nearby tree. She pulled the neck of her shirt over her mouth to hide the clouds of vapor that were pouring out of her lungs. The boy had to think she had given up and gone back to the other girls.

When the sound of footsteps disappeared, Carea snuck out from her hiding place. She studied the ground. There were broken twigs and smashed leaves, not to mention a dirt path that clearly marked a trail leading somewhere well traversed. This meant one of two things. One, either everyone in this camp was terrible at tracking these mobsters, or two, they were a very scary bunch and no one *wanted* to track them for fear of *finding* them. Considering the generally deviant sort of population sent to this camp, she bet on the latter. ...Hmmmm, that meant she had better be careful. Maybe hand-to-hand combat wasn't smart just yet. She decided to turn back and find out more about this group from camp. Knowledge was important for her success if she was up against many. It would protect her from making stupid mistakes that might get her killed. She'd have to devise a recovery strategy for the rest of the supplies. This attack would have to wait for another day. Carea was disappointed. She wanted to prove herself to the girls. Now she would return with only her supplies. Shrugging, she decided that was OK. It would show she had at least *some* success. She was sure that was worth something.

Backtracking, Carea found her pile of supplies. Picking them up, she glanced over her shoulder. Just to make sure no one was behind her. The area was clear.

Snap!

Carea stopped! That was a twig! Her heart thumped in her chest as her muscles quivered in readiness. There *was* someone behind her! Quickly, she turned about and scanned the trees as well as all the spaces around them. Her senses told her she was being watched. Who was it? ...She couldn't see anyone, but she knew he or she was out there—watching *her*—studying *her*. Now she was the pursu*ee* instead of the pursuer. *She hated that!* The tables had turned.

Carea considered the supplies in her arms. It wouldn't be good if she was attacked now. She wouldn't be able to do a thing, and she wasn't willing to give them up. There was only one choice. She had to get back to camp fast.

Carea quickened her pace and rushed back the way she came. "Around the rock wall, then to the right and over the stump. Now, under the branch and to the left," she rehearsed to herself. "I came from the right, so go left," she doubled checked herself as she remembered the way she had come. She was confident in her memory since everything seemed familiar. She could see the clearing where she and the other girls had been dropped off through the trees. It was just a little way ahead, down the hill.

Behind her, Carea could hear footsteps. They were growing louder. Whoever was following her, was gaining on her. *"Not today,"* she whispered to herself as she put on a burst of speed. There had been a low hanging birch branch up ahead, she remembered. It was just around the corner. The skin of the birch was smooth, like a bar used in gymnastics. She thought maybe she could use the branch to climb into a tree to ambush whoever was following her from above, but if she was going to do that, she had to get ahead now to buy some time.

The footsteps behind her grew faint as she increased speed. The branch was ahead. She could see it. Just a few more seconds...yes, it was perfect. "One—two—three!" Carea counted to herself and then she threw the blanket and supplies behind a bush and with a leap, she took a last step and jumped, catching the smooth limb with her hands and allowing her body to swing with the speed of her run. The momentum of her weight swung her body over the branch. She landed with her hip bones against the limb with her legs dangling down. With a quick thrust, she pulled her feet up to the branch as she caught another one above her with her hands. Climbing higher, she sought refuge in the leaves of the other branches. Now, breathing hard, she'd wait and catch her breath.

The person, who had been chasing Carea, slinked along the path cautiously. It was obviously another boy, or small man. He had a black fur-like coat. The long mangy fur made him look like a bear creeping along the ground. Was this the same boy she had followed into the woods? After watching, she decided, no, this was someone different. This one was *sent* out after her. He must be good at something. Maybe he was a good fighter. If that was the case, she'd better not take any chances and make sure her first blow was a good one. She'd use her bodyweight as her weapon. It was her best chance to assure this boy could not fight back.

The boy hovered over her last footprint in the soft, moist ground. He studied the path, looking for her next step. Carea smiled to herself as she knew there wasn't another one because she had caught the branch there. The boy looked baffled, but Carea knew it wouldn't be long until he figured out where she was. It was time to come down.

Quietly Carea descended one branch, and like a cat, poised for her attack. She waited for the perfect moment. Just a few seconds more...she'd let him move directly underneath her...another foot...a couple more inches—now! Carea jumped from the tree.

Thud!

Carea landed square on the boy's back with both of her feet on the top of his shoulder blades. She felt the force of her body sink into his as he fell forward, and then unmistakably, she heard two sickening pops that came from under her feet.

"Ahhhheeeha!" the boy screamed in an uncontrolled yell, and then he went silent as the air was knocked out of him.

Carea cringed. She knew instantly she had broken something in his body. A revolting feeling jabbed her in her gut as she rolled off the boy. She had meant to surprise him, even hurt him, but she didn't mean to break his *bones*!

"Hey!" yelled someone off in the distance. "Carea!"

Carea looked up worried. Who was calling her?

"Wahoo!" screamed one girl as she ran waving her arms in the air.

"Way to go, girl! Way to put that guy *down*!" yelled the gorilla girl as all the girls from the bus ran towards her. "Who's this guy?" she asked when she arrived.

"Did you find our stuff?" asked Octavia, her bus seatmate, breathing heavily from running.

"Yeah," said Carea. "I was able to get one pack and blanket. It's behind that bush," she said, pointing behind her.

"I think you broke *both* his arms," said the vampire girl, crouching down to study the boy who obviously had fainted. Standing back up she laughed as she rolled the boy over with her foot.

Carea felt a little numb, as if she was going into shock herself. She looked down at the young man. Both of his arms lay across his chest, bending in the wrong places. It was clear she had busted both of his forearms.

"Who'd think a little thing like you could do something like *that*!" continued the large girl as she patted Carea hard on the back.

Carea gazed around at the circle of girls that had congregated. Despite her shock, she instinctively knew this was a moment she could use in her favor. "We'll use this guy to get the rest of our stuff back," she said, feeling horrible inside but covering it up. "His buddies will come for him and we'll work a trade."

"Yeah!" said Octavia with a bucked-tooth smile. She had a fist in the air.

"Yeah!" echoed the rest of the group.

"Way to take the bull by the horns," said the gorilla girl. "By the way, I'm Bones. I think you've earned the right to know my name."

"Bones. That's a great name. I'm glad to meet you," said Carea nodding and trying to maintain an air of confidence. "I know we'll be a good team."

"Yeah, we will be!" exclaimed Bones to the other girls who cheered loudly.

Carea could see that she had won some respect points today. Considering their situation, that was good. It gave her hope.

Looking back at the boy, she swallowed. She really hadn't meant to hurt him this bad. She felt somewhat nauseous as the memory of the sound of his arms breaking echoed in her head. Blinking hard she refused to explore the memory any further. No, this was perfect. This is what needed to happen. She had to establish herself as someone with leadership skills and right now, in this group, she had done that. There was no need for guilt because who knew what this boy would have tried to do to her if she hadn't stopped him. She had defended herself.

"Now, we need to get this guy to some shelter," said Carea squatting down to help pick up the boy's upper body. "He'll be going into shock and he'll be no good to us dead."

"Right," said Bones with a generous smile. "Let's take him to our bunk."

"We have a bunk?" Carea asked looking up at Bones as she waited for some help.

Bones pointed off in the distance. "Yes, the camp was expecting us and we have a place of our own. It's the oldest one of the bunch and rickety and falling apart, but we can call it home for a while."

"Great," said Carea looking over her shoulder and seeing some A-frame cabins for the first time. "Something's better than nothing."

"Some guys from my hood are here too," said Bones as she retrieved the pack and blanket from behind the bush. "They've hooked us up with food and old blankets until we can get ours back."

"There's a bonfire too," piped up Octavia.

"Great. I'd love to roast myself next to the fire. It's cold out here."

"Yep," said Bones, handing the supplies to another girl and bending down to help Carea lift the boy. "That's why we have to get our things back."

"I know," said Carea as they lifted the boy off the ground in unison. "Don't worry, I'm on that one. I've got a plan," she said nodding.

"I hoped you did," said Bones.

"Let's go," coaxed Carea.

Two or three other girls moved alongside the boy's body and together they carried him to their cabin. As they walked under the heavy weight, Carea's mind worked. She looked at the boy as she walked backwards. This stranger was their captive—a prisoner of war. Carea worried about the next couple of days. Was she ready for this? Maybe these other girls were used to this kind of thing, but she wasn't. How was she going to keep it together with her limited experience? How was she to maintain this respect that was handed over to her so automatically? There was no doubt about one thing; she'd have to be as wise as a serpent and bite like one too.

Welcome Home

Provo, Utah
3:22 p.m.

"Get-up-sleepy-head!" said Nebraska as she jumped on the outdoor trampoline. "Get up! Get up! I know you aren't dead!"

Nebraska's curls bounced in the warm sunlight. She was smiling. The air was fresh—

Suddenly, a black form swooped out of the sky and took Nebraska. *She was gone!*

"Nooooooo!" Dane screamed. He sat up abruptly taking in a big gulping breath.

"Get up!" said Nebraska, with her face in Dane's. "You sleep too long!"

Dane grabbed Nebraska and, feeling sweat break out on his back, he hugged her tight, closing his eyes in thankfulness.

"You're *squishing* me!" said a little voice from his chest.

Dane looked down and Nebraska was peering out at him with one eye and a red face.

Dane let out some pent-up air with a laugh of relief as he released her. "I'm so glad you're here!" he said, feeling so glad he wasn't dreaming.

"Yep!" she said getting to her feet again and jumping on the bed. "I'm-here-I'm-here!" she chanted, and then she did a seat bounce, bouncing twice on her behind. Looking at Dane with a smile she said, "I like your bed, it's bouncy!"

"I do too!" said Dane, taking Nebraska down and tickling her. "That's why I was sleeping till you woke me up!"

Nebraska let out a peal of laughter.

"Hey, I don't want to break up the fun, but I think we need to think about going," said Louise from the bedroom door.

"OK," said Dane, conceding and sliding out of bed. Aside from his nightmare, sleep felt good!

"There's some Spam and green beans on the table. I know you must be hungry."

"Spam?" asked Dane, as he tried to make the bed as Nebraska resumed her jumping. "What's Spam?"

"It's yucky!" said Nebraska between jumps.

"It's food," said Louise. "And Nebraska, your stomach is full. You ate it, so it couldn't have been that bad," she said teasingly.

"Blah!" said Nebraska, letting her tongue hang out for a second.

"You don't know what Spam is?" Louise asked Dane.

Dane thought a minute as he made one last useless tug on the covers. "Well, maybe I do. I think my dad made it for us once when I was a kid, but I think I agree with Nebraska. It wasn't my favorite."

Louise looked slightly disappointed. "Well, it's what was in the cupboards."

"But, I'm sure my tastes have changed since then," said Dane, scrambling to recover as he headed for the door. "I'm so hungry right now, I could eat roadkill."

"What's roadkill?" asked Nebraska.

Dane hesitated, looking at Louise with second thoughts. "Woops, I shouldn't have said that." Turning back he said, "It's nothing. Don't worry about it. You wouldn't like that either."

Nebraska quickly did another seat bounce and then slid off the bed and followed Dane and Louise. "Where do we go now?" she asked.

"We're going to go to my house," said Dane. "You're going to meet my brothers."

Nebraska crinkled up her nose. "Boys are mean. I don't like boys."

Dane nodded as they walked down the hall towards the kitchen. "I know boys are mean. I hope my brothers will be nice, though. I think they'll like you because you're so cute."

"Maybe," said Nebraska, innocently.

Dane sat at the table. The food looked so good. It smelled good. Real food! It had been a few days! Five, to be exact. Dane was so grateful. After a quick silent prayer, he ate. And as long as he ate, Louise cooked. He must have eaten four cans of spam and three cans of beans all by himself. But it was so good! In that moment, everything was great!

ξξξξξξξ

"There it is. My house is just up here, at the end of the street," said Dane. "It's the one on the corner with the smoke coming out of the chimney."

"That one?" asked Nebraska, pointing.

"Yep," said Dane.

"On the corner?" asked Louise, looking a little nervous. "The log cabin?"

"Yep," he said again. "We used to have a stone cottage-like house but the dam broke and it had to be demolished. We used to plant purple cabbages and giant sun flowers along the front making it look like something out of a fairytale book."

"That must have been darling," said Louise.

"Maybe," said Dane. "I didn't notice stuff like that then."

"I like daisies," said Nebraska abruptly, obviously thinking she was adding to the conversation.

"Ohhhh, to stand in front of a roaring fireplace," Louise said, rubbing her arms and looking up in the chilly September air. "Now *that* will feel good! Won't that feel good, Nebraska?" asked Louise.

"Uh huh," said Nebraska in her chipper voice.

After a moment of silence, Louise asked Dane in a subdued tone, "Are you sure I won't be a bother to your family?"

"I'm sure," said Dane, confidently. "Don't worry."

"I don't want to inconvenience anyone."

"We have lots of house, food and supplies. My mom and dad were big on being ready for anything," said Dane. "We definitely have enough for you, I promise."

As they approached the last ten yards of their journey, Dane couldn't help but smile as he imagined the faces of his family when he entered the front door. Studying the window, a wonderful feeling flowed over him. There, behind the glass were the people he loved. He closed his eyes as emotion welled up inside him. Soon he would be in their arms. It was too good to be true.

Stepping up the stairs, Louise asked, "Should we knock?"

"Yeah," said Dane thinking the knock would add effect to the shock. A dramatic entrance would be fun. "Be my guest," he said still absorbed in his imagination.

Louise and Dane stood before the large wooden door and she knocked politely.

Tap, tap, tap.

"No, no," said Dane shaking his head. "You have bang on that door to get noticed, or no one will hear you. Normally, it's pretty loud in there," he said with a chuckle. "I don't know where everyone is right now, but I'm sure they're busy doing something."

"Knock louder," said Nebraska.

"Yes, OK," said Louise. Making a fist she deliberately pounded on the door.

Rap, rap, rap.

"That's better," said Dane.

Louise, Nebraska and Dane waited but no one answered the door.

"Don't you have a doorbell?" asked Louise looking around.

Dane shook his head. "No, sorry. Here, I'll knock this time." With a strong arm he pounded on the door.

Bam, bam...

Abruptly, Dane stopped knocking. He heard a voice on the other side, one he didn't recognize; wondering for a split second if maybe his family had moved. He listened.

"Bishop, I worked hard for my food and I deserve every bit of it," said the voice on the other side of the door.

"Who's that?" asked Louise. "Is that your dad?"

Nebraska was silent. Her eyes were huge.

Dane shook his head. "No, my dad is the bishop of our ward."

"What's a ward?"

"My church group."

"Oh, he's a preacher," said Louise nodding.

"Kind of," said Dane. "He's more like a father figure, or a spiritual leader. He watches over the people. Someone must be talking with him." Dane was secretly relieved when he heard his dad's voice. He turned his attention back to the door.

The voice continued, "I hope you understand I can't afford to give any of my food away. It's not that I don't care, or understand, it's that I can't afford to."

"No one can afford to, Brother Carpenter. It's hard times. But we have to help each other," said Bo. "That's what Zion is all about."

"That second voice, *that's* my dad," said Dane.

Louise nodded.

"Are we going to go in?" asked Nebraska.

"Shh," said Dane gently, still listening.

"Well, I can't be swayed by other people," said Brother Carpenter, "I can't be held accountable for other people's choices. The Church believes in consequences of choices. Sometimes people just have to suffer for theirs. Don't mean to be harsh, but..."

"OK, Brother Carpenter. I understand," said Bo.

Then the door opened and a red faced man exited quickly, closing the door behind him, totally involved with his thoughts.

Suddenly, the man swallowed as he stopped and gazed at Louise and Nebraska. Looking twice at Louise, a look of shock came across his face. He whispered something under his breath, and then ran off as if someone had rammed him with a hot poker.

"What was that about?" asked Dane to Louise. "Did you know him? Did he recognize you?"

Louise shook her head thoughtfully as she brought a hand to her hair. "I hope not. Did you know him?"

Dane shook his head. "No. He must be new." Dane turned back. "I can't believe that guy shut the door on us." *Bam, bam, bam.* Dane banged hard on the door.

"I'll get it!" yelled a voice inside.

"No! I'll get it!" yelled another. There were sounds of children running down stairs.

"Mooooom! He pushed me! ...*Don't push*!" yelled the first.

Dane laughed. "Sounds like nothing's changed."

The doorknob turned and the door opened a crack. Roc's face appeared in the opening. His eyes showed his shock and he yelled *"Daaaaaaaane!"* as he threw open the door and jumped onto Dane with a vice-like hug. *"You're home!"*

"Who's home?" asked Ry, stepping out of the doorframe. *"Daaaane!"* yelled Ry who also jumped on his brother with a great smile.

"What's going on?" asked Jax who looked outside at the strange sight. *"Oh! Dane! You're home!"* exclaimed Jax, giving Dane a rough hug over his other brothers. They were still hanging on to Dane like spider monkeys, but smiling from ear to ear. Stepping back he yelled into the house, *"Mom! Dad! Dane's home! He brought a lady and a girl here!"*

Dane looked at Louise as she watched him try and pull his brothers off with an amused smile. "What can I say? They love me," he said as Roc and Ry continued to hold on to Dane's waist.

"We won't let go!" yelled Roc.

"Nope!" yelled Ry in agreement.

"Dane?" called his mother from the top of the stairs, *"Are you home?"* she asked, as she rushed down the stairs.

Dane was trying to move through the door, heavy with his brothers' bodies. He figured he better get off the porch and into the house, otherwise the whole neighborhood might be out soon to welcome him home. Dragging his laughing brothers who had now slid down his legs, he took two labored Frankenstein steps into the house. "Mom! Dad!" he said cheerfully, as his mother flew happily into him and his father came in from the other room. "I'm home."

"Son!" exclaimed Bo, with moist eyes. "You made it!" he said with a laugh, making eye contact, shaking his hand and giving him a hug. "And you brought guests."

"Yes, this is Louise Anderson, a professor who teaches at the University of Las Vegas, and Nebraska, she's five."

"I'm five," said Nebraska, holding up five fingers.

"It's great to meet both of you," said Corrynne as she studied Louise as if surprised.

Louise nodded in agreement. "Thank you. You, too."

Dane sensed his mother look at Louise a little too long, but he was too overwhelmed and honestly, didn't care. He was so glad to be home, he held out his arms and hugged everyone he could grab, enfolding his brother Jax and his Mother and Father in a large group hug all at the same time. Then he cried. They all did.

"Yes, I made it," said Dane, continuing to cry like a baby, not caring who was watching or even trying to be tough. "I'm home!"

"Dane?" called a feminine voice from above.

Dane looked up surprised. He wiped his face with a hand and looked up. "…Brea?" he choked out. "You're here?"

"Yes! Brother!" she said affectionately, as she descended the stairs, holding onto the handrail, with Striynna and Strykker sliding down after her. She had a bright, warm smile. "I'm home too!" she said. "I got home just a little while ago."

"I can't believe this! *This is great*!" said Dane wiping his eyes again.

Brea reached the bottom of the stairs and joined the family. "I love you, Dane!" she said as she hugged him tight.

Dane shook his head. His heart was so full. No words could escape any longer. For a long time, no one could say one word more. All of them rejoiced in each other.

Hospital

Provo, Utah
11:40 p.m.

Corrynne scanned her intra-department computer messages at work. She wanted to stay home with Dane and Brea that night, but they were tired and someone had to work. Since Bo had been out of a job, she had to work. They were lucky. Nursing had been paying the bills when nothing else did. Not very many people had gas to heat their homes, or electricity, but they still did. She should be thankful she *could* work.

A message popped up as she scrolled down her screen. It was written in red. Obviously, it was important. She opened it.

"Each employee will be expected to apply for their new ID as soon as possible. Due to multiple breaches in security, no hospital employee will be able to enter the hospital after October 1st without it. Be on notice that only those with a **valid ID** will continue to be employed after that date."

Corrynne re-read the note to herself.

"...only those with a ***valid ID*** *will continue to be employed after that date."*

This note bothered her. Many things bothered her. What valid ID? She had a valid ID. What was going on now?

Corrynne shook her head. That would mean she'd have to walk to the hospital during the day on her day off. What a pain! She hated the hospital controlling her life. Healthcare didn't make sense anymore...she felt like *quitting*...but she couldn't.

Bang!

Corrynne jumped and looked out the ICU entrance window. The sound had come from there.

A man was out in the hall, sick and pale with wild eyes. He was looking at her because she was sitting at the computer nearest the door.

"Let me in!" he yelled. *"I'm going to die if you don't! I'm bleeding to death! I've been hurt real bad."* Then he held up a mangled and bleeding hand in the window. *"Please! My leg is worse!"*

Corrynne looked away from the window and pushed a button under the desk. The man had obviously snuck in somehow. He wasn't *authorized.* She could only give care to those who were *authorized.* Her computer would have told her he was coming—if he had money.

Corrynne looked away from the man's pleading eyes as her heart ached. She was unable to help him. If she used the hospital's limited resources for any unauthorized patient, she would be fired and arrested. She couldn't afford that so she would do as policy dictated.

Within a minute, there were four security guards, wrestling the man away from the ICU door.

"No! Help! You don't understand! What are you guys? *Animals?*" he yelled as he was pulled from the door. "What happened to this country?" Corrynne could hear the man ask the security guards. *"I'm bleeding! You can't throw me out!"*

Then the man let out a strangled scream. Corrynne knew he had been tasered. The thought made her stomach churn.

Corrynne put her face in her hands. She couldn't put up with this much longer. Things were wrong on so many levels. With a sigh, she logged out with a finger stroke and got up from the desk. She wanted to hide from that window, just in case someone else snuck in.

Walking into her patient's room, she surveyed the equipment. Seven pumps were neatly stacked, one above the other. The tiny things glowed with numbers as each infused a life-sustaining clear fluid to the patient through a central line in the neck. The ventilator delivered metered breaths, as the dialysis machine cleaned the blood.

The swollen patient was lying in a coma on the bed, the sheets lying neatly across his waist. The room looked perfect. Not one thing out of place.

This was a retired politician with an influential family. He was dying. He had no chance to live—well nearly. Because he was rich, she'd keep him alive with her machines and so would the nurse after her until he would die another day—or until he ran out of money.

Corrynne logged into her computer screen in the room. She looked over the patient's medications, but she wasn't really looking at them. Instead, she was wondering if working in the hospital was even moral. She had gone into nursing to make a difference, to save people, for life, not to refuse care to those who could survive and give care to those who couldn't...it was all so backwards. But what could she do about it?

Nothing.

Cash was king, even in her life.

Notes to "Control"

Daunting Numbers

[1] "...The greatest resource available to a bishop is the strength of the individuals and family units within his ward" (Marion G. Romney, "Principles of Temporal Salvation," *Ensign*, April 1981, pg. 3).

[2] The situation presented in the text is an extreme circumstance. Today, we are encouraged to be self-reliant, try everything in our power to solve the situation and refrain from turning to the bishop for support. To assure that we do not have to call on the bishop it is suggested we 1) be out of debt, 2) live within our means, 3) develop a savings of emergency money, 4) become educated in a marketable skill, 5) learn how to creatively make do with what we are blessed with, 6) store food and clothing, and if possible fuel for a year, 7) learn how to garden and eat from it and store its excess, 8) obtain adequate health, home, and life insurance, 9) be willing to forego luxuries, and 10) become spiritually prepared to be able to hear God's desires concerning us. If we have done everything in our power to accomplish the above and still are wanting, we should go to family for help first, and then the bishop, in that order. For articles on these topics, see www.lds.org Gospel Library Search, "welfare," "food storage," and "self reliance."

[3] "A bishop is ordained with an everlasting endowment, and it is lost only through unworthiness which brings Church discipline, even to excommunication. He is set apart as bishop of a ward to provide it leadership. He becomes the judge, spiritual advisor, inspirer, counselor, discipliner. He becomes by ordination and setting apart the father of his people and should know them individually by name and nature and weakness and strength. He should foresee and forestall possible problems and, if some develop, be able and ready to help in their solution. His ward family should be his enlarged family and receive the same general interest as his own flesh and blood children" (Spencer W. Kimball, *Teachings of Spencer W. Kimball*, pg. 474).

[4] "Jesus knew how to involve his disciples in the process of life. He gave them important and specific things to do for their development. Other leaders have sought to be so omnicompetent that they have tried to do everything themselves, which produces little growth in others. Jesus trusts his followers enough to share his work with them so that they can grow" (Spencer W. Kimball, *Teachings of Spencer W. Kimball*, pg. 482).

[5] "Sadly, surveys show that there are many of us who have not followed this counsel [becoming prepared], believing evidently, that the Church can and will take care of us" (Marion G. Romney, "Principles of Temporal Salvation," *Ensign*, April 1981, pg. 3).

"From President Thomas S. Monson, First Counselor of the first Presidency of the Church of Jesus Christ of Latter Day Saints, we hear: 'Many more people could ride out the storm-tossed waves in their economic lives if they had their year's supply of food … and were debt-free. *Today we find that many have followed this counsel in reverse: they have at least a year's supply of debt and are food-free.'* ...We call upon priesthood bearers to store sufficient so that you and your family can weather the vicissitudes of life" (Keith B. McMullin, "Lay Up in Store," *Ensign*, May 2007, pgs. 51–53).

[6] "Now, the bishop is a man of varied responsibilities and of many duties. He visits the 'fatherless and the widows'; he blesses the sick; he buries the dead; he calls to responsibility; he appoints and releases; he conducts meetings and supervises all the numerous activities in the ward; he counsels, advises, calls to repentance, disciplines, and sometimes must handle people for their fellowship and membership. He is called of God and promised divine guidance and he will be led to make right decisions and follow proper courses as he is in total attunement with the Lord" (Spencer W. Kimball, *Teachings of Spencer W. Kimball*, pg. 475).

[7] "...The bishop, as one of his first responsibilities, has the charge to teach the value of self- and family-reliance—indeed, as the Lord's shepherd, he is to teach every principle of the gospel with its power to lift, sustain, maintain, renew, purify, sanctify, make full, and satisfy our every need and righteous desire. He is to help those who request help to assess their own circumstances, to determine their own goals and objectives, to determine their own plans and their own solutions to their problems—to safely pilot their own course. The bishop is not there to do it for us. His primary role is to be a facilitator, a counselor, a confidant. He will help us deal with any immediate and pressing

needs. But the measure and extent of his assistance will be determined by what we and our immediate family have done to solve the problem" (Marion G. Romney, "Principles of Temporal Salvation," *Ensign*, April 1981, pg. 3).

[8] "In the Church, the concept of providing for one's family and of relying on one's family for growth, mutual care, and help—or family reliance—is equally fundamental to self-reliance. The family is the basic organizational unit of the Church. No agency or institution can or should replace the family. By sacred covenant and eternal priesthood government, the eternal family unit is established. By virtue of the commitment made as a part of that covenant, husbands are obligated to provide for their families. Thus, in the words of the Lord: 'Women have claim on their husbands for their maintenance, until their husbands are taken.' 'All children have claim upon their parents for their maintenance until they are of age' (D&C 85:2, 4). And through Paul the Apostle we have the sentiment: 'But if any provide not for his own, and especially for those of his own house, he hath denied the faith, and is worse than an infidel' (1 Timothy. 5:8)" (Marion G. Romney, "Principles of Temporal Salvation," *Ensign*, April 1981, pg. 3).

[9] "In this last dispensation, the Lord has again spoken plainly on the subject. 'Thou shalt not be idle,' he said. 'For he that is idle shall not eat the bread nor wear the garments of the laborer' (D&C 42:42). 'And the idler shall not have place in the Church, except he repent and mend his ways' (D&C 75:29). In light of these scriptures, no member should desire or seek to voluntarily shift the responsibility for his own maintenance to another. Rather, each member, through work, should seek to find great satisfaction in personal achievement; and thus, he will be entitled to the fruits of his labors—both temporal and spiritual" (Marion G. Romney, "Principles of Temporal Salvation," *Ensign*, April 1981, pg. 3).

[10] "In one of the most classic confrontations in the Bible, the Lord asked Cain, 'Where is Abel thy brother?' Cain answered, 'Am I my brother's keeper?' (Gen. 4:9). I put to each of us that same query: Are we our brother's keeper? King Benjamin taught, 'Ye will teach them to love one another, and to serve one another' (Mosiah 4:15). '...Ought not ye to labor to serve one another?' (Mosiah 2:18). And we will have learned the wisest answer to that question when we learn that 'when ye are in the service of your fellow beings ye are only in the service of your God' (Mosiah 2:17). Are we our brother's keeper? In Galatians, Paul told the Saints that they should love and serve one another (see Gal. 5:13–14). In James, pure religion and undefiled before God is spelled out: 'To visit the fatherless and widows in their affliction, and to keep himself unspotted from the world' (James 1:27). And who can forget the great message that Peter gave outside the gates of the temple when the lame beggar pleaded for alms: 'Silver and gold have I none; but such as I have give I thee' (Acts 3:6). The 81st section of the Doctrine and Covenants says, 'Succor the weak,' and I like this language: 'Lift up the hands which hang down, and strengthen the feeble knees' (D&C 81:5). The Doctrine and Covenants also reminds us of the judgment by which we are all judged: 'Remember in all things the poor and the needy, the sick and the afflicted, for he that doeth not these things, the same is not my disciple' (D&C 52:40). Are we our brother's keeper? Yes!" (James E. Faust, "Go Bring Them In from the Plains," *Ensign*, July 1997, pg. 2).

[11] "...It is imperative that we understand that God's chief way of acting is by persuasion and patience and long-suffering, not by coercion and stark confrontation. He acts by gentle solicitation and by sweet enticement. He always acts with unfailing respect for the freedom and independence that we possess. He wants to help us and pleads for the chance to assist us, but he will not do so in violation of our agency. He loves us too much to do that, and doing so would run counter to his divine character. Brigham Young once said: 'The volition of [man] is free; this is a law of their existence, and the Lord cannot violate his own law; were he to do that, he would cease to be God. ...This is a law which has always existed from all eternity, and will continue to exist throughout all the eternities to come. Every intelligent being must have the power of choice' (*Journal of Discourses,* 11:272)" (Howard W. Hunter, "The Golden Thread of Choice," *Ensign*, November 1989, pg. 17).

[12] "Let him that is ignorant learn wisdom by humbling himself and calling upon the Lord his God, that his eyes may be opened that he may see, and his ears opened that he may hear" (D&C 136:32).

CHAPTER FOUR

BLACK DEEDS, WHITE LIES

"For we must all appear before the judgment seat of Christ; that every one may receive the things done in his body, according to that he hath done, whether it be good or bad" (2 Corinthians 5:10).

00:03:06, 13:24:01, Zulu
Wednesday, September 24th

No Deposit, No Return

Denali National Park, Alaska
1:36 a.m.

It was dark.

Abruptly, Carea sat up. A cold feeling crept over her, clawing at her security. Something was wrong. All her senses focused as she held her breath. She felt someone outside, moving through the howling wind.

Knock, tap…scrape.

The sounds were faint, but she heard them. Instantly she knew it wasn't a tree branch or garbage blown against the wall. It was a person, sneaking around outside. Back at the gym, her beloved Sonseng had worked hours to help her refine her defensive senses. No one would sneak up on her tonight!

Standing carefully, she steadied the old wooden joints of her cot. "No squeaking!" she inaudibly commanded the elements in the cot, more to steady her mind through diversion than anything else. Luckily, the wood stayed silent.

With darting eyes, Carea searched the darkness for the wounded boy she and her roommates had captured. Was he still in his bed? Her heart skipped a beat as she realized that for her to maintain leverage, he had to be! As her eyes focused, she saw a mangled blanket and arms sticking out from underneath. Yes, he was there.

Carea scoffed at her own worry. *Of course he was there.* Where would he have gone in his underwear? It was way too cold outside to attempt a getaway and expect to survive. She knew that and so did he. That's why she and her girls had stripped the boy down so he wouldn't attempt to escape. Now he wore only his t-shirt and boxers under a pile of blankets. It wasn't the most ideal situation for him, but for her, it was the most humane idea she could think up and still keep him hostage. *She had to keep him hostage.* That was the key to her plan.

Carea listened. The boy's breathing was even and steady. He was asleep. She was glad. Sleep was probably the only relief he might get from the terrible pain she had caused him. …She *hated* that she had broke *both* his arms! She hadn't meant to break the boy, darn it! Carea shook her head. …Oh well, what could she do? The situation was what it was. She wished she could have set his arms, or something but she couldn't. She didn't know how and no one in her cabin did either. After all, they were all still just a little more than kids! At least the boy was warm and out of the wind. She hoped *his* people knew what to do to help him. In the meantime, she'd try and do her best to make up for what she had done by being kind. She hoped someday he'd forgive her.

Pushing her heavy guilt down, Carea turned her thoughts to the window. She crouched down and crept to it. She noticed her arms and legs felt stiff. It was because the night had grown colder. She stretched them briefly as she moved up against the frame. Cautiously, Carea peered out the hard clear plastic window. Who was outside?

A black form passed by the window, causing shock to pulse through Carea's body as she gasped and pulled back.

Leaning flat against the wall, she felt her body shake. She had been right! There was someone outside and he or she was probably trying to get in!

Carea's palms began to sweat as another night like this haunted her memory. She remembered the pale face at her bedroom window at home. The boy had been from her school. He had taken her from her bedroom without anyone knowing. Today, she didn't remember how that happened, but that had been when she received the chip in her forehead. With a soft stroke Carea touched her skin at the top of her face. She could still feel the bump underneath. She shook her head. Nothing like that would *ever* happen to her again! But, now was not the time to think about such things. They would make her weak. She had to center her thoughts and close out unwanted emotions.

Taking a deep breath, Carea concentrated and closed her eyes for a moment. Wiping clean all threatening thoughts and memories, she took control of her mind. Now all she thought about was combat. Now—she was ready.

Scrape…tap.

This time, the sound was on the other side of the cabin.

Quickly, Carea pulled her blanket off of her cot and wrapped it around her shoulders. She would face whoever was out there outside. Maybe catch them off guard.

With a few steps, Carea was at the door. Quietly turning the knob she opened it. A knife-like cold blast hit her face. She tightened her jaw as she forced herself to go outside and close the door behind her.

"Hey!" called a man's voice.

Carea froze like a tiger prepared for a fight. The light was better out here and immediately she spotted two members of what she now called the Fur Clan, both in characteristic black, right off the porch.

"Give us back our tracker," growled a deep and menacing voice.

Carea didn't respond, but instead sized up the two in the moonlight. One was broader across the back and the other was thin and tall. Each of them had a carved stick.

"Are you deaf? I said give us back our tracker!" snarled the larger man, tapping his stick threateningly in his hand.

"Your tracker?" asked Carea.

"Yes," said the thinner man.

Something clicked inside Carea. If the word "tracker" meant animal tracker, the boy inside her cabin was more valuable than she thought. Out in the wilderness a good tracker could mean the difference between starvation and survival. "Does he find your food?" she asked.

"Give him back," said the tall one, apparently unwilling to reveal anything more.

"What makes you think that's an option?" asked Carea. "Maybe *we* want a tracker."

"These sticks say you don't get one," said the one with broad shoulders.

Carea nodded. "Ahh, I see." Her mind whirled to figure out what to say next. "How about we strike a deal?"

"No deals," growled the thin one. "Us two against you says we win. No need to strike a deal."

Carea had experience with the Kendo sword in martial arts training so their sticks didn't intimidate her, as long as she had one too. She looked around the base of the trees for one. She didn't see anything worth fighting with. To stall for time, she said, "Ahh, come on guys. I'm sure there's a way we can work things out."

Both men took a couple of steps forward. "Get our tracker, *now*!" demanded the thin man.

"Or we'll bust in and get him ourselves," added the broad-shouldered one.

Carea held her hand out defensively. Maybe if she could steal one of the sticks, then that would level the playing field. Considering just how she would do this, she said, "Alright, tell you what. You guys put down the sticks and just take me on, like real men instead of scared little boys that need sticks for security."

The two men looked at each other and laughed mockingly. The broader one said, "You? Against us? You're crazy."

Carea shrugged and said, "Maybe…maybe not. The only stipulation is if I clean your clocks, you listen to me."

"Why? What do you want to say?" asked the thin one.

"Well, I think I want to give back your tracker, but not until I get all of the new stuff back that you guys took from us."

The big guy shook his head and said, "The way things work around here is that we get the new stuff and the new detainees get the old stuff. That blanket around your shoulders works well enough for you. You won't die of cold. Gruff makes sure everyone has what they need. So no, no deal."

"Who's Gruff? Is he your leader?"

"Yeah. He's the brains."

"I see. And he sent you guys."

"Yeah, we're the muscle," said the tall guy with a sly smile.

Carea nodded. "I see. So really I'm wasting my time with you, right? You can't make any decisions anyway. You guys are just lunkheads. Might as well just teach you a lesson and get it over with." Carea went into her fighting stance.

The men looked at each other and then back.

"Whatever," said the larger man with a smile spreading on his face.

"Yeah. Whatever you say, missy," said the other, continuing to tap his stick in his hands.

Carea could tell that neither of the men thought she was a threat. That was good. She'd surprise them. That would give her the upper hand. However, in the back of her mind she knew that even if she won this fight there might have to be more fighting to get their things back. She hated that, but she knew it was necessary in this environment. Sooner or later it would have to work.

Carea whispered a prayer for protection. She remembered Ammon had to cut off the arms of many bad guys in order to win the respect of the king. She figured this was the same kind of situation. All she wanted was good for her girls. That good would lead to greater good and that's what she was here for.

The big guy took a menacing step towards Carea. He was just close enough. Quicker than lightning, she kicked his hand with a powerful flick and the stick he had flew into the air.

The man was astonished and all of them watched it arc, hit the cabin behind Carea, then roll to her.

Carea bent down and picked up the stick. "Thanks. I needed that."

"Whatcha doing?" complained the tall one hitting his partner in the shoulder. "You gave her your stick!"

"I didn't *give* it to her, she knocked it out of my hands!" said the bigger, closer, man.

"You're an idiot!" said the tall one.

"What's going on here?" asked Bones from the door. "Yo, Carea, you need back up?"

"Sure," Carea answered, while keeping her stare on the men. "Friends are good."

Suddenly, the group of bad-tempered looking girls filled the doorway. All of them had rocks or sticks of their own.

"No, wait a minute. You said, just you against us," said the big guy with a raised hand.

Carea nodded. "I'll make good on all my offers if you bring back our goods."

"Are you going to break these guys' arms like you did the other one?" asked Bones with a sneer, taunting the boys.

"Maybe," said Carea, lying.

"Yeah," started Bones. "She snapped both your boy's arms in one second. You guys sure you want to mess with her? Because I wouldn't if I were you. This girl doesn't need a weapon because she *is* a lethal weapon. That stick is just for show."

The men looked at each other. "You're bluffing," said the unarmed one.

"No, not really. She broke your arms, didn't she precious?" called Bones back behind her.

There was a scream of pain.

"Tell them what happened to you! Who broke your arms?" demanded a voice inside.

"Yes, yes! Don't touch me! *My arms! Please!* Get me out of here!"

The looks on the men's faces changed. The tall one stepped back. "Ahh, so you want a trade, huh?" he asked, backpedaling.

"Yep," said Carea whipping the stick she had from side to side and then hitting her sword fighting stance again. With her hand she signaled for both the men to advance. "I want that, and *you.* Come on. Let's go!"

The big guy looked helplessly around on the ground. "I need…"

"Ahh, we need to go talk to Gruff and tell him your terms," said the tall one.

"That'd be a great idea," said Bones, nodding over Carea's head, staring the men down the way only Bones could. "*Because we want our stuff.*"

"We'll be back," said the big guy.

"I'll be waiting," said Carea. "Tell Gruff, Carea Rogers is waiting for his decision. In the meantime we'll take good care of your tracker."

In response, the men slinked off into the night.

Family Affairs

Provo, Utah
8:15 a.m.

Corrynne smelled food as she opened the front door after work. Good, someone had made the children a warm breakfast. Now she felt a little bit better about getting home late. She *always* made it a point to get home for their morning routine and send the children off to school after a night shift. That was the benefit of working a night shift. But today, she was forced to stay later than normal. *Stupid work,* she thought to herself. The distaste for her job and its misplaced priorities still lingered.

Corrynne closed the front door and stood in the entryway, hesitating, listening. The house was quiet except for adult voices in the kitchen. It looked like her little guys had successfully left for school. Good, things looked like they were under control. At least *someone* was on the ball.

"Bo? Are you cooking?" she called from the living room as she put her bag down beside the front door and took off her coat.

"It's Dane and I, Mom," replied a feminine voice.

"Brea? Dane?" called Corrynne, feeling happier just to hear their voices.

"Yeah, Mom, it's us," said Dane.

"What are you cooking?" she asked moving towards the kitchen. "It smells so good!"

"We had pancakes and eggs," said Brea.

Corrynne rounded the corner to see her son and expectant daughter sitting at the table across from each other. Brea looked rosy-cheeked and happy. Dane, who turned back with a glance, looked a little thin, but he was smiling too. It was such a good sight. "Hello you two!" said Corrynne, giving both of them a hug and a kiss on the cheek.

"How was work?" asked Brea.

Corrynne frowned as she took a seat at the table next to Dane. "I don't want to talk about work. I want to talk about this morning. How did it go? Where's Dad?"

"Dad's still sleeping," said Dane. "We let him sleep in."

"That was nice," said Corrynne, nodding.

"And don't worry, Mom, we had morning scriptures and prayer with Jax, Ry, and Roc, and now they've gone to school."

Corrynne sighed with relief. "You are too good to me," she said, feeling emotional. "You just automatically filled in, smoothing out the rough spots. Thank you."

"Sure," said Dane.

"We kind of know the routine, Mom. Of course we'd fill in," said Brea. "But I wasn't sure if there *was* school, so I hope I did the right thing."

Corrynne nodded. "Yes, there is, as I understand it, but school probably won't last long if things stay the way they are. It's good they went today."

"Well, Jax and Ry said school was still functioning, so I sent them on their way."

"Good," said Corrynne, as she shook her head and placed her hands on her children's arms. "Thank you for pinch hitting. I'm *so* thankful both of you are home." Tears came to her eyes easily. "It's been hard without you."

"Ahh, Mom," said Dane putting an arm around his mother and patting her shoulder. "You missed us."

Corrynne laughed and cried at the same time as tears fell from her eyes. She quickly wiped them away. "More than you know!"

Dane turned and gave his mother a true, full hug. "Well, we're here now."

"I'm so glad," said Corrynne, taking in the energy from Dane's body. She loved being embraced by him. His presence was feeding her, regenerating her from her night of no sleep and the days before filled with mourning and secret longing for her grown children. She had tried to be strong but now she couldn't help herself. "I'm sorry," said Corrynne pulling away. "I don't mean to cry."

"You're tired," said Brea with concerned eyes.

Corrynne nodded. "I am, but I don't want to go to bed. If you don't mind, I'd like to sit here and talk with you guys for a while. I'm just enjoying seeing you and hearing your voices."

"We'd love you to stay," said Brea, grasping her mother's hand gently over the table.

"Then I will," said Corrynne with a smile and a nod. Sniffing she asked, "Where're the twins?"

"They're still sleeping, too."

"They are?" asked Corrynne looking at her watch. "They never sleep this late. Sometimes they get up at five!"

"I think everyone's tired today," said Dane. "Last night was an exciting night."

"I agree. And Louise and Nebraska?" asked Corrynne. "Are they still sleeping, too?"

"Snoozing away," said Dane. "They deserve the rest."

"What about you?" asked Corrynne. "Dane, don't you need more sleep?"

"Nah. I'm good," Dane said with a shrug. "Anyway I'm too interested in Brea and her secret life. She could start her own mini-series."

"What do you mean?" asked Corrynne, looking at Brea.

"Not everyone has an assassin for a father-in-law," he said with a disrespectful laugh.

"Dane, that's not funny," said Corrynne, surprised Brea had told Dane about Matt's father. She had thought his true identity and intentions were secret. "Brea's safety is at stake. That's not funny, Dane."

"It's OK, Mom," said Brea, shaking her head. "I'm starting to laugh about it myself. If you think about it, my whole situation is ridiculous."

"I don't know about that," said Corrynne. "Aren't we supposed to keep everything quiet about MD?" she asked. "Won't Dane knowing the details put him, as well as you, at risk?"

Brea shook her head. "Dane won't tell anyone. Anyway, I don't think things can get any worse, do you, Mother?"

Corrynne nodded. "Yes, they can get worse. I know what it's like to live without you and for me, losing you would make things unbearable."

"Well, that's not going to happen," said Brea, smiling. "Matt's making sure of that."

"Let's hope so," said Corrynne.

"Mom," said Dane with intensity. "Have you heard about her toys?"

"What *toys*?" asked Corrynne, not having any idea what Dane was talking about.

"She has a cloaking device as well as a computerized home under ground," continued Dane.

"No, I don't have it yet, Dane. It's still being built," corrected Brea.

"Mom, she'll have a state-of-the-art home under ground where no one will even suspect it's there!" continued Dane. "She'll be able to turn the lights up and down by voice and her floor will vacuum itself!"

Corrynne smiled at Brea. "Sounds nice. Matt's coming through for you, then?"

Brea opened her mouth to answer, but Dane interrupted. "Why didn't you tell me all this was happening? Half the fun is knowing. I didn't even know you were rich!"

"I didn't know I was rich!" said Brea emphatically.

"Tell me about this underground home," said Corrynne. "Is it up in the canyon? Matt told us he had picked out a spot."

"No..." began Brea, as she stood and headed to the counter. "Would you like some food, Mother?"

"Sure," said Corrynne. "But tell me about your home."

"OK..." said Brea, thinking.

"Tell her about the cloak first," suggested Dane. "That thing is amazing. Almost out of the pages of Harry Potter!"

"What cloak?" asked Bo abruptly from the entrance to the kitchen.

"Dad!" said Brea, jumping a little. "I didn't notice you there."

"I just got here," said Bo scratching his bed head.

"Would you like some powdered eggs, whipped up to look like real ones? Dane and I made breakfast today," said Brea with a smile.

"Yes, thank you," he said. "I'll have whatever else you're dishing out too. What cloak?" asked Bo, redirecting the conversation.

"Well..." started Brea, but didn't continue as she dished up food onto two plates.

"Is it some sort of device to make you translocate?" asked Bo, sounding skeptical as he took his seat across from Corrynne and next to where Brea had been sitting. "In my mind, that's the only way Matt would be happy, if he could just pluck you out of here whenever he wanted to. He didn't want you at our house."

Brea smiled and nodded. "You're right, Dad, Matt didn't want me here, but it wasn't personal."

"Oh, I know that," said Bo, but it didn't look that way to Corrynne. He seemed a little bothered. It was probably just talking about Matt that irritated him. Corrynne knew Matt wasn't his favorite person right now.

Brea set the plates in front of Corrynne and Bo and said, "But after many heated discussions, it became apparent that I *needed* to be here."

"I would agree with that," said Corrynne, picking up a fork, "considering your nearing delivery date."

"Also, considering my divorce..." she said as she sat back down, next to her father.

"Divorce?" asked Dane, looking confused.

Corrynne gave Dane a firm look and shook her head.

Dane got the hint and nodded, putting up his hands in defense and sitting back a little.

"Oh, Brea," whispered Corrynne, as she returned her thoughts to her daughter, shaking her head in sadness. She felt empathy for her daughter's hard situation. She didn't deserve what was happening to her.

Brea looked at her mother abruptly. With sudden fire in her eyes she exclaimed, "Well, I need to say it as it is, right? No need for sugarcoating. I'm alone, *right*?"

"Right," said Corrynne, agreeing quickly, feeling a sudden heaviness for changing the feeling of the conversation. She hadn't meant to cause problems.

Brea continued. "The reality of this situation is that Matt won't be part of my life in the foreseeable future, so I had to ultimately decide what was good for me. I out-voted Matt. *I* decided I wanted to be here, *despite* the risks."

"You're being very mature about your separation," said Corrynne, trying to be as supportive as possible.

"It's a divorce, Mother, not a separation."

"OK, your divorce," said Corrynne, hating the sound of her own words.

Brea shook her head. "And I'm really not mature. There are times I kick and scream and throw tantrums because I can't have the life I expected for myself. But, I'm fine right now."

Corrynne reached across the table and said, "Well, don't worry. We'll raise your children together."

"Good," said Brea, shedding a single tear and wiping it away with a shaking hand. "At least one of them," she said under her breath.

"What's that?" asked Dane.

"Not now, Dane," whispered Corrynne.

Dane nodded. "OK," he said with a look of resignation.

Another tear fell. Brea hit the table softly with her fist and said, "Now, *I'm* crying, *darn it*!"

"It's OK," said Corrynne, feeling like crying again herself, but controlling her emotions. "Mascara runs in our family! It's genetic," she said with a big smile, trying to make a joke and lighten the mood.

Brea smiled. "That one *was* funny, Mom."

"Thanks!" said Corrynne, smiling and squeezing her daughter's hand.

"Dane, you should learn from Mom," said Brea, with a partial smile through her tears.

Dane smiled back and said, "Fine, mock me. I can take it."

Brea grew serious again and said to her mother, "But, I have to tell you—I mean," Brea stopped and looked at her father. "I have to tell both of you some things."

"Go ahead," said Bo. "We're listening."

"I'm going to level with both of you and tell you that, yes, I am in hiding from MD, but let's be honest, we all know MD already knows where I am."

"Are you sure?" asked Corrynne.

"Sure he does, Mom," said Brea with a shrug. "He's a smart man. And if he doesn't, he will."

"But you're talking theoretically. You don't *know* that he knows you're here, right?" said Bo.

Brea nodded. "You're right. I don't know anything. But I'm sure he's assuming I'd come home to have these children. Any intelligent person would."

"I see," said Corrynne, looking at Bo. "Doesn't that make you nervous?" she asked Brea.

"Yes," said Brea. "But what am I going to do? Not come home?"

"Stay in hiding," said Bo.

Brea shook her head. "I can't do it, Dad. I did it for one week and I nearly went crazy. I need to have a certain amount of freedom or I'll become a basket case."

"Yes, but you must be careful," said Corrynne. "We can't protect you from MD. He's stronger than we are."

"And you have to consider the risk you bring to your little brothers and sister," said Bo.

Brea frowned. "Of course, Dad, that's why Matt and I came up with our plan: to *protect* your family—and mine."

"So tell me about this plan," said Bo.

Brea looked at the ceiling and then said, "It's simple. If he can't see me, he can't find me."

"So you're going to stay out of sight."

"Right," said Brea. "I never want MD to have any evidence that I'm here. And even if he came looking for me, he'd have a hard time, if not an impossible time, finding me."

"How's that?" asked Bo.

"Well, first of all, the way MD normally finds people is by tracking their chip. I don't have one, so he can't directly track me."

"Thank heavens for that!" Corrynne sighed.

"Secondly, that dark cloak that I have—"

"The dark brown one you had on last night?" asked Bo.

"Yes. It's made of a special heat absorbing material so that not only am I invisible to any satellite eyes but I'm invisible to heat sensing equipment."

"So you can move around outside, at night, without being sensed," said Dane with enthusiasm.

"Right," said Brea.

"OK, so that's good at night, but what about during the day?" asked Bo.

"I don't come out during the day," said Brea, looking back and forth between her parents. "I stay at home."

"Whose home?" asked Corrynne.

"My home."

"You have a home already?" asked Bo. "I thought Matt was going to build you a home in a mountain."

Brea looked troubled. "He wanted to, but I dug my heels in on that one. I'd be too far away from you guys."

"But isn't that optimal," asked Corrynne. "I mean, I want you close, but I want you safe, too."

"Underground is just as safe as in a mountain," said Brea. "The important thing is that the house is in the earth to block MD's global monitoring devices."

"You know what's good about that?" asked Dane.

"What?" asked Corrynne, trying to be patient with Dane's interruptions.

"Brea's computerized home will be protected from any solar flares or electromagnetic pulses. Energy can't travel through the earth. Louise and I had a discussion about that on our way home."

"That's good," said Corrynne. "At least her phones will work."

"No they won't," said Bo. "If she's connected to any power grid or telephone relay station on the outside world, her power, phones and everything else will go down along with the rest of ours."

"No, Dad," said Dane. "What I'm saying is that, eventually, the solar flares will become more and more damaging, not just interrupting service, but melting down motherboards."

"Oh," said Bo, nodding. "You're right. Having our computers in Brea's home would protect them. That's a great idea, son."

"So tell us where your home is going to be built," Corrynne encouraged Brea.

"Right here," said Brea as she tapped the table and smiled.

"Under our house?" asked Corrynne, with raised eyebrows. "Is that possible?"

"I don't think that's wise," added Bo, shaking his head.

"No, not *under* your home, but *near* your home," said Brea. "Very near your home."

"Where?" asked Dane.

"Haven't you noticed the digging on Old Man Griffin's property?" asked Brea.

Corrynne's mouth dropped open. "Across the street?"

Brea nodded and smiled. "Yes, across the street. That's where my home will be. In fact, there's a part that will be finished enough that I can move in next week. I'll be sleeping in my living room for a while, but that'll be OK."

"Wow, that's fast!" said Corrynne. "How is it being built so quick?"

"Money will do that for you, I guess," said Brea with a shrug.

"That's sweet," said Dane. "Too bad you're divorcing the guy."

Brea stood and gave Dane a quick hit in the shoulder.

"Ouch!" said Dane, snickering. "Mom, you're going to let her do that?"

Corrynne nodded. "You deserved that one."

"You're *not* funny, Dane," said Brea with a smirk meant to resemble the death stare she used to give him when they were little. "I think I told you that already."

"Yeah, you told me that," said Dane. "But I couldn't help myself."

"Well, *learn*. It will help you when you're married."

"Right. My wife will think I'm hilarious. We'll have a marriage made in heaven," he said as he covered his heart with his hand and looked dramatically up to the ceiling.

"Whatever!" said Brea. "That's what you think."

"Time out!" exclaimed Corrynne, good-naturedly. "Brea, get back to what you were saying!"

Brea turned back to her parents and continued. "Now before I was so *rudely* interrupted, I was saying that Matt bought the land and set the house up. Oh, and by the way, you should meet Mr. Griffin. He might not be a member of our church, but he's the nicest and most generous man you'd ever meet."

"Was he paid well?" asked Bo with a flat tone.

"Very well," said Brea.

"Good. We wondered what was happening over there," said Bo. "Normally in times like these, all construction stops, but I noticed that it didn't across the street. I hope Matt took precautions with his money so MD doesn't find you."

"I'm sure he did," said Brea. "He's good at details. One good thing about the origin of Matt's money is that it's immune to our banks closing."

"Why?" asked Dane.

"Because Matt *is* the bank," said Brea. "Well—at least his father is."

"He is?" asked Dane.

"Yes, his father controls all the banks in America and most around the world."

"So it's your husband's family's fault the world is falling apart," said Dane.

"Absolutely," said Bo, boldly.

"Hmm," said Dane as he nodded slowly. As if thinking about something. "What did you say Matt's father's name was again?"

"MD," said Brea, looking back to Dane. "His real name is Matthew Daimler Senior, but he goes by MD."

"I see," said Dane.

There was a pause in the conversation then Bo said, "So, tell us when your home will be done."

"This week the last of the materials were taken down underground. Next week the ground will be replaced, complete with Mr. Griffin's hay, so he can continue growing it and harvesting it as normal."

"Wow, that's a great idea," said Corrynne.

"No one will even know there's a house under there. That will let the building continue underground," said Dane nodding. "That's smart."

"So even if MD looks here, he won't find me," said Brea.

"Unless he tears up all the land around here," said Dane.

"Why would he do that?" asked Brea, with a look of frustration.

Dane shrugged. With raised eyebrows he said, "I don't know, I was just saying…"

"He wouldn't, unless there was a reason," said Bo. "We just won't give him a reason. Brea will be out of sight, *period*."

"Right," said Corrynne with a nod.

"So I feel relatively safe," said Brea.

"OK, what about food?" asked Bo.

"Well, that's the bad news. I'll have to depend on you guys for my food," said Brea with a grimace, "since the stores aren't open."

"That's fine," said Corrynne. "We have your portion of food supply still."

"Good. I knew that you did," said Brea. "Don't happen to have diapers still do you?"

Corrynne shook her head and said, "No, but we have rags and towels. We'll make diapers."

Brea looked unsure.

"It'll work," said Corrynne. "There's always a way."

"OK, I'll depend on you to help me figure all that out."

"I'm excited to do it," said Corrynne with a smile.

"Tell me where the entrance to your home will be," said Bo.

"There will be a tunnel leading from my home to a grove of trees down the road from here about a block. The door will just look like grass, so when it's shut, it'll be camouflaged."

"Good," said Bo.

"So it's not near our house?" asked Corrynne.

"No," said Brea. "I made sure of that. If MD ever did come looking around here, I didn't want him to think you guys were hiding me. That could be bad. This way, I'm hiding myself and no one else is involved."

"What about church? Are you going to go to church?" asked Dane.

"Why? Are you worried I might get out of it?" Brea joked with her brother.

"No, I was just wondering," said Dane defensively. "What? Now I can't even ask questions!"

Brea laughed, "Of course. I'm just giving you a bad time—*little* brother."

Dane laughed and shook his head.

Brea turned to her father and asked, "Dad, I'm still in your ward, if I live in that field out there, aren't I?"

Bo thought a moment and then said, "I believe you would be."

"And Dad's the bishop, right?" asked Brea, looking at her mother.

"Right," said Corrynne.

"So Jax can bring me the sacrament, and if you don't mind, I'll listen in to the meetings through you. You can record the meetings for me."

"That's not a problem," said Bo. "We already do that for a few home-bound ward members now. We'll just add another recording to our list."

"Thanks, Dad," said Brea.

"And who knows…as time continues, maybe things will change. Maybe…" Brea stalled.

"Maybe Matt will take over MD's business and it will all be over?" asked Corrynne.

"Yes, maybe that will happen," said Brea thoughtfully.

"But doesn't MD have to *die* first?" asked Bo.

"Bo!" said Corrynne in a warning voice.

"Well, I was just double checking to see if that was still true," said Bo.

Brea shook her head. "I don't know. I get exhausted worrying about it, but I do know Matt is planning a takeover of some sort. I don't know the details, but he's been working on it for a while. So maybe this underground house and all our secrets will only be short term."

"But for now, it will be fine," assured Corrynne.

"I hope so."

"Talking about Matt, have you heard from him lately?" asked Bo.

Brea shook her head. "I'm not expecting to until after the babies are born."

"Why?"

"The last communication I had from him wasn't very clear. He called me on a cell phone but it kept cutting out."

"It was those solar flares," said Dane. "No one could call anyone anywhere."

"What did he say?" asked Corrynne.

"He told me his father was watching him carefully and monitoring all his communications. Since we were supposedly getting divorced, not to expect any communication unless he could figure something out that couldn't be traced."

"Supposedly?" asked Dane. "Is there part of this story I'm not hearing?"

"Brea and Matt are divorced legally, but not in reality," said Corrynne. "It's just for show to please his father."

Dane looked confused. "Now wait, isn't the legal part what makes marriage—marriage?"

Brea looked at Dane with a bored stare again.

"What?" he asked defensively. "I'm not being funny this time. I'm just asking."

"Don't worry about it, Dane. It's complicated," said Brea.

"I can understand complicated," said Dane. "Try me."

"I'll tell you later," said Corrynne. "Brea doesn't want to go into it."

"No, I don't," she said, looking at the table.

There was a creaking right outside the kitchen entrance.

"Who's there?" called Corrynne, expecting her little twins any minute.

"Oh, I'm sorry," said a sleepy Louise as she poked her head into the kitchen. "Where's the bathroom?"

"Oh, ahh, you're almost there," said Corrynne, pointing. "Continue down the hall and it's on the left."

"Thank you," said Louise, as she disappeared.

Bo looked at Dane pointedly for a moment, almost with an amused look on his face.

"What, Dad?" Dane asked defensively.

Bo didn't answer immediately but smiled, as if he was thinking about picking on him.

"What's going on here?" asked Dane. "Everyone's got it out for me or something."

"We're not picking on you," said Corrynne, as she hugged her son from the side.

"He's going to," said Dane, pointing at his father across the table. "I can see it in his eyes!"

"I'm not going to pick on you, son. I'm just going to ask you who Louise really is."

Dane hesitated and looked around the table. Everyone was waiting for him.

"She's a lady who helped me get home. She didn't have food, or a family, so I told her she could come and eat our food and stay with us. Why?"

"Dane, do you know the President of the United States is missing?"

Dane nodded. "Sure, Dad."

"Did you ever think that Louise might look like her?" said Bo, glancing at Corrynne, who nodded.

Dane shrugged. "Maybe," he said. "Isn't the president pretty tall though?"

Bo shook his head, "No, she's about five-eight, just like Louise. Don't you know what the president looks like?"

Dane paused. "I guess I've never paid close attention to her looks. They weren't important."

Bo shook his head. "They are, in *this* situation. Son, I'm not trying to make trouble; I'm just stating the obvious. Now that I've seen that woman again, I'm convinced Louise is *not* a professor, and she *never* taught at the University of Las Vegas."

"So, what are you saying, Dad?" asked Dane.

"Well," said Bo with a smile. "First of all, I think that woman *is* the President of the United States—I'd bet my life on it! And second of all, I think she knows a thing or two about Braun."

Corrynne was stunned. That was true! *Braun had disappeared from the White House!* With an open mouth she felt a new hope grow within her. Could this woman know about her son? Could she help get him back? Miracle of miracles! Could Heavenly Father have sent such a tender mercy to a family with breaking hearts?[1]

Corrynne shook her head, in the strongest tone she could muster she asked, "Dane, tell us! Is Louise the President or not? *We need to know!*"

Dane stared at his family. He didn't respond right away. With a conflicted stare he said, "I—I—can't tell you..."

"What?" asked Bo, almost in anger.

Corrynne cringed. *What was happening here?*

Bribery

Denali National Park, Alaska
8:22 a.m.

Forlorn people milled about the camp, none of them seemed to have a purpose. All of them had gray, ripped blankets wrapped tightly around their heads and bodies as each fought off the near freezing autumn air of Alaska. The gray color fluttered everywhere, adding to the gloom of the overcast sky.

Carea was astonished at the despair she saw all around her. What was wrong with the people in this place? Sure it was a prison camp, but it wasn't like *they* were in jail. Everyone here was only being held until the hysteria calmed down in America. It'd be over soon. She felt like these detainees needed to get a grip and take their lives back and stop acting like victims![2] Nothing was more poisonous in a survival situation than self-pity!

Carea wandered over to a fire where a pot of something was boiling. Her stomach growled loudly. She was very hungry. Carea looked deep into the boiling liquid.

"What's in there?"

"Soup," said the woman tending the fire.

"Good, I'm starved," said Carea. "What kind of soup?"

"Bone soup," said the woman.

"What kind is that?"

"The only kind we've got. Do you have a problem with that?" asked the woman angrily.

Carea stared at the woman for a moment and then said, "It's obvious to me that someone's given you a bad time about your soup."

"Yes, and I'm sick and tired of it," said the woman, stirring the pot a little with a stick. "I'm not a magician, you know. Can't cook what I haven't got. This is all that's left."

"From what?"

"The last delivery of food."

"The last delivery? Who says?"

"I say."

Carea folded her arms and took a step back. Was this woman telling the truth or just dishing out pessimism? "OK, why do you think that?"

"No more food's comin'. There's no gas, so no trucks can bring it up here. So, we're just going to sit around and watch each other starve. That's how I see it."

"Well, that's just dumb," said Carea, feeling angry the suggestion was even brought up. "Are you in the business of passing dismal rumors?"

"Someone's got to say it how it is. No use living in a fantasy world."

Carea didn't want to fight with this single-minded woman. It seemed she received some sort of personal reward by making others miserable. Carea was going to stop this right now.

Stepping up on a large boulder, she called, "People! I understand from this woman that all of you believe there's no hope and we are just counting the days till our death. Is this true?"

A couple people turned their heads toward Carea but didn't seem very interested. Carea could see that their eyes were dull.

"Let me ask you a question. Even if the government isn't going to bring any more food or supplies, why would we just lie down and die? Why are we so willing to rely on the government to feed us and so willing to die if they don't?"[3]

A group of people turned, looking like they might gather to listen.

Carea took that gesture positively. She hoped she was earning their interest.

"Whatcha doing girl?" asked Bones as she quickly approached the circle.

"I'm telling these people to wake up and realize we aren't helpless. We can do something about our situation. We can make things better. People throughout time have lived on this planet without handouts and succeeded!"

"What do you have in mind?" asked a sickly looking boy who approached slowly.

"What do I have in mind?" asked Carea. With a finger in the air she said, "People! There's *game* in these woods! We're in Alaska! One of the richest parts of the world for wild game! There are animals everywhere here, not like Los Angeles, New York, or any other area you people have been transplanted from, but real live animals that can give us nutritious food to keep us alive! Anyone in the mood for a barbeque?"

There were a couple hoots and claps, but they were sparse. It was a start.

A woman who had come close asked Carea with a hollow stare, "Do you know how to hunt?"

Bones nodded. "My girl can do anything!" she said with a nod and a smile. "If anyone can pull miracles out of a hat, I'm convinced this one can."

Carea smiled at Bone's support. She continued to address the crowd that was forming. "I don't know about miracles, but I do know about effort! To be honest I don't know how to hunt, but there are people in this camp walking around with animal fur coats on. Black fur coats. Obviously *someone* not only knows how but is actively hunting and being very successful!"

"That gang won't share," said someone off to the left. "They *want* us to die."

"Are you going to give them what they want?" Carea waited for a response. "Huh?" she asked, challenging the people.

No one offered anything.

"I can't believe what I'm seeing! *Wake up people!* Become a power to be reckoned with! Let's learn how to bring the water to us. Let's learn how to insulate our cabins. Let's learn how to be self-sufficient! Get a grip! If you're going to die, *die for something*, not just because no one wanted to share with you! Where's your will to survive? Come on!"

"Tell them what you have in mind, Carea," yelled Bones with a twinkle in her eye, obviously feeling the spirit of the situation.

Carea pointed. "Those people out in the woods, those people are just like you! They are here for the same reason you are here! The only difference between you and them is that they decided to change their lot. They decided to fix their problems rather than accept them! We can do that, too! Sure we might have to entice the hunters to teach us to hunt, but what's wrong with that? Exchange of goods and services is what society's all about!"

"Hey! Are you Carea Rogers?" asked a voice from behind her, interrupting her speech.

Carea turned.

There was a group of six members of the black fur clan standing expectantly, looking at her.

"Yes?" asked Carea, suddenly feeling pleased. These people showed up right on cue! "Speak of the devil!" she said to the people as she stepped off her rock. "What do you want?" she asked.

Bones and five other scary-looking girls moved in behind Carea for support.

"You are Carea, right?" the boy asked again.

"Yes, I am. I already told you that."

"Gruff wants to see you."

Carea smiled patiently and said, "Does this mean he's ready to make a trade?"

Three of the members pulled backpacks off their backs and threw them on the ground in front of Carea.

"What's this?" asked Carea, feeling the crowd thicken to watch what was happening. A person came from the periphery and quickly tried to snatch one of the bags.

"Don't touch that bag!" commanded Carea, pointing.

Bones stepped between the person and the bag.

"No, these supplies are just a token of good will," said one of the clan members. "Think of them as a gift. There's more to come if you come with us to see Gruff. He wants to talk about the terms of our trade."

"I like how that sounds," said Carea, nodding. "But, how do I know this isn't a trap?"

"No trap."

"What's my guarantee?"

"We'll leave two of our people in your custody in return for your trust."

Carea thought for a moment. "I don't know. We're not in the business of taking care of captives. We don't even have enough for ourselves, let alone two more people. I think I'd rather have a meeting in a neutral place surrounded by my people, just in case. You understand, don't you?"

The spokesperson for the clan looked troubled.

"So take these supplies back and tell Gruff I would be more than happy to meet with him, but it has to be in a neutral place."

Slowly they picked the bags back up. "We'll tell Gruff what you said."

A murmuring began behind Carea. She ignored it. "Great," said Carea. "I'll be waiting for his word."

The clan members turned and left together.

A different woman nearby began to cry.

"What's wrong?" asked Carea, going to her.

"Why would you let those supplies go? We need them."

Carea's heart broke. In a kind voice she said, "Believe me, it's better that we don't take bribes. We need to hold out for the best solution for everyone. We want supplies for the whole camp, not just for three people."

The woman shook her head. "You don't understand. You're not very hungry yet, you just got here. We're starving to death. Our bodies can't stay warm. We can't wait for another time."

Carea wrapped an arm around the stranger. "I know what you're saying. You're right. I'm not suffering like you are yet and I hope I don't have to. I'm trying to do what's best for all of us. Those bags wouldn't have been enough. We want more and I think we can get it. Keep your chin up. Things will be fine. That's a gift I hope to give to everyone here."[4]

Carea turned and approached the woman making the bone soup. She asked, "May I have a bowl of your delicious soup?"

The woman smiled briefly and poured a metal cup full, then waited for Carea to taste it.

Carea took a drink and held up the cup high. "This is the best bone soup I have ever tasted. I invite all of you to have some! And tomorrow, I personally guarantee, it will be even better! Everyone! Take some, it will make you warm, and tell this woman, 'Thanks!'" With a wink, Carea walked away with plans forming in her head.[5]

"What's going on?" asked Bones. "I can tell you're thinking."

"This despair has got to end," Carea exclaimed. "Contribute or starve. That's just how it's going to be," she said as she kicked a rock out of her way. "Food for labor. That will be the first step. Now, first on the agenda, find the food…."

"*Yes!*" said Bones with a wide smile. "I was hoping you'd say that!"

Notes to "Black Deeds, White Lies"

Family Affairs

[1] "But behold, I, Nephi, will show unto you that the tender mercies of the Lord are over all those whom he hath chosen, because of their faith, to make them mighty even unto the power of deliverance" (1 Nephi 1:20).

"...The Lord's tender mercies are the very personal and individualized blessings, strength, protection, assurances, guidance, loving-kindnesses, consolation, support, and spiritual gifts which we receive from and because of and through the Lord Jesus Christ. Truly, the Lord suits 'his mercies according to the conditions of the children of men' (D&C 46:15). ...We should not underestimate or overlook the power of the Lord's tender mercies. The simpleness, the sweetness, and the constancy of the tender mercies of the Lord will do much to fortify and protect us in the troubled times in which we do now and will yet live. When words cannot provide the solace we need or express the joy we feel, when it is simply futile to attempt to explain that which is unexplainable, when logic and reason cannot yield adequate understanding about the injustices and inequities of life, when mortal experience and evaluation are insufficient to produce a desired outcome, and when it seems that perhaps we are so totally alone, truly we are blessed by the tender mercies of the Lord and made mighty even unto the power of deliverance" (David A. Bednar, "The Tender Mercies of the Lord," *Ensign*, May 2005, pg. 99).

Bribery

[2] "Part of enduring to the end is related to our attitudes toward ourselves. When we have a high enough regard for ourselves, we can overcome setbacks and still go forward. It is difficult to defeat a person who is determined to endure in this sense. ...Raise your own spirits by finding something to do that will lift others. Nothing seems to have a greater power for turning us away from our own self-pity and despondency than to focus upon something good we can do for someone else who has a need" (Dean L. Larsen, "The Peaceable Things of the Kingdom," *New Era*, February 1986, pg. 4).

[3] "Each of us should make every effort to become economically independent...Avoid looking to the government for handouts or future security. ...A government which is unable to pay its own bills can hardly be depended upon to pay yours. ...Any government powerful enough to give the people all that they need is big enough to take all they have" (Ezra Taft Benson, *An Enemy Hath Done This*, pg. 220).

[4] "The most important sphere of giving …is not that of material things, but lies in the specifically human realm. What does one person give to another? He gives of himself, of the most precious he has, he gives of his life. This does not necessarily mean that he sacrifices his life for the other—but that he gives of that which is alive in him; he gives him of his joy, of his interest, of his understanding, of his knowledge, of his humor, of his sadness—of all expressions and manifestations of that which is alive in him. …He does not give in order to receive; giving is in itself exquisite joy. But in giving he cannot help bringing something to life in the other person, and this which is brought to life reflects back to

him; in truly giving, he cannot help receiving that which is given back to him" (Erich Fromm, *The Art of Loving*, pgs. 24–25).

[5] "Even during these difficult times, members 'armed with righteousness' can do so many things. (1 Nephi 14:14) We can have love at home, even though the love of many waxes cold in the world. (See Matthew 24:12.) We can have inner peace even though peace has been taken from the earth. (See D&C 1:35.) We can keep the seventh commandment even though others break it and mock it. We can render individualized, humanitarian service even though the mass of human suffering seems so overwhelming. We can use our tongues to speak the truth in love, while refusing to use them to bear false witness. (See Ephesians 4:15; Ex. 20:16.) We can stand fast 'in holy places' even though in the world 'all things shall be in commotion.' (D&C 45:32; D&C 88:91) We can reach for 'hands which hang down,' even if some refuse our proffered hands of friendship. (D&C 81:5) We can hold to the iron rod even if others slip away and a few end up mocking us from 'the great and spacious building.' (1 Nephi 8:26–28) Like Nephi, we may not always know the meaning of things happening to us or around us. Nevertheless, like Nephi, we can still know that God loves us! (See 1 Nephi 11:17.) Yes, 'the enemy is combined,' but when we are combined with the Lord's 'chariots of fire,' then 'they that be with us are more than they that be with them!' (2 Kings. 6:16–17) Furthermore, the divine promise is that no weapon formed against the Lord's work shall finally prosper; this 'is the heritage of the servants of the Lord.' (Isaiah. 54:17; D&C 71:9)" (Neal A. Maxwell, "'Behold, the Enemy Is Combined' (D&C 38:12)," *Ensign,* May 1993, pg. 76).

CHAPTER FIVE

FACES OF PRIDE

"Pride goeth before destruction, and an haughty spirit before a fall" (Proverbs 16:18).

00:03:06, 07:35:21, Zulu
Wednesday, September 24th

Is There a God?

Provo, Utah
9:25 a.m.

Nebraska peeked around the corner of the kitchen with a finger in her mouth and her curls all frizzy.

Dane's eyes lit up. "Hello, Nebraska! Come in here. Are you hungry? I have some food for you."

Nebraska cautiously moved into the kitchen, but she stayed close to the corner of the wall. Slowly, she looked from person to person sitting around the table. She didn't answer.

The bathroom door opened and Louise appeared behind Nebraska. "Hello, sweetheart," she said over her head, peering down at her.

Nebraska turned around and held her hands up to Louise.

Louise picked up the seemingly frightened little girl and hugged her close as Nebraska hid her face in Louise's shoulder.

"She's being a little shy," apologized Louise. "She'll warm up."

"It's OK," said Corrynne with a smile as she and Brea stood to prepare plates for the guests.

"Come sit down and we'll feed you both breakfast," said Brea.

Louise sat down at the table with Nebraska on her lap. "Thank you. We'd like that." Looking around the kitchen, Louise smiled. "This is a cute kitchen."

"Thank you," said Corrynne dishing up eggs. "It's nothing like what you're used to, I'm sure."

Louise shook her head. "It's perfect. Thank you for allowing us to stay with you. Your family is too kind. Lately, Nebraska and Dane have been my family, and I can't tell you how wonderful that's been. Thank you for letting me borrow your son."

Dane smiled and nodded.

"Our pleasure," said Bo, looking pleased with his son. "We're glad he helped you out."

"Tell us about this cute little girl," said Brea, as she set a plate in front of Nebraska. "When I first saw her, I thought she was yours."

Corrynne put a plate in front of Louise, and then both Brea and Corrynne sat back down.

"She's not mine, but I'd like her to be," said Louise, brushing a hand lovingly through Nebraska's hair. "Heaven knows I love her like my own," she said as she gave Nebraska a squeeze. "Huh, little one?"

Nebraska nodded as she took her first bite of eggs.

"I rescued her out of a sewer drain in New York," said Dane to the others.

"A sewer drain?" asked Corrynne, with surprise.

"It's a long story. I'll tell you later," said Dane, making motions indicating the subject was too dramatic to go through with Nebraska sitting with them.

"Where's her family?" asked Brea in a hushed tone.

Dane looked at Brea and shook his head. With a finger across his throat, he made a face indicating that wasn't a topic they should talk about either.

Brea nodded and grimaced slightly.

"Ah, we don't know where her parents are," started Dane, trying to act normal again. "But we'd like to find them if we can, wouldn't we, Nebraska?" he said, trying to help the little girl feel more comfortable.

Nebraska nodded again as she chewed her food. "My grandma lives in Washing machine D.C.," she said, spitting egg.

Dane took a napkin and wiped the few egg spots on the table. Nodding, he said, "Yes, her grandma lives in Washington, D.C.," then shaking his head he said, "we couldn't find her. But we went there and looked, didn't we Nebraska?"

"Yep," she said, swallowing. "I was sleeping, so I couldn't find her."

Brea and Corrynne looked at each other and smiled. Nebraska was too cute!

"I'll find her another day," said Nebraska.

"So, tell me again how you managed to get home," Brea asked Dane, changing the subject. "Weren't you stationed on the East Coast?"

"I was," said Dane. "Louise had a car with no gas, and I had gas without a car. We both wanted to come out this way so we partnered up."

"How did you find gas," asked Bo, "because there's little if any gas around here. Is it different on the East Coast?"

Dane shook his head. "No. All the gas stations are out of fuel that we saw."

Louise nodded in agreement.

"The only gas we found available was from the UN relief stations."

"Then tell us what happened," said Brea.

"I found a speed boat still running in the water in New York. It held 200 gallons."

"Two hundred gallons?" asked Corrynne. "And it was full?"

"No, but it was about 3/4ths full. That gas was enough to get me to a UN relief station in Lexington, Maryland. That's where I met Louise."

"I was a poor homeless woman begging for gas, and Dane was kind enough to have mercy on me," said Louise, as she speared eggs onto her fork.

"You weren't homeless," said Dane. "You weren't poor either."

"Yes, I was, not one dime to my name," said Louise, looking pointedly at Dane.

"Maybe that's how you are today, but you've never been poor a day in your life," said Dane arguing for the sake of arguing.

"Today *counts* as part of my life. My life hasn't ended," said Louise, refusing to back down. "Don't mess with me, boy, I'm the *queen* of debate."

"Ha, ha!" exclaimed Brea. "I'd listen, Dane. She'll clean your clock. I see it in her eyes."

Dane studied Louise, looked at Brea and then smiled, saying, "OK, you win. I'll stay out of your story."

Louise nodded. "Thank you," she said and took another bite.

"How did you know he had gas, Professor Anderson?" asked Brea.

"Call me Louise, please."

"OK, Louise."

Louise shook her head slightly as she pushed a piece of pancake into a pool of syrup. "I didn't. I begged anyone who crossed my path. He just happened to be the one who said yes."

"Uh-uh," said Nebraska as she shook her head. "Dane said *'no!'*"

All the adults looked at each other again with amused smiles.

"Now *she's* debating," said Corrynne with a laugh. "She fits right in!"

"So is Nebraska right? Did you say no?" asked Brea, looking at Dane.

Dane nodded. "At first I did. I didn't know Louise or anything about her. I wanted to save the gas for Nebraska and me."

"What changed your mind?" asked Bo.

"I thought I had lost the boat from the high tide and I started praying to figure out what I should do. Suddenly I was told exactly what I should do."

"What was that?" asked Louise with interest, as she sat up a little straighter.

"I was to give the gas to you."

"What?" asked Louise, astonished. "You were *told* to give me the gas?"

"Yes," said Dane.

"You never said anything about that," said Louise, looking overwhelmed as her face pinked up.

"It was a private experience," said Dane. "I don't normally do anything important till I pray and get an answer."[1]

"So you prayed to God about helping *me* and he answered you?" asked Louise again, now her face turning even redder.

"Yes," said Dane. "It was very clear. I was to give you my gas and that would make it possible for all of us to get to Utah."

"And that's..." Louise shook her head in amazement as she struggled to finish her sentence. She swallowed and tried again. "And that's what happened. Against all odds, when logic dictated we wouldn't make it, our car worked until we got here."

"Of course it did." stated Dane. "The Lord helped us all along the way."

Louise put on a painful smile and said, "That would mean that God knew what was going on with us. He knew what we were doing."[2]

"Right," said Dane nodding.

"And he knew I had a car without gas."

"Yes, he did."

"And he heard..." Louise faltered.

"What?" asked Dane. "What did he hear?"

"...My prayers," said Louise, her face soft with thought.

Dane lifted his eyebrows in surprise. "Yes. If you said them, he heard them! God answers prayers. He answers all our prayers."[3]

"Even mine," said Louise with a delicate voice as she gazed at the kitchen table. Suddenly looking up at everyone she said, "I know this family is religious and you'll have to excuse me, I'm a baby when it comes to this kind of thing. I've never had any kind of spiritual experiences, ever. God being real, takes a little getting used to."

"God knows all of us," said Bo. "He loves all of us."

"Including you," said Dane, pointedly.

Louise pursed her lips and nodded her head. "Including—me," she repeated slowly. Then she shook her head again. "That's twice in a short period of time I've been told God knows me by two different people I trust and who had nothing to gain. I'm not quite sure what that means."

"Take it the way it's offered," said Bo. "At face value—maybe God is reaching out to you. Maybe he's trying to tell you something through people you feel comfortable with."

"Well, God would have to reach pretty far down to find me, if you know what I mean. I've lived a very sordid life and made many bad choices. God wouldn't want me."[4]

Bo shook his head. "All of us are sinners.[5] None of us are perfect enough.[6] That's why God gave his son for us, to atone for our sins. He knew we would need a Savior."[7]

"All he wants from us is for us to try," said Brea. "He wants us to do our best to be the best we can be, knowing what we know.[8] He wants us to find him and choose to be like him."[9]

"But it has to be our choice," said Dane.

"Right," said Corrynne, nodding.

Louise put her fork down and hugged Nebraska who was finishing up the food on her plate. "Oh, if it were only that easy."

"It is that easy," said Dane.

Louise shook her head. "You know, all of you are lucky. Believing in a higher power comes so easily to you and your family. But for me, it's been a struggle."

"Why?" asked Dane.

"Because," Louise paused as she gathered her thoughts. "I have some serious questions."

"Like what?" Dane pressed.

Louise looked unsure.

"...Louise?" interrupted Nebraska as she touched Louise's chin so she would look at her.

"What, honey?" asked Louise in a quiet voice.

"Can I go look around? Where are—the boys?"

"They're at school," said Corrynne. "Go ahead. Go look around. There are some toys in some of the bedrooms. You can play with anything you find."

"OK," said Nebraska as she slipped off Louise's lap and tiptoed out of the room.

Dane caught Louise's eye and said. "Don't worry about asking questions with this group, we love to have deep discussions like this, don't we?" Dane asked his family.

"Sometimes that's what we do as a pastime, delve into the philosophical," said Brea. "We're strange that way."

Louise looked at each person at the table, and then she said, "OK, then, I'm going to be bold and ask you—how you can believe in a God when there's so much suffering in the world? Why does he allow bad people to influence the world? Why does he allow little children to suffer? Why does he allow evil to take advantage of the good? I mean *where is he* when all this is happening?"[10]

Bo, Dane, Brea and Corrynne looked at each other, as if trying to decide who should go first in explaining answers to Louise's questions.

"May I?" Bo asked the others as well as Louise.

"Please," said Louise.

"To answer your question, we must ask another one."

"What's that?" asked Louise.

"Why are you here?"

"Why am I here?" asked Louise, looking confused. "In your house?"

"No, why were you born on earth? Where were you before you were born, and where will you be when you die?"

Louise blew out her breath in a sigh. "Those are big questions. I can't even begin to answer them. Tell me what you believe, because I'm not sure."

"First of all, do you believe in the scriptures?" asked Bo.

Louise nodded. "I believe in most things written in the Bible. Some things I'm not so sure about, but maybe that's just because I don't understand them as I should."

Bo nodded. "That's the way it is for all of us. It's a hard book to understand. But once you begin to read the scriptures, soon understanding comes.[11] In the Bible, we learn that we lived before we were born.[12] God knew us.[13] We were his spirit children and he was our Father."[14]

"OK," said Louise, nodding.

"We, being his children, wanted to be like him. We wanted all the power he possessed. We wanted a physical body like his and we wanted to learn all the things he knew."[15]

"I can see that," said Louise. "If it's true we are his children, I could see that we would want to be like our parent."

"Right. And our father wanted us to grow up to be like him too. He loved us and wanted us to be all we could be, but to be like him meant we had to be born, or receive a physical body, and then learn to live all the laws he lived. We had to become strong and valiant like he was,[16] but to do that, we had to have opposition, resistance or conflict."

"Why?" asked Louise, shaking her head.

"Simple. How does a muscle become strong? How do bones become strong? How do we gain the inner strength we need to have our own beliefs, to choose our own paths despite all the voices in the world telling us what to do?"

Louise thought for a moment and said, "Practice?"

Bo nodded. "Yes, we practice lifting heavier and heavier weights. We practice running hard at the gym. We practice following our intuition rather than following the crowd. Through that practice, being consistent and increasing in intensity, we become equal to the task."[17]

"We become strong," said Louise.

"Exactly," said Bo

"That's called opposition. We have to have opposition so we can grow strong. We must practice what is good and right in the face of opposition and as we practice, we become strong like our Father in Heaven. We become like him."

"So, you're saying, life is hard to make us strong?"

"Yes, I am, but it's more than that. We can make our life hard or easy by our choices," said Bo. "That's part of the plan too. That we learn from our choices."[18]

"I like to think of it this way," said Dane. "Our life is the ultimate reality game. For example; it's our choice what we do in life. We can make our life financially easier by going to college or learn a trade and becoming marketable, or we can avoid that and struggle financially the rest of our lives. We can have a strong mind by avoiding toxins like drugs and alcohol, or we can kill off brain cells by deciding to indulge in those things, inviting all sorts of potential brain disorders."

"What about choosing to play the games of politics, manipulating money, cheating and using my contacts to become rich and pampered?" asked Louise with a coy look in her eye.

Bo stopped his next comment and looked at Corrynne in surprise. She in turn looked at Dane.

Dane didn't respond, but kept his face expressionless.

"Did you do that?" asked Brea, looking back and forth between her parents and Louise.

Louise thought for a moment and then nodded. "I did. I did it knowing what I was doing was wrong,[19] but thinking those choices would make my life better."

"Did it?" asked Dane with seriousness that Corrynne hadn't seen in her son for a while.

Louise stared at Dane for a few tense moments. There seemed to be some sort of communication going on between them, and then she shook her head. "No. It didn't. There were costs I hadn't considered. I'm not happier."[20]

There was silence in the room for a few seconds. Then Louise sighed. "I think I know what you're saying, if I can paraphrase."

"Go ahead," said Bo.

"Here, we have choices," started Louise. "We can choose to bring peace to the world by our presence here, or bring the world and people in it terror and pain.[21] God allows everyone to play whatever game they choose so they can learn lessons brought on by their choices, or be held responsible for those choices."

"Yes, that's everyone's right. God won't rob anyone of the lessons of their choices. Each person has the right to do good or do evil,[22] but there is a catch."

"What's that?" asked Louise.

"Judgment day is coming and for those who choose righteously, all injustices will be made whole. All suffering will be healed, and all sadnesses will be turned to joy. Justice will be done."[23]

"And for the evil?" asked Louise.

"They'll reap what they sow,"[24] said Dane.

"What's that?" asked Louise.

"A world without progress, an eternity of memories highlighting their bad choices, and never obtaining that which they desperately wanted in life, happiness and satisfaction."

"In other words, damnation," said Louise nodding.

"Yes, damnation,"[25] said Dane.

"That's what I was afraid of," said Louise painfully.

"But for those who repent, there's a second chance.[26] Every day holds another chance.[27] That's called mercy. [28] God loves those who turn to him and give up the world.[29]"

"I've heard that before," said Louise, "I just don't know if I believe it."

"Oh, it's true," said Bo. "God's whole purpose is to lead us to greatness,[30] not to condemnation.[31] All we have to do is take hold of the atonement and allow it to take away our past.[32] Jesus Christ's sacrifice was given to us for that purpose, to give us life forever in happiness.[33] It's up to us to pray about what we learn and then find out what's truth."[34]

Louise stood up from the table.

The men at the table also stood out of respect.

"Thanks to all of you. I've learned some valuable information and you've given me much to think about."

"President—I mean...*Professor,*" said Bo, but he didn't finish.

Louise looked at Bo with surprise in her eyes and then shifted her look to Dane.

"Excuse, me," apologized Bo, looking at his son too. "Ahh, I..." he said, searching for something to say.

"Louise, while you stay here, you're welcome to come to our scripture study. We have it every day," said Dane, not even responding to the tension in the air. "It might help answer some of your questions."

Louise nodded. "Thank you. I think I might. But for now, I'm in need of a good shower."

Corrynne stood. "How about I get you some things to wear and a towel and you can take one. Then, I think I'm going to go to bed. I need a nap."

"Thank you," said Louise, suddenly looking very stately, despite her dirty clothes. "Do you also have some hair dye? I need to cover this gray."

"I might," said Corrynne smiling.

"I also might need to cut my hair. Does anyone in your family cut hair?"

Corrynne nodded. "Brea does."

"Good," said Louise as she smiled at Brea.

Brea nodded and smiled back.

Bo took a step out from the table. He didn't look at Louise again. Corrynne thought he looked flustered. It was obvious he had dropped his previous question. "I have some interviews scheduled so I'll be gone for a while too."

"Dane and I will watch Nebraska and the twins," said Brea smiling at her mother. "I think they'll like each other."

"That would be great!" said Corrynne. "Now, come with me." Corrynne held out her hand to Louise, gesturing towards the stairs.

When everyone was gone, Brea turned to Dane, but didn't say a word.

"What?" asked Dane after a moment of Brea's intense look.

"What do you mean, *'What?'* You know."

Dane stood from the table. "No, I don't."

"Well, *is she?*" Brea asked.

"She's a very nice woman," said Dane. "And she needs her space."

"No! You know...*is she the President*? Because if you don't tell me, I have ways to find out. I'll know the moment I touch her hair. I have my ways of knowing."

"Well then why are you asking me?"

"Because I think you should tell me."

"Why? Would you treat her any differently?" asked Dane.

"No," said Brea.

"Good," said Dane, then he moved to leave the room, but at the last second he stalled and turned back. "Just remember, *I* didn't tell you a thing."

Brea nodded and smiled. "I'll remember," she said.

Pictures

Provo, Utah
11:45 p.m.

"Hey, Nebraska, sweetheart, don't take things out of the closet," said Louise, as she came up the stairs and saw a mess of albums spilling out the closet door and all over the floor. Nebraska and the twins were sitting in the middle of the hall looking intensely at each page. There were some loose pages on the floor, obviously torn by one of the twins. Louise bent down to pick them up. "I'm sure their mommy doesn't want these books ripped up like this."

As Louise started picking up the pages, she realized these were scrapbooks of the Rogers family. Happy faces riddled the torn pages. Pictures of children doing silly things, pictures of proms and graduations, they touched her. As she gazed at the pictures, she wondered how it would have been to have such childhood experiences...it certainly was different from her lonely past. She would have liked a family.

Louise scanned the images with amusement, losing herself for a moment in the longing of it all. She looked at the floor to pick up more, now out of interest more than duty to clean up, when she saw a familiar letterhead. It was from the UN. Who would be receiving a letter from the UN in this house, she wondered. It was addressed to...**who?** *"Braun Rogers?"* and it was an invitation to serve as a student assistant to the...*Secretary-General*? Quickly, she searched for a date and found it. It was dated a year ago.

"Braun...?" said Louise to herself. She couldn't believe what she was seeing. *"The* Braun Rogers from the White House?" A sick feeling pulsed through her body as she realized it was true! Quickly, she looked through the other pictures. Searching for an image—a familiar picture—a recent picture...and then—she found it! There, in full color was a large photo of Braun Rogers. Yes, it was him, the same dark brown hair, the same kind eyes, the easy-to-trust face. Yes, this had been her aide. Louise shook her head as she thought, looking up at the ceiling. *What was happening? Was this some joke?* Again, she looked at the picture. Surely she was wrong! Yes, Dane and Braun had the same last name, but that didn't mean.... As she gazed at the picture again, she realized, she wasn't wrong. *This—was—Braun.* She was living in *his* house! How could this have happened?

Louise looked at Nebraska. She loved that little girl. What should she do? Should she take Nebraska and leave? Where would she go? How would they eat?

As thoughts raced through Louise's mind, she remembered standing in MD's office and watching his face contort into ugly giddiness as he confessed his works. She remembered him reveling in his trickery as he told her that kind, dependable Braun had been his unsuspecting mole. Then it clicked! Braun was just like Dane! They were both intelligent, kind and—*and religious*! No wonder! They were *brothers*! What a sucker she was. MD would know she would trust Dane, just as she had trusted Braun. Surely, Dane was another mole! He must have been put in her path with just the perfect amount of gas to get her to where he wanted her to be. She bet his story about praying about her was just another ruse!

Another thought hit her and then twisted inside her. *The snipers!* That's how they knew where she was! Dane was their man! They were following him! That was the only answer! He must have a chip after all!

Louise shook her head. She was so *stupid*! She had walked happily, thankfully, into a trap. Make a mistake once, maybe understandable, but make the same mistake *twice*?

Louise shook her head. She was dead! It was only a matter of time.

Widowed and Hungry

Provo, Utah
11:50 a.m.

"Hello, Sister Crane," said Bo, with a smile and a handshake.

The young woman, with a baby on her hip, shook his hand, smiled nervously, and then took a seat.

"How are you doing?" he asked. "We missed you at our meeting."

Sister Crane took a deep breath and folded the collar of the outfit her little one was wearing. "I know, but my baby was sick. I'm sorry," she said, with eyes filled with unspoken burdens.

Bo nodded. "It's OK. That's hard, isn't it, especially with other children to care for?"

"Right," the young woman said, "...And, with my husband gone..."

Bo waited for Sister Crane to finish, but she couldn't. Her lips began to tremble with emotion.

Bo wanted to comfort the young mother. With a kind voice he said, "I know your situation must be very hard."

Sister Crane nodded. "It is, Bishop. I miss my husband. He was killed only three months ago."

"I know," said Bo, digging deep for something to say. "What can we do for you to ease what you're feeling?"

Sister Crane shook her head. "I'm just worried. I don't know how we're going to eat."

"Why?" asked Bo. "Tell me your situation."

"Well," she said, and then she paused, trying to control her emotions. "I need the basics."

"Like what?" Bo asked.

"I have no food."

"Nothing?" asked Bo.

Sister Crane shook her head. "Nothing except for oatmeal my mother just happened to bring over a month ago, thank goodness. We've been eating that for every meal for the past three days. And..." Sister Crane's voice faltered as she hid her face in her baby's chest and cried.

Bo stood and moved to Sister Crane's side. He placed a comforting hand on her shoulder and waited for her to gain her composure.

After a minute, Sister Crane looked up at Bo and said, "I don't even have milk to feed my baby. I'm afraid I'm going to kill her!"

Bo shook his head as he squatted down to eye level with the young mother. "No, you're not going to kill your baby. We'll find milk for you. We'll find food for your children."

Sister Crane nodded and wiped her eyes.

Bo stood and retrieved a notebook of blank paper from his desk. "I want to take notes so I remember everything we've talked about."

Sister Crane nodded again as she reached for a Kleenex out of the box Bo had on his desk.

"What do you have in your cupboards?"

"I have spices," Sister Crane said with a shrug. "I might have another day's worth of oatmeal, and maybe a can or two of tomato soup, but that's it. When my husband was deployed, we already had very little."

"Do you have any vegetables left in a garden?" asked Bo.

Sister Crane shook her head. "I don't. We didn't have a garden this year. Taylor was working 80 hours a week, and I was sick after I had the baby in March, so neither of us could put one in."

"Do you have family nearby?"

Sister Crane shook her head. "My family lives in Idaho."

"And your husband's family?"

"They live in California."

Bo looked down at his notes. His shoulders felt heavy. This woman was the fifth person that day to inform him of their great need. What was he going to do?

Bo paused for a moment to ask Heavenly Father what he should do. A feeling of peace came to his heart. In a moment he knew, somehow the answers to this difficult situation would be made known. Somehow, as he worked through all his ward member's needs, there would be enough. With that thought, he said, "Everything will be fine, Sister Crane. Your baby will grow up healthy and strong, your children will have enough to eat. The Lord is aware of you and the heavy burdens you carry by yourself. Turn to him, and he will lighten your load, giving you the strength and the understanding to be the powerful influence he desires in your home."[35]

Sister Crane looked at Bo with hopeful eyes.

"For the next little while, I want you to come to my house for your meals until I can figure out other arrangements," said Bo.

Sister Crane shook her head in gratitude. "Thank you, Bishop."

"I promise. Your family will not starve."

Sister Crane stood and shook the Bishop's hand, "You are wonderful, Bishop Rogers. May the Lord bless you *forever*."

"I'd like that," said Bo nodding, feeling exhausted.

Truth or Dare

Provo, Utah
12:05 p.m.

Louise stood at the top of the stairs, looking into a mirror on the wall. She eyed her dark brown hair color. Was it different enough? She had really wanted a haircut before she ventured out into the streets again. She must not be recognized. She checked her clothes. They were slightly worn, baggy jeans, a large, blousy sweater in a style she'd never wear if she had a choice, and Nike sneakers. She looked frumpy enough. She hated it, but maybe it was distracting from her normal looks and therefore, good.

After looking for a few more seconds she decided, OK, *now* she looked like a homeless woman without a dime to her name. Those acknowledgements made her want to laugh hysterically and scream with frustration at the same moment. Louise shook her head. How did her life get so hopeless? What was she going to do? Closing her eyes in misery, Louise knew it was the end of the line for her. Her life was over, one way or another.

Louise, full of anxiety and depression, was about to take a step down off the top stair when she stalled to gaze back at her sweet Nebraska. Wistfully, she sighed. Nebraska had been a spark of joy in her dismal life. It ripped her heart apart to think she was going to have to leave her, but she knew she couldn't bring the little girl. It would be difficult enough to provide for herself, let alone Nebraska. No, it was the right choice to leave her here and get out of the Rogers' home, but she had to leave now, otherwise, she was sure MD would find her again.

"Louise," called Brea.

Louise jumped as she looked down the hall. Brea was coming out of one of the bedrooms. "Yes?" she asked, forcing a smile.

"I found the scissors," Brea said, holding up a pair.

"Oh, that's great."

"Let's cut your hair in the kitchen."

Louise looked at Nebraska, back to Brea, and then down the stairs. Should she stay? Did she have time?

Suddenly, Brea slowed as the smile disappeared from her face. "Where are you going?"

Louise was surprised. How did Brea know she was leaving? "Ahh, why do you think I'm going anywhere?"

"I've just got a sixth sense about these things," Brea said as she stepped over the scrapbook mess in the hall. "Something's bothering you. Is there something I can do to help?"

Louise shook her head. "No, I'm doing just fine."

Brea put the scissors in a hidden pocket and placed a hand gently on the railing. She had an odd look about her, as if she were thinking hard about something.

"I'm just going downstairs," said Louise.

Brea shook her head. "I get the distinct impression you're leaving."

Louise was astounded. "Why do you say that?"

"Let's just say I have a gift. I can sense other people's intentions."

Louise shook her head. "I'm sorry, you're wrong this time. I'm not going anywhere."

Brea nodded thoughtfully. "OK, good. How about we go downstairs and I cut your hair. I could freshen up your blunt cut..."

As Brea spoke, Louise decided she couldn't afford to delay. Who knew when MD would send his men out after her again?

"...I could make it frame your face..."

"No," said Louise abruptly. "No, not right now, thank you, maybe later."

"OK, then," said Brea, looking a little jilted, but she recovered quickly. "I guess I'll walk with you downstairs. I have to make lunch anyway. What are you hungry for?"

Louise laughed, taking the first steps. "Oh nothing. I can make myself something. You don't have to wait on me."

"It's no problem," said Brea, following close behind.

Both the women finished walking down the stairs.

Louise paused at the bottom stair as she remembered she hadn't said good-bye to Nebraska. She couldn't leave without doing at least *that*.

Brea brushed Louise as she moved passed her. Suddenly, Brea gasped and turned back, staring at Louise with wide eyes.

"What's wrong?" asked Louise surprised by Brea's response.

"You *are* leaving!" said Brea. "You're hesitating because of Nebraska."

"What?" asked Louise, not knowing what to think.

"There's more. You think Dane has set you up. You think you aren't safe here."

Louise was mystified and she shook her head. This couldn't be happening. It was some trick. "No...I...."

Brea continued, "But you *are* safe here. You have everything backwards in your head, Madame President. Be careful. You're thinking your friends are your enemies. That will only cause you to do something you'll regret."

Louise stared at Brea. There was no use denying anything any more. "What's happening here?"

Brea shook her head. "MD is a terrible man, but I assure you none of us are in league with him."

"Stop!" said Louise, as she swiped her hands in the air. *"Just stop!"*

Brea closed her mouth.

"Now, I'm going to ask you again, *what's going on here*?"

Brea thought for a moment and said, "I have a gift. I can discern the intentions of other people.[36] Then there are other times, through the Holy Ghost, I can touch a person and read their specific thoughts.[37] I read your thoughts, Ma'am, not necessarily on purpose, mind you, but I read them all the same. The Lord wanted me to know your thoughts so I could stop you from leaving. He's protecting you."

Louise put a hand on her hip and tried to figure out what to do next. She didn't know what to believe. With squinted eyes she asked, "So, you have a spiritual gift that helps you read minds?" clarified Louise.

"Not really 'read,' but 'perceive' thoughts. If that's what you mean, then yes, that's right."

"And the Holy Ghost, as in the Holy Trinity, is the source of this gift?"

"Right," said Brea, nodding.

"I don't know what to think of that," said Louise, remembering Braun had a gift he claimed was from God, too. Could all of this be real?[38]

"I know it's hard to believe, but it's true. The Holy Ghost is the source of all spiritual gifts for everyone. [39] My gift helps me identify and separate the good people from the bad.[40] You're a good person. Conflicted, but good."

"You sure about the good part?" asked Louise, hoping Brea was right, but knowing she had too many flaws for it to be true.

Brea nodded. "I can feel the Lord loves you. He's watching out for you. Maybe you should believe him." Then with a shrug, she said, "Maybe he needs you to do something for him. You should find out."

Louise thought about Brea's words. Could it be true? Could God be sending her messages, protecting her, calling to her? And, if that was true, what would that mean? All those questions swam in her head and began to cloud her thinking. She couldn't think about those things right now. Business first. Clearing her throat she said, "First of all, despite what God is doing or not doing," Louise began, "it's imperative that no one know I'm the President. My life depends on that remaining a secret."

Brea nodded. "I agree."

"Secondly, I'd appreciate it if you'd be quiet about anything else you have pulled from my mind. Most of it is classified and very sensitive information."

Brea smiled. "There's nothing to be afraid of here. This home is a safe house for you."

Louise looked around still not sure what to believe. "Tell me, can anyone else read thoughts in this family?"

"Not that I know of," said Brea.

"So you're the only one."

"Correct," said Brea.

Louise wondered if she could use Brea's talent to put her worries to rest. "Would you do something for me?"

"Sure."

"Would you touch your brother, Dane, and make sure he doesn't have a tracking device on his body?"

Brea smiled. "There's no way he has a chip anywhere, he'd rather die than have a chip implanted."

"That's what he told me, but I just want to make sure."

Right then Dane came around the kitchen corner. "Hi," he said as he looked back and forth between Louise and Brea. "Are we having a convention on the landing?"

Brea patted her brother's back gently. "Wouldn't you like to know?"

Dane shrugged. "Fine, don't tell me," he said, as he moved past the women and headed up the stairs, two at a time. "I have important things to do anyway."

"Good!" called Brea.

"So does he?" asked Louise in a low voice.

Brea shook her head. "Nope. There's nothing."

Louise ran her fingers through her hair in relief. "How sure are you?"

"One hundred percent," said Brea. "And just for the record, he's the most honest, forthright man on the face of the planet. He hides nothing. So if you want to know something about Dane, just ask him. He'll tell you the truth every time."

Louise nodded. "That's good to know. I'm not used to such honesty."

"Can we go into the kitchen, so I can make the children lunch?" asked Brea. "I'd be glad to answer any of your other questions in there."

"Sure. Of course," said Louise. She had many more questions spinning in her head. She was starting to relax. It was obvious Brea was very gifted, as well as honest.[41] When she spoke, she looked directly into Louise's eyes. Louise liked that. She could tell that Brea was as candid as her brother.

Brea took some homemade bread out of a plastic bag and began to cut it. "Braun is a good guy, too," said Brea. "He was never a spy for MD. MD had him imprisoned while he was at the UN and forcibly shot a chip under his skin. Braun had no idea the chip had the capabilities that it did. He would have never come to the White House if he had known."

Louise shook her head, astounded with every word that came out of Brea's mouth. "You are amazing. You are a wealth of information! How do you know all these things?"

"Let's just say I'm connected," said Brea, as she unscrewed the lid of the jelly.

"And all those thoughts you took from my head, you downloaded all of that from one little touch?"

Brea laughed. "It's not always like that, but today it was. Your thoughts were intense and quick."

Louise was so amazed. "Boy, could I have used someone like you on my cabinet!"

Brea shook her head as she unscrewed the peanut butter lid. "Then I'd end up like Braun, off in Siberia to hide from MD."

Louise couldn't believe this! A sick feeling dropped into her stomach. "Is that what happened to him?"

Brea nodded as she spread the peanut butter. "Yes. Braun had worn out his usefulness to MD. He was influencing you too much."

"Ahh," said Louise. "That sounds about right. So Braun is in Siberia?"

"Yes. He's being taken care of, but yes, that's where he is."

"And how do you know? That information was not in my head," said Louise.

"Because the father of my twins is Matthew Daimler, Junior, his son," said Brea as she put the pieces of the bread together in sandwiches.

Louise's jaw dropped and she almost fell off her chair.

Notes to "Faces of Pride"

Is there a God?

[1] "Counsel with the Lord in all thy doings, and he will direct thee for good," (Alma 37:37).

[2] "Now my brethren, we see that God is mindful of every people, whatsoever land they may be in; yea, he numbereth his people, and his bowels of mercy are over all the earth" (Alma 26:37).

[3] "Be thou humble; and the Lord thy God shall lead thee by the hand, and give thee answer to thy prayers" (D&C 112:10).

[4] "If we have felt disheartened or inadequate, we need only turn to our Heavenly Father and plead for his help. He will give it! It is a promise he has made to us that he will not break. Thus, so long as the Spirit is striving with us, there is always hope. But when we attempt to excuse our actions by saying, 'This is the way I wish to live' or 'I am different' or 'God made me this way' or 'My parents or society are responsible,' then we have arrived at a tragic state in our relationship with ourselves and with God. If we will earnestly seek our Heavenly Father's help and apply the steps that constitute the doctrine of repentance, then we will find peace and joy both in this life and in eternity" (Spencer W. Kimball, "The Gospel of Repentance," *Ensign*, October 1982, pg. 2).

[5] "For all have <u>sinned</u>, and come short of the glory of God" (Romans 3:23).

[6] "If we say that we have no sin, we deceive ourselves, and the truth is not in us. If we confess our sins, he is faithful and just to forgive us our sins, and to cleanse us from all unrighteousness" (1 John 1: 8-9).

[7] "Wherefore, redemption cometh in and through the Holy Messiah; for he is full of grace and truth. Behold, he offereth himself a sacrifice for sin, to answer the ends of the law, unto all those who have a broken heart and a contrite spirit; and unto none else can the ends of the law be answered" (2 Nephi 2:6-7).

[8] "We cannot keep all the commandments without first knowing them, and we cannot expect to know all, or more than we now know unless we comply with or keep those we have already received" (Joseph Smith, *Teachings of the Prophet Joseph Smith*, pg. 256).

[9] "I would commend you to seek this Jesus of whom the prophets and apostles have written, that the grace of God the Father, and also the Lord Jesus Christ, and the Holy Ghost, which beareth record of them, may be and abide in you forever" (Ether 12:41).

[10] "Life's most challenging questions seem to be those that begin with the word why. 'Why is life so hard?' 'Why is there so much sorrow, hate, and unhappiness in the world?' 'Why does death take the young?' And 'why must the innocent suffer?' We all have wrestled with such questions from time to time as we struggle with the vicissitudes of mortality...We mortals have a limited view of life from the eternal perspective. But if we know and understand Heavenly Father's plan, we realize that dealing with adversity is one of the chief ways we are tested. Our faith in our Heavenly Father and his beloved Son, Jesus Christ, is the source of inner strength. Through faith we can find peace, comfort, and the courage to endure. As we trust in God and his plan for our happiness with all our hearts and lean not unto our own understanding (see Proverbs 3:5), hope is born. Hope grows out of faith and gives meaning and purpose to all we do. It can give us comfort in the face of adversity, strength in times of trial, and peace when we have reason for doubt or anguish. By focusing on and living the principles of Heavenly Father's plan for our eternal happiness, we can separate ourselves from the wickedness of the world. If we are anchored to the correct understanding of who we are, why we are here on this earth, and where we can go after this mortal life, Satan cannot threaten our happiness through any form of temptation. If we are determined to live by Heavenly Father's plan, we will use our God-given moral agency to make decisions based on revealed truth, not on the opinions of others or on the

current thinking of the world" (M. Russell Ballard, "Answers to Life's Questions," *Ensign*, May 1995, pg. 22).

[11] "Search the scriptures; for in them ye think ye have eternal life: and they are they which testify of me" (John 5:39).

[12] "Man was also in the beginning with God. Intelligence, or the light of truth, was not created or made, neither indeed can be" (D&C 93:29).

13 "Before I formed thee in the belly I knew thee" (Jeremiah 1:5).

[14] "God that made the world and all things therein...for in him we live, and move, and have our being; as certain also of your own poets have said, for we are also his offspring" (Acts 17:24, 28).

[15] "The Church of Jesus Christ of Latter-day Saints, basing its belief on divine revelation, ancient and modern, proclaims man to be the direct and lineal offspring of Deity. God Himself is an exalted man, perfected, enthroned, and supreme. By His almighty power He organized the earth and all that it contains, from spirit and element, which exist coeternally with Himself. He formed every plant that grows and every animal that breathes, each after its own kind, spiritually and temporally...Man is the child of God, formed in the divine image and endowed with divine attributes, and even as the infant son of an earthly father and mother is capable in due time of becoming a man, so the undeveloped offspring of celestial parentage is capable, by experience through ages and eons, of evolving into a God" (First Presidency, "The Origin of Man," *Ensign*, February 2002, pg. 26).

[16] "Now the Lord had shown unto me, Abraham, the intelligences that were organized before the world was; and among all these there were many of the noble and great ones; And God saw these souls that they were good, and he stood in the midst of them, and he said: These I will make my rulers; for he stood among those that were spirits, and he saw that they were good and he said unto me: Abraham, thou art one of them; thou wast chosen before thou wast born. And there stood one among them that was like unto God, and he said unto those who were with him: We will go down, for there is space there, and we will take of these materials, and we will make an earth whereon these may dwell; And we will prove them herewith, to see if they will do all things whatsoever the Lord their God shall command them; And they who keep their first estate shall be added upon; and they who keep not their first estate shall not have glory in the same kingdom with those who keep their first estate; and they who keep their second estate shall have glory added upon their heads for ever and ever" (Abraham 3:22-26).

[17] "The man who never had to toil,
To heaven from the common soil,
Who never had to win his share
Of sun and sky and light and air,
Never became a manly man,
But lived and died as he began.

"Good timber does not grow in ease;
The stronger wind, the tougher trees;
The farther sky, the greater length;
The more the storm, the more the strength;
By sun and cold, by rain and snows,
In tree or man, good timber grows."
(Douglas Malloch, comp. Al Bryant, *Sourcebook of Poetry*, pg. 456.)

"The gospel will show us a way through and around our troubles. It promises no crown without a cross, no triumph without a battle. Remember, the storms beat upon the house built upon the rock, even as they do upon the one built on sand. True, the pathway may be strewn with rocks that bruise our feet, but when we contemplate our goal, they only tend to toughen and strengthen our resolve, and we recall that "great works are performed not alone by strength but by perseverance." (Samuel Johnson, Rasselas XIII.) If we banish hardship we banish hardihood; out of the same door with calamity walk courage, fortitude, triumphant faith, and sacrificial love. If we abolish the cross in the world, we make impossible the Christ in man" (Hugh B. Brown, "Salvation Is My Goal," *New Era*, December 1974, pg. 4).

[18] "In this life we have to make many choices. Some are very important choices. Some are not. Many of our choices are between good and evil. The choices we make, however, determine to a large extent our happiness or our unhappiness, because we have to live with the consequences of our choices. Making perfect choices all of the time is not possible. It just doesn't happen. But it is possible to make good choices we can live with and grow from. When God's children live worthy of divine guidance they can become 'free forever, knowing good from evil; to act for themselves and not to be acted upon'" (James E. Faust, "Choices," *Liahona*, May 2004, pgs. 51–54).

[19] "For behold, the Spirit of Christ is given to every man, that he may know good from evil; wherefore, I show unto you the way to judge; for every thing which inviteth to do good, and to persuade to believe in Christ, is sent forth by the power and gift of Christ; wherefore ye may know with a perfect knowledge it is of God. But whatsoever thing persuadeth men to do evil, and believe not in Christ, and deny him, and serve not God, then ye may know with a perfect knowledge it is of the devil; for after this manner doth the devil work, for he persuadeth no man to do good, no, not one; neither do his angels; neither do they who subject themselves unto him" (Moroni 7:16-17).

[20] "Do not suppose, because it has been spoken concerning restoration, that ye shall be restored from sin to happiness. Behold, I say unto you, wickedness never was happiness. And now, my son, all men that are in a state of nature, or I would say, in a carnal state, are in the gall of bitterness and in the bonds of iniquity; they are without God in the world, and they have gone contrary to the nature of God; therefore, they are in a state contrary to the nature of happiness" (Alma 41:10-11).

[21] "But wo unto him that has the law given, yea, that has all the commandments of God, like unto us, and that transgresseth them, and that wasteth the days of his probation, for awful is his state!" (2 Nephi 9:27).

[22] "Wherefore, men are free according to the flesh; and all things are given them which are expedient unto man. And they are free to choose liberty and eternal life, through the great Mediator of all men, or to choose captivity and death, according to the captivity and power of the devil; for he seeketh that all men might be miserable like unto himself" (2 Nephi 2:27).

[23] "Therefore remember, O man, for all thy doings thou shalt be brought into judgment. Wherefore, if ye have sought to do wickedly in the days of your probation, then ye are found unclean before the judgment-seat of God; and no unclean thing can dwell with God; wherefore, ye must be cast off forever" (1 Nephi 10:20-21).

[24] "For behold, I, God, have suffered these things for all, that they might not suffer if they would repent; But if they would not repent they must suffer even as I; Which suffering caused myself, even God, the greatest of all, to tremble because of pain, and to bleed at every pore, and to suffer both body and spirit—and would that I might not drink the bitter cup, and shrink—Nevertheless, glory be to the Father, and I partook and finished my preparations unto the children of men" (D&C 19: 16-19).

[25] "For behold, this life is the time for men to prepare to meet God; yea, behold the day of this life is the day for men to perform their labors. And now, as I said unto you before, as ye have had so many witnesses, therefore, I beseech of you that ye do not procrastinate the day of your repentance until the end; for after this day of life, which is given us to prepare for eternity, behold, if we do not improve our time while in this life, then cometh the night of darkness wherein there can be no labor performed. Ye cannot say, when ye are brought to that awful crisis, that I will repent, that I will return to my God. Nay, ye cannot say this; for that same spirit which doth possess your bodies at the time that ye go out of this life, that same spirit will have power to possess your body in that eternal world. For behold, if ye have procrastinated the day of your repentance even until death, behold, ye have become subjected to the spirit of the devil, and he doth seal you his; therefore, the Spirit of the Lord hath withdrawn from you, and hath no place in you, and the devil hath all power over you; and this is the final state of the wicked" (Alma 34:32-35).

[26] "And no unclean thing can enter into his kingdom; therefore nothing entereth into his rest save it be those who have washed their garments in my blood, because of their faith, and the repentance of all their sins, and their faithfulness unto the end" (3 Nephi 24:19).

[27] "...there was a space granted unto man in which he might repent; therefore this life became a probationary state; a time to prepare to meet God; a time to prepare for that endless state which has been spoken of by us, which is after the resurrection of the dead" (Alma 12:24).

[28] "Listen to the voice of Jesus Christ, your Redeemer, the Great I Am, whose arm of mercy hath atoned for your sins" (D&C: 29:1).

[29] "For the natural man is an enemy to God, and has been from the fall of Adam, and will be, forever and ever, unless he yields to the enticings of the Holy Spirit, and putteth off the natural man and becometh a saint through the atonement of Christ the Lord, and becometh as a child, submissive, meek, humble, patient, full of love, willing to submit to all things which the Lord seeth fit to inflict upon him, even as a child doth submit to his father" (Mosiah 3:19).

[30] "For behold, this is my work and my glory—to bring to pass the immortality and eternal life of man" (Moses 1:39).

[31] "...In obedience there is joy and peace unspotted, unalloyed; and as God has designed our happiness…he never has—He never will institute an ordinance or give a commandment to His people that is not calculated in its nature to promote that happiness which He has designed, and which will not end in the greatest amount of good and glory to those who become the recipients of his law and ordinances" (Joseph Smith, *Teachings of the Prophet Joseph Smith*, pgs. 256–57).

[32] "Wherefore teach it unto your children, that all men, everywhere, must repent, or they can in nowise inherit the kingdom of God, for no unclean thing can dwell there, or dwell in his presence" (Moses 6:57).

[33] "And this is life eternal, that they might know thee the only true God, and Jesus Christ, whom thou hast sent" (John 17:3).

[34] "The gift of the Holy Ghost comes after one repents and becomes worthy...The Holy Ghost bears witness of the truth and impresses upon the soul the realty of God the Father and the Son Jesus Christ so deeply that no earthly power or authority can separate him from that knowledge" (James E. Faust, "The Gift of the Holy Ghost—a Sure Compass," *Ensign*, April 1996, pg. 4).

Widowed and Hungry

[35] "The Savior said, 'Come unto me, all ye that labour and are heavy laden, and I will give you rest' (Matthew 11:28). Many carry heavy burdens. Some have lost a loved one to death or care for one who is disabled. Some have been wounded by divorce. Others yearn for an eternal marriage. Some are caught in the grip of addictive substances or practices like alcohol, tobacco, drugs, or pornography. Others have crippling physical or mental impairments. Some are challenged by same-gender attraction. Some have terrible feelings of depression or inadequacy. In one way or another, many are heavy laden. To each of us our Savior gives this loving invitation: 'Come unto me, all ye that labour and are heavy laden, and I will give you rest. Take my yoke upon you, and learn of me; for I am meek and lowly in heart: and ye shall find rest unto your souls. For my yoke is easy, and my burden is light' (Matthew 11:28–30). ...As we struggle with the challenges of mortality, I pray for each of us, as the prophet Mormon prayed for his son, Moroni: 'May Christ lift thee up, and may his sufferings and death, … and his mercy and long-suffering, and the hope of his glory and of eternal life, rest in your mind forever' (Moroni 9:25). I testify of Jesus Christ, our Savior, who invites us all to come unto Him and be perfected in Him. He will bind up our wounds and He will heal the heavy laden" (Dallin H. Oaks, "He Heals the Heavy Laden," *Ensign*, November 2006, pgs. 6–9).

Truth or Dare

[36] "The gift and power of discernment in this world of contention between the forces of good and the power of evil is essential equipment for every son and daughter of God. There could be no such mass dissensions as endanger the security of the world, if its populations possessed this great gift in larger

degree. ...Every member in the restored Church of Christ could have this gift if he willed to do so. He could not be deceived with the sophistries of the world. He could not be led astray by pseudo-prophets and subversive cults. Even the inexperienced would recognize false teachings, in a measure at least. With this gift they would be able to detect something of the disloyal, rebellious, and sinister influences which not infrequently prompt those who seemingly take pride in the destruction of youthful faith and loyalties. Discerning parents will do well to guard their children against such influences and such personalities and teachings before irreparable damage is done. The true gift of discernment is often premonitory. A sense of danger should be heeded to be of value. We give thanks for a set of providential circumstances which avert an accident. We ought to be grateful every day of our lives for this sense which keeps alive a conscience which constantly alerts us to the dangers inherent in wrongdoers and sin. (Stephen L. Richards quoting Joseph Smith, *Conference Report*, April, 1950, pg. 163).

[37] To know the specific thoughts of others is also a gift of the Spirit. See the following scriptural accounts:

Alma contending with Zeezrom:

"Now Zeezrom, seeing that thou hast been taken in thy lying and craftiness, for thou hast not lied unto men only but thou hast lied unto God; for behold, he knows all thy thoughts, and thou seest that thy thoughts are made known unto us by his Spirit; (Alma 12:3).

Ammon speaking to King Lamoni:

"And it came to pass that Ammon, being filled with the Spirit of God, therefore he perceived the thoughts of the king. And he said unto him: Is it because thou hast heard that I defended thy servants and thy flocks, and slew seven of their brethren with the sling and with the sword, and smote off the arms of others, in order to defend thy flocks and thy servants; behold, is it this that causeth thy marvelings? I say unto you, what is it, that thy marvelings are so great? Behold, I am a man, and am thy servant; therefore, whatsoever thou desirest which is right, that will I do. Now when the king had heard these words, he marveled again, for he beheld that Ammon could discern his thoughts" (Alma 18:16-18).

Jacob teaching the Nephites in the temple

"But behold, hearken ye unto me, and know that by the help of the all-powerful Creator of heaven and earth I can tell you concerning your thoughts, how that ye are beginning to labor in sin, which sin appeareth very abominable unto me, yea, and abominable unto God" (Jacob 2:5).

Amulek answering the lawyers in Ammonihah

"Now they knew not that Amulek could know of their designs. But it came to pass as they began to question him, he perceived their thoughts, and he said unto them: O ye wicked and perverse generation, ye lawyers and hypocrites, for ye are laying the foundation of the devil; for ye are laying traps and snares to catch the holy ones of God" (Alma 10:17).

[38] "Wo unto him that spurneth at the doings of the Lord; yea, wo unto him that shall deny the Christ and his works! Yea, wo unto him that shall deny the revelations of the Lord, and that shall say the Lord no longer worketh by revelation, or by prophecy, or by gifts, or by tongues, or by healings, or by the power of the Holy Ghost!" (3 Nephi 29:5-6)

[39] "...Deny not the gifts of God, for they are many; and they come from the same God. And there are different ways that these gifts are administered; but it is the same God who worketh all in all; and they are given by the manifestations of the Spirit of God unto men, to profit them" (Moroni 10:8).

[40] "People are liable in many ways to be led astray by the power of the adversary, for they do not fully understand that it is a hard matter for them to always distinguish the things of God from the things of the devil. There is but one way by which they can know the difference, and that is by the light of the spirit of revelation, even the spirit of our Lord Jesus Christ. ...Consequently, it becomes us, as Saints, to cleave to the Lord with all our hearts and seek unto Him until we do enjoy the light of His Spirit,

that we may discern between the righteous and the wicked, and understand the difference between false spirits and true" (Brigham Young, *Journal of Discourses*, October 6, 1855, Vol. 3, pgs. 43-44).

[41] "It is for this purpose that these gifts are bestowed, that those who do obey the commandments of God shall have privileges, blessings and powers that those who do not take this course cannot have. The bestowal of these is to create a distinction between the people of God and those who are not His people, to give them that superiority which the enjoyment of these gifts bring" (George Q. Cannon as quoted by Jerreld L. Newquist, *Gospel Truth*, pg. 154).

CHAPTER SIX

EXPOSURE

"...The righteous, and the wise, and their works, are in the hand of God" (Ecclesiastes 9:1).

00:03:06, 04:40:19, Zulu
Wednesday, September 24th

Selfishness

Provo, Utah
12:20 p.m.

"Hello, Brother and Sister Thompson," said Bo, with a forced smile, as the previously wealthy, elderly couple entered his office. Shaking both their hands, he said, trying to be friendly despite his weariness, "I missed you at our meeting yesterday."

The wife looked at her husband, then back, as they sat down in chairs in front of Bo's desk. "My husband has poor health. It's hard for us to get out," she said apologetically.

"But we're here now," said the husband, with an arrogant set of his jaw and a pointed look.

Bo nodded, "Yes you are, Brother Thompson. Thank you for that."

"So what's this interview all about, Bishop?" asked Brother Thompson.

Bo could feel the environment becoming tense. It seemed Brother Thompson was already defensive and they hadn't even started! Bo hesitated, wondering if this meeting was more trouble than it was worth, but then he checked himself. Maybe he was casting his own feelings of frustration and fatigue upon these two. He decided to forge forward.

"Brother and Sister Thompson, because of the shortness of time, I'm just going to jump right into the concerns I have."

"What concerns are those?" asked the elderly man, unblinkingly.

"There is a family near your home that lacks food to eat. I was hoping that you, being blessed with the fruits of a successful life, would have a good supply of food, and would be willing to take a young widowed mother and three little children under your wing, and make sure they had the food they needed."

Brother and Sister Thompson looked stunned as they cast a look at each other and then back.

Bo waited for an answer, but neither offered a word, so he continued. "I prayerfully considered who could come to the rescue for this little family and your names came to my mind."

Brother Thompson's face turned a few shades of red as Sister Thompson continued to look at Bo with a blank stare.

Bo continued, now trying to convince. "The Lord needs your sacrifice in their behalf..."

Brother Thompson interrupted, "Excuse me, but am I my brother's keeper? What am I, a *welfare service*?"

Bo looked down at his folded hands, trying to keep his patience. He nodded. "Since you asked, yes, Brother Thompson, we are our brothers' and sisters' keepers. We are responsible to look after the well-being of our neighbors."[1]

"Says who?" asked Brother Thompson. "I'm not responsible for anyone but myself and my wife."

"That's not true. Have you forgotten the most simple of commandments, 'love your neighbor as yourself,' and the Golden Rule?[2] Brother and Sister Thompson, we all should do unto others as we would have others do unto us."[3]

"Don't be quoting scriptures to manipulate me," said Brother Thompson, pointing a finger at Bo.

"I'm not," said Bo. "Those scriptures were not written to manipulate you. They were written to inspire us to love each other and to remember what's important in this life.[4] I'm not going to put any pressure on you to do anything you're not comfortable with, but I just want you to think about this question. If you needed help, wouldn't you be grateful if others would care enough to help you?"

The old man pursed his lips angrily as his stare bore into Bo. "Surely I'm not the only one with food around here," said Brother Thompson, avoiding the question. "There must be others that can help out that family. I'm just as poor as everyone else now. Lost everything."

Bo nodded. "I know, and I'm sorry. I'm not asking for money, I'm just asking you to share what you have. We're asking everyone in the ward to contribute to each other and work things out so no one has to suffer. Most of the families in our ward had food storage but there are a few that didn't…"

Brother Thompson banged his hand on his arm rest. "Where's the Church Welfare Service? Where's my tithing money gone? Where's my fast offerings gone? Where is the food we've canned at the cannery?" asked Brother Thompson. "I've paid thousands of dollars, no, hundreds of thousands of dollars to this church. *Where is it?*"

"Your money has done what you meant for it to do. It has supported the Church and the poor within it, but now each ward has been cut off from each other. We need to help each other..."

"No!" said Sister Thompson, with closed fists, as she hit the armrests, too.

Sister Thompson's response surprised Bo and he turned his attention to her.

"We have given *enough*," she said, mirroring her husband's tone. "In the past, we have given when we didn't know where the next meal was coming from, haven't we, John?"

Brother Thompson nodded. "Yes, we have."

"Now, I think it's time to say 'no,'" Sister Thompson continued. "You can't ask us to donate because we gave money in the past. We won't let you or anyone take us for granted. We aren't a free lunch!"

Bo was speechless. He didn't know quite what to say. So he nodded. "Alright. I just thought I'd give you a chance to help out, and maybe chalk up some blessings."

"Blessings?" asked Brother Thompson, standing. "*Blessings?* What kind of double talk is that? The word 'blessing' is what Church leaders throw around when they want your stuff but won't pay for it. Forgive me, but the word *'blessings'* sets off alarms in my head. All I've had since the previous Bishop told me I'd be blessed, is *colon cancer*. Great blessing, huh? No, no. I don't trust anyone who claims I'll get blessings for something. Blessings can't be counted on, let me tell you!" said Brother Thompson, as he took a seat again, and shook his head.

"We've done our helping," said Sister Thompson. "Let someone else shoulder some burdens. It will be good for them. It builds character."

Bo shook his head as he clenched and unclenched his jaw. There was no reasoning with this hypocritical couple. Bo saw no other choice but to try and smooth things over. "I can see we don't see eye to eye."

"No we don't," said Brother Thompson. "I don't need guilt from my bishop to give food to anyone. I'll give if I want to give, and I won't give if I don't want to."

"I'm sorry, Brother Thompson."

"I'm a good man," said Brother Thompson, defensively.

"I know," said Bo.

"And he's a hard worker!" said Sister Thompson, nodding.

"I know he is," said the Bishop. "And we appreciate everything the both of you do."

"Thank you," Brother Thompson said with a nod.

"Then I guess our meeting is over," said Bo, with a hand extended.

"No wait," said Sister Thompson. "We haven't told you what *we* need."

Bo sat back down and folded his hands. With extreme self-control he said, "Do you need something?"

"Yes, my husband has terrible pain because of his cancer."

Bo nodded. "I'm sure you do," he said, but as he looked at him, more and more he perceived Brother Thompson was using his cancer as an excuse to abuse prescription narcotics.[5] He certainly didn't seem to be in any pain.

"We need pain medicine," said Sister Thompson. "Can we get that from the Church?"

Bo shook his head. "I'm sorry. I have no pain medicine to give."

"Isn't there a doctor nearby who could figure that out for us?" asked Brother Thompson.

"I don't know who. That's not something doctors donate. It's a controlled substance."

"How about your wife? She works at the hospital. Surely she can pull a few strings."

"No," said Bo, shaking his head. This conversation was only getting worse. "Corrynne doesn't have access to medications like that."

"What about Brother Harrison?" asked Sister Thompson. "He has a clinic."

"He's a veterinarian," said Bo.

"Yes, but he must have pain medicine for animals. Couldn't they use that for humans?"

Bo shook his head. "I don't know."

"Could you find out?" asked Sister Thompson.

Bo couldn't believe these two. He leaned forward and with the kindest voice he could muster, he said, "The Church does not provide narcotics for its members, I'm sorry."

"So what am I supposed to do?" asked Brother Thompson, with an angry stare. "I have real pain."

"I don't know," said the Bishop.

"I have cancer!"

"I understand that," said Bo. "We can offer you a blessing."

"A blessing?" said Brother Thompson, standing. "I don't want a blessing![6] I want pain medication!"

"Let's go, John," said Sister Thompson, beginning to shake with anger. "I told you we couldn't get help here."

"You were right," said Brother Thompson, standing again. "But I thought I'd give this bishop a chance to earn some *blessings*. Have a good day, sir."

Bo stood out of respect. "You too, Brother Thompson."

Sister Thompson ushered her husband out of the office and the door slammed behind them.

Bo sat, feeling empty and disappointed. All he could do was shake his head.

In God's Hand

Provo, Utah
12:30 p.m.

"Let me get this straight," said Louise, feeling like the air had been knocked out of her. "You're the Brea, married to the Daimler heir that was featured in People magazine?"

Brea nodded as she brought the sandwiches to the table. "In person—although they didn't represent me very well."

"They never do," said Louise. "Are you on good terms with your in-laws?" she asked, wondering if Brea being related to MD was another issue that might put her at risk.

Brea shook her head. "I'm on a hit list, just like you. I'm in hiding, just like you. MD likes to kill off those who don't do what he wants, as you know."

Louise nodded. Did she ever!

Turning, Brea walked to the stairs and called, "Dane, could you bring the twins down here for lunch? Nebraska, time to eat!"

Louise watched Brea. It was obvious her time of delivery was nearing. She felt sorry for the girl. With America's downward spiral, she imagined how hard Brea's children might have it, especially being cut off from the Daimler fortune.

Dane called down. "We'll come down in a minute. We have to clean up this mess."

"OK," said Brea, returning to the table.

"One last question before the troops invade," said Louise.

"Yes?"

"How in the world did three siblings, you, Dane, and your brother, Braun, all from the small town of Provo, Utah, become so intertwined in the affairs of this nation and the powers that run the world? Do you know the odds of that happening to a family that's not in politics or having an exorbitant amount of wealth?"

Brea sat down at the table with a knowing look. "Yes, I can see how that seems impossible."

Louise continued. "Right. The chances are nil. That's why I was sure MD had arranged Dane to conveniently rescue me."

"I understand, but, Madam..."

"Call me Louise."

"Louise, you're missing a big piece of the puzzle," said Brea.

"How's that?"

"I believe you haven't considered *all* the powers in the political realm. There's someone other than MD who has an influence over what's going on today, someone even more powerful."

"Explain yourself," said Louise, intrigued. Did this girl know more than even she did? Was she talking about Vladimir? Maybe Wormwood...

Brea took a deep breath and flipped her hair over her shoulder. "I believe like you do, that none of this is coincidence."

"Continue," said Louise. "Who are the players here? Who is more powerful than MD?"

"To answer that question, I have to tell you three stories. They're quick."

"Go ahead," said Louise.

"First story," said Brea. "I was a freshman at BYU and a beautiful and charismatic man asked me to lunch. He was smart, good, and in time, we fell madly in love, but before I would marry him, I had to pray to ask if I should.[7] After all, who knows more about the future than God?"

Louise looked sideways at Brea. She wasn't talking about Vladimir or Wormwood. She wasn't talking about a person at all. "Are you telling me it's *God* who's more powerful than MD?" she asked, feeling disappointed.

Brea nodded. "Yes, he is. Until you realize his true power and involvement in your life, you'll always have a skewed view of things. God is infinitely more powerful than MD, and MD's days are numbered.[8] So back to my story..."

Louise nodded. "The floor is yours."

"I'm going to ask you again, and I want you to really think about my question. Who knows more about the future than God?" asked Brea.

Louise didn't know much about religion. She shook her head as she took a stab in the dark. "If you believe that God is all powerful,[9] all knowing,[10] and can see into the future,[11] I presume the answer is, no one knows more about the future than God."

"Exactly," said Brea. "Being omniscient, he knows the skeletons in every person's closet. He knows the secret desires of our hearts.[12] I leaned on the Lord to tell me if Matt Daimler was a worthy husband."

"Did you receive an answer?" asked Louise.

Brea nodded. "I did. My answer was very clear. With Matt, I could achieve all my hopes and aspirations. I was told he'd be a protective father as well as husband and that, yes, it was a good choice to marry him."

"How do you feel about that answer now that—I assume you aren't together any more, right?"

Brea shook her head. "No, his father has forced us apart, but we'll find each other again."

"You seem sure."

"I am sure," said Brea. "And because I'm so sure, I know Matt will still be a wonderful father and husband. He'll still help me achieve all my hopes and aspirations. Things just haven't turned out the way I expected. That doesn't mean they're wrong, or that I was wrong in asking. All that means is that I need to trust in his answers,[13] keep asking, and keep receiving information that will guide me through this complicated situation. I have to lean on the Lord to give me the vision of the future to help me stay focused, just as I leaned on him to make that decision in the first place.[14] Now for story number two...."

Dane came rumbling down the stairs with a sibling under each arm. "Zooooom!" he said, as he sat each baby in high chairs that were situated at the end of the table.

"I'm hungry," said Nebraska.

"Good, little one," said Louise, as she tussled Nebraska's golden hair. "Here are some sandwiches for you."

"Yea!" said Nebraska, as she sat.

"Dane, will you say the prayer?" asked Brea.

Dane nodded and bowed his head as the little twins did the same.

Nebraska looked up at Louise, who motioned she should fold her arms, too.

Nebraska folded her arms and bowed her head.

"Our dear Heavenly Father," began Dane. "We thank thee for this wonderful bread our Father has made for us. We thank thee for Brea that she made our sandwiches. We thank thee for our home, and that it's warm and dry. Most of all, we thank thee that Nebraska and Louise have come to live with us. We pray for protection for all of us and that this food will help us be strong and healthy. In the name of Jesus Christ, amen."

"Amen," said Brea.

"A-nen," said Striynna, while Strykker just bounced his body twice, as if that counted for "amen."

Louise smiled. This little family was so cute. Tears threatened to come to her eyes as she suddenly felt so grateful to be within these walls. Looking at Dane, she nodded in thanks for his simple prayer for the children.

"Are you ready for story number two?" asked Brea.

Louise looked at the children. "Can we?"

Brea nodded. "Sure. It's a good story."

"OK then," said Louise.

Dane looked at Brea and Louise. It looked like he was going to say something, but Brea began talking before he could swallow.

"Braun, my oldest brother, was just off his mission in South America and was planning his life when one day the feeling came strongly to him to apply to the UN for an internship."

"A feeling?" asked Louise, not knowing what that meant.

"The feeling was an urging given to him by the Lord[15] to apply."

Louise nodded. "Do you think so? Does the Lord do that?"

Brea nodded. "Of course! He was planning on being a physician, so this impression came out of the blue for him. It wasn't his desire to ever be involved in politics or government, so he knew his feeling didn't come from his own mind; it came from outside his own thoughts. It came from God."

"If you say so," said Louise, with raised eyebrows, not sure how anyone could decide what God's thoughts might feel like.

Brea continued. "So Braun applied among thousands of other qualified applicants, and he was chosen."

Brea made a good point. "Yes, that does seem amazing; however, he is a very extraordinary person," said Louise, rationalizing.

Dane stopped chewing and looked at Brea and Louise questioningly, but again, didn't say a word.

"Once he was at the UN and had received a couple of extensions," continued Brea, "he had another impression, and that was to go and be an aide at the White House."

Louise nodded. She remembered that time. "I jumped at the chance to have him, since I heard he had dream-like premonitions telling of the future. The Secretary General swore they were real, and to tell you the truth, he interested me."

"Maybe there was more than one reason he interested you," said Brea, with a glint in her eye.

Dane swallowed as he finished watching the interaction between Louise and Brea. "Boy, you two have become chummy."

"Girl talk," Brea said to Dane. "Now don't interrupt."

Dane gave his sister an irritated glance.

"What are you getting at?" asked Louise, studying Brea.

"The Lord knew you'd be interested in Braun, that's why he was sent to the White House. He had a message for you."

Louise looked at the table. "Yes, he did..." she said, but didn't finish. She was remembering the conversation about a falling America. It had seemed so impossible at the time, but now, it had unfolded just as Braun had explained.

Brea took a breath and said, "You know, going to the White House was hard for Braun. He knew danger lurked, circling him like a shark, but he went anyway. The Lord expected him to do as he asked, and he obeyed, in spite of the risks."[16]

Louise shook her head. "And now he's running for his life."

"He is?" asked Dane, looking back and forth between Louise and Brea.

Brea held up a hand. "Later, Dane."

"I see where you're going with this," said Louise, thoughtfully.

"Then there's Dane," said Brea looking at him with a steely stare.

"Me?" asked Dane, with a hand to his chest. "Don't bring me into this. I was just curious..."

"You asked for it," said Brea, with a wry smile. "You shouldn't have interrupted."

"Heeyyyy," said Dane, looking from Louise to Brea.

Pointing at her brother, Brea said, "Now, this guy could have acted selfishly and avoided you when you were stranded, but again, a thought came to him to give you his gas, as you know."

"So you're saying that God is putting us all together."[17]

Brea nodded as Dane nodded and relaxed.

"That is exactly what I'm saying," said Brea. "God is the power greater than MD,[18] and through God's plan, He will bring MD down. We can see the beginnings of his plans in our involvement. Why else would you be brought to our home?"

Louise was struck by Brea's question. ...Yes—why else? She couldn't say anything was a coincidence anymore. The one fact that stood out was that she was the *only* one in this home *not* regularly praying to God. Maybe that should change.

Louise looked at Nebraska who was finishing up her sandwich and then back at Brea. "I think I'll be staying for lunch and a salon treatment," she said jokingly, as she ran her fingers through her simple hair. "The cut is included, isn't it?"

Brea laughed and stood up. "Absolutely. It's the special of the day."

"Oh, good," said Louise.

"I'll get you a sandwich."

Generosity

Provo, Utah
4:45 p.m.

Brother Stow entered the Bishop's office. He was bent over with age, with silver hair, and an eternal smile on his face. He was the last of a series of interviews that day meant to check personally on the status of each family in the ward.

Sitting down and with both hands on his cane, Brother Stow asked, "Bishop, how are you?" His expression was caring.

Bo raised his eyebrows. To tell the truth to this kind man would be cruel.[19] "I'm good, Brother Stow. How are you?"

"I've never been better," said Brother Stow, light almost bursting from his presence.

Bo smiled, feeling intense gratitude for the good people of his ward. They made his pain almost worth the agony. "Thank you, Brother Stow. I needed a smiling face today."

Brother Stow pulled his chair right up to Bo's desk. Then with a kind hand, he patted Bo's arm. "I'm here to support you and lift your burdens,"[20] he said, genuinely. "I've been in your position, and I see its weight on your shoulders."

Bo studied Brother Stow. Warmth and love emanated from him. There was no doubt about it, this man was happy![21] Despite trials and the world falling down around him, he was happy![22] Bo was amazed. Now this was the perfect example of how all Saints could be if they would give up pride and practice what they claimed to believe![23]

"What is it I could do for you?" asked Brother Stow.

"I need your food storage," said Bo, almost without thought. It was so automatic that he surprised himself. *Boy, that was blunt!* He scolded himself.

Brother Stow winked. "Whatever you need, it's yours," he said.

Bo blinked hard. Did he actually hear Brother Stow correctly? He felt like jumping up and doing a jig! Bo laughed out of pure happiness. "Brother Stow, Heavenly Father sent you, didn't he? You knew what I was going to ask, didn't you?"

Brother Stow nodded. "Of course, Bishop. But anyone could have guessed what's happening inside this room. You desire for your people to eat. What choices do you have? There's people with needs, and those with extra. We all just need to play nice, and then everything will be fine, right?"

Bo looked down at the table as he took in Brother Stow's words. With a lump in his throat he said, "I'm not good at this, Brother."

Brother Stow laughed heartily and nodded. "Oh, yes you are. You're doing just fine, and these people, will *be* just fine."

Bo let out a sigh and said, "Hearing those words, those simple words, have made me feel so relieved! You're right. Why am I so weighed down?"

"Because you're the Bishop! Your mantle is broad. Just remember to allow the Lord to carry your burdens, too."[24]

Bo nodded. "Excellent advice. Excellent advice."

"So, where do you want me to bring my food?"

Bo looked at Brother Stow in confusion, but then he realized that this man's desire to help was so strong, he was willing to give all of his food to his neighbors. "No, no, I don't want you to bring it anywhere," said Bo. "I just want you to be aware of the needs of some of the families in our ward and just do the best you can in watching over them. You'll get a list."

Brother Stow bowed his head and nodded. "I understand, Bishop, and I will help in any way I can. Just tell me who and consider it done."

"But you know you will not be expected to give more than you can. There are others that can help, too."

"I appreciate that, Bishop," said Brother Stow, nodding.

"Do you have any questions for me?" asked Bo.

"Nope. The Lord blessed me with what I have and I have always promised to share it willingly."

Bo shook his head in continued amazement. "You are a very unselfish and kind man, Brother Stow. You will be blessed beyond measure because of your willingness to help others."

"Thank you." Tears came to Brother Stow's eyes without apology. "Thank you," he repeated, with a quick dab of Kleenex to his eyes. "I need blessings. We all do. Since my wife has passed on, and my daughter, Michelle, and her two little ones died in that car accident, not much else matters but the Lord's will. Mankind is now my family. I want to do all that I can to share what I have and ease other's suffering."

"Your life has been hard, hasn't it?" asked Bo, feeling very sympathetic.

"I have no complaints," said Brother Stow.[25]

"Well, you are appreciated and loved. Thank you for your generosity," said Bo, wishing he could do and say more.

"No problem," said Brother Stow. "Food is temporal. It's the Lord's acceptance I seek. If I can achieve that by giving some flour, then so be it."

Bo stood and walked around to Brother Stow, who shook with age. With arms out wide, he gave the man who had seen more hardship in his years than seemed equitable, a strong embrace. "I promise you as I stand here, you will have more joy in this life, because of your love for Christ and his people."

"Thank you, Bishop," said Brother Stow. "So will you, Bishop...we all will."

Victory

Denali National Park, Alaska
9:22 p.m.

It was night. The tracker had been whimpering all day and now continued into the night. Carea, after checking to see what could be wrong, noticed that the tracker's arms didn't look so great. His fingertips were white and his hands were blotchy, not to mention the arms were two times the size they had been. There was something wrong. She didn't know what, but she knew there was nothing she could do about it. She wished she knew about medicine, and then at least she could fix the things she broke.

A quiet tap came from the window. It sounded like a rock.

Carea frowned. What was that? She looked around at the other girls in her cabin. None of them acted like they had heard it.

Another tap came from the window.

"I hate windows," said Carea, as she moved cautiously to the window and peered out through its blurriness. Someone was outside, once again. She could see their dark form. Was it more black fur clan members? Why would they be throwing rocks at her window? Didn't they learn last time?

The person outside motioned for her to come out.

She considered this request. Was this another trap? An ambush? She decided to ignore the hail.

Carea returned to her bed, and stared down at the tracker, who slept on a cot next to hers. He looked so helpless. She had to look away.

Knock, knock, knock.

Carea looked up. "Someone's at the door!"

Bones frowned. "I don't like it that someone's knocking this late."

Carea stood up. "What time is it?"

"Nearly 9:30. Around here, nothing good happens after dark," said Bones. Then with a voice of authority, she said, "You sit down, girly. You're not going to that door."

"Why?" asked Carea. "I did fine last time."

"Why?" asked Bones, looking at the door, in almost an excited manner. "Because you're backing me up this time. It's only fair I get some fun, too."

Knock, knock, knock.

Carea smiled and nodded. "OK," she said. "I'll stand back here," she whispered, as she tiptoed to stand behind the door.

Bones opened the door. "Yes? …Back so soon? …Do you have something for us?"

"No, I need to talk to Carea," said a familiar voice.

Carea frowned. Where had she heard that voice before? It was different than anyone else's she had met at the camp.

"No one talks to Carea till we get our supplies," growled Bones.

"That wasn't the deal," said the voice.

"The deal's changed," said Bones, as she moved to close the door, but it hit something and bounced back. "Hey! Get your foot out of the door or I'll have to cut it off!" she threatened through clenched teeth.

"Ask Carea how her family is," said the voice.

"No, I won't ask her that. She misses her family. That would be wrong."

"No, I mean, ask her if she's seen Kessa lately."

"Kessa?" asked Carea, feeling her heart drop. Kessa used to be her best friend! Who knew Kessa? She pulled the door back and shock ripped through her. *"Jack!"* she exclaimed, with almost a strangled voice, as she looked at the familiar face. "What are *you* doing here?"

Jack smirked underneath his overgrown blonde hair. "What do you mean 'what am I doing here?' I was sent here a long time ago by your brother, remember? The Raves?"

Carea's mouth hung open. She didn't know what to say. Of course she remembered….

"You know this person?" asked Bones, looking sideways at Carea.

Carea nodded as she swallowed. The truth was, secretly, she had been in love with this guy before he had gone bad and joined the Bats. They had grown up together, gone swimming together, played games long into late summer nights together. "Yeah, I know him," she said, trying to gain her composure.

"Is he a good guy?" asked Bones.

Carea studied the smiling, weathered, but still beautiful face of her long-lost friend. "Yeah, I think so. At least he used to be," she said, with a modest smile.

Jack held up his hands and confidently sauntered by Bones. "Thanks for inviting me in."

"I didn't invite you in," said Bones, looking like she was pumping up her muscles, making her tall stature look monstrous. "But since you *insist* on coming in here...." She slammed the door, giving the impression she had Jack right where she wanted him.

"Hey, Carea, call off your pit bull," said Jack with a thumb over his shoulder.

Bones jumped at Jack and popped him in the lip.

"Bones! Stop!" yelled Carea.

Blood dripped from Jack's mouth. Anger flared in his face, but he controlled himself.

Bones slowly retreated. "Tell him to be respectful then," she said, with an angry stare.

Carea gave Jack an irritated look. "Don't come in here saying things that make people hate you."

Jack wiped more blood from his split lip and said, "People *I like* don't hate me" he said, keeping his eye on Bones.

"Be nice, Jack, or get out," said Carea, with a warning glare.

Jack held up his hands and said, "OK, OK, I'll be good."

Bones crossed her arms and asked, "I'm assuming you came alone."

Jack looked around the cabin and shrugged. "My men are outside, but I did come to be alone with...Carea," he said with a sudden flirtatious smile.

Bones looked suspiciously at Carea. "What's this about?"

Carea raised her eyebrows and shrugged. "I'm not sure, but I'll find out." She felt her heart beat a little faster. She had to admit she was flattered he had sought her out. Jack's familiar face made her very happy and very—uneasy at the same time. She had to be careful that her attraction to him didn't cloud her judgment. "What can I do for you, Jack?" she said, folding her arms too.

Jack approached Carea.

Carea stood her ground.

With a slow hand he gently stroked Carea's arm. "There are many things you can do for me," he crooned.

"Don't play with me, Jack. Get to the point," Carea said, pretending she was unaffected, but hiding her true feelings. She tried to ignore the part of her that was actually enjoying his touch.

"Can you come away with me?" asked Jack, with an intense stare.

Carea was surprised. "Come away, what does that mean?"

"You know, get out of here. We need to be alone."

Carea shook her head. That would not be good. "Why?" she asked with a sideways glance.

Jack shrugged. "We need to get reacquainted. We need to talk about old times—and new times." Jack leaned forward, just enough so Carea felt uncomfortable. Then he said in a quiet voice in her ear, "A crowded cabin is no place for that."

"He's playing you, girl," warned Bones.

Carea looked at Bones and knew she was right. "I'm sorry, Jack. I don't think so."

"Why? You said yourself, I was a good guy."

Carea shook her head. "I don't know you anymore, Jack. Who knows what you've become, especially living here. And to be honest, the only thing I want from you is information."

"About what?" he asked.

"Like, when are your people going to give back our stuff?" asked Bones, interrupting in a loud voice.

Jack looked at Bones and then back to Carea.

Carea nodded. "She's right. People here are suffering. I think your group, clan, or whatever you call yourselves, can help. We have skills that I think your people would benefit from, as do you for us. I think we should create an alliance."

Jack studied Carea's face and then said, "And who would enter into an agreement if an alliance was to occur?"

Carea looked at Bones.

Bones nodded in support.

"I would," said Carea.

"You would?" asked Jack.

"Yes, I would. I would in behalf of the people in this camp. I want to make a pact with Gruff. Can you get me an audience and give me a guarantee of safety?"

"And what makes you think you can negotiate anything with Gruff? Who are you? You just got here," said Jack.

"I might have just got here, but I know how to fix the problems here, and I have enough energy and desire to do it."

"You do?" asked Jack.

"Yes, I do."

"And what would you do?"

"For starters, around here," started Carea, "everyone just walks around, moping and sitting in corners, not doing anything about not having food, or enough warm blankets and clothing for the coming winter. That's suicide! They have no hope, and that equals only one thing, death."

"So let them die. More food for us," said Jack.

"No!" said Carea, with strength. "You're thinking the wrong way. More people, equals more work force. Everyone can benefit by a working economy."

"And what if they don't want to be productive?" asked Jack.

"Then they don't receive the benefits."

Jack nodded. "Interesting thoughts."

"By the way, tell me something," said Carea.

"What?"

"Obviously you've found a food and a clothing source by how healthy you look, and I'm not talking about the pillaging you've been doing. I'm talking about those warm fur coats. Whatever animal they belonged to, I'm sure was very good eating."

"Bear."

"Bear what?" asked Carea.

"This fur is bear. There's lots of them around here and we figured out how to kill them. One bear can feed and clothe seven of our clan."

Carea looked at Jack with amazement. "Wow. I can't believe that!" Then Carea had an idea. "I wonder if you can breed bears for food."

"What are you talking about?"

"Well, it's one thing to hunt bears, but sooner or later, you kill too many and they're gone. If you make sure they can reproduce at least as fast as you hunt them, then that will never happen."

Jack looked intrigued. His look changed. "I think you have some good points. I think I'll take them back to Gruff."

Carea shook her head, "No, I want to talk to Gruff. Let me pitch it to him."

Jack shook his head. "No one talks to Gruff but me."

"Why's that?"

"That's just the way it is. This is a violent crew and Gruff has to be untouchable. Anyway, what does it matter? You want your supplies, you want your ideas heard and I have an in. Let me go to bat for you."

Carea bit her lip and shook her head. "I don't know…"

Jack smiled and started for the door and said, "Here, I'm sure this will make you feel better."

"What?" asked Carea, smiling now.

Jack opened the door and then whistled through his fingers. Suddenly, out of the darkness came many people, clad in fur, holding their supplies. Within minutes, the floor was covered with food, brand new blankets, boots, hats, and other supplies.

Carea was beside herself. "What? I can't believe this! You brought our stuff back!"

"Plus more," said Jack, with a satisfied smile and a wink. "A token of our good intentions."

"And I didn't even have to beat up anyone!" chided Carea. "You've come a long way, Jack!"

"Thanks," he said. "Hey later, you're going to have to show me some of your moves. I hear you're a pretty amazing martial artist."

Carea laughed with satisfaction. Nodding she said, "I've practiced some."

Jack gave the signal for his people to retrieve the tracker. Quickly, the cabin filled with the bear clan, and then gently they picked up the cot the tracker was lying on, and piled blankets on top to keep him warm. With one who seemed to know something about medicine calling out instructions, they backed out of the cabin.

"I'd never want to meet you in a dark alley, Carea," said Jack. Then with a sly smile, he stalled. "Or, maybe, secretly, under different circumstances, I might." Winking, he closed the door.

Carea smiled. Flattered and contented, she couldn't help it! This was a major victory!

The cabin erupted in ecstatic happiness. *Yes!* Things were changing!

Notes to "Exposure"

Selfish

[1] "Every man seeking the interest of his neighbor, and doing all things with an eye single to the glory of God" (D&C 82:19).

[2] "The Savior gave us the Golden Rule: 'All things whatsoever ye would that men should do to you, do ye even so to them' (Matthew 7:12). Satan's position is the opposite. He sponsors self-interest, raw and unrefined by any other consideration" (Dallin H. Oaks, "'Brother's Keeper'," *Ensign*, November 1986, pg. 20).

[3] "'Seek ye first the kingdom of God, and his righteousness; and all these things shall be added unto you," [Matt. 6:33] and "Love one another.' [John 13:34] In these two statements can be found the key to the solution of all those problems which are causing such misery and trouble for individuals, communities, nations, and the world. By accepting and living according to these two doctrines, we could have joy unspeakable here and eternal happiness hereafter. These are the blessings for which we all should be seeking" (N. Eldon Tanner, "Love One Another," *Ensign*, October 1972, pg. 2).

[4] "The world today tells you to leave your friend alone. He has the right to come and go as he pleases. The world tells you that persuasion to attend church or priesthood meeting or to discard a bad habit might lead to frustration and undue pressures; but again I repeat the word of the Lord: You are your brother's keeper, and when you are converted, you have an obligation to strengthen your brother" (Robert L. Simpson, *Conference Report*, October 1971, pg. 114).

[5] "I raise my voice with others throughout the world who warn against abuse of drugs beyond prescribed limits, and the recreational or social use of chemical substances so often begun naively by the ill-informed. From an initial experiment thought to be trivial, a vicious cycle may follow. From trial comes a habit. From habit comes dependence. From dependence comes addiction. Its grasp is so

gradual. Enslaving shackles of habit are too small to be sensed until they are too strong to be broken. Indeed, drugs are the modern "mess of pottage" for which souls are sold. No families are free from risk. ... Agency, or the power to choose, was ours as spirit children of our Creator before the world was. (See Alma 13:3; Moses 4:4) It is a gift from God, nearly as precious as life itself. Often, however, agency is misunderstood. While we are free to choose, once we have made those choices, we are tied to the consequences of those choices. We are free to take drugs or not. But once we choose to use a habit-forming drug, we are bound to the consequences of that choice. Addiction surrenders later freedom to choose. Through chemical means, one can literally become disconnected from his or her own will!" (Russell M. Nelson, "Addiction or Freedom," *Ensign*, November 1988, pg. 6).

[6] "For it is not meet that the things which belong to the children of the kingdom should be given to them that are not worthy, or to dogs, or the pearls to be cast before swine" (D&C 41:6).

In God's Hand

[7] "Pray about the important things of your life—about attending school, about going on a mission, about the girl you will marry or the boy you will marry. The Lord will bless you and guide you" (Gordon B. Hinkley, Montreal, Quebec, Canada, 6 August 1998).

[8] "And he shall speak *great* words against the most High, and shall wear out the saints of the most High, and think to change times and laws: and they shall be given into his hand until a time and times and the dividing of time. But the judgment shall sit, and they shall take away his dominion, to consume and to destroy *it* unto the end. And the kingdom and dominion, and the greatness of the kingdom under the whole heaven, shall be given to the people of the saints of the most High, whose kingdom *is* an everlasting kingdom, and all dominions shall serve and obey him" (Daniel 7:25-27).

[9] "Believe in God; believe that he is, and that he created all things, both in heaven and in earth; believe that he has all wisdom, and all power, both in heaven and in earth" (Mosiah 4:9).

"Unless God had power over all things, and was able by his power to control all things, and thereby deliver his creatures who put their trust in him from the power of all beings that might seek their destruction, whether in heaven, on earth, or in hell, men could not be saved" (Joseph Smith, *Lectures on Faith, Vol.* 4 pg. 12).

[10] "Does God know all things? He does. Is there anything he does not know? There is not. Is he progressing in knowledge and learning new truths? He is not. He is not a student God. His knowledge and Supremacy are not limited to a sphere or realm beyond which there are higher spheres and greater realms. He is an Eternal God, an infinite being, an omniscient man, one in whose person all knowledge, all power, and all truth center" (Bruce R. McConkie, *New Witness for the Articles of Faith*, pg. 176).

"Without the knowledge of all things God would not be able to save any portion of his creatures; for it is by reason of the knowledge which he has of all things, from the beginning to the end, that enables him to give that understanding to his creatures by which they are made partakers of eternal life; and if it were not for the idea existing in the minds of men that God had all knowledge it would be impossible for them to exercise faith in him" (Joseph Smith, *Lectures on Faith*, Vol. 4, pg. 11).

[11] God can definitely see the future. He resides in the past, present and future all at the same time and knows all the consequences of our choices. We are counseled to seek his perception of our future so to make the best choices. See the following:

"[God lives] on a globe like a sea of glass and fire, where all things for their glory are manifest, past, present, and future, and are continually before [Him]" (D&C 130:7).

"...God perceives time as instantaneously as we perceive space. For us, time is difficult. Lacking higher facility, we are as blind about time as a sightless man is about space. ...Equally complete now is each of our lives before the Lord. We explore them sequentially because we are time-blind. But the Lord, perceiving time as space, sees us as we are, not as we are becoming. We are, for him, beings without time. We are continually before him—the totality of our psyches, personalities, bodies, choices and behaviors" (*Continually before the Lord*, Commissioner's Lecture Series, Brigham Young University Press, pgs. 5-6).

[12] "[God] looketh down upon all the children of men; and he knows all the thoughts and intents of the heart; for by his hand were they all created from the beginning" (Alma 18:32).

[13] "Did I not speak peace to your mind concerning the matter? What greater witness can you have than from God?" (D&C 6:23).

[14] "Trust in the LORD with all thine heart; and lean not unto thine own understanding. In all thy ways acknowledge him, and he shall direct thy paths" (Proverbs 3:5-6).

[15] "The power of the Holy Ghost is one of the great resources of the Latter-day Saints if they will only use it. ...The Holy Spirit is truly a guide to us in our daily activities. Each of us has a conscience. When our conscience bids us avoid anything, or when we have fallen into trouble and it urges us to repentance, it is the Spirit influencing us. It can be our salvation. Let us remember that the glory of God is intelligence (D&C 93:36) and that the glory of mankind is also intelligence. When the Spirit of God works upon us, we may receive help from the divine intelligence that gives light and direction to our own intelligence (spirit). The Savior taught us that the Holy Spirit is the Spirit of Truth, and 'he will guide you into all truth...and he will show you things to come' (John 16:7-16)" (Mark E. Petersen, "The Gift of the Holy Ghost," *Tambuli*, July 1979, pg. 16).

[16] "Submission to God, among many things, requires us to strip ourselves of our pride in order to be obedient to Him. In that process we make ourselves so much more useful in the achievement of God's purposes among His children" (Neal A. Maxwell, *Not My Will but Thine*, pg. 88).

[17] "What is it that kindles such special divine displeasure? Ingratitude, to be sure, but surely our meek and perfect Lord is not asking for mere ritual acknowledgment or for superficial praise of the tongue. Instead, we are told about our loving Father, 'In all thy ways acknowledge him, and he shall direct thy paths' (Proverbs 3:6)" (Neal A. Maxwell, *That ye May Believe*, pg. 25).

[18] "[The beast will] make war with the Lamb, and the Lamb shall overcome [him]: for he is Lord of lords, and King of kings" (Revelation 17:14).

Generosity

[20] "Patient endurance permits us to cling to our faith in the Lord and our faith in His timing when we are being tossed about by the surf of circumstance. Even when a seeming undertow grasps us, somehow, in the tumbling, we are being carried forward, though battered and bruised" (Neal A. Maxwell, "'Endure It Well'," *Ensign*, May 1990, pg. 33).

[20] "Wherefore, be faithful...succor the weak, lift up the hands which hang down, and strengthen the feeble knees. And if thou art faithful unto the end thou shalt have a crown of immortality, and eternal life in the mansions which I have prepared in the house of my Father" (D&C 81:5-6).

[21] "And moreover, I would desire that ye should consider on the blessed and happy state of those that keep the commandments of God. For behold, they are blessed in all things, both temporal and spiritual; and if they hold out faithful to the end they are received into heaven, that thereby they may dwell with God in a state of never-ending happiness. O remember, remember that these things are true; for the Lord God hath spoken it" (Mosiah 2:41).

[22] "...Plant this word in your hearts, and as it beginneth to swell even so nourish it by your faith. And behold, it will become a tree, springing up in you unto everlasting life. And then may God grant unto you that your burdens may be light, through the joy of his Son" (Alma 33:23).

[23] "When pride has a hold on our hearts, we lose our independence of the world and deliver our freedoms to the bondage of men's judgment. The world shouts louder than the whisperings of the Holy Ghost. The reasoning of men overrides the revelations of God, and the proud let go of the iron rod. (See 1 Nephi 8:19-28, 1 Nephi 11:25; 1 Nephi 15:23-24.)" (Ezra Taft Benson, "Beware of Pride," *Ensign*, May 1989, pg. 4).

[24] "...Every one of us carries around burdens and fears that wear us down and greatly oppress us. ...According to a recent study of mental health in America, plain old-fashioned worry is one of the few emotional problems that is on the increase, for reasons that are not altogether clear to physicians and

behavioral scientists. Dr. Claire Weekes, in trying to discover a pattern for such emotional and spiritual worry, said, "The basic problem is fear. Guilt opens the door to fear. Anxiety, worry, dread, conflict, even sorrow are only variants of fear in different guises." (*Hope and Help for Your Nerves* [New York: Hawthorn Books, 1969], p. 21.) It is in response to these very modern challenges that God comes to us as 'the Father of mercies, and the God of all comfort.' What a reassurance and reward just to know that such all-encompassing help is available to us in our anxious times. No wonder we lovingly call him Father. ...With humility, express your gratitude for every blessing, every good thing you enjoy. Share with him your problems and fears. Talk to him about each one and pause long enough to receive his counsel. I promise that you will learn his shoulders are broad enough for your burdens. ...When we hand our fears and frustrations to him in absolute confidence that he will help us resolve them, when in this way we free our heart and mind and soul of all anxiety, we find in a rather miraculous way that he can instill within us a whole new perspective. He can fill us with 'that joy which is unspeakable and full of glory' (Helaman 5:44), even in the midst of our anguish" (Jeffery R. Holland and Patricia T. Holland, *On Earth as it is in Heaven*, pg. 36-37).

[25] "Sadness, disappointment, and severe challenge are *events* in life, not life itself. I do not minimize how hard some of these events are. They can extend over a long period of time, but they should not be allowed to become the confining center of everything you do. The Lord inspired Lehi to declare the fundamental truth, 'Men are, that they might have joy' (2 Nephi 2:25). That is a conditional statement: 'they *might* have joy.' It is not conditional for the Lord. His intent is that each of us finds joy. It will not be conditional for you as you obey the commandments, have faith in the Master, and do the things that are necessary to have joy here on earth. Your joy in life depends upon your trust in Heavenly Father and His holy Son, your conviction that their plan of happiness truly can bring you joy. Pondering their doctrine will let you enjoy the beauties of this earth and enrich your relationships with others. It will lead you to the comforting, strengthening experiences that flow from prayer to Father in Heaven and the answers He gives in return. A pebble held close to the eye appears to be a gigantic obstacle. Cast on the ground, it is seen in perspective. Likewise, problems or trials in our lives need to be viewed in the perspective of scriptural doctrine. Otherwise they can easily overtake our vision, absorb our energy, and deprive us of the joy and beauty the Lord intends us to receive here on earth. Some people are like rocks thrown into a sea of problems. They are drowned by them. Be a cork. When submerged in a problem, fight to be free to bob up to serve again with happiness" (Richard G. Scott, "Finding Joy in Life," *Ensign*, May 1996, pg. 24).

CHAPTER SEVEN

PLANS WELL LAID

"Fret not thyself because of evil men, neither be thou envious at the wicked; For there shall be no reward to the evil man; the candle of the wicked shall be put out" (Proverbs 24:19-20).

00:03:00, 08:55:28, Zulu
Tuesday, September 30th

Report

Frankfurt, Germany
4:05 p.m.

"What's the status of the United States and the relief effort?" asked MD, as he leaned back in his leather chair. He was in his office with Matt. A cloud of cigar smoke hung low in the room.

"The UN has relief centers in the main metropolitan areas. There are one hundred of them," said Matt. He tried to point at the computer screen but lost his grip on his stylet and dropped it on the keyboard. His state-of-the-art prosthetic hands still had difficulty with fine motor movements.

"Is that enough?" asked MD.

"Far from it," said Matt, catching the stylet before it could roll off the edge of his computer.

"That's OK," said MD, as he blew out a ring. "We'll branch out to other areas after we reach implantation saturation."

"If there's anyone still left alive," said Matt to himself, as he once again grasped his stylet firmly between the thumb and third finger of his right hand.

"What did you say?" asked MD. "My hearing's going."

Matt looked up at his father. "Oh, I said, 'if there's anyone left alive.' I don't think too many people will survive without us."

"Oh, yes," said MD. "Good. You're right. Not many will. Tell me how many deaths do we have to date?"

Matt tapped the screen and a new window appeared containing satellite images of the devastation in the United States. He clicked through them. "The exact number is unknown. We have mass deaths in the largest cities due to the gas that was released and more due to lack of clean water."

MD drew in on his cigar. "Give me an estimate," he said with smoke billowing out his nose.

"I'd say, fifty million."

MD shook his head and set his cigar into a tray. "That's not enough. We need more. We need to take the population from 400 million down to about 40. We can feed and control forty million."

Matt's stomach turned. He held his face still, his expression flat. He had to be stoic. "I'm sure time will do that for us. All farming has stopped and there isn't any food in the stores. It's just a matter of time."

MD nodded. "I agree. I'm not worried," he said, as he interlaced his hands across his abdomen.

"We've tagged about three hundred thousand is all."

"Well keep going till you meet 40 mil. Then kkkkkkichchchc," said MD, with a thumb drawn across his neck. "That's it."

"OK," said Matt, writing a note to himself.

"Have you heard any backlash concerning the deaths? What's going on in the heads of the survivors?"

Matt shook his head. "Nothing. We—I mean, the UN is distanced from all of this. Generally, people aren't aware of what's happened, or who did what. Most people are isolated so they only see what's happening locally."

"What about New York and Washington?"

"We have the gassed cities roped off and quarantined. No one is going in or out, thus the quantity of deaths inside are unknown by the general population."

"Are crews cleaning up the bodies?"

"There's no way to get to all of them. They're doing the best they can. They're understaffed. We might just have to burn the place."

"Hmmm, oh well, that would do."

"Yes, sir."

"How's the UN looking? The aid must be increasing public opinion."

"People think we're the best thing since chocolate."

MD chuckled. "Why do you say that?"

"The handheld video communicators we're distributing are like candy to America's psyche. They were an extra expense, but I think in the long run, they'll pay for themselves in loyalty."

"I see. Tell me about what you hope to accomplish."

"Just what you said. A positive public perception."

"How are you doing that?"

"Through the media. Our media is doing a great job selling the UN."

"And are people believing it?"

"Hook, line, and sinker," said Matt.

"Good. Excellent! Positive propaganda is an excellent idea. Keep the video feeds rolling. America needs to trust us. They need to love us and never want to live without us. We are taming the shrew."

"Got it," said Matt.

"Handheld video communicators, huh? Who thought of that one?" asked MD, with a hint of approval.

"I did."

"Good move," said MD, with a nod.

"I was just cashing in on the previous perceptions of the Americans. They trust the news media. Now that they don't have their media, they'll trust ours."[1]

"Tell me more about these genius little gadgets."

"They have cell, video, and Internet capabilities. As each person enters the system, they can talk to others in the system. Another good thing that has come from the hand devices is connections. Americans have felt deaf, dumb, and blind, as they lost track of their loved ones. We're publicizing stories of reconnections as families find each other again."

"I love it!" exclaimed MD, as he smacked his desk with his palm. "This is just what we want."

Matt didn't quite know how to take all this positive feedback. He stood uncomfortably and tapped his stylet, waiting for the next item of business.

"Are you offering mortgage support yet?" asked MD, blowing a circle of smoke in the air.

"Yes, we're offering food, utility, and mortgage support. In some areas we're matching skills with employment."

"That's good. How can anyone resist such a package? We'll have everyone chipped before long!"

"Actually, some are refusing."

"Who?"

"Those who are religious."

"Any reason for that?"

"Most believe our chip is something predicted in the Bible associated with the devil."

"That's funny—because they're *right*!" said MD with a deep laugh. He laughed for a while, finally red-faced and sweating, he said, "Oh, well! I say, let them starve! If they want to refuse free food and support, that's up to them. They can die, for all I care. More resources for everyone else and one less plague we'll have to arrange. In fact, put the pressure on them. Take away their homes, their medical care, and kick their kids out of school. Let's see how long they can endure that one, two, three punch! Soon, those self-righteous hypocrites will be coming over to our side in droves!" MD squished his cigar out repeatedly in his ashtray as he chuckled. "Yes, yes, that should push things along nicely."

Matt nodded but kept his face unemotional. Inside, his stomach twisted in disgust, but he had to stay calm. No remarks. No hint of irritation.

"Carry on, son!" said MD.

"Yes, sir," said Matt.

"By the way, get our video team to create some really bad stuff about those religious folks. Get everyone riled. A little war would be just what we need to wipe out those idiots. I'll follow up with some really good stuff for later. Maybe we'll make an international announcement that will help nail their coffins shut."

"Yes, sir," said Matt again.

"Oh yes—*this* is going to get *good*," said MD, as he flicked his wrist and dismissed his son with a roar of self-indulgent laughter.

Matt turned with relief and left the room. Enough was enough! He thought he might get sick!

Enticement

Provo, Utah
5:20 p.m.

"This is a message sponsored by the UN..." The deep voice was coming from a bullhorn outside.

"What was that?" asked Jax, looking up at his brothers. "Did you guys hear anything?"

"...A relief station will be set up at Crestview High School to service this neighborhood..."

Jax went to the window. There was a white truck outside driving slowly by with a horn mounted on top. On the side of the truck it said "UN" in big, bold, black letters. "You guys! Come look."

Roc and Ry ran to the door and opened it. The message repeated as the truck rolled by.

"This is an announcement sponsored by the UN. For anyone out of work or out of food, there will be a relief station set up at Crestview High School. There's also gas and clean, bottled water. The relief station will be open tomorrow at 8:00 a.m."

Little Strykker pulled the door open and bolted out and onto the sidewalk. "Ice-keam!" he yelled happily.

"Get him!" yelled Jax.

Ry and Roc started to laugh to each other. "He thinks that's an ice cream truck," said Roc.

"Guys! Get him!" said Jax, as he watched Strykker disappear down the sidewalk.

"You get him," said Ry, defiantly. "Dad told you to watch him while he went downstairs."

Jax growled with frustration as he took off after his little brother. "Watch Striynna!" he called over his shoulder.

"Get some ice cream while you're out there!" yelled Roc, laughing hysterically with Ry as he closed the door.

As Jax ran after his little brother, he noticed that his neighbors were trickling out of their homes and onto the sidewalk. There was Brother Thomson, hobbling along with his cane, mean Brother Reiser with his killer dog following him, and crazy Sister Carver. None of them noticed Strykker rushing to catch up to the truck; instead all of their eyes were glued to the truck as it slowly rolled by.

Jax finally caught up with his baby brother. "Strykker Rogers!" he called authoritatively. "Where are you going?" he asked, grabbing the little guy by his arm.

"Ice-keam!" Strykker pleaded, pointing, fighting against his brother's grip.

"That's not an ice cream truck! That's a—a—" he didn't know what to call it. "It's a police truck. They don't like little children," he said, knowing he was wrong. "They don't have ice cream."

"Ice-keam!" called Strykker now falling to his knees to pull away from Jax. "Ice-keam!"

"Come on!" demanded Jax, in the lowest and loudest voice he could manage. "Get up!" He picked Strykker up around his torso and started for home.

Strykker kicked and screamed, arching his back in anger.

"Jax!" called a woman from behind.

Jax turned around. "Yeah?" he asked, over his brother's crying. He took a deep breath as he struggled to keep Strykker in his arms.

"Is your father home?" asked Sister Carver, rushing towards him, her thighs jiggling in a frightening speed-walk.

"Yeah, he's working on something in the basement," said Jax, straining to speak while getting kicked in the shins. "I'm supposed to be watching the kids so he doesn't get bothered," he managed to say over the pain.

Brother Reiser, who was quickly approaching, must have heard their conversation. "Get your father. We need to talk to him," he demanded.

Sister Carver nodded wide-eyed in agreement.

Jax set Strykker on the ground as he noticed about ten other people approaching. They looked weird as they all came toward his house! It was like one of those undead movies.

"Come on, Strykker. I'll get you a treat," Jax bribed.

"Treat?" asked Strykker, with a hopeful stare.

"Yeah," said Jax, as he watched even more people gather behind him. He stood tall and asked, "What are all of you following me for?"

"We're not following you, honey. ...We want to talk to your father," said Sister Carver, with a patronizing look.

"All of you?" Jax asked, not understanding.

"Yes," said Brother Reiser, with an impatient tone. "Get your father."

Jax nodded. He felt irritated, too, as he turned and pulled Strykker along. He hated that Brother Reiser was never nice to him.

The crowd of people had grown to about twenty. They all followed Jax up the stairs and onto the porch.

Jax opened the front door and said, "Might as well come in. I'll get my dad."

The crowd filed into the Rogers' home one by one and spilled over the entryway into the living room.

"But, don't let the babies out!" Jax added.

"What are all these people doing in our house?" Roc whispered, as he stared and leaned against the hall wall to stay out of the way.

"They're here to see Dad—take Strykker," Jax said, as he handed his little brother to Roc. "Don't let him get away this time."

"OK," said Roc, still looking at the neighbors in wonder.

Jax opened the downstairs door. He trotted down the stairs calling, "Hey, Dad!"

"What?" his father responded. Jax couldn't see him but it sounded like he was straining to do something somewhere in the room.

"There's tons of people here to see you."

"Why?" asked Bo.

"I don't know," said Jax, "but they're waiting in the living room."

Bo appeared from around the corner, wiping his hands on a cloth. "Tell them I'll be right there."

"OK," said Jax, climbing the stairs. At the top, he announced. "My dad's coming."

Sister Carver smiled. "Thank you, dear," she said with a wink.

Jax cringed inside. That lady gave him the willies. She smelled funny. Despite this thought, he nodded politely and stole down the hall. Too much attention made him embarrassed. He'd go see what the other kids were doing.

ξξξξξξ

"Sister Carver? How's your husband?" asked Bo warmly.

"He's OK," she said. "He'll survive today."

"Good," said Bo nodding. "That's all we can ask." Turning to Brother Reiser he asked, "And what can I do for you?"

"Did you hear that announcement, Bishop Rogers?" Brother Reiser didn't waste any time on pleasantries.

"What announcement?" asked Bo.

"Something wonderful has happened!" added Sister Carver, with her hands clasped. "Our prayers for relief have been answered!"

"How's that?" asked Bo. He felt like he had somehow stepped out of the loop when he went into his basement.

"The UN is in our part of town and will be setting up a relief station at Crestview High," gushed Sister Carver.

"They'll be handing out food and water in the morning," continued Brother Reiser.

"Do you want us to send someone out to tell others in the ward?" asked Sister Carver.

Bo frowned as a feeling of dread hit him in the chest. Hadn't Dane told him that the UN was handing out biochips in return for food and water? That scenario didn't sit right with him. "No, I don't think so," said Bo, shaking his head. "At least not yet..."

"Why not?" asked Brother Reiser, interrupting Bo, with a look of shock. "That's relief food! We deserve relief. *We don't have any work!*"

Bo held up his hands and said, "I know the relief supply sounds like a great deal, but I really don't think it is."

"Why not? It's free," said Sister Carver, looking like she might cry. "Don't you think this is the help we all need?"

Bo nodded. "I know, it might appear that way but I believe if we pull together, we can help each other adequately. We don't need help from the UN."

"Yeah, but if they're offering, why not take it?" said Brother Reiser. "It makes economic sense to let them feed us so we don't dip into our stores. We don't know how long this dry spell is going to last."

"I understand your thinking, and ordinarily, I'd say, 'Sure, go,' but right now, I can't do that."

"Why?" asked Sister Carver.

"Because as you know, my son, Dane, just came home from the military, and he told me that those relief stations do give out food and water, and sometimes even gas…"

"Yes, I bet they would have gas," said Brother Reiser, nodding to others in the room. "It was a truck that went by, and it obviously had gas."

"I know," said Bo, "but listen. I know firsthand that the relief they are offering comes at a price."

"No, it's *free*," repeated Sister Carver, shaking her head.

"It might not cost you any money, but it's by no means *free*."

"What do you mean?" asked Brother Reiser, frowning.

"According to my son, in order to receive relief, you must agree to have a computer chip placed under your skin to facilitate the UN's support."[2]

"What's wrong with that?" asked Brother Reiser. "There's got to be some sort of accounting system in place. How else can they know who to bring relief for?"

Bo studied the man who just a few days ago had been independently wealthy. Going from having millions to fighting for every crumb he could find must be taking its toll. "Brother Reiser, computer chips are not necessary to know how much food to bring. Everyone in the United States is starving, whatever they bring won't be enough, I promise."

"I think you're just being paranoid," said Brother Reiser. "There's nothing wrong with those chips. I've studied them. They're the way of the future. They can act like cash in some places. Everyone in Europe has one and petty theft and stolen identities are a thing of the past."[3]

Bo nodded. "I know those things, if used appropriately, can be very useful, but in our situation, they aren't necessary."

"Come on, Bishop. The chips are harmless," said Brother Reiser. "My brother has MS and has one implanted to hold his medical records.[4] And that's here in America!"

"I know, Brother Reiser. I'm not going to argue the pros and cons of the chip with you. I'm just going to tell you what I feel. I, as your bishop, am telling you, I have bad feelings about this situation. I encourage you to stay clear of Crestview High tomorrow."

The crowd was silent. It looked like everyone was disappointed and weighing in their minds if they were going to listen to the Bishop.

Bo continued. "No one should allow anyone, man, machine, corporation, or government, to infringe upon their privacy. You are a free man right now, Brother Reiser. No one owns you…"

"What good is being free, if you die from hunger?"

"You won't *die*, Brother Reiser."

"Who says?" he asked, looking back at the crowd for support. "Sure we have some food, Bishop, but we all know we don't have enough. There's a lot of things we don't have enough of."

"And what about our water?" asked Sister Carver. "Boiling water, every time you want a drink is not how I want to live my life."

"Those are the choices you're going to have to make," said Bo, nodding. "As your bishop, I will not stop you from walking up that hill tomorrow to receive food and water. Like I said before, all of you are free. You can do with your life as you see fit."

"Life's a string of economic choices, Bishop," said Brother Reiser. "Eating is pretty high on my list. The cost of that choice seems pretty clear to me."

"I understand," said Bo, nodding. "But before you make that choice, know that there may be costs you aren't aware of at this time. Ones we haven't discussed"

"Like what?" asked Sister Simonson from the back of the room.

Bo looked out across the people that filled his living room. With a sigh, he said, "My wife, as you know, is an ICU nurse. She has personally cared for patients who have lost their lives because of the chip. The chip can be used for more than just a means of monetary exchange, tracking,[5] or identity purposes. They can be tools of control. In severe cases, I know the chip has caused sickness and death."[6]

"Are you trying to scare us, Bishop?" asked Brother Reiser.

"No, you can look up each case. All of them were in the paper."

"How, Bishop. We have no newspapers," said Brother Wright, who was standing beside Brother Reiser.

"OK, then, you'll just have to learn from *my* experience," said Bo. "If you remember, my son received a chip at the hands of the Bats, and from that chip, bacteria poured into his blood and it nearly killed him."

"That's true, I remember when that happened," said Sister Jensen, thoughtfully. "I visited him at the hospital."

"But the Bats are a gang. How can you compare the UN with a local drug gang?" asked Brother Reiser. "That's a ridiculous comparison."

Bo felt frustration well up inside him. Keeping his patience he said, "Ask yourself these questions: Why did a lowly drug gang need *biochips*? How did they even obtain them? What were the biochips used for? Where are the Bats now?" Bo waited for a response. "Anyone?"

No one answered.

Bo continued. "Since *my* son was directly involved and there were police investigations concerning him, I'll tell you. The Bats obtained biochips from the same man who created the UN's chips. Incredible? Unbelievable? Am I just being paranoid? You might think I could be until it's discovered that the Bats were a test group. They were guinea pigs; an expendable segment of society that could be implanted and studied by very rich, powerful and manipulative men. And how do I know? Because my wife uncovered this plan when she saw people die at the hospital. Through her efforts some Bats were saved and their lives changed, and others were hauled away." Bo looked at his friends, feeling his eyes filling with emotion. "Come on. All of you know this information. It was all over the news!"

Bo's neighbors remained silent. He could feel embarrassment filter through them, but it didn't stop him.

With emotion making his voice shake, Bo continued, "And now, I believe that out of some sick retaliation effort, a chip was forcibly implanted in my daughter and she too, was carted away to the prison camps in Alaska...we didn't even get to say good-bye." Bo was becoming overwhelmed and feeling like he needed to leave the room.

"Bishop…" said Brother Reiser, shaking his head. But then he stopped and silence hung heavily over the gathering.

After a few moments, Bo regained his composure and looked at Brother Reiser. "So, Brother Reiser, I *know* firsthand, without a shadow of a doubt, the abuses that can be inflicted by these chips."

"Yes, but the UN would never…" started Brother Reiser again.

Bo was astonished. "They wouldn't? Putting aside everything I told you about my own experiences, let me ask you a couple of *other* questions."

The group remained silent so he continued. "Who runs the UN? Did you vote for them? Do you know if they are good, forthright, upstanding citizens that you want to trust with your life, identity, and freedom?"[7]

Brother Reiser stood silent and didn't answer.

"And even if the UN was run by good people, who's to guarantee that the ones that follow them will be good. What mechanism is in place to protect you?[8] *Who controls them?*"[9]

The silence in the room continued as each person looked down. No one wanted to look the bishop in the face.

Suddenly, from the back a voice spoke up. "I'm going to Crestview tomorrow, Bishop," said the new member of their ward, Brother Carpenter. "I respect your experiences, but my family and I need relief. We don't have near enough food and I don't expect anyone to carry me as a burden."

Bo looked down at the floor, his hands on his hips. "We can help you, Brother Carpenter. All of us can pitch in and help you."

"No thank you, Bishop. These are good folks and all, but I was unwise when there was food, and now that there isn't food. I know I'm at fault for that. No one should give up one crumb for me, and I'm willing to do whatever it takes now to make up for my weaknesses, even if it means I have to give up some freedoms."

"I understand," said Bo. "That's your right. We'll love and serve you the same no matter what choice you make."

"I appreciate that," said Brother Carpenter, as he opened the front door and exited quietly.

The heater turned on. The blowing air accented the silence of the group.

"OK," said Bo finally, feeling full control return. "I know what's going through your minds, because it's going through mine, too. You want to know what the Prophet thinks of all of this.[10] I don't blame you. I do too. It's driving me crazy not to be able to pick up the phone and talk to my leaders, so I'll tell you what."

The ward members gazed at Bo expectantly, waiting for his next words.

"I'll walk to President Baum's home first thing in the morning and talk to him about this situation. There's ham radio communication between the stakes and the headquarters of the church. If he doesn't know anything about this situation, I bet we can get some answers by radio. I should have an answer for you from the First Presidency by morning."

"That's fine," said Sister Carver, nodding and looking at her neighbors. "Isn't it?"

Most of the neighbors nodded.

"OK," said Brother Reiser. "Now let's get out of this poor man's house," he said to the crowd. "Let's let him do his work."

Old Man Griffin

Provo, Utah
6:30 p.m.

"Brea, is it dark enough outside for you to walk with me out in the open?" asked Corrynne.

Brea looked at the horizon. "I think so. The sun's down."

Corrynne scanned the purple and pink sky. "Well, the sun is still setting. It will still be about a half hour till it's completely dark."

"I think it'll be fine," said Brea. "Especially since we'll be inside in just a moment."

"OK," said Corrynne, adjusting a pot full of homemade soup that she was holding in her hands. "Just making sure."

"Mom," said Brea, with a softened look to her face, as they crossed the street leading to a hidden gate in a large leafy hedge. Lifting the lever, Brea opened the gate. "Mr. Griffin's the nicest man you've ever met! He's an Evangelical Christian. He's so unselfish and kind. You're going to love him."

"I'm sure I will," said Corrynne. As they moved through the gate she noticed how happy Brea seemed. That made her happy, too.

Looking around Mr. Griffin's yard, Corrynne smiled as she took in the storybook home. "Look how sweet this place is!" she said, as she gazed at all the pansies that adorned the borders and landscaping of the house. "And look at this fruit!" said Corrynne, looking up into monster apple trees. "There's enough to feed an army!"

"I know," said Brea. "He might let us pick some."

"That would be great," said Corrynne, as she continued to look around. "I love those little dormer-like doors and the little Juliet porches! Living here would be like living in Disneyland! No wonder Mr. Griffin keeps the world out behind those tall walls and hedges. I would too. What does this man do for a living?" asked Corrynne.

"I don't know," said Brea, as they walked up a little trellised pathway leading to the front door. "But I know he owns this house and the land outright."

"He does?" asked Corrynne, amazed.

"That's what he told me a couple of days ago."

"How did that topic come up?" asked Corrynne.

"He told me that he didn't want to sell any of his land because it was all paid off free and clear, which was near impossible to do before the banks crashed."

Corrynne nodded. "Right. I can understand that one. Now it's even more impossible."[11]

"But when Matt offered him some obscene amount of money to build *under* his land, where he could still have his land and continue to use it for grazing and farming," continued Brea, "Mr. Griffin jumped at the opportunity."

Corrynne laughed. "I bet so! Lucky us! How much did Matt offer him?"

Brea shrugged. "I don't know, and I don't care. As long as my little family will be safe, what he offered was just right."

"Right," said Corrynne, impressed with her daughter. She had grown up to be so level-headed.

"Want to hear something sad Mr. Griffin told me?" Brea asked, as she stopped a few steps from the porch stairs.

"Sure."

"He told me that most of the people who built houses the same time he did sold out a long time ago. Now that his children are all grown and gone, and his wife passed on, he's all alone in our neighborhood. He told me that his only regret in life was not being brave enough to make new friends."

"He feels alone?" asked Corrynne, thinking of the many houses that lined Mr. Griffin's land.

"Yes, he said since he's not Mormon, he feels out of place, so he just keeps to himself."

"Oh, that's not how it should be," said Corrynne.

"But that's how it is," said Brea. "We live less than a block away from Mr. Griffin and have we once gone over and said hello to him?"

Corrynne frowned. It was true, they hadn't. The thought hadn't even occurred to her. The wall and the hedge made the home seem so inaccessible. "You've got a point, but now, we're here, and we can change all that," she said, deciding she owed this stranger something, considering he was doing for her daughter something she could not. "I'm glad you've been able to get to know this man. Maybe we can help him feel less lonely," she said to her daughter, hoping to be forgiven for her blindness toward this neighbor.[12]

Corrynne and Brea climbed the steps and stood before the large oak door with a huge gold knocker. "Go ahead. You knock," said Brea.

Corrynne held the pot against her hip with one arm and took hold of the heavy knocker with the other. She hit the door three times.

There was some scuffing on the floor and then the doorknob turned. The door opened a crack, and a man who looked very similar to Albert Einstein answered. Suddenly, a broad smile spread across his face.

"Brea! You've come to visit me!"

"Yes I have, and I brought my mother. Mother, this is Mr. Griffin. Mr. Griffin, this is my mother, Corrynne Rogers."

With a warm and gentle hand, he took Corrynne's hand in his. "It is so good to meet you. Brea has been a light in this old man's normally dingy and monotonous life."

"Good, I'm glad," said Corrynne, taking in his gentle demeanor. "Thank you for allowing her to build her home here."

"My pleasure! Come in! Please come in!" said the man, as he opened the door wide and held out a hand of welcome. "It's getting chilly outside. Come by my fire."

"Oh, thank you," said Corrynne. "That would be wonderful."

Brea and Corrynne entered the neat, but cluttered house filled with books, papers, boxes, and furniture covered in sheets. There was a fire burning in the fireplace.

Mr. Griffin quickly pulled a sheet to uncover one of his couches and gestured to Brea and Corrynne to sit. "It's been a while since I've had visitors. I don't live in this part of the house, so it's become a kind of storage room, if you will. You were lucky I built the fire today. Normally, it sits unused."

"Where do you live, if you don't live here?" asked Brea.

"I live in a little apartment downstairs."

"Why, when you have this whole house?" asked Corrynne.

"Because I don't need the big thing. I like more of a cozy space. I'm just too stubborn to sell it, so here I sit, living in a little room in my basement."

"Hey, it's your house," said Brea, as she let her hood fall from her head. "You should live in it as you like."

"That's right," said Mr. Griffin. "That's right," he said, repeating himself thoughtfully.

"How is it, if you don't mind me asking," began Corrynne, "that your house was untouched by the dam breaking?"

"Oh it was damaged," said the old man. "My sons and I fixed it. Water filled my basement."

"Yes, but it wasn't destroyed," said Corrynne.

Mr. Griffin scratched his head with his thumb. "No, it wasn't. We're on a little hill here, if you haven't noticed, and I have a concrete fence that goes from the ground up to about twelve feet. My May thought I was silly for building such a sturdy fence, but it saved my livestock and most of my house."

"That's amazing," said Brea.

"I'd say it was a miracle," said Corrynne.

"I'm making coffee in the kitchen, would you ladies like some?" Mr. Griffin asked, as he moved toward the kitchen.

Brea and Corrynne looked at each other and Brea said, "We don't drink coffee, but thank you."

"Oh, I'm so sorry," said Mr. Griffin turning a couple shades of red. "I knew that. What can I get you?"

"Eggs," said Brea.

The old man stopped. "Eggs?"

"Yes, we've brought you some homemade soup in hopes you'd trade with us."

Mr. Griffin laughed. "I'm so glad you want my eggs! I have so many eggs I don't know what to do with them! The little country store that used to sell them for me has closed up and now I'm stuck with them. Please take them. Take all of them. Give them to your friends! I'm so tired of eggs I never want to eat them again!"

Brea and Corrynne looked at each other and laughed. "Are you serious?" asked Corrynne.

"Of course I'm serious! And how about milk? Do you have any boys that can milk my cows? They're going to dry up if no one milks them. I'll let you have all the milk you can pull."

Corrynne put a hand over her mouth. "Fresh milk?"

"Sure, sure, I've got so much, it's overflowing my refrigerator. Please take some. Bring your friends, bring your boys. I'm sure there's someone in this neighborhood that needs it."

Corrynne was overwhelmed. "Oh, Mr. Griffin, you are so generous! I don't know what to say!"

"Say you'll help an old guy out and milk my cows."

"We'll milk your cows!" said Corrynne, wanting to jump for joy. "We'll cut your hay, pull your weeds, can your tomatoes, *and* pick your apples. We'll do anything you'd like us to do!"

The old man looked touched. He came close to the couch and took Corrynne's hands in his. "You are an angel."

Corrynne shook her head as she felt tears threaten. Guilt filled her. "You don't know the half of it, Mr. Griffin. *You* are the angel, we are the miserable, selfish, shortsighted neighbors who have been neglectful of *you*."

Old Man Griffin shook his head. "No, my dear. You haven't been neglectful. You have been busy raising children and being a good mother. I can tell by this jewel you have at your side," he said, with a delicate touch on Brea's chin. "My sweet wife would have liked both of you."

Corrynne looked down. "Thank you, Mr. Griffin."

With a pat on Corrynne's hand, the man said, "Now go, tell your friends, invite your neighbors to come get as much food as they need from my land. What's mine is theirs." Behind his hand, he said in a whisper, "But bring *your* family first."

Corrynne smiled as did Brea. "We will," said Corrynne. "You're a true example of a Christian."[13]

"I hope so, my dear. I hope so," he said, as Brea and Corrynne stood to leave. "...Oh, but, wait...."

Brea and Corrynne stopped and turned back.

Mr. Griffin looked hungrily at the pot Corrynne was carrying. "You say there's homemade soup in there?"

Corrynne laughed. "Of course there is. I was so amazed at your offer I forgot to give it to you. Here, it's all yours."

"I love homemade soup," Mr. Griffin said with wide eyes.

"We'll make you all you could ever want," said Brea.

"Yes, we'll keep that pot perpetually full for you," said Corrynne, with a broad smile.

"Mmmmm," said Mr. Griffin, as he shuffled close to sniff what was in the pot. "Yes. I think I like that idea."

"Thank you, Mr. Griffin," said Brea.

"Yes, thank you," said Corrynne, as she handed over the pot. "I'm going home to tell my husband the good news."

"See you soon," said Mr. Griffin, with a large smile, lifting the lid and gazing at its contents once again.

Notes to "Plans Well Laid"

Enticement

[1] "...Most television and a lot of radio programs are a waste of time, if not corrupters of morals or distorters of truth. The less newspapers have to say of value and of truth, the more pages they seem to take to say it. Usually a few minutes is more than sufficient to read a paper. One must select wisely a source of news; otherwise it would be better to be uninformed than misinformed. The subscribers of some mass magazines and newspapers are ever reading but seldom able to come to a knowledge of the truth in the areas of most vital concern (see 2 Timothy 3:7)" (Ezra Taft Benson, "In His Steps," *1979 Devotional Speeches of the Year*, pgs. 61-62).

[2] This storyline is not so fictitious anymore. The VeriChip, a tracking, data-storage computer chip, has been FDA-approved for human injection.

"FAST FACTS: The chips are inserted in the upper right arm with a hypodermic-type needle. The cost of the procedure: $200. VeriChip uses a patented process, called bio-bind, to secure the chip to muscle tissue and prevent migration. Medical personnel wave a scanner within 12 inches of the chip. A 16-digit identification appears to identify the person. VeriChip maintains the patient's records in its database. Customers pay an annual fee, from $20 to $80, to keep a medical file" (Ivan Penn, "Are ID chips too invasive? An FDA-approved chip implant raises Big Brother concerns," *The Consumer's Edge*, Published July 28, 2007 by Tampabay.com. available online: http://www.sptimes.com/2007/07/28/news_pf/Business/Are_ID_chips_too_inva.shtml).

[3] A cashless society is very possible and being touted as superior because of its anti-theft qualities according to the following global security conference held in Paris.

"At a global security conference held today in Paris, an American company announced a new syringe-injectable microchip implant for humans, designed to be used as a fraud-proof payment method for cash and credit-card transactions. The chip implant is being presented as an advance over credit cards and smart cards, which, absent biometrics and appropriate safeguard technologies, are subject to theft, resulting in identity fraud. Identity fraud costs the banking and financial industry some $48 billion a year, and consumers $5 billion, according to 2002 Federal Trade Commission estimates. In his speech today at the ID World 2003 conference in Paris, France, Scott R. Silverman, CEO of Applied Digital Solutions, called the chip a 'loss-proof solution' and said that the chip's 'unique under-the-skin format' could be used for a variety of identification applications in the security and financial worlds" (Sherrie Gossett, "Bio-chip implant arrives for cashless transactions, Announcement at global security confab unveils syringe-injectable ID microchip," *Worldnetdaily.com,* November 21, 2003, available online: http://www.worldnetdaily.com/news/article.asp?ARTICLE_ID=35766).

[4] Microchips to safeguard medical history is supported by the American Medical Association.

"It appears that the effort to implant microchips into humans is not only alive and well but moving ever closer to getting under everyone's skin. Delray Beach firm VeriChip, the nation's only FDA-approved company allowed to produce microchips for injection into people, got a boost recently from the American Medical Association. The AMA said such devices "may help to identify patients, thereby improving the safety and efficiency of patient care." ...Scott Silverman, chief executive officer of VeriChip, says the primary aim is to help high-risk medical patients such as those with diabetes, Alzheimer's, cancer, and heart conditions. The chip, implanted in the upper right arm, allows medical personnel to access a patient's medical history in the event the person is unconscious or otherwise unresponsive. The person's data is stored in VeriChip's database. Sounds a little spooky, and makes George Orwell seem more like a prophet than a novelist. Silverman says it could save lives, 'it's fairly safe and there have been no side effects'" (Ivan Penn, "Are ID chips too invasive? An FDA-approved chip implant raises Big Brother concerns," *The Consumer's Edge*, Published July 28, 2007 by Tampabay.com. available online: http://www.sptimes.com/2007/07/28/news_pf/Business/Are_ID_chips_too_inva.shtml).

[5] Tracking people through RFID chips has already started in America. The following are just a few examples of how this technology is already tracking people.

"2005 patent application by American Express itself describes how RFID-embedded objects carried by shoppers could emit 'identification signals' when queried by electronic 'consumer trackers.' The system could identify people, record their movements, and send them video ads that might offer 'incentives' or 'even the emission of a scent.' RFID readers could be placed in public venues, including 'a common area of a school, shopping center, bus station or other place of public accommodation,' according to the application, which is still pending — and which is not alone. In 2006, IBM received patent approval for an invention it called, 'Identification and tracking of persons using RFID-tagged items.' One stated purpose: To collect information about people that could be 'used to monitor the movement of the person through the store or other areas.' Once somebody enters a store, a sniffer 'scans all identifiable RFID tags carried on the person,' and correlates the tag information with sales records to determine the individual's 'exact identity.' A device known as a

'person tracking unit' then assigns a tracking number to the shopper 'to monitor the movement of the person through the store or other areas.' But as the patent makes clear, IBM's invention could work in other public places, 'such as shopping malls, airports, train stations, bus stations, elevators, trains, airplanes, restrooms, sports arenas, libraries, theaters, museums, etc.' (RFID could even help 'follow a particular crime suspect through public areas')" (Tod Lewan, "Microchips Everywhere; a Future Vision," *Yahoo News*, January 26, 2008, available online:
http://news.yahoo.com/s/ap/20080126/ap_on_hi_te/chipping_america_iii).

[6] Although the scenario in this series is fictional, the scriptures are clear that there will be sores and sicknesses associated with this mark of the beast necessary to participate in the economy of the world (Revelation 16:2). The implantable microchip has, in its preliminary stages, has been shown to grow tumors in a percentage of lab animals and implanted pets. See the following:

"When the U.S. Food and Drug Administration approved implanting microchips in humans, the manufacturer said it would save lives, letting doctors scan the tiny transponders to access patients' medical records almost instantly. The FDA found 'reasonable assurance' the device was safe, and a sub-agency even called it one of 2005's top 'innovative technologies.' But neither the company nor the regulators publicly mentioned this: A series of veterinary and toxicology studies, dating to the mid-1990s, stated that chip implants had 'induced' malignant tumors in some lab mice and rats. 'The transponders were the cause of the tumors,' said Keith Johnson, a retired toxicologic pathologist, explaining in a phone interview the findings of a 1996 study he led at the Dow Chemical Co. in Midland, Mich. Leading cancer specialists reviewed the research for The Associated Press and, while cautioning that animal test results do not necessarily apply to humans, said the findings troubled them. Some said they would not allow family members to receive implants, and all urged further research before the glass-encased transponders are widely implanted in people. ...Published in veterinary and toxicology journals between 1996 and 2006, the studies found that lab mice and rats injected with microchips sometimes developed subcutaneous 'sarcomas,' malignant tumors, most of them encasing the implants.

"A 1998 study in Ridgefield, Conn., of 177 mice reported cancer incidence to be slightly higher than 10 percent, a result the researchers described as 'surprising.'

"A 2006 study in France detected tumors in 4.1 percent of 1,260 microchipped mice. This was one of six studies in which the scientists did not set out to find microchip-induced cancer but noticed the growths incidentally. They were testing compounds on behalf of chemical and pharmaceutical companies; but they ruled out the compounds as the tumors' cause. Because researchers only noted the most obvious tumors, the French study said, 'These incidences may therefore slightly underestimate the true occurrence' of cancer.

"In 1997, a study in Germany found cancers in 1 percent of 4,279 chipped mice. The tumors 'are clearly due to the implanted microchips,' the authors wrote.

"When the FDA approved the device, it noted some Verichip risks: The capsules could migrate around the body, making them difficult to extract; they might interfere with defibrillators, or be incompatible with MRI scans, causing burns. While also warning that the chips could cause 'adverse tissue reaction,' FDA made no reference to malignant growths in animal studies" (Todd Lewan, "Chip Implants Linked to Animal Tumors," *Washingtonpost.com,* September 8, 2007, available online:
http://www.washingtonpost.com/wp-dyn/content/article/2007/09/08/AR2007090800997_pf.html).

[7] "Those who voluntarily put power into the hands of a tyrant or an enemy, must not wonder if it be at last turned against themselves" (Aesop, *Great Quotations,* pg. 746).

[8] "And others will he pacify, and lull them away into carnal security, that they will say: All is well in Zion; yea, Zion prospereth, all is well—and thus the devil cheateth their souls, and leadeth them away carefully down to hell" (2 Nephi 28:21).

[9] "There is one safeguard known generally to the wise, which is an advantage and security to all, but especially to democracies as against despots. What is it? Distrust" (Demosthenes, 384-322 B.C. *Familiar Quotations*, pg. 277).

[10] "Could any people have a greater blessing than to have standing at their head one who receives and teaches the will of God concerning them? We need not look far in the world to know that the wisdom of the wise has perished and that the understanding of the prudent has come to naught. (See D&C 76:90) That wisdom for which the world should seek is the wisdom which comes from God. The only understanding that will save the world is divine understanding. 'Surely the Lord God will do nothing, but he revealeth his secret unto his servants the prophets.' (Amos 3:7) It was so in the days of Amos and in all the years when men of God spake as they were moved upon by the Holy Ghost. (See 2 Peter 1:21) Those ancient prophets not only warned of things to come but, more important, became the revealers of truth to people. It was they who pointed the way men should live if they were to be happy and find peace in their lives" (Gordon B. Hinckley, "'We Thank Thee, O God, for a Prophet'," *Ensign*, September 1991, pg. 2).

Old Man Griffin

[11] "If you must incur debt to meet the reasonable necessities of life—such as buying an automobile, a house, or furniture—then I implore you, as you value your solvency and happiness, buy within your means and use credit wisely. Resist the temptation to plunge into property far more pretentious or spacious than you really need. How much better off you will be, especially young families just starting out, if first you buy a small house which you can expect to pay for in a relatively short time. Such a house in a neighborhood where values are increasing will usually provide the basis for a very large down payment on a bigger home when you are ready for it. True, you can sometimes buy with little or no down payment, and on long terms. But these terms mean that a very large part of your total payments will go to pay interest charges, not to retire the principal of the debt. Remember, interest never sleeps or takes a holiday. Such payments of interest can easily become a tremendous burden, especially when you add to them taxes and repair costs" (Ezra Taft Benson, "Pay Thy Debt, and Live," *Ensign*, June 1987, pg. 3).

[12] "We worship the Lord, declare His divinity and His living reality. We reaffirm our love for Him and our knowledge of His love for us. There are some who do not regard us as Christians. That is not important. How we regard ourselves is what is important. We acknowledge that there are differences between us. Were this not so, there would have been no need for a restoration of the gospel. I hope we do not argue over this. We simply, quietly, and without apology testify that God has revealed Himself and His Beloved Son in opening this full and final dispensation of His work. We must not become disagreeable as we talk of doctrinal differences. But we can never surrender that knowledge which has come to us through revelation. Let us never forget that this is a restoration of [the Savior's Church]. We can respect other religions, and we must do so. We must recognize the great good they accomplish. We must be tolerant and friendly toward those not of our faith. I am in receipt of a letter from a man who is not a member of the Church. He says that his little daughter has been [purposely left out of things] by her schoolmates who are Latter-day Saints. He sets forth another instance of a child who had a religious medal ripped from his neck by a Latter-day Saint child. I hope this is not true. If it is, I apologize to those who have been offended. Let us rise above all such conduct. Let us be true disciples of the Christ, observing the Golden Rule, doing unto others as we would have them do unto us" (Gordon B. Hinckley, "Come Listen to a Prophet's Voice: We Bear Witness of Him," *Liahona*, February 2003, pgs. 2–3).

[13] "The nun Mother Teresa, caretaker of the poor and the dying, was the winner of the Nobel Peace Prize in 1979. She dared to fight against the immeasurable suffering and misery in Calcutta, India. She exemplifies the second quality, courage. In the beginning people only smiled at her activities. They said, 'Such a sacrifice, such an effort makes no difference in a city where every day hundreds of people have to starve and die anyway.' They said her efforts were like drops of water on hot stones—they amount to nothing and do not change anything. Also mentioned was the blame the poor shared in their own misery. We all recognize such rationalizations which we use to smooth over our guilty consciences when something requires courage, willingness to sacrifice, and time. Mother Teresa was not bothered by these arguments. Most important to her was the individual person. She believed that a world in which one less person suffers is a better world. This is exactly what we learn from King Benjamin about how to be a true Christian: 'And also, ye yourselves will succor those that stand in need of your succor; ye will administer of your substance unto him that standeth in need; and ye will not suffer that the beggar putteth up his petition to you in vain, and turn him out to perish. Perhaps

thou shalt say: The man has brought upon himself his misery; therefore I will stay my hand, and will not give unto him of my food, nor impart unto him of my substance that he may not suffer, for his punishments are just—But I say unto you, O man, whosoever doeth this the same hath great cause to repent; and except he repenteth of that which he hath done he perisheth forever, and hath no interest in the kingdom of God' (Mosiah 4:16–18). Mother Teresa once suggested that we expand our prayers from 'Give us this day our daily bread,' to 'Give us this day our daily bread, and give our poor fellowmen theirs through our hands'" (Hans B. Ringger, "Serenity, Courage, and Wisdom," *New Era*, November 1987, pg. 4).

CHAPTER EIGHT

MARK OF THE BEAST

"And he causeth all, both small and great, rich and poor, free and bond, to receive a mark in their right hand, or in their foreheads: And that no man might buy or sell, save he that had the mark, or the name of the beast, or the number of his name" (Revelation 13:16-17).

00:02:30, 08:40:02, Zulu
Wednesday, October 1st

Stake

Provo, Utah
8:20 a.m.

Bo knocked at his stake president's door. "I hope President Baum's home," he said to Jax. "It should be early enough to catch him," he said, as he looked at his watch.

"What happens if he's not here?"

"Then we'll go somewhere else, maybe President Johnson's house. He lives only a couple of miles away," said Bo, as he looked off in the distance. "He's in the Seventy."

"Would he know what to do?" asked Jax.

"I think so, if not, he'd know how to find the answers." Bo shook his head as he let out a big sigh. "...Is it time for a nap yet?"

"Dad," said Jax with a laugh, "You just woke up!"

"I know, but I'm already feeling tired. That's what happens when you get old."

"You're not old, Dad," said Jax.

"Yes, I am, see my gray hair?" said Bo, leaning over to show Jax his salt and peppered part.

Just then the door opened. A very tall, stately, older gentleman with perfectly combed white hair answered the door.

"President Baum! I'm so glad you're home," said Bo, with a smile and a chuckle of relief. "I have a serious problem I need to talk to you about."

"Well, come on in, Bishop," said President Baum warmly. "Is this your boy?" he asked, patting Jax on the back with his big hand.

"Yes, this is Jax."

"How old are you, son?" asked President Baum.

"I'm twelve," said Jax.

"A deacon, huh?"

"Yeah," said Jax nodding, thrusting his hands in his pockets.

"That's good," said President Baum. "Well, have a seat, Bishop," he said, gesturing to his couch. "Excuse the cold. Sarah and I don't have central heat anymore."

"My furnace was on the fritz too," said Bo, as he sat down, "but I jimmied it and now it seems to be working again."

President Baum shrugged as he, too, sat down and said. "We had it turned off."

"Turned off?" asked Bo, perplexed.

"Better off than us owing someone money," said the President.

Bo understood. Even in this house, the necessities of life were becoming expendable. Not wanting to embarrass his leader, he got right to the purpose of his visit. "I hope you don't mind us coming to see you."

President Baum shook his head and leaned forward. "I'm glad you're here. What's on your mind?"

"Have you heard anything about the UN's relief station being set up at the high school? I understand that in order to receive aid, each person must have an identification chip inserted under their skin. Now, I don't know about you, but that sends warning bells off in my head. What do you think?"

President Baum held up his hand as he stood and walked over to an end table. There were a stack of papers on top. "Well, it's a good thing you're here. You saved me a trip. I just received this," he said, as he picked up the top page and brought it to Bo.

"What's this?"

"Well," said President Baum, as he took a seat again. "Without telephones we've been using the ham radio, as you know, to communicate between the First Presidency and the wards..."

"Right," said Bo, nodding.

"So the ham radio operator for our stake received this information from the Prophet today."

"So it's started, huh?" asked Bo, looking at the paper in his hands that represented the beginning of how things were going to operate for a while. It was so surreal in his mind. The transition between *what was* and *what is*, had been so quick. "What's this about?"

"He tells us to stay far away from what the UN is offering. There are bad intentions attached to the food.[1] We are to look within for support."[2]

Bo nodded. "That's what I thought. This is going to be hard, President."

"What is?"

"To tell the ward members they can't have food, water, gas and everything else the UN is offering. It will be a huge trial for the Saints.[3] I just had twenty of my nearest friends and neighbors all but tell me I'd better give my permission or they'd veto my leadership."[4]

"Hmmmm," said the President contemplatively. "What's your feeling about all of this?"

"I agree with the Prophet and the First Presidency. We are entering a very dangerous time in our nation's history.[5] All our freedoms are being hijacked in the name of survival."[6]

"That's an interesting way of putting it."

"My question is, will we, without outside help, have enough?"

The stake president studied Bo without answering.

"Because, I have been looking at the inventories of food in my ward and I'm sorry to say, we aren't as ready as we thought we were," continued Bo. "We have too many deficits to service everyone in our ward, even if we lived the law of consecration—I mean, sure, we might be able to barely survive, but we definitely don't have all that we need."

President Baum nodded. "But that's OK. We must be tried in all things."[7]

Bo stared at him. "That's OK?" asked Bo. "No, I don't think you understand. We won't be able to make it, President. Even to spring, to plant new crops. I'm afraid of the very things my neighbors are, and that is survival."

The stake president's expression became very kind and he said, "It will all work out, Bishop. Things will shake out so that the Saints will survive."[8]

"Yes, but how many will die in the meantime?" asked Bo, feeling helpless. "We have elderly, we have newborns, we have people with medical problems..."

President Baum held up a hand and said, "Bishop, I'm not telling you people won't die. Some will. Through all time, people have died. Today is no different.[9] Maybe during this transition period, we'll even see more than we're used to, but we have to realize God knows our burdens and our limits, and he will make our burdens light if we but ask."[10]

"I know," said Bo, nodding thoughtfully.

"Our hardships are ours for a purpose," continued President Baum, "and after everything is said and done, the end result will be a strong and vibrant people."[11]

Bo shook his head and placed his forehead in his hands. He was feeling very weak at the moment. "I know what you are saying is true. Right now, I just don't see the path through it all."

"It's a time of refining, Bishop. Even for us. All of us must be tried and found worthy to inherit the promised blessings. The Lord will refine those he loves, so that they might inherit his blessings.[12] Keep your vision focused on Christ, and all things will become clear."[13]

"I know," said Bo, sniffing and blinking back tears. "I've learned that lesson. Maybe that was to prepare me for today. I just love my ward. I love every single person in my ward."

"Sure, they're your stewardship. You should love them."

"But I won't be able to protect all of them."

"No, you won't, because that's an impossible task. Protection is left up to the individual," said President Baum, "Not you. You can only protect those that have protected themselves."

"What do you mean?" asked Bo.

"The Lord will fulfill all his words concerning his Saints. He'll lead us all along, protecting those that have heeded the words of the prophets, and prepared themselves physically and spiritually. These are they who will not waver during these hard times because they knew what was coming. These are they who will stand steadfast by your side, experiencing the blessings of confidence in a time of turmoil, receiving protection and peace."[14]

Bo stopped and thought a moment. He was right. Bo felt the truth of those words sink deep in his heart. A dividing process was occurring. This was the time everyone must choose which side they were on.[15] This was the time each person reckoned with the status of their hearts.[16] "Those that want to be protected, will come together," said Bo, as a new understanding spread through him.

"Right, and those that don't will separate themselves from us. In every age this has happened. The righteous will flee to each other for safety."[17]

"Right," said Bo nodding.

"And the righteous—Bishop—" the stake president paused obviously.

Bo looked at him to understand all the nuances behind what he was saying.

"...Are those that are prepared,"[18] finished the stake president with a wink.

Suddenly Bo understood. Help was coming. "So you're saying, as the righteous gather together to support each other, our resources will actually grow, because the righteous have been obedient and have saved up for a rainy day such as this one."

President Baum smiled and nodded.

"So they'll bring more to the table," said Bo, understanding something he hadn't before.

"Yes, that's what I'm saying. Those that cannot bear the adversity will decide on their own to separate from us, going other places for their needs, while those that have faith in the Lord's promises will gather, bolstering our strength as a people."[19]

Bo shook his head in amazement. He hadn't thought of that. Of course that's how things would happen. Everything would work out. All he had to do was be patient and let it happen. "So you're saying, let those that want to go to the UN, go."

"What other choice do you have, Bishop?"

Bo stared at the carpet. "None. No other choices."

"Right. You can't force them to stay home, nor should you try."

"I know," said Bo. "That's what I told them. I told them that I wouldn't stand in their way."

"Good. You gave your neighbors proper counsel, so don't worry."

"It's hard not to."

"I know," said President Baum, with a reassuring hand on Bo's shoulder.

"For sure, some of your friends will go to the UN for help. For a while, it will seem fine. Nothing bad will happen immediately because of their choice. It might even seem to others that they're better off because they went against your counsel, and then more will go."

"I can see that happening," said Bo.

"But know, through all of that, that you've warned them. You have fulfilled your responsibility in trying to lead your ward away from danger."

"Alright," said Bo.

"Keep your chin up. Whether your ward listens to you or not, doesn't reflect on you. Each person has the agency to choose, and they will."[20]

"OK," said Bo, nodding.

"All of this has been prophesied to happen," continued President Baum, "and it will continue just as the Lord has spoken it.[21] Keep the faith, Bishop. Your responsibility is to teach and counsel your ward members to seek God's will in all things, but despite your efforts, there will always be those who will not, no matter the love and direction we show them."

Bo smiled with relief. His way seemed much clearer now. His job was to deliver messages from the First Presidency, support, love, and admonish, but he could release himself from any guilt attached to those that decided not to listen.[22] Only they would be held accountable for their choices and his garments would be washed clean because of his service. Suddenly he felt free and light. All the dark self-doubt had disappeared. All that was happening was a good thing. It was a cleansing of the church, a natural division, that would give God a pure people and it would happen whether Bo wanted it to or not.[23] His job wasn't to fight it, but to understand it.

"Thank you, President," said Bo, standing.

"You're welcome," said President Baum, as he winked. "You'll be fine."

"Good luck, young man," said the President, shaking Jax's hand. "Take care of your father. Help him do good."

"I will," said Jax, as the door opened.

"Good bye, President," said Bo.

"Good bye."

Valid ID

Provo, Utah
10:00 a.m.

Corrynne stalled as she pushed the twin stroller around the corner of the crowded sidewalk to the hospital. A UN flag was flying on the flagpole. She frowned. "What's this?" she wondered. It was strange enough that there were so many people milling around, but now she saw there was a packed crowd of people sitting on the lawn and completely filling the parking lot. Something was happening.

There was a large woman with frizzy hair sitting on a blanket near the edge of the sidewalk.

Corrynne leaned down and asked, "What's happening here?"

"They're giving out medicine in the ER," the woman said, pointing to the doors.

Corrynne looked at the huge crowd. "What kind of medicine?" she asked, wondering what could cause people to camp out like this.

"Whatever you need," said the woman.

"What are *you* waiting for?" asked Corrynne, trying to get a feel for who these people were by what they were after.

The woman looked at Corrynne with a sour face and then said, "That's *my* business."

Corrynne was surprised, "I wasn't being nosy, just wondering what was available."

"How should I know?" said the woman. "Get in line."

Corrynne raised her eyebrows. She wasn't going to get in line! She didn't have to. With a thrust, she moved the stroller out of the grass and back onto the sidewalk. She would go into the hospital herself to figure out the answers.

"Hey! You can't cut!" yelled the woman.

Corrynne didn't turn around. She didn't have to explain herself. With effort, she weaved the stroller around people as she made her way to the doors. If it weren't a double wide, it would have been easier, but to hold two wiggly toddlers firmly in belts, it had to be. "Excuse me!" she called to a gentleman with gray hair, who sat right in the middle of the sidewalk. "Can I get past you?"

The man turned and looked at her. "Nope," he said. "You ain't passin'"

Corrynne was so amazed. These people were so rude! "I need to get by."

"No you don't," said the old man, and then he clenched his toothless jaw in determination.

"I'm a nurse," said Corrynne. "I'm not here to stand in line. I don't want the medicine."

The old man looked Corrynne up and down and then looked at Striynna and Strykker. "You ain't lookin' like no UN nurse," he said.

Corrynne pulled her badge from her pocket and showed it to him. "See? I'm not a UN nurse, but I work here. I'm off duty. I have to get in there to fix a problem with my job."

The man studied the badge and then looked at Corrynne, comparing her face to her picture, as if he were the police.

"So if you don't mind, I need to get by you."

The man still wouldn't move.

"Fine!" said Corrynne, as she tipped the stroller with difficulty on its side, and went around him. She was so angry she could have kicked the guy as she passed, but she used restraint and ignored him instead.

At the glass door, Corrynne swiped her badge. The lock on the door lit red instead of the green she was used to. She tried the handle, but it was locked. She tried again. Again it lit red. Corrynne cupped her hand and looked in through the dark glass. There was a woman with a name tag near the door. Corrynne knocked.

The woman, who was an older, unhappy-looking person, glanced at her, but then looked away, obviously busy processing people.

Corrynne knocked again and put her badge up to the window. "I work here!" she yelled. "Let me in!"

The woman looked bothered, but she left her place behind the desk and slowly walked to the door. Unlatching the lock, she opened the door a crack and asked, "What do you need?"

Corrynne showed the woman her badge and said, "I have to get a new ID or I can't work here. Today's the last day."

"No, honey. Yesterday was the last day. Today, that badge is invalid and you are unemployed."

Corrynne was shocked! "What? No, no, no, that's not true. My e-mail said that after October 1st, which is today, I'd be locked out. It said nothing about yesterday."

"I'm sorry," said the woman. "The early bird gets the worm, I guess. There's nothing I can do," as she began to close the door.

"*Wait, wait, wait!*" Corrynne said in a panic. "There has to be something I can do! My family needs my income. There are too many people who depend on me!"

"You can re-apply at the UN relief center at the high school," the woman said with a bored face.

"Why at the UN relief center?" asked Corrynne.

"Because they've taken over this facility. We work for them now," said the woman, as she closed the door.

The lock engaged, mocking Corrynne. She stared at her badge. It was useless. She shook her head in shock. Now what should she do? What should she say?

Struggling to turn the stroller around, she began the frustrating journey through the people again. When she got to the old man, he suddenly stood and gave her passage. With cynical grin, he said, "Told you, you weren't no nurse," he said cruelly.

Corrynne didn't even reply. She was way too angry.

Hands and Hearts

Frankfurt, Germany
6:20 p.m.

Matt wiped his mouth with his napkin. "Mother, this meal was very good," he said.

Matilda blushed. "Thank you, Matt. I found this pheasant dish at a cute little restaurant in town. I couldn't resist bringing it home for you."

"It was very good," said Matt again, as he scooted his chair back. "Now, if you'll excuse me, I'm going to retire to my quarters."

"Certainly," said Matt's mother with a nod. "Tell Brea hello for me. I wish she could have come to dinner, too. I hope she feels better soon."

Matt looked at his mother and then at his father in confusion.

MD shook his head with a smile, an indication for Matt to play along with his mother's delusions. Matt nodded. It would be easier to play along than to remind her again that Brea was not in Germany. "I will tell her hello for you. She'll be happy you are concerned about her."

"Take her some pheasant," said Matilda, as she dished up another plate, complete with all the sides, then placed a napkin over the top and handed it to Matt.

Matt took the plate, with a look in MD's direction.

MD flicked his hand, indicating that Matt should take the food to his room as he chewed vigorously.

Matt nodded again and stood with the plate in his hand and turned to leave.

"Matt," said MD.

"Yes?" asked Matt, turning back.

"I've been noticing you've been leaving your television on at night to those fuzzy off network channels."

Matt nodded. "I like the white noise."

"Is that a new thing?" asked MD, with squinted eyes.

"Yes. I've found it helps me sleep deeply and I dream less."

"It does, does it?"

Matt nodded. "You can find many studies on white noise and sleep. You should try it."

"No thank you. I like my nights absolutely quiet," said MD.

"Our nights aren't quiet," said Matilda. "Your snoring is so loud there could be a robber breaking all the glass in the house, and you wouldn't know it. I can even hear it through the walls."

"Well, good thing you have your own room then, isn't it, snook-ems?" said MD, in a patronizing tone.

"Yes, it's a very good thing," said Matt's mother, as she refolded her napkin.

"Good night," said Matt.

"Good night, sweetheart," said Matilda.

"Be sure to lock up before you leave," MD said, with a meaningful look.

Matt nodded, knowing what was implied. His father didn't mean lock up the doors before bed. No, Matt knew exactly what he meant. "I will," he said compliantly, and then he left the room.

Matt didn't go to his quarters. Instead, as had become his nightly ritual, he entered the library. Pushing a thumb onto a lit area on the trophy case, there was a buzz, and then the doors popped loose. Quietly, he opened the case. Inside were medals and trophies from all over the world celebrating his father's victories over dangerous, mammalian prey. There was nothing his father loved more than to conquer big game. However, hidden in the back of the cabinet were two empty spaces; there were two trophies missing from is father's collection, but not for long....

Matt rolled up his sleeves, and then rolled down the rubbery, flesh-like silicone skin of his prosthetics, first the right, then the left, releasing the suction that held his prosthetic hands securely on his wrists. The left bionic hand was removed first and put in its place in his father's trophy case. To remove the right hand, Matt had to sit and use his thighs to hug the appendage. With a twist it came loose. Then with his stubbed forearms he managed to place it next to the left.

Matt quietly pushed the doors of the trophy case closed with his right stub, and it automatically locked. It was a time lock. He wouldn't be able to open it until seven in the morning.

Matt looked down at his mutilated arms. The scars, although thin from the work of excellent plastic surgeons, were still bright pink. He imagined opening and closing his hands. He could still feel them, even though they were gone.

Matt shook his head. He wished with all the desire in him that he could just leave all this ugliness behind him. But then, who would do what only he could do? His knowledge and his contacts made his decisions for him. He was the world's last chance for freedom. Because of that, he couldn't afford to be selfish. He would stay—even if it killed him....

MD was afraid of Matt. That's why Matt lost his hands. Back in the days of kings and thrones, fathers killed their sons to stop their ascension. His father decided instead, to put a chip in his head and removed his hands so that after hours, when Matt was away from his father's sight, he could be assured that Matt could not plot against him through any kind of communication: written, vocal, or typed.

Matt looked at the plate full of pheasant, creamed potatoes and vegetables. He closed his eyes as the pain of loneliness hit him. Brea…he loved his Brea. She should be by his side and eating this great meal, but it was an impossible dream. With an angry thrust, Matt pushed the food off the ledge of the trophy case into the nearby garbage. The plate shattered. It was appropriate. It matched his life.

Matt swallowed as he tried to gain control of his emotions. His father loved it when he lost his temper, and watched constantly on his video recordings that were transmitted from the chip in his head for those moments. It was his sick form of entertainment. Matt was sure he'd hear about this one. Good thing his father couldn't read his thoughts.

Matt turned and left the room. Tonight he had work to do. Despite all the precautions his father had taken to try and eliminate Matt as a threat, he had failed. His father would fall. If it was the last thing he would do, he would fall. MD might be smart, but Matt was smarter. By the time he was through, Matt knew his father would rue letting his son live, but he would wish that from the depths of hell. Matt would make *sure* of it.

Choices

Gently unbuckling the sleeping twins from the stroller, and with effort, lifting one to each shoulder, Corrynne quietly tip-toed into their bedroom and laid them, one by one, in their beds. She hesitated at the door as she looked at her sleeping babies. There was so much on the line. What should she do about the hospital?

Turning, she ran right into Bo, who had his arms full of papers.

"Well, hello there!" he said, with a smile, taking Corrynne in his arms. "So nice to bump into you."

Corrynne looked at the kind, smiling face of her husband. He was such a good man. They had so much together....

"What's wrong?" asked Bo. "You look like you just lost your favorite puppy."

Corrynne managed a smile but pushed away from Bo. "I have a lot on my mind," she said.

"Like what?" asked Bo. "Do we need to talk?"

Corrynne looked at Bo and nodded. Her heart was breaking.

Bo led Corrynne into their bedroom and sat her down on the bed. "Tell me everything."

Corrynne stared at her hands. She didn't know where to start.

"What's happening? Are the twins OK?" asked Bo.

Corrynne nodded but as she did, a tear dropped into her palm. She shook her head and looked up, wiping her eyes with her finger. "I'm sorry, Bo. I'm feeling overwhelmed."

"Well, lay it on me, baby," said Bo sitting by Corrynne. "I've found my shoulders are much stronger lately."

Corrynne smiled and put her hand in Bo's. With a deep shuddering breath, she said, "I lost my job."

Bo stared at Corrynne with a stunned look on his face, but then he looked at the carpet and reset it. Forcing a smile, he said, "That's OK. It was bound to happen sooner or later."

Corrynne shook her head. "No, you don't understand. I tried to fix it. I went to the high school like they told me but they wanted me to..." she stopped as tears flowed down her cheeks.

"Wait, wait!" said Bo. "Slow down and tell me what happened. Start at the beginning."

Corrynne took a deep breath and said, "OK, I went to the hospital to get my new ID, but I found the UN had taken over the whole hospital."

"The UN?" asked Bo. "How did they do that?"

Corrynne shook her head. "I don't know. All I know is that I'm not employed at the hospital anymore, and I think that's why. There must have been a sudden sell-off and since I wasn't at the hospital to claim my place, I got locked out. A woman there told me I could go re-apply at the high school..."

Bo's face turned red, "The high school?" he asked. "I don't want you *near* the high school!"

Corrynne nodded. "I know, but I went anyway."

"What?" asked Bo, as he stood.

"Sure, I had to get my job back. It's the only income we have!"

Bo began to pace. "No way, Corrynne. I don't care if they paid you a *million dollars*, it still wouldn't be enough. Stay *away* from the high school."

Corrynne shrugged. "Do you want to hear what happened when I went, or do you want to just continue to rant?"

"And you took the twins with you?" asked Bo, with large eyes.

"Of course!" said Corrynne, what was she supposed to do? Hide them in the bushes?

"Do you have a chip?" asked Bo, pointedly.

Corrynne stared at her husband. He was acting crazy. "No, I don't have a chip."

"Do the twins have a chip?"

Corrynne shook her head. "No! They don't have a chip!"

Bo held up the papers he had been carrying. "See these?" he asked.

Corrynne read the headings. She got the gist of what they said. "Sure, those must be notices to the ward not to get chips."

"Yes, and do you know why?"

Corrynne shrugged. "I'm sure it's because they're dangerous, but no one knows that as well as I do, Bo," said Corrynne, with a serious stare.

"That's right. The Prophet has told us not to take the chip. He said that through them, we'll lose the freedoms that we now have."

Corrynne nodded. "Bo, I know, and it's true. They would control everything in our life, our money, our jobs, and our future. But when I was at the high school, I saw some benefits that right now, may be outweighing those issues."

"Corrynne..." started Bo, with a breathless voice.

Corrynne forged forward. "I'm not going to lie. I considered getting a chip. We need my job, not only for money, but in case something goes wrong, we need the medical care."

"No we don't," said Bo. "If the Prophet says we don't, *then we don't*."

Corrynne shook her head. "It's not that easy, Bo."

"Yes it is, Corrynne. It's that easy. No! *We don't take the chip!*"

Corrynne bit her lip. Bo wasn't letting her tell her story. He was too wound up. She got up from the bed and headed for the door.

"Where are you going?" asked Bo. "We're not done."

Corrynne looked at her husband. His shoulders were tense, his face was taut, and he looked like he might explode. She didn't need any more stress and neither did he. "I'm sorry, Bo, but you're not letting me say anything. I might as well go unwind somewhere else."

"Fine!" said Bo, taking a seat on the bed and looking down at the carpet. "Go ahead. I'll listen."

Corrynne laughed a little, but it wasn't because she was amused. It was because she didn't know what else to do. She leaned against the doorjamb and said, "You know, with this new ID chip, my job would be so different. I'd be treated like a queen. I'd never have to swipe anything. Doors would open automatically, just because I was approaching. I wouldn't have to log in on the computer at the stations, our whole family would receive free health care, a car would pick me up for work and take me home and on top of all that, we'd receive all the usuals, at least one person's allotment of mortgage support, food, water, and a utility allowance."

Corrynne waited for a response, but Bo remained quiet. She continued, "They need my intensive care skills at the hospital, Bo, and I found they're willing to pay well. We'd never have to worry about anything. How many people can say that?"

Bo nodded as he looked up at Corrynne, then he said, "They have you, don't they?"

Corrynne shook her head. "No, they don't. I didn't take the stupid chip."

"But you want one."

Corrynne nodded slightly. "I can't believe I'm saying this, but from an economic perspective, it would make our lives easier."

Bo jumped up from the bed. *"Corrynne? What's going on?"*

"Nothing, I'm just telling you what I think. I'm not going to do it, I'm just talking."

"No, there's something else happening here."

"Bo, what if *I* took the chip and no one else did? We have enough food so that no one else needs one, but just for the sake of my job..."

Bo was up and pacing. *"No!"* he interrupted.

"It's not a sin, Bo. Taking a chip is not against the commandments."

Bo looked at Corrynne in amazement. Corrynne knew that look. He was disappointed in her. She closed her mind to that. She needed to talk. She wanted to continue. "Think about it, Bo," said Corrynne, trying again. "If I took the chip, only I would be in danger of whatever might happen. Everyone else would be fine. I'm willing to take that chance so my children can have a warm house and medicine when they need it, and I would still go to the celestial kingdom. I'm sure the Prophet is just warning all of us of the risks we already know about. If I take a chip, knowing what can happen, then I, and only I, choose that outcome, right? There's nothing evil in that. The Lord will see my good intentions. He'll see I'm willing to sacrifice myself for the good of my family. Isn't that what Christ did for us? Didn't he sacrifice himself so that all of us could live?"

Bo shook his head. "I can't believe this. Corrynne, your logic is all messed up."

Corrynne looked down at her shaking hands and then back up. "I'm scared, Bo," she said, feeling the need to cry again. "I want to do what's right for my family, but I don't know what that is!"

Bo took his wife in his arms. He ran his fingers gently through her hair as he said, "We'll get through this Corrynne. You and I. We'll do it together, without the UN."

Corrynne cried with unrestrained tears. She didn't know if they could.

Elementary Propaganda

"Freaks like you are u-ga-ly, u-ga-ly, u-ga-ly," sung a little girl with curls and a warm, fluffy, pink coat. She was singing to the tune of *Mary Had a Little Lamb.* "Freaks like you are u-ga-ly and real-ly du-mb, too."

Ry looked at her with the best sneer he could manage. "Oh, yeah?" he asked, as she started her song again. He refused to listen to her by beginning his own chant. *"I know you are, but what am I?"* he taunted rebelliously, as he climbed the stairs to the slide. *"I'm rubber, you're glue, whatever you say, bounces off me, and sticks to you!"* he chanted trying to drown the girl out with his own voice. Suddenly, his stomach felt a little queasy.

From the ground the little girl and two others yelled, "You're a *loser*! *Go home you little loser!*"

Ry sat on the slide and thrust himself forward. At the bottom, he said, "The only loser I see is *you*!" but then he felt an overwhelming feeling to vomit. "Brrrglah!" the noise he made was kind of a gurgling choking sound. He could hear it from inside as everything moved in slow motion. Without meaning to, he threw up all over all three of the rotten, stinky girls.

As soon as he finished, he couldn't help himself, he started to laugh. The girls' hair and fluffy coats were now coated in barf. "Yes!" he said, as he wiped his face.

The little girls ran off screaming and crying.

Ry couldn't help himself. Barf was a pretty good weapon! He liked that—but then quickly—he barfed again.

ξξξξξξξ

Ry, feeling weak from too much throwing up, dragged himself into his class. He wanted to go home, but the teacher wouldn't let him. He was in trouble for getting the girls all gross, but it wasn't like he did it on purpose. His stomach just didn't like lunch. But it didn't matter what he said, the teacher said he was in trouble, and that after school, she was going to go to his house and make sure he was punished.

Whatever! He thought to himself as he rolled his eyes. He wished the school nurse was there, she'd tell his teacher that throwing up was an accident.

"World peace. What does that mean?" the teacher asked the class.

Children around the class raised their hands eagerly.

"Sasha?"

"It means we don't fight."

"Right," said the teacher. "And that's what we want, isn't it?"

"Ah, huh," answered the class in unison.

"Now who knows what the UN stands for?"

Ry raised his hand. He had heard that term at home.

"Ry?"

"It means United Nations."

"Right," said the teacher. "Isn't it wonderful that we have a governing body named, 'United Nations'? See? If we're all united, then we aren't fighting, isn't that true?"

"Ah, huh," said the children.

Ry hated that. The teacher liked the children to answer together. He thought it was stupid. It made them all sound like girls.

"You children are so fortunate to live in the world today," said Miss Adams, with a bright smile. "With the help of the UN, it will finally become what it should be. A glorious future is yours as you grow up and become leaders in a brave new world. Now take out your video devices."

Many of the children rummaged in their backpacks or their coat pockets.

Ry watched the other kids. He didn't have a video device.

Ry raised his hand. "Miss Adams?" he called.

"Yes, Ry?"

"I don't have a video device."

Miss Adams' faced changed. "You don't?"

Ry shook his head.

"Who else doesn't have a video device?"

About half the class raised their hands.

"Well, pair up everybody. Choose someone to share with."

Ry moved next to Rodney, his best friend. He had one. It was shiny and black.

"You should tell your families to get these video devices. The UN is handing them out and they are free to everyone," said Miss Adams.

"My parents won't let me have one," whispered Ry to his friend.

"Why?" asked Rodney.

"They say the UN is bad and if we get a video device, they'll just tell us lies."

Rodney raised his hand. "Teacher?"

"Yes, Rodney?"

"Is it true that the UN tells us lies on the video devices?"

Miss Adams gasped. "Of course not! The UN would *never* lie to us. They're good! They care about us. They give us food, water, and jobs. And right now, they're supporting this school. We are very, very fortunate to have such wonderful help in a very difficult time. Why did you think that, Rodney?"

"Ry told me so."

Miss Adams' eyes fell on Ry.

Ry was already in trouble, and he could tell he was again. He shrunk down in his chair.

"Why would you say such things, Ry?"

Ry didn't know what to say for a minute. "Ummm," he began. "Because—it's true?" he said with a weak smile.

"No it's not, Ry," corrected Miss Adams. "If it wasn't for the UN, you might be dead right now."

Ry shook his head. "No I wouldn't. My parents take care of me, not the UN. And my parents don't like the UN," he added, feeling like there was still more to say. "And, they wish they would just leave us alone and get their big fat noses out of our business!"

"Well!" sighed the teacher, in obvious frustration. "If your parents don't support the one organization that is keeping this community alive, then they must not be patriotic. You should teach your parents about the good the UN does, because if you don't, you might get sick, or need food, and no one will be there to help you."

Ry looked at Rodney's video device. It was nice. He wanted one. He wanted to be healthy. He wanted his parents to like the UN. Miss Adams was right. He'd have to tell them....

Notes to Mark of the Beast

Stake

1 "We must resolutely refuse to exchange principles for government handouts. We must realize that giving without earning, rights without responsibilities, and freedom without vigilance are but figments of an imagination gone wild. Never must this choice nation be permitted to fall prey to a mammoth, centralized, paternalistic government on the pretext that such a government can by decree create and dispense health, wealth, and happiness to a subservient people" (Ezra Taft Benson, *So Shall Ye Reap*, pg. 331).

2 "There are certain events awaiting the nations of the earth as well as Zion; and when these events overtake us we will be preserved if we take the counsel that is given us and unite our time, labor and means, and produce what we need for our own use; but without this we shall not be prepared to sustain ourselves and we shall suffer loss and inconvenience thereby" (Wilford Woodruff, *Journal of Discourses*, May 8, 1874, Vol. 17, pg. 70).

3 "...Saints will be put to tests that will try the integrity of the best of them. The pressure will become so great that the more righteous among them will cry unto the Lord day and night until deliverance comes" (Heber C. Kimball, *Deseret News*, May 23, 1931, pg. 3).

4 "There is not another people on the earth whose faith and works are directed for the accomplishment of good like the Latter-day Saints. But we do not obey counsel as we should. Yet when we look at them and at others on the face of the earth, we have reason to say we are proud of the Latter-day Saints. But are we all where we should be? No. *We must learn to listen to the whispering of the Holy Spirit, and the counsels of the servants of God, until we come to the unity of the faith*" (Brigham Young, *Journal of Discourses*, July 25, 1868, Vol. 12, pg. 241, italics added).

5 "Yes, we have traveled a long way down the soul-destroying road of socialism. (You young men and women today little realize that the federal government has taken over what once was the exclusive domain of the local government or the individual citizen.) How did it happen? Men of expediency ascended to high political offices by promising what was not theirs to give, and citizens voted them into office in the hopes of receiving what they had not earned. You can, therefore, see how the violation of one commandment-Thou shalt not covet-has weakened our entire system of government and led to a partial loss of liberty" (Ezra Taft Benson, "Be True to God, Country, and Self," 11 February 1979, Young Adult Fireside, Logan, Utah as quoted in *Teachings of Ezra Taft Benson*, pg. 685).

6 "I fear for the future when I realize that our once-free institutions-political, economic, educational, and social-have been drifting into the hands of those who favor the welfare state, and who would 'centralize all power in the hands of the political apparatus in Washington. This enhancement of political power at the expense of individual rights, so often disguised as 'democracy' or 'freedom' or

'civil rights,' is 'socialism,' no matter what name tag it bears.' (Admiral Ben Moreell)" (Ezra Taft Benson, *Title of Liberty*, pg. 62).

[7] "My people must be tried in all things, that they may be prepared to receive the glory that I have for them, even the glory of Zion; and he that will not bear chastisement is not worthy of my kingdom" (D&C 136:31).

[8] "...There is safety wherever the people of the Lord live so worthily as to claim the sacred title of citizens of the Zion of our Lord. Otherwise the name Zion is but an empty sound. The only safety that we can expect in this or any other calamitous time lies in our conformity to gospel requirements" (John A. Widtsoe, *Conference Report*, April, 1942, pg. 33).

[9] "I explained concerning the coming of the Son of Man; also that it is a false idea that the Saints will escape all the judgments, whilst the wicked suffer; for all flesh is subject to suffer, and 'the righteous shall hardly escape;' still many of the Saints will escape, for the just shall live by faith; yet many of the righteous shall fall a prey to disease, to pestilence, etc., by reason of the weakness of the flesh, and yet be saved in the kingdom of God" (Joseph Smith, *D.H.C.*, September 29, 1839, Vol. 4, pg. 11).

[10] " Come unto me, all *ye* that labor and are heavy laden, and I will give you rest. Take my yoke upon you, and learn of me; for I am meek and lowly in heart: and ye shall find rest unto your souls. For my yoke *is* easy, and my burden is light" (Matthew 11:28-30).

[11] "And I will bring the third part through the fire, and will refine them as silver is refined, and will try them as gold is tried: they shall call on my name, and I will hear them: I will say, It *is* my people: and they shall say, The LORD *is* my God" (Zachariah 13:9).

[12] "It matters not what the minds and feelings of men are, the Lord is determined to raise up a people that will worship Him; and if He has to whip, and scourge, and drive us through a whole generation, He will chastise us until we are willing to submit to righteousness and truth, or until we are like clay in the hands of the potter. The chastisements we have had from time to time have been for our good, and are essential to learn wisdom, and carry us through a school of experience we never could have passed through without. I hope, then, that we may learn from the experience we have had to be faithful, and humble, and be passive in the hands of God, and do His commandments" (Wilford Woodruff, *Journal of Discourses*, February 25, 1855, Vol. 2, pg. 198).

[13] "And if your eye be single to my glory, your whole bodies shall be filled with light, and there shall be no darkness in you; and that body which is filled with light comprehendeth all things" (D&C 88:67).

[14] "Brethren and sisters, we are living in a time of urgency. We are living in a time of spiritual crisis. We are living in a time close to midnight. There is an urgency to meet the worldwide spiritual crisis through action now. It can only be accomplished by performance. Procrastination is a deadly weapon of human progress. ...It can be properly and appropriately concluded that the ten virgins represent the people of the Church of Jesus Christ, and not alone the rank and file of the world. The wise and foolish virgins, all of them, had been invited to the wedding supper; they had knowledge of the importance of the occasion. They were not pagans, heathens, or gentiles, nor were they known as corrupt or lost, but rather they were informed people who had the saving, exalting gospel in their possession, but had not made it the center of their lives. They knew the way, but were foolishly unprepared for the coming of the bridegroom. All, even the foolish ones, trimmed their lamps at his coming, but their oil was used up. In the most needed moment there was none available to refill their lamps. All had been warned their entire lives. Today thousands of us are in a similar position. Through lack of patience and confidence, preparation has ceased. Others have lulled themselves to sleep to a complacency with the rationalization that midnight will never come. The responsibility for having oil in our personal lamps is an individual requirement and opportunity. The oil of spiritual preparedness cannot be shared. The wise were not unkind or selfish when they refused oil to the foolish in the moment of truth. The kind of oil needed by all of us to light up the darkness and illuminate the way is not shareable. The oil could have been purchased at the market in the parable, but in our lives it is accumulated by righteous living, a drop at a time. . . Let us not procrastinate. Midnight is so far and yet so close to those who have procrastinated. 'But behold, your days of probation are past; ye have

procrastinated the day of your salvation until it is everlastingly too late, and your destruction is made sure'(Helaman 13:38). There is an urgency in this day for us to prepare for the coming of the Lord. For you who have heeded the warning and continue in your preparations to accumulate the oil of righteousness in your lamps, great blessings are yours" (Marvin J. Ashton, "A Time of Urgency," *Ensign*, May 1974, pg. 35).

[15] "I know thy works, that thou art neither cold nor hot: I would thou wert cold or hot. So then because thou art lukewarm, and neither cold nor hot, I will spue thee out of my mouth" (Revelation 3:15-16).

[16] "...the *LORD* seeth not as man seeth; for man looketh on the outward appearance, but the Lord looketh on the heart" (Samuel 16:7).

[17] "And it shall come to pass among the wicked, that every man that will not take his sword against his neighbor must needs flee unto Zion for safety" (D&C 45:68).

[18] "In preparation for that marvelous event [the Second Coming] the Master counseled: 'Watch therefore: for ye know not what hour your Lord doth come. Therefore be ye also ready: for in such an hour as ye think not the Son of man cometh.' Then there was this promise to His servants who had been living faithfully: 'Blessed is that servant, whom his lord when he cometh shall find so doing' (Matthew 24:42, 244, 46; see also Joseph Smith—Matthew 1:46, 48, 50). When an earthquake strikes, every person might be taken as he is then living—if at a movie, or a tavern, or in a drunken stupor, or whatever. But the true servants of God, those who are doing their duty, will be protected and preserved if they will do as the Lord has counseled..." (Harold B. Lee, *Teachings of Harold B. Lee*, pg. 411).

[19] "Let the righteous among this people abide in their righteousness, and let them cleave unto the Lord their God; and if there are those among them who will not keep his commandments, they will be cleansed out by the judgments of which I have spoken. But if the majority of this people will be faithful, the Lord will preserve them from their enemies, from sword, pestilence and plague, and from every weapon that is lifted against them" (Orson Pratt, *Journal of Discourses,* March 9, 1873, Vol. 15, pg. 362).

[20] "All rational beings have an agency of their own; and according to their own choice they will be saved or damned. ...The volition of the creature is free; this is a law of their existence and the Lord cannot violate his own law; were he to do that, he would cease to be God. He has placed life and death before his children, and it is for them to choose. If they choose life, they receive the blessing of life; if they choose death, they must abide the penalty. This is a law which has always existed from all eternity, and will continue to exist throughout all the eternities to come. Every intelligent being must have the power of choice, and God brings forth the results of the acts of his creatures to promote his Kingdom and subserve his purposes in the salvation and exaltation of his children" (John, A. Widtsoe, *Discourses of Brigham Young*, pg. 62).

[21] "What I the Lord have spoken, I have spoken, and I excuse not myself; and though the heavens and the earth pass away, my word shall not pass away, but shall all be fulfilled, whether by mine own voice or by the voice of my servants, it is the same" (D&C 1:38).

[22] It is the desire of all leaders/parents/prophets to be held blameless for the choices of the people they serve. "Therefore, as I said unto you that I had served you, walking with a clear conscience before God, even so I at this time have caused that ye should assemble yourselves together, that I might be found blameless, and that your blood should not come upon me, when I shall stand to be judged of God of the things whereof he hath commanded me concerning you" (Mosiah 2:27).

[23] "For I will raise up unto myself a pure people that will serve me in righteousness" (D&C 100:16).

CHAPTER NINE

CHAINS

"O that ye would awake; awake from a deep asleep, yea, even from the sleep of hell, and shake off the awful chains by which ye are bound, which are the chains which bind the children of men, that they are carried away captive down to the eternal gulf of misery and woe" (1 Nephi 1:13).

00:02:26, 06:28:36, Zulu
Sunday, October 5th

Pope

Provo, Utah
10:32 a.m.

Bo entered the house after his morning meetings. He had walked back from the church building to help Corrynne get his family to Sacrament on time. "Everyone ready?" he asked his wife. "It's nearly time to go," he said, as he looked at his watch.

Corrynne nodded. "Pretty much." She held Striynna on her hip as she surveyed the children rushing about her. "That shirt is dirty," she called to Roc. "You need to change it—hurry!"

"Aw!" said Roc, as he quickly started to climb the stairs passing Strykker, who was inching his way down one step at a time.

"Watch out for the baby," called Corrynne, as Roc almost stepped on him.

"I hate it when you make me change!" continued Roc, as he stomped up the stairs.

"Then put on clean clothes the first time by using your eyes to see the dirt," Corrynne called after her eight-year-old as he disappeared around the corner at the top. "And put your shirt in the dirty clothes so it can be washed!" she added.

"Are Louise and Nebraska coming with us?" asked Bo, looking down the hall and up the stairs for a sign of the pair.

Corrynne nodded as she smoothed Striynna's frilly Sunday outfit. "I think so. Louise borrowed one of my dresses."

"Good," said Bo. "I didn't know if she would. If I was her, I don't know if *I* would."

"Why?" asked Corrynne. "She's Christian. We're Christian. I don't see the problem."

"That's not it. What if someone recognizes her?" asked Bo, referring to her presidential identity. Brea had disclosed that tidbit of information, confirming their suspicions the other day.

"What if?" asked Corrynne.

"That's not what she wants, is it?" asked Bo. "Maybe she should stay out of sight with Brea."

Corrynne shrugged, "She cut and dyed her hair, and we gave her glasses and a big hat too. It'll be fine. She looks totally different."

"Sounds good," said Bo, catching Jax by the arm as he rushed by. Bo straightened his tie. "Don't go anywhere, bud," he said to his son. "We're leaving soon."

"OK," said Jax, who flopped onto the couch.

Corrynne inspected Ry, who was dressed in his suit. She scanned his clothes. "You look good, mister."

"Thanks," he said, but he had a solemn, slightly sick look.

"Are you feeling OK?"

Ry nodded but seemed like he wasn't quite sure.

Bo looked at Corrynne with concern. "Will he be alright?"

Corrynne nodded. "I'll bring him home if he feels worse. He hasn't thrown up today. I think he's getting better. He doesn't have a fever," she said, with a hand to his forehead. "The last few days have been hard, haven't they, honey?" she asked Ry.

Ry nodded weakly. "I hate barfing."

"OK," said Bo with a resigned sigh. "No throwing up on anyone today. I don't want another lecture from your teacher at church like I received from your teacher at school."

"No one's going to lecture the bishop, Bo," said Corrynne. "They might lecture the mother, but *never* the bishop. You seem to be protected by politics."

"I wouldn't be so sure," said Bo. "Politics hasn't protected me from much lately."

"Dad, I want a UN video device," said Ry quietly. "We need them for school. ...They're free."

"Shhh, Ry," said Corrynne, shaking her head. "We don't want to discuss that right now."

"Why?" asked Ry. "I'm practically the only person without one."

"That can't be true," said Bo.

Ry looked down and shrugged. "Well, lots of kids have them, and my teacher says you're not patriotic if you don't."

Corrynne threw an irritated look at Bo and then lifted Ry's chin up so she could see his face. "Sweetheart, I know it must be hard not to have a video device, but we're not getting one."

"But..." said Ry.

Corrynne shook her head as she put Striynna in the nearby stroller. "No, Ry, listen."

Ry stopped talking, and with sad eyes, he patiently waited.

"I know your teacher thinks the UN is a great organization," Corrynne continued, as she retrieved Strykker and buckled him into the stroller. "Granted, it's normally a good thing to listen to your teacher, but I'm afraid this time she doesn't know the things we know." Standing and motioning to Jax to take the stroller, she continued. "Braun worked in the UN. We know that the UN is dangerous. There are bad men who want to trick us into giving them our rights and our freedom. We can't do that. Do you understand? The Prophet has told us to stay away from the UN, and we're going to do what he says, OK? That's the only way to stay safe."

Ry looked worried. He hesitated and then nodded.

"It'll be fine," said Corrynne, as she lovingly ran her fingers through Ry's hair. "Don't worry, baby," she said, as she gave him a hug.

"OK," called Bo as he turned to the upper level of their house. With a breath he yelled from the bottom of the stairs, "Everyone out! Time for church!" Then, quickly, he moved to the front door and opened it.

One by one, the Rogers straggled out of the house. On the street, Bo, Corrynne, and Ry walked together as Nebraska, Dane, and Louise walked a few feet in front of them. Jax pushed the twins in the stroller as Roc skipped, galloped, and walked to stay out in front. Suddenly, the sound of approaching vehicles surprised the family.

"Car!" called Corrynne to her children.

"Get to the curb," said Bo.

The group responded by looking back at the on-coming cars and moved to the sidewalk. They had become accustomed to walking in the street since vehicles rarely had gas anymore.

Bo studied the cars as they passed by. He recognized the drivers. "There go the Carpenters, the Carvers, and the Simonsons. You'd think they'd avoid driving around at this time, knowing the ward is all *walking* to church because we don't have any *gas*. They might as well wear a red stamp across their forehead that says, 'I've been chipped!'"

"Bo," said Corrynne, in a scolding tone.

"What?" he asked, challenging her.

"I think you're just jealous you can't drive to church too.'"

Bo nodded. "I *am* jealous," he said. "I'm the one who has twenty meetings every week and have to walk back and forth to the church building," he said, kidding, but still feeling a twinge of irritation.

Rocwell chased a paper that was blowing along the sidewalk. With a leap, he caught it under his foot.

"What do you have there?" asked Bo, watching his son as he and Corrynne walked up behind him.

Roc lifted his foot and the wind caught the paper causing it to take off again. Roc chased it and leaped, catching it under his foot just as before. Carefully, he lifted a toe and pulled the paper from under his foot. "It's a picture of an ugly guy," he said, as he let it go in the wind again. "Ew," he said, as he pretended to shiver. "You don't want to look at him, *believe* me!"

"I want to look at him," said Bo, with a hand out. He wondered who was on the flyer. Paper was hard to come by now. It was rare to find a piece just flying around in the neighborhood. "Catch it again, Roc. I want to see that ugly guy."

"OK," said Roc, shrugging. He took off running after the lilting paper as it rode on the air currents.

Ry joined Roc in the pursuit. "I'll catch it for you, Roc," he said, leaping, but missing.

"Be careful, Ry. Take it easy," warned Corrynne. "I don't think you're quite back to normal yet."

"Dad told *me* to get it!" said Roc defensively, pulling on Ry's suit coat. *"I found it!"*

"Guys!" called Corrynne. "Cool it! We're walking to church. Start thinking about being reverent. If you don't start now, it won't happen later."

Ry looked back at his mother and stopped chasing the paper. He fell back into a casual, slightly pouty walk beside her.

Roc caught the piece and brought it to Bo. "Here, Dad."

"Thanks, son," said Bo, as he scanned the flyer. The face on the front wasn't ugly, like Roc had said. The picture was merely smeared. It had black pock marks from Roc's shoes scraping it across the sidewalk, giving the picture a deformed look.

The flyer was produced by the UN. One more sign that people in his neighborhood were receiving aid. The picture on the front looked familiar to Bo. He looked closer, and then a vague memory returned to him. "Hey, isn't this Imam Mahdi?" he asked Corrynne, showing her the flier.

Corrynne peered at the flyer. With a wince as if she had a hard time looking at the picture, she said, "Yes, that's him! Where'd you get that?"

"Roc was just playing with it. It's from the UN relief organization."

"What's *his* picture doing on that flyer?"

Bo thought for a moment. "He must be the UN's new poster-boy."

"For what?" asked Corrynne.

Louise, turned back slightly. She walked a little slower for a few steps as if she had something to say. Then she obviously changed her mind and returned to a faster step, maintaining her distance just ahead of Bo and Corrynne.

Bo noticed the subtle signs of her interest in their conversation—he bet Louise knew something he didn't—since she *was* the President. Maybe she would be willing to explain things in greater detail. Bo cleared his voice and said, "Mrs. Anderson?"

She turned "Yes?"

"Do you know anything about this man?" Bo held out the paper for Louise to see.

"I want to see," said Nebraska, hand-in-hand with Louise.

Louise showed Nebraska the page.

"Ew, he's *ugly*," she said, mimicking Rocwell and then laughing.

"Hey, I know that guy," said Dane, as he looked at the picture too. "I thought he died."

"He did," said Corrynne.

"No," said Louise. "He couldn't die because he was immortal."

"Well, that's what he *said*," said Corrynne. "But we all know that was a hoax. That man died during the earthquake. A steal bar went through his head."[1]

"I know that's what it looked like, but through a miracle, he lives. The world is a witness to his immortality," said Louise. "And now humankind accepts him as the pope, the resurrected Jesus Christ, Imam Mahdi, and Vishnu, come to bring peace to the world, to every people, and every nation under heaven."[2]

Dane looked like he had been slapped. "Come again?"

"I don't believe that," said Corrynne, shaking her head. "No matter what anyone says, I will *never* believe he's immortal or that he's our Savior. It's all a trick."

"Well, besides what people believe," began Bo, trying to get back to the original topic, "why would a religious figure—any religious figure, be pictured on a UN flyer? He's religion. The UN is government."

"There's a new feeling in politics," Louise explained, as they continued to walk. "Believe it or not, internationally, government and religion are joining hands, becoming *one nation under God*."

"That's ironic," said Bo, feeling like this conversation was heading in the wrong direction.

"Hey, they stole that statement from America," said Dane.

Louise shrugged and winked. "It sounds like a good motto, and America isn't using it anymore..."

"You're kidding, right?" asked Corrynne looking sideways at Louise.

Suddenly, Louise smiled coyly. "You people are too smart. Independent thinkers are no fun."

Dane started to smirk. "OK, you had me going there."

"But, honestly, it's not a joke," said Louise. "Maybe you don't believe the 'god' package, but most other people do. This man," said Louise, pointing at the picture, "was a cardinal in the Catholic church.[3] His real name is Apollo Ramius. He was the youngest and most elevated Cardinal in history, that is, until he sold his soul and face to the devil to become not only pope, but all the other promised religious leaders in the world. MD arranged it all."[4]

"MD had something to do with his position, too, huh?" asked Bo.

"Of course," said Louise. "He was groomed by MD from the time he was in the seminary. That's how almost all the leaders of the civilized world are cultivated today. MD hand-picks them when they are young and promotes them through the political ranks."[5]

"I've never met MD, but I understand he's a pretty slick talker,"[6] said Corrynne.

"Oh, yes," said Louise. "Because of his money and power, his words are nearly omnipotent. But, Brea told me you knew that already."

"Yes, we did," said Corrynne looking at Bo. "Wish we didn't, but we do."

"What else can you tell us?" asked Bo.

Louise pressed her lips together, and then she said. "More than you might want to know."

"My question is, how'd the cardinal take on the looks of Imam Mahdi?" asked Dane. "Because I would swear they look identical."

"They do look identical," said Louise, "for a good reason. When Imam Mahdi died, MD transplanted his face onto Cardinal Ramius."

"What?" asked Corrynne.

"That's gross," said Dane, with a grimace.

"Why?" asked Bo.

"To impersonate God. To claim a miracle. He had to pull together two of the greatest religious factions on the earth: those religions that followed Imam Mahdi, already thinking he was the Messiah, and those that followed the pope."

"Oh, that's just evil,"[7] said Corrynne.

"Ahh," said Bo. "And what better way to do it than to take the elected pope and give him the face of Imam Mahdi?"

"Right," said Louise. "Then through science and the work of holograms, MD presented the pope to the world. First, as he looked before the transplant, then, before the world's eyes, he morphed the pope's old looks and his new ones until he stood, changed, in front of a crowd and television cameras to witness. It was the first of many televised miracles."

"I remember when that happened," said Corrynne. "It was spooky. Then after that, lightning struck, with pin point accuracy, killing cardinals who were standing at his feet."

"Yes," said Louise, nodding. "And for the rest of the story—those cardinals were suspicious of the pope and had insinuated that MD had planted him in the papal seat. They were causing discontent and trouble within the church, so MD had to get rid of them fast. He wanted a public massacre at the hand of God to communicate a lack of tolerance for anything but support."[8]

"Well, he got that," said Bo.

"It was pretty dramatic, wasn't it?" asked Louise. "It was meant to be a good show. In fact, that was a preview of what's to come."

"What do you mean," asked Corrynne.

"Well, ironically, the plan is to eventually have the pope, who's supposedly the promoter of peace, become the head of MD's punishing arm," said Louise.

"For who?" asked Dane.

"The world. You do something against any law or offend anyone and *fitz,* you're dead," said Louise. "No prisons, no trials, only curses from God."

"That's crazy," said Bo.

"How would that happen?" asked Corrynne.

"The biochip, of course,"[9] said Louise. "It will have the capability to kill."

"It already does," said Dane, rubbing his hand.

"It will be known as the Praetorian Guard to those on the inside, when it's used for social control."

"Wow," said Bo, feeling a little breathless. This plot ran much deeper than he had ever suspected. He knew the chip had deadly potential, but to hear how it was all planned from the very beginning from someone with clout, like the President. That gave everything a different perspective.

"You talk about this so nonchalantly," said Dane. "How can this not bother you?"

Louise smiled. "I've been around it for a long, long time. Nothing MD does surprises me anymore. He's ruthless, and no one knows that better than I."

The group walked on in a brief moment of silence, as each thought about what they had been told. It especially weighed heavily on Bo.

"Didn't they test Imam Mahdi to see if he was who he said he was?" asked Dane.

Louise nodded. "Yes. His blood, teeth, fingerprints, DNA and hair were tested by three independent labs."

"What did the tests say?" asked Corrynne.

"Exactly what you'd expect; his eyes, teeth, fingerprints and hair were that of Imam Mahdi, but his blood, which was rare, was that of the pope. It was a perfect unification, physically and symbolically, of both religious leaders, satisfying everyone that he was truly the Savior, come to unify the world."

Corrynne nodded in comprehension. "So even his teeth, eyes, hair and fingerprints were transplanted from Imam Mahdi."

"Yes," said Louise.

Corrynne shook her head. "That is truly amazing. I've heard of face transplants, but have never seen one performed."

"So you think the world bought the whole transformation?" asked Bo.

Louise nodded. "Absolutely." Pointing at the picture, she continued, "There is a growing majority of people as well as heads of state who believe that this man is *truly* God."

"Really?" asked Corrynne in frustration.

"Yes, and it gets worse," said Louise. "Not only do people believe he's God, some governments are already demanding that people give up all other religions and worship only him, or be killed."

"That's harsh," said Dane.

"No, it only demonstrates the strength of religion. MD understands the strong relationship between religion and compliance, and that's why now we're seeing a religious figure speak on behalf of the UN."

"So instead of fighting people's religion, MD has decided to fulfill the people's expectations, and bring God to the people."

"Right," said Louise. "The pope is simply a tool to bring people into compliance. He's a light for the moth, the honey for the bee. He is the lure for the world to fall in line and cooperate with the objectives of the UN. [10] After all, who would fight against the unbeatable power of God?"

"Especially if he can strike you down with a lightning bolt,"[11] said Dane, as the group stepped down from the sidewalk to cross the street to the church.

"Right. And I'm a witness that MD furnishes the best science so that the pope can do his thing, causing some lightning here, some there, and maybe a little healing, turning water to wine, so on and so on, and voila, you have a god and total obedience from the people. It's a perfect partnership."[12]

"That's ingenious," said Bo, shaking his head in awe.

"Now you see why it's nearly impossible for anyone to fight MD. He's all powerful.[13] He has all the aces in his hand, especially now that America has fallen. No one will challenge him," Louise said, as they all stepped up to the sidewalk leading up to the church building. "It's all a magic trick and you know what they say about magic…" said Louise.

"No, what?" asked Dane.

"Magic is only magic because you don't know how it's done."

"Touché," said Bo as he opened the chapel door, wishing he could talk more about this subject with Louise, but knowing time wouldn't allow it right now. One fact was obvious, however. The need to urge his friends and neighbors to refuse the biochip was urgent.

"Ladies and children first," Bo said with a nod, hiding his thoughts. As Louise passed by, he said, "Thank you, Ma'am for your time and valuable information."

Louise nodded. "Any time, Mr. Rogers. It's the least I can do for your life-saving hospitality." Then she moved into the foyer with the rest of the Rogers clan.

Bo let the door close behind him as he wadded up the face of Imam Mahdi and made a basket into the trash.

Sacrifices

Bo stood and approached the pulpit. He gazed at the congregation, feeling the anxiety that hung over the people. He saw many look up at him, some with hope, others with disdain, still others with openness and an eagerness to know what he would say concerning the words of the Prophet and their food supply.

Bo's stomach turned with concern. How would his message be taken today? He knew even now that some would use this talk against him, and others would love him for his desire to help them. It was a varied and angry world right now, where forces threatened the Saints constantly. That made normally calm men frantic and logical men wild with strange, emotional thoughts. He had to have patience for the trauma the people were going through. Things weren't normal.

With shaking hands, and knowing the topic to address, but not knowing the right words to say, he began. "Ummm...." He turned to the book of Revelation. Next he folded his hands over his scriptures and smiled out at the crowd. For a moment he didn't say anything, but waited for inspiration to come. He stood in silence, smiling, waiting...for inspiration. It didn't come. He had to say the right words. The clock ticked. It didn't come. People shifted in their seats. Bo swallowed as he felt sweat break out on his brow. Still it didn't come.

Clearing his throat, Bo gazed down at his book. Revelation, Chapter 13, lay open under his hands, and then suddenly he *knew* what to say. He began as the words almost tumbled from his mouth.

"Brothers and Sisters, we have before us an unsettling new world. It's a transition, if you will, from yesterday's security, routine, and interconnectedness, to today's loss of communication, loss of connections to loved ones in other parts of the nation, and wonder concerning our own futures. We are confused and unsure. Fear is settling in among us as we look for answers. We're used to providing for ourselves and being independent of each other, but suddenly we're in the throes of chaos, and unable to do that which will provide food for our tables. Strangely, our skills have been devalued and we find ourselves here together, strangers among friends, in a familiar land, but not knowing the way to satisfaction, hungering for even the simple things, not knowing what to do to obtain them."

"Ry? What's going on? Are you OK?" Corrynne called into the men's bathroom. She waited but only heard retching. She knew it was her son.

"Hello? Is anyone in here?" she called.

No one answered.

"I'm coming in," she warned. She tiptoed into the bathroom looking for her son. She found the bathroom empty except Ry in the last stall, bowed over the toilet. "Are you throwing up again?" she asked, bending down to see her son's face.

Bo studied the congregation solemnly. "I know these thoughts and these feelings, because I have them too. I feel panicked inside, too. I look at what I've stored over the years and I see so many holes in my planning. I find myself wondering, 'How could I not have done better? I knew this day was coming.' But I'm here to tell you that those kinds of emotions, such as fear, panic, frustration, anxiety, and self-punishing thoughts, do not help us. [14] They hurt us. They cause us to run about aimlessly from some unidentified enemy. Rise above them![15] If we continue to allow our fear to control us, we will eventually turn on each other. We cannot let that happen! Look to the Lord for relief!"[16]

Ry turned with tears streaming down his face. "Mom, there's something wrong with me."

"You're sick. We'll go home," Corrynne said.

"I can't."

"Why not?" asked Corrynne.

"I can't walk," replied Ry.

"Can't walk?" asked Corrynne, looking at her son. "What do you mean?"

Ry turned and sat on the toilet, and then he lifted his pant legs, exposing his ankles. They were three times their normal size.

Bo looked to the left side of the room. "Our safety lies in each other, my friends. Our future lies in each other. We have been told that from the time we could read the scriptures that Zion[17] was the place of solace, of satisfaction, of safety.[18] And where is Zion?"[19] Bo pointed to his heart. "It can be right here. Is it here?" Bo turned to the right. "No. It isn't. Not yet. As long as we are searching other places for our needs and hopes, it isn't."[20]

"What happened to your ankles?" asked Corrynne, looking at both, repeatedly, wondering if maybe Ry had broken them because of the swelling.

Ry shook his head and wiped his face with his sleeve. "I don't know, Mom, they're just big...and, they hurt."

Corrynne couldn't believe what she was seeing. Both her son's ankles had knobs on them the size of soft balls. "Did you trip? What happened?"

"Nothing," cried Ry. "They just swelled up."

Bo looked straight on. "I perceive this ward is not joined into one. It's splintered. Our hearts are not unified. We are afraid of our neighbors. We're afraid we're going to have to share our food. We're afraid someone's going to rob us of what we 'deserve.' Those are prideful thoughts, angry thoughts, and will rip us apart rather than pull us together. Fight these feelings![21] We have to rid ourselves from this plague of destruction,[22] in order to find health and happiness. Do you want to be happy? Do you want to be safe? Do you want to have safety for your children? I know I do. I want those things! I pray for those things. So I ask you, how do we achieve it? I'll tell you. It's a mystery. The answer to that mystery is change. We must be changed.[23] We must seek the charity of Christ and love each other.[24] We must participate in a miracle. Yes, Brothers and Sisters, a miracle through the power of Jesus Christ must transpire within us all, to bring us together.[25] Then and only then can we have those things we seek. Can it happen? Yes! Will it? That's up to us,[26] and I testify to you, right now," Bo pounded the pulpit with each word, "There-is-no-other-way!"[27]

"Is anything else swollen?" asked Corrynne, beginning to pull Ry's jacket off.

Ry nodded. "My fingers aren't working right."

Corrynne quickly rolled up Ry's sleeves to look at his arms. His finger joints, wrists, and elbows looked like they were balls of fluid too. She squeezed them gently. "Does that hurt?"

Ry nodded. "Everything hurts, and I have bruises too."

"Where?" asked Corrynne.

"Here," said Ry, twisting his arm so that the underside was visible.

Corrynne's eyes widened as she looked at four bright purple spots the size of dimes.

Bo took a breath and narrowed his eyes. "This morning I saw something that was very disconcerting. I saw a flier blowing along the sidewalk. It had the face of the pope on the front. He was admonishing us to come together in peace and unity, and join the world economy in the name of God. We were invited to participate in the UN's relief effort, taking their aid today, and then entering their work force tomorrow. It said that all the nations were donating to help the United States so that the citizens of the United States might be able to in turn bolster the economy, and pay back what they received. Sounds fair enough, right? In fact, not knowing any other issues, it sounds great! I guess that means I have some pretty stiff competition to help provide for this ward, huh?"

Some of the ward chuckled while others looked on.

"According to the flier, the UN was offering food, water, utilities, emergency medical aid, mortgage support, and job placement. They even offered to throw in a cell videophone to give us up-to-date news from around the world. That is an amazing offer! How can they do that? It seems like a miracle, doesn't it?" Bo shook his head and looked down at the pulpit. "Does it sound too good to be true?" he asked as he looked around. "Does it seem reasonable? What's the catch?"

"Did you hit your arm on something?"

Ry shook his head. "No, Mom, the bruises just appeared. I saw them when I got up this morning, but then they were just little. But now they're growing!"

"Come on," said Corrynne as she struggled to pick up her ten-year-old.

"Where are we going?" asked Ry.

"I'm not sure," said Corrynne. "Something's wrong with you, and we're going to figure it out."

"Here, look to the scriptures," said Bo. "The Prophets of the ages have seen our day and have been warning us for thousands of years. Our prophet, the messenger of the same God as the ancient prophets, has warned us that the day is here. He has admonished us to turn away from the UN's aid—but we being so weak and mortal, wonder why.[28] Turn to Revelation, chapter 13, verse 11. Read with me."

"Brother Simonson," whispered Corrynne from the foyer doors. He was sitting on the back row.

"Yes?" he said, leaning forward.

"I need your help."

"What can I do for you?" he asked, coming out into the foyer.

"Ry is very sick. I don't know what's wrong with him. Please, will you give me a ride to the hospital?"

"Sure," said Brother Simonson, looking back towards the chapel. "You sure it's OK with your husband?"

Corrynne shook her head. "No, but Ry needs help. Please, help me." Corrynne pulled Ry's sleeve up to expose the growing blood spots on his arms and the inflating joints.

Brother Simonson nodded quickly and said, "Come with me."

"My teacher from school said I might get sick," said Ry, as they moved out through the doors. "She was right."

Corrynne stopped short, right outside the glass doors. "No, she wasn't right," said Corrynne with a flash of anger. "This has *nothing* to do with what she said, do you understand me?"

Ry frowned as if he was going to cry and then nodded. He didn't say another word, but laid his head on his mother's shoulder.

"'And I beheld another beast coming up out of the earth; and he had two horns like a lamb, and he spake as a dragon.'[29] Who could this beast be?" asked Bo looking about the room.

"The beast in this verse, seems harmless, that's why it's described as a lamb. However, even though this beast to all the earth seems good, it speaks the words of Satan, the dragon. I propose that this entity is an unnamed power or kingdom that through its influence will eventually fulfill the words of Nephi. It will oppress the Saints of God with a yoke of iron and bind them down into captivity.[30] So what does this say to us? It says that an organization perceived by the world as good, maybe even seeming to come in the name of Christian principles, in its works, for example, aid and unity and peace,[31] actually has subversive objectives to bind and to capture people through the words of Satan.[32] Now, I don't know about you, and I can't say who all the players are, but food being offered by the UN as a token of good will, in return for captivity of the biochip, to me comes very close to this warning scripture."[33]

The hospital was a mile away from the church. Brother Simonson's car whisked Corrynne and Ry to the emergency doors in minutes.

"Thank you," said Corrynne as she struggled to get Ry out of the car and back in her arms.

"Do you want me to wait?" asked Brother Simonson.

Corrynne shook her head. Forcing a smile, she said, "I don't know how long we'll be, but I appreciate your help."

Brother Simonson nodded.

Turning, Corrynne carefully carried Ry across the sidewalk in her Sunday heels. It was difficult, but she did it. At the emergency doors, she gently set her son down.

Ry winced in pain as he stood on his feet, but he didn't complain.

Corrynne pounded on the locked doors.

A nurse came to the door.

"Dr. Stevens. I need to talk to Dr. Stevens," Corrynne demanded. "Tell him Corrynne Rogers is here, and it's an emergency!"

The nurse nodded and disappeared.

"Who is Dr. Stevens?" asked Ry.

"He's my friend. He'll help you."

Bo held up the letter he had received from the Stake President. "I have here a letter from the First Presidency of the Church. It was received through our Stake ham radio operator directly from Salt Lake City. This communication was written down by the operator and then transcribed for each ward in the Stake by President Baum. Within this letter is an 'admonishment,' and I say that because of course, each of us has a choice in this matter.[34] It's an admonishment from the First Presidency to not go to the UN for aid. We are to turn to each other for the things we need. We are to be creative and inventive, patient, industrious, and frugal, just as the Saints before us.[35] We are promised if we apply these principles, we will be able to not only have our needs met, but it will serve as a catalyst to bring Zion into our community. That's a great thing! Through this service to each other, we will have that change come upon us spontaneously. We should be thankful for our hardships, because in bearing them together, they will bring us the refined nature we seek."[36]

"Corrynne, what's wrong?" asked Dr. Stevens. He had pulled her into a private room in the Emergency Department.

"It's my son. He has been vomiting for almost a week, unable to eat anything. I think he's lost too much weight."

"I see," said the doctor, looking at Ry, listening to his heart and lungs.

"And today, his joints started swelling. He can't walk. In addition, purple spots that look like bruises have started to appear on his arms."

Dr. Stevens nodded as he pulled Ry's sleeve up and inspected the spots that were now covering the whole upper area of his arms. After looking for a while, he turned to Corrynne. "This boy has an autoimmune disease."

"Autoimmune?" asked Corrynne with a hand to her forehead. "Autoimmune diseases are terrible! I've never seen this kind of thing. What's it called?"

"Henoch-Schonlein Purpura."

"What's that?" asked Corrynne, feeling as if the floor had just fallen out from under her feet.

Bo put the letter down on the pulpit. "But there's another issue here, one of freedom. I understand that the UN is offering aid, but for that aid, it's expecting in return to mark those it's giving aid to. A microchip is being implanted in those who receive aid in order to supposedly guarantee continuous, uninterrupted aid to American citizens. Sounds more like an Internet ad than a relief ad, doesn't it?"

Some of the ward members smiled and nodded.

"We know this chip will forever track, identify, and count us. But, it may also exclude, punish, control, or even kill those who carry it. Who actually knows the capabilities of this chip, and who do we trust to tell us? I propose that the information you are receiving at the hands of the UN is what's called propaganda. It's advertisement to tell you what they want you to know and nothing they don't. I have no doubt, however, that if you take the chip, short term you will be full, you will be warm, and you will not lose your home. But long term, I'm warning you, there will be dire consequences. Again, I exhort you to refuse the chip. No matter how inviting it might seem. Refuse it! Do as the Prophet has suggested, and turn to each other for help, rather than to the world. We know that through the scriptures, in Revelation chapters 13, 14, 15, 16, 19, and 20, a mark is discussed explaining that it's something put in the hand or the forehead.[37] It will act as a form of money for trade where you can't buy or sell without it,[38] that it will cause you to be counted a part of a society, and that it will demand that you worship the organization from which you received it, seeking death from you if you don't.[39] I don't know, but doesn't that sound like all the capabilities that a computer chip might give a government over a people?"

"Is this disease terrible?" asked Corrynne.

The doctor shook his head. "Not really. A little steroid would fix this guy right up. It'd take a day or so and he'd be as good as new."

"Good. Let's do it then," said Corrynne feeling instantly relieved.

Dr. Stevens didn't move.

"What? Doctor?"

He still didn't answer, but instead stared at Corrynne with troubled eyes.

"Mark, what's wrong?" asked Corrynne, her anxiety returning.

"How are you going to pay for this, Corrynne?"

Corrynne shook her head as she tried to think of solutions. "I don't know, what do you suggest?"

"If you worked here, we could deduct it from your pay."

"I can't work here. I can't afford to take the chip. It's just not an option."

"I do have to point out that the scriptures say that those who have the mark, after they are fed and clothed, eventually they will suffer with noisome sores,[40] never rest day or night,[41] and be thrown into the lake of fire and brimstone with its maker.[42] I don't know about you, but that's not what I want."

"So, is what I'm telling you true? Is it possible that the Prophet, all the local leaders of the Church, and the scriptures, could be wrong? That's up to you to decide. I just ask you to please, don't give up your inheritance, freedom, for a bowl of pottage. I know it's hard to see right now, when we are hungry and hurting, and all we see is easy relief from our burdens if we just give in. But like a spider, the desires of conspiring men are reeling in unsuspecting Americans in order to make them and all the other people of the world slaves to their economy. Don't let that happen to you."

"Get a chip and I can treat your son."

Corrynne shook her head. "I can't, Mark. My husband and my religion are against it.'

"Then get your husband and your religion to fix your son," said the doctor, with a condescending tone.

"Mark!" gasped Corrynne, flabbergasted with his response. "What has happened to you?"

"Nothing. I'm just telling you that I—can't—help—you. No matter how much I want to, *I can't.* You know how it is."

Corrynne shook her head. She couldn't believe it was coming to this.

"My hands are tied. The UN runs this place. They write the rules," finished Dr. Stevens as he started to leave.

"OK, Mark, wait!" said Corrynne with a hand out. "What happens if Ry doesn't get the steroid?"

"The symptoms continue," he said simply.

"For how long?"

"Sometimes a month."

"*A month?* Ry can't afford not to eat for a month! Look how skinny he is! He might die!"

"I can't help that," said Dr. Stevens, as he shook his head.

"What about his joints?"

"They'll stay swollen."

"That will make him an invalid! Please! You have to help us!"

Dr. Stevens gave Corrynne a frustrated look. "Help yourself. It's your choice."

"J. Reuben Clark once said, 'I say to you, with all the soberness I can, that we stand in danger of losing our liberties, and that once lost, only *blood will bring them back....*'"[43]

"So, please *think*. Do not give up your liberty! Reach out to each other! Do not listen to the promises of a government you did not elect, nor have any power over. Go to the Lord and seek his counsel. He will lead you in the ways of self-sufficiency and peace."[44]

"In the name of Jesus Christ, Amen."

"Amen," echoed the congregation.

Notes to "Chains"

Pope

[1] This storyline is a play on the words in Revelation. "...And I saw one of his heads as it were wounded to death; and his deadly wound was healed: and all the world wondered after the beast" (Revelation 13:3). Imam Mahdi was wounded with a deadly wound to his head in book 3, and then miraculously he rose from the dead, causing the world to wonder after him. Now we know that not only did Imam Mahdi not rise from the dead, but also, he wasn't the beast.

Although no person on earth claims to completely understand the symbolic allusion of one head of the beast dying and regaining its health through a sort of resurrection, through other clues from the scriptures we can begin to feel a better interpretation of its meaning.

In Revelation 17, the meaning of the seven heads of the beast is defined by an angel as having two meanings: 1. Representing seven mountains often interpreted to refer to Europe. John states that "the seven heads are seven mountains, on which the woman sitteth" (Revelation 17:9). "The allusion to seven hills best fits Rome, which was called the city of seven hills (15) and certainly manifested the spirit of the great beast in John's day. However, Rome itself stands as a symbol of the archetypal Babylon. As the number for completeness, seven not only symbolizes the power exercised by Rome in John's day, but it also denotes the political powers of the latter days" (Richard R. Draper, *Opening the Seven Seals*, pg. 193).

2. Representing seven kings who enjoyed complete power over the civilized world. (Revelation 17: 10-11). The last king, or the seventh king, according to the scripture, as defined above, would live in the last days and potentially rule from Europe, the seat of the beast. The analogy of this king being wounded to death could refer to his power. It may be that whoever this seventh king is in our day might have had complete power at one time, but then lost it, or feigned losing it, leading the world to the conclusion that his power was dead. Later, however, this king could recover his power causing the world to wonder how it could have possibly happened.

For the purposes of this book, the choice was made to have the seventh king (who is a ruling power, not necessarily in a political position) who is wounded to death, to represent international secret combinations who have wished to control the world through socialistic principles. For at least a century, taking into account all the other clues about the beast desiring to control the world through both war and unification of the world (see Daniel 8:23-25) and the many warnings by President Ezra Taft Benson about Communistic designs, the healing of the head could represent that secret combination power rising again in the last days, being reclaimed by the same socialistic principles once thought dead.

[2] "And I beheld another beast [the antichrist] coming up out of the earth; and he had two horns like a lamb, and he spake as a dragon" (Revelation 13:11).

"The lamb is Antichrist working miracles and teaching false doctrines in the name of salvation. Later in the revelation this lamb is called the 'false prophet' (16:13; 19:20; 20:10, KJV) and uses counterfeit prophetic knowledge as a means of deception. The two horns represent feigned benevolent authority. Note John's words carefully. He says that the beast had horns 'like a lamb,' not like the Lamb. Therefore, the second beast, the fraudulent Christ, imitates the Lord" (Richard Draper, *Opening the Seven Seals*, pg. 146).

[3] The involvement of the Catholic Church is fictional.

[4] MD and his political power represent the symbolic beast mentioned in Revelation.

"I stood upon the sand of the sea, and saw a beast rise up out of the sea, having seven heads and ten horns, and upon his horns ten crowns, and upon his heads the name of blasphemy" (Revelation 13:1).

" 'The beast,' states Elder McConkie, 'is being used to symbolize certain unnamed kingdoms on earth and to show their dealings toward the saints and the cause of righteousness. Further, 'the beast does not represent all the world, but only selected kingdoms' (Bruce R. McConkie, Commentary, Vol. 3, pgs. 520-21). ...Ambiguity also surrounds the meaning of the word 'kingdom,' though 'political entities' seems to best fit the context" (Richard Draper, *Opening the Seven Seals,* pg. 142).

[5] "...And power was given [the beast] over all kindreds, and tongues, and nations" (Revelation 13:6).

[6] "And there was given unto [the beast] a mouth speaking great things" (Revelation 13:5).

[7] "...the dragon [Satan] gave [the beast] his power, and his seat, and great authority" (Revelation 13:2).

[8] "[The antichrist] cause that as many as would not worship the image of the beast should be killed" (Revelation 13:15).

[9] "And [the antichrist] causeth all, both small and great, rich and poor, free and bond, to receive a mark in their right hand, or in their foreheads" (Revelation 13:16).

[10] "And [antichrist] exerciseth all the power of the first beast before him, and causeth the earth and them which dwell therein to worship the first beast, whose deadly wound was healed" (Revelation 13:12).

[11] "And [antichrist] doeth great wonders, so that he maketh fire come down from heaven on the earth in the sight of men" (Revelation 13:13).

[12] "[The antichrist] deceiveth them that dwell on the earth by *the means of* those miracles which he had power to do in the sight of the beast" (Revelation 13:14).

[13] "...Who is like unto the beast? Who is able to make war with him?" (Revelation 13:4).

Sacrifices

[14] "We must not lose hope. Hope is an anchor to the souls of men. Satan would have us cast away that anchor. In this way he can bring discouragement and surrender. But we must not lose hope. The Lord is pleased with every effort, even the tiny, daily ones in which we strive to be more like Him. Though we may see that we have far to go on the road to perfection, we must not give up hope" (Ezra Taft Benson, *Teachings of Ezra Taft Benson*, pg. 397).

[15] "We can rise above the enemies of despair, depression, discouragement, and despondency by remembering that God provides righteous alternatives. As it states in the Bible, 'There hath no temptation taken you but such as is common to man: but God is faithful, who will not suffer you to be tempted above that ye are able; but will with the temptation also make a way to escape, that ye may be able to bear it' (1 Corinthians 10:13)" (Ezra Taft Benson, *Teachings of Ezra Taft Benson*, pg. 398).

[16] "We live in a world of fear today. Fear seems to be almost everywhere present. But there is no place for fear among the Latter-day Saints, among men and women who keep the commandments, who place their trust in the Almighty, who are not afraid to get down on their knees and pray to our Heavenly Father" (Ezra Taft Benson, *Improvement Era,* pg. 57).

[17] "And the Lord called his people Zion, because they were of one heart and one mind, and dwelt in righteousness; and there was no poor among them" (Moses 7:18).

[18] "And that the gathering together upon the land of Zion, and upon her stakes, may be for a defense, and for a refuge from the storm, and from wrath when it shall be poured out without mixture upon the whole earth" (D&C 115:6).

[19] "Zion is people. Zion is those whose sins are washed away in the waters of baptism. Zion is those out of whose souls dross and evil have been burned as though by fire. Zion is those who have received the baptism of fire so as to stand pure and clean before the Lord. Zion is those who keep the commandments of God" (Bruce R. McConkie, *Millennial Messiah*, pg. 286).

[20] "[That] we have not yet attained this high state of righteousness is clear, for few among the saints see the face of the Lord while they are in mortality, to say nothing of the Lord coming and dwelling with the whole body of his people as he did anciently. Thus, Zion is built up by righteousness and destroyed by wickedness, for Zion is composed of righteous people, and if they cease to keep the commandments, they are no longer Zion. ...And it is the building of Zion in the last days that the Lord says: 'And Zion cannot be built up unless it is by the principles of the law of the celestial kingdom; otherwise I cannot receive her unto myself' (D&C 105:5)" (Bruce R. McConkie, *Millennial Messiah*, pg. 286).

[21] "Behold, I say unto you, there were jarrings, and contentions, and envyings, and strifes, and lustful and covetous desires among them; therefore by these things they polluted their inheritances" (D&C 101:9).

[22] "Nevertheless, Zion shall escape if she observe to do all things whatsoever I have commanded her. But if she observe not to do whatsoever I have commanded her, I will visit her according to all her

works, with sore affliction, with pestilence, with plague, with sword, with vengeance, with devouring fire" (D&C 97:18-26).

[23] "...Behold, I ask of you, my brethren of the church, have ye spiritually been born of God? Have ye received his image in your countenances? Have ye experienced this mighty change in your hearts? ...I say unto you, can ye look up to God at that day with a pure heart and clean hands? I say unto you, can you look up, having the image of God engraven upon your countenances?" (Alma 5:14,19)

[24] "Let thy bowels also be full of charity towards all men, and to the household of faith, and let virtue garnish thy thoughts unceasingly; then shall thy confidence wax strong in the presence of God; and the doctrine of the priesthood shall distil upon thy soul as the dews from heaven" (D&C 121:45).

[25] "Behold, I will gather them out of all countries, whither I have driven them in mine anger, and in my fury, and in great wrath; and I will bring them again unto this place, and I will cause them to dwell safely: And they shall be my people, and I will be their God: And I will give them one heart, and one way, that they may fear me for ever, for the good of them, and of their children after them: And I will make an everlasting covenant with them, that I will not turn away from them, to do them good; but I will put my fear in their hearts, that they shall not depart from me. Yea, I will rejoice over them to do them good, and I will plant them in this land assuredly with my whole heart and with my whole soul" (Jeremiah 32:37-41).

[26] "'And blessed are they who shall seek to bring forth my Zion at that day'—the day in which we live and the day that is yet to be—'for they shall have the gift and the power of the Holy Ghost; and if they endure unto the end they shall be lifted up at the last day, and shall be saved in the everlasting kingdom of the Lamb; whoso shall publish peace, yea, tidings of great joy, how beautiful upon the mountains shall they be' (1 Nephi 13:37)" (Bruce R. McConkie, *Millennial Messiah*, pg. 288).

[27] "If Zion is true and faithful in all things, he said, 'she shall prosper, and spread herself and become very glorious, very great, and very terrible. And the nations of the earth shall honor her, and shall say: Surely Zion is the city of our God, and surely Zion cannot fall, neither be moved out of her place, for God is there, and the hand of the Lord is there; And he hath sworn by the power of his might to be her salvation and her high tower.' That is, if Zion in the last days becomes like Zion was in the early days, the same preserving care from on high will rest upon her, the Lord will dwell in her midst, and the wicked of the world will have no power over her" (Bruce R. McConkie, *Millennial Messiah*, pg. 287).

[28] "Independence and self-reliance are critical to our spiritual and temporal growth. Whenever we get into situations which threaten our self-reliance, we will find our freedoms threatened as well. If we increase our dependence on anything or anyone except the Lord, we will find an immediate decrease in our freedom to act. As President Heber J. Grant declared, 'Nothing destroys the individuality of a man, a woman, or a child as much as the failure to be self-reliant' (*Relief Society Magazine,* Oct. 1937, pg. 627)" (L. Tom Perry, "Becoming Self-Reliant," *Ensign*, November 1991, pg. 64).

[29] Revelation 13:11.

[30] See 1 Nephi 13:4-6.

[31] "And in the latter time of their kingdom, when the transgressors are come to the full, a king of fierce countenance, and understanding dark sentences, shall stand up. And his power shall be mighty, but not by his own power; and he shall destroy wonderfully, and shall prosper, and practise, and shall destroy the mighty and the holy people. And through his policy also he shall cause craft to prosper in his hand; and he shall magnify *himself* in his heart, and by peace shall destroy many: he shall also stand up against the Prince of princes; but he shall be broken without hand" (Daniel 8:23-25).

[32] "...The dragon gave him his power, and his seat, and great authority... And there was given unto him a mouth speaking great things and blasphemies" (Revelation 13:2, 5).

[33] "Behold the formation of a church which is most abominable above all other churches, which slayeth the saints of God, yea, and tortureth them and bindeth them down, and yoketh them with a yoke of iron, and bringeth them down into captivity. And it came to pass that I beheld this great and abominable church; and I saw the devil that he was the founder of it" (1 Nephi 13:5-6).

[34] "Wherefore, men are free according to the flesh; and all things are given them which are expedient unto man. And they are free to choose liberty and eternal life, through the great Mediator of all men, or to choose captivity and death, according to the captivity and power of the devil; for he seeketh that all men might be miserable like unto himself" (2 Nephi 2:27).

[35] "May we walk in the footsteps of our great forebears—that our children and our children's children following in our foot-steps will safely walk the way of truth and right. ...Were these indomitable pioneers to express in words their fundamental beliefs, so manifest in their acts, surely they would counsel us to believe: In the dignity of work; that the world owes no man a living, that it owes every man an opportunity to make a living. They would counsel us to believe: in the supreme worth of the individual and in his right to life, liberty, and the pursuit of happiness—that these are inalienable rights, guaranteed by our Constitution and sacredly upheld by the Church whose basic purpose is to build men and women to become Godlike in their attributes and powers. That we cannot strengthen the weak by weakening the strong. That truth and justice are fundamental to an enduring social order. They would counsel us to believe: in the sacredness of a promise; that a man's word should be as good as his bond; that character—not wealth, power, or position—is of supreme worth to individuals and nations. That every right implies a responsibility! Every opportunity an obligation; every possession a duty. That the law was made for man and not man for the law; that government is the servant of the people, not their master. They would advise us, that we cannot produce prosperity by discouraging thrift; that thrift is essential to well-ordered living and that economy is a prime requisite of a sound financial structure, whether in government, business, or personal affairs. That we cannot establish sound security on borrowed money. That we cannot build character and courage by taking away man's initiative and independence. They would counsel: that you cannot help men permanently by doing for them what they could do and should do for themselves; that the rendering of useful service is the common duty of mankind, and that only in the purifying fire of sacrifice is the dross of selfishness consumed and the greatness of the human soul set free. Yes, they would urge us to believe: that love is the greatest force in the world; that in love there is no fear; that love alone can overcome hate; that right can and will triumph over might; that there is an all-wise and all-loving God, and that the individual's highest fulfillment, greatest happiness, and widest usefulness are to be found in living in harmony with his divine will" (Ezra Taft Benson, Reed A. Benson, *So Shall ye Reap*, pgs. 313-314).

[36] "I, the Lord, will contend with Zion, and plead with her strong ones, and chasten her until she overcomes and is clean before me. For she shall not be removed out of her place" (D&C 90:36-37).

[37] "And he causeth all, both small and great, rich and poor, free and bond, to receive a mark in their right hand, or in their foreheads" (Revelation 13:16).

[38] "...No man might buy or sell, save he that had the mark, or the name of the beast, or the number of his name" (Revelation 13:17).

[39] "...And cause that as many as would not worship the image of the beast should be killed" (Revelation 13:15).

[40] "...And there fell a noisome and grievous sore upon the men which had the mark of the beast, and *upon* them which worshipped his image" (Revelation 16:2).

[41] "...And they have no rest day nor night, who worship the beast and his image, and whosoever receiveth the mark of his name" (Revelation 14:11).

[42] "If any man worship the beast and his image, and receive his mark in his forehead, or in his hand The same shall drink of the wine of the wrath of God, which is poured out without mixture into the cup of his indignation; and he shall be tormented with fire and brimstone in the presence of the holy angels, and in the presence of the Lamb" (Revelation 14:9-10).

[43] J. Reuben Clark, Jr., *Conference Report*, April 1944, pg. 115.

[44] "Brigham Young instructed the Saints, 'Instead of searching after what the Lord is going to do for us, let us inquire what we can do for ourselves'" (*Discourses of Brigham Young, Selections of John A. Widtsoe*, pg. 293).

CHAPTER TEN

THE FALL OF GREAT NATIONS

"Prepare ye, prepare ye for that which is to come, for the Lord is nigh; And the anger of the Lord is kindled, and his sword is bathed in heaven, and it shall fall upon the inhabitants of the earth" (D&C 1:12-13).

00:02:25, 22:08:23, Zulu
Sunday, October 5th

The Fall of Rome

Provo, Utah
6:52 p.m.

Bo was sitting in the living room with a book and notes all about him. He was deep in thought. "The Fall of Rome..." he mumbled to himself. "...The fall—of America..." he said, pointing to his notes. There was something here he needed to understand. He just couldn't get his mind wrapped around it.

The front door closed.

Bo looked up to see who had come in. It was Corrynne. She was carrying Ry in her arms. "Hello there," Bo said. "I understand you went to the hospital."

Corrynne nodded as she moved into the living room from the entry. "Ry became sick during church."

"How did you get in?"

"It was an emergency. They let us in," said Corrynne.

"Why are you carrying Ry?" asked Bo in confusion. "Isn't he too old to carry like that?"

"Probably," said Corrynne, as she sighed and sat Ry down on the couch.

"I can't walk very well," Ry offered.

"What?" asked Bo. "Why not?" as he looked at Corrynne.

"Ry has an autoimmune disease."

"What's that?" Worry began in Bo's gut.

"It's when the immune system attacks the body."

"The immune system?"

"Yes, that's the part of the blood that normally fights bacteria and viruses. Sometimes it becomes confused and begins breaking down the tissues of the body."

"What tissues?" asked Bo.

"The tissues in his joints, blood vessels, and intestines. That's why he's been vomiting for the last few days without a fever. His intestines are swollen with extra fluid, making it nearly impossible for food to be digested. Today his joints swelled, making it hard for him to walk. Then he began to get these blood spots on his arms," Corrynne explained. She pulled Ry's sleeve up to show Bo the now huge purple areas that almost took up the whole circumference of Ry's arms.

Bo cringed. "Is it painful?" he asked.

Corrynne shook her head. "The blood spots don't hurt, but the swollen joints are very painful. Aren't they, Ry?"

Ry nodded. "But Mom got me some medicine, so I'm going to get better."

Dread entered Bo's heart as his focus shifted from Ry to Corrynne. He hesitated, not really wanting to know the answer but asked anyway, "How did you manage that?"

Corrynne looked at Ry and said, "I have friends in high places. Ry should be better very soon."

Bo waited for more, but Corrynne didn't offer anything else. He debated whether to ask her more questions, but he decided not to. Letting go of his anxiety, Bo rationalized that he trusted Corrynne. She'd tell him if there was anything else to know. Right now, he was in the middle of something he had to figure out, and if Ry was fine, that's all that mattered. "Anything else?" he asked, returning his thoughts to his notes.

"No," said Corrynne.

"I'm glad you're home," said Bo, with a smile. "I would have worried, but Brother Simonson told me where you were."

"That's good," said Corrynne.

"Mom, I've got to go to the bathroom," said Ry.

"I can help him," said Bo, standing and moving to his son.

Corrynne shook her head. "No, it's OK. I think I'll take him upstairs and then he can play with a game while I lay down. You sit, Bo. It's been a long day."

"It has for you, too," Bo said, as he picked up Ry for his wife.

Corrynne took her ten-year-old and adjusted him in her arms.

"You sure you're OK?" he asked.

Corrynne nodded. "Sure. He's not too big to carry—yet," she said with a smile, as she looked at Ry. Then, checking down the hall, she asked, "Where are the twins?"

"Brea has them in her new place," said Bo. "She asked for them to come and stay the night with her tonight. I took them there after dinner."

"Oh, that's fun! A sleepover," said Corrynne, as she started up the stairs. "That means I can sleep tonight. Wahoo."

"Yes, you can," said Bo, smiling.

"See you later," she said, with effort as she climbed.

"I'll come up in a while," said Bo.

"OK," said Corrynne.

Suddenly, Nebraska ran out from the hall into the center of the living room, seemingly unaware of Bo. "Neener! Neener!" she said, as she wiggled her body and waved her hands with her thumbs stuck in her ears.

Bo looked around. Who was she playing with? Then he saw Roc peering around the corner of the wall. He looked like he was stalking her.

"Rah!" he yelled, jumping out with his hands curled like claws.

Nebraska squealed and ran down the hall as Roc took off running after her.

Bo smiled. They seemed like they were getting along.

Next, Louise entered the room. "Oops," she said, seeing Bo with all his papers strewn across the table. "Oh, excuse me. I'm just passing through."

"No problem," said Bo.

Louise had almost left the room when she hesitated at the doorway leading to the kitchen. Turning slowly, she said, "I was impressed with the speech you gave today."

Bo was confused. "What speech?"

"In your church. To your people."

"Oh, my talk?" asked Bo.

"Yes, your talk."

"Thank you. I hope it made a difference."

"It was heart-felt and good. I could tell people were affected."

"Well, thank you. That's fantastic," said Bo, flattered to receive a compliment from the President! "I had hoped it might come across that way. I meant every word."

"And you were spot-on concerning the biochip. It *will* whittle away what's left of America's freedom."

"Thanks," said Bo as he hesitated and studied Louise. Maybe Louise could help him make some connections between the fall of Rome and the fall of America. He would guess that she, being the President, would have very valuable insights. "I have a question for you, Louise. Would you have a few minutes to have a mental spar?"

Louise hesitated for a moment and then nodded. "Sure, what's on your mind?" asked Louise, as she took a seat on the adjacent couch.

"I've been studying about the rise and fall of different historical governments..."

"Why?" asked Louise. "I'm not questioning you, just trying to understand the purpose behind our discussion."

"Because I think all of us should study history so we don't repeat it."[1]

"And what will you do with that knowledge?" asked Louise.

"More of what I did today—try to help people see what they can do to avoid the mistakes of history and change their future."

"Don't you think it's too late?"

Bo shook his head. "It's never too late."

"Why?"

"Because, if we want to be fatalistic, we say, 'OK, this is it. We're done for,' then we just lie down and die. But, if we want to be optimistic and see that a time like this is just the springboard for a new life, then we say, 'What can I do to improve my situation?'"[2]

"But what good do you expect from all this thinking? What can you do? This is just a little neighborhood," said Louise.

"It might be a little neighborhood," said Bo, "but as far as we're concerned, it's all we have. It's our world, and I believe if you can move a pebble, you can move a mountain."

Louise smiled and with a sideways glance, she said, "Now I see where your children get their fortitude and optimism."

Bo chuckled. "If that were only true."

"Oh, it's true," said Louise, nodding. "OK, give me what you've got."

Bo cleared his throat and looked down at his notes. "If we look at the history of Rome..."

Louise nodded and said, "That's a good place to start. Rome is an appropriate archetype for our decline. It symbolized all our fears and now represents all our realities."

Bo was surprised with Louise's comment. It was very intuitive. He smiled. "Right—OK, I guess we're on the same page."

"What are you thinking?" asked Louise, enticed by the potential of this conversation.

"I have discovered the first step of the Roman society's destruction. Do you know when that point was?"

"Not particularly," said Louise.

"It was when the citizens of Rome undermined the dignity and the sanctity of the family. Since the foundation of humanity and of every society *is* the family, if that's eliminated..."

"...Then a structure without a foundation falls," said Louise, finishing his sentence.

Bo nodded, "A society with no foundation leads to no society, exactly. Second step," said Bo. "Guess what that one was," he said, with a smirk.

"I have no idea," said Louise shaking her head.

"*Democrats*—er, no, I mean taxes," he said laughing under his breath.

Louise looked at Bo with a bored stare. "Democrats are not the only ones who raise taxes."

"Hit a nerve, did I?" asked Bo, finding great enjoyment in this conversation, considering who he was talking to.

"No," said Louise. "Get on with it. What's the second step?"

"I said it. Higher and higher taxes. Rome spent public money to give people free bread and entertainment."

Louise smiled. "Are you making a parallel to our welfare system?"

"I'm making a parallel to our government, its hunger for higher and higher tax rates, and its equally gross misappropriation of our public money. Yes."

"Every person a critic," said Louise, rolling her eyes. "What's the third step?"

"Third, Romans turned from family and religion as sacred priorities, and replaced them with obtaining pleasure, sports, and continual hunger for more brutality and excitement in their entertainment."

"In other words, lots of dessert and no meat makes you weak," said Louise.

"And morally flabby," added Bo, thinking he was pretty clever.

Louise smiled slightly. "Is that all?"

"No," said Bo. "Then the Romans built gigantic armaments when the real enemy was within."

Louise closed her eyes and then shook her head. It seemed this conversation was starting to get to her.

"Are you OK?" asked Bo.

Louise looked out the window and nodded. "Sounds like America," she said, in a reflective voice. "We had lots of military toys and thought we were so strong. Look where that got us. Little did we know our enemies had already infiltrated us and we were teetering on the edge of a cliff that no amount of weapons could save us from."

Bo was quiet. It seemed Louise needed a break. Maybe he had pushed her too hard. He looked down at his notes.

"What's next?" Louise asked, her face emotionless, as if she was numb with pain.

Bo considered ending their conversation. "Louise, if you'd rather, we don't have to go on."

"No," said Louise, looking at Bo. "Continue. I want to see how obvious our downfall was. I want to see why we couldn't see it coming. What else did we do wrong?"

Bo studied Louise and then nodded. "This one is a biggie."

"Let me have it," said Louise.

"In Rome, when the people lost their way, and they were heading for disaster, their leaders didn't warn them. Instead, they told them they were strong and nothing was wrong. They catered to the people, telling them what they wanted to hear. The politician's goals were to be popular rather than protective. Their leaders lost their sense to warn and guide the people appropriately."[3]

Louise nodded thoughtfully, "Or just didn't."

Bo looked at Louise. She was right. He echoed her words, nodding. "Or just didn't."

Louise stood and rubbed her arms. "It's a big, bad world out there. When you're in the midst of the boiling pot, it's hard to see or feel anything but the heat of the water. One gets caught up in it, thinking that's all there is."

Bo picked up his pencil and said, "I know that personally. Leading people in the safest course is often not the most popular thing to do."

"Right," said Louise. "For example, today, no one wanted to hear you say to stay away from the UN. Everyone wanted you to say, 'There's the solution to all your problems. Go get it.' If you would have said that, you would have been the most popular bishop around."

"It wasn't an option," said Bo.

"Sure it was, especially if you were *running* to be bishop," said Louise.

"But I'm not, so it's not."

Louise nodded. "I guess that's a good thing."

Bo shrugged. "I don't know. I guess I'm not as popular as I could be."

"Maybe not, but you're wise."

"People don't value wisdom," said Bo.

"They do when you're *dead*," said Louise. "Look at Abraham Lincoln. Everyone loves him now."

"Great," said Bo, shaking his head.

Louise sat back down with resolve. It looked like she had something to say. With a finger pointing into her palm, she began. "The truth is, your research is right. History fails to record a *single* precedent in which nations subject to *moral decay* have not passed into political and economic decline, leading ultimately to disaster.[4] The fate of America has been written on the wall for some time, and if we are truly honest, we'd say that the disaster we have experienced in America was *orchestrated* but couldn't have succeeded if the people didn't want it to. The desire for Americans to be constantly fed with material goods, larger and better homes, more cars, more money, and more selfishness, has led to politicians playing up to their appetites, and their enemies *investing* in their appetites. Americans were led along to their destruction and eventual captivity.[5]

"As you said this morning, Americans have grown weak. They don't know how to provide for themselves. They've been spoon-fed for too long. No one grows gardens, makes their own clothes, and raises animals anymore. Without those skills, we have become dependent on society for every need![6]

"So what's the response when everything goes belly up? I hear it already. I hear it here, in your little neighborhood. They say, 'Who will help me?' People are acting like lost little babies instead of grown, independent, true Americans.[7] *'I will survive!'* is the voice of the strong. *'I will survive!'*" Louise repeated again. "*That* is the voice of a true American!"

Turning to Bo, Louise asked, "Do you know what that 'gimme' attitude does for us in a disaster like this one?"

"No, what?" asked Bo, watching Louise almost in amusement now.

"It creates an environment perfect for *Communism*![8] We're *prime* for the taking."

Bo nodded. "I agree."

"Doesn't that shock you?" asked Louise.

"Not really," said Bo. "People want a government to do all the work for them, not understanding what price it will demand.[9] To me, that spells trouble."

"Exactly. That's why what you said this morning was *perfect*!" said Louise, pounding a fist into the palm of her other hand. "People need to hear that! They need to know what they're facing if they start on the path down the road to dependency!"

"I agree," said Bo. "In fact, one of our prophets said that Communism, or a system that was willing to be everything to everyone, was the most satanical threat to peace, prosperity, and the spread of God's work on the face of the earth,"[10]

"Well, he was right. One thing I've learned here is that your prophets are smart men," said Louise, with a focused look.

"Ezra Taft Benson, another one of our prophets, said that in society, 'we go from bondage to spiritual faith, from spiritual faith to courage, from courage to freedom, from freedom to abundance, from abundance to selfishness, from selfishness to complacency, from complacency to apathy, from apathy to fear, from fear to dependency, from dependency to bondage.'[11] That's the stage we're in now."

"Dependency to bondage?" asked Louise thoughtfully.

"Well, yes, fear to dependence and then from dependence to bondage. We are driven to accept *bondage* through *fear*."

"Yes, you're right," said Louise, with light in her eyes. "But we shouldn't. We should be brave and do what it takes to *keep* our freedom, no matter the cost!"[12]

"Right," said Bo. "But here's the big question. How do you get the people to see that point of view and love it to the point they're willing to fight for it?"

Louise sat back in the couch and thoughtfully looked around the room. "That's a very hard question, Mr. Rogers. I suppose it comes from giving your vision to the people. Let them see what you see. You must talk, and talk a lot. Have others who think like you talk about it, too. It's a hard road to travel, but the harder the goal, the more glorious the triumph."

Bo thought about what Louise said. He remembered his dreams and his admonitions to be a leader in the way of righteousness in the last days, to support the brethren and fight for the cause of truth. No one said it would be easy, only that he should serve in that capacity.[13] Bo nodded. "You're right. I need to fight hard for the souls of my friends."

"Yes, fight *hard*," said Louise, looking relieved. "You'll be happy you did. Today, you might feel like you're the last American left, but know there are others like you, and they will march behind you to support you."[14]

Bo smiled and picked up his pen again. Taking a deep breath, he looked at his notes. His talk with Louise had connected all the dots. Now he knew what he had to do, and that was help his people hunger for freedom.

"I've enjoyed our talk," said Bo.

"So have I," said Louise, standing. "Just remember you're fighting for the greater good. That's always worth it."

Bo nodded. "Wise words."

With a satisfied smile, Louise left the room.

Bo stretched out and whistled. Wow! He thought. What he could do if he could give speeches like—*the President*!

Evil Temptations

Within the mind
10:45 p.m.

Brea moved through the tunnel that led up to the street. She put a hand to her back. A contraction pulled on her abdomen, taking her breath away. Contractions came and went more often lately. A baby kicked, and then another poked. "Soon," she whispered down to her children. "Your day is coming."

It was dark outside as Brea left her underground house to visit her family. With one hand, she pulled the hood of her cloak over her head, and with the other, she assured it covered her whole body. Nothing could be showing, and nothing was.

With a firm jerk, she pulled the hydraulic lever that would open a grass-covered door leading to the outside. Slowly, the hatch opened and cool, fall air poured in. Brea took a deep breath of the freshness and smiled. It was good to be outside.

She liked her high-tech home with its robot vacuum cleaner and artificial environmental porches, complete with tropical sunsets. Soon, when the construction was finished, Brea would have a master suite with a star-lit ceiling, warm night breezes, and a queen-sized, suspended-air hammock to sleep in at night. Not to mention the tear-drop Jacuzzi tub with the retractable cover in the middle of the room. She had been joking when she had described her perfect bedroom to Matt, but despite that, he remembered every detail, and built it into the design of her underground home. Yes, her house was nearly perfect—but not quite, because...it was missing Matt.

Brea smiled again as she shook her dismal thoughts from her head and took in another full breath of autumn air. Yes, technology was fun but there was no substitute for God's own nature.

Brea climbed the stairs leading to the outside. Suddenly, a different cold chill passed through her, one that sank deep into her bones. Instantly, she was petrified and froze. *What was that?* She wondered, as she slowly peeked over the foliage that was eye-level. The last time she had felt a chill like that was in her father-in-law's mansion! It was a distinct feeling of evil, an evil not of the physical world.

Brea scanned the grounds near her. She saw nothing out of the ordinary. Taking another cautious step, she focused her senses. Something was different. Another chill shot through her and she stopped, ducking low. There was no mistaking it, evil was near. *What or who was out here?*

"Tell him," Brea heard an old woman's voice whine.

Brea stayed low, crouching near the ground. The voice came from near her.

"Throw the rock," taunted a boy's voice. "Go ahead! It will feel good!"

"No, he should tell the man off first and *then* throw the rock," said the old female spirit.

"Shut up, woman! This guy is too chicken-livered to do that! He's the kind that throws the rock and then runs and hides so no one knows he did it," said the boy.

Brea left the tunnel and quietly shut the hatch door by remote. Silently, she crossed the street and moved down the sidewalk to her parent's house, careful to stay hidden in the bushes that lined the way. There was trouble in the voices she had heard and she felt an obligation to find out what was going on.

Brea found a place to hide behind a large bush near the corner of her parent's home. She peeked through the branches and saw a man standing on the sidewalk in deep contemplation. In his hand, he held a rock with black writing on the edge. On either side of him were two translucent forms, one an old bent-over woman with strings of grey hair hanging off her head, the other a young punk kid dressed in leather and dripping in chains.

"Smash that rock into your bishop's face," said the old woman again, with almost a joyful lilt. "He deserves it. He made you lose your house, didn't he? Now you have to ask for help and look like a spineless fool!"

"This guy *is* a spineless fool," said the young man with an agitated sigh.

"Shut up, boy! I think he's breaking. Work with me here!" said the woman, looking deeply into the man's face.

"What are we doing?" asked the boy in frustration. "We're supposed to be looking for that girl."

"That's OK. We can have fun along the way can't we?" said the old woman, still staring at the man as if willing him into action.

Brea blinked hard and shook her head. What was she seeing? A shiver shook her, leaving her skin prickly. Evil spirits made her feel this way. If she had to guess, these were *powerful* wicked spirits. What were they doing here, outside her parent's house?

Suddenly, another spirit appeared. Brea gasped as she realized it was the butler from Matt's house! Brea's heart beat heavily in her chest as she remembered him. Her knees buckled slightly. Now she knew why these spirits were lurking around. They were after *her*! Had she lured these spirits here? Would they hurt her family?

"Did you find her?" The butler asked the other two.

"No, but I know she's around here somewhere," said the boy. "This was her house. If I know anything, I know she's not far from here."

"Could she be inside?" asked the butler.

"I don't know!" said the boy. "The house is layered in protection. I can't get near enough to sense her."

Protection? What was he talking about? Brea looked behind her at her parent's house. She noticed there was a gentle white hue coming from the walls. Was that the protection they were talking about? Was the Lord protecting their home?

"Why don't you just go in?" taunted the old woman. "You said this would be easy."

"I can't, woman! Stop being stupid!" snarled the boy.

"Well, at least I have a plan," said the woman. "This guy gets angry, throws the rock, and then Bo will get angry too, and because of his temper, he'll invite us in."

"Enough!" hissed the Butler, looking around. "We're wasting time when we should be searching for Brea."

There! The butler said it. They *were* looking for her! Brea pressed herself up against the stone of her parent's house to catch her breath and to think what to do. After a moment of consideration, she decided she *was* doing exactly what she needed to do. She had the upper hand; after all, the spirits didn't know they were being watched. Maybe they'd expose their plans to her unknowingly. Cautiously, Brea peeked once again through the branches.

The butler was silent, as if he was listening for something. He turned Brea's way.

Brea's muscles tensed in fear.

"I can sense her. She's near," she heard the butler say.

Brea was surprised. How could he know? Could he sense her like she could them?

"Good thing you've met her before then. I just knew her sister, Carea," said the boy.

Brea couldn't contain herself any longer. She bolted for the back door, feeling an intense need to get inside her parent's house. Instinctively, she knew she'd be safe there.

As Brea turned the corner to the back of her house, she saw an *additional* tall spirit standing guard. She dropped behind another bush. Now, who was *this* guy, she wondered. After a minute, she realized this spirit was different than the three in the front. He was not transparent like the others, but a brilliant bright white with a glowing countenance. He was dressed like a warrior with gold armor, helmet, and large shield. In his hand he held a long, thick spear at his side.

Brea closed her eyes to try and sense the nature of this spirit warrior. Was he good or bad? A peaceful feeling flowed over her like a gentle waterfall. This spirit-man was good, *very good.* Her fear dissipated slightly. Was this a guardian angel sent to protect her family? Had he always stood watch over her house? If he had, she hadn't seen him before.

Slowly, Brea walked around the bush and approached the door.

The warrior looked down and smiled at her.

"Hi," Brea whispered, not knowing what else to say to a good guardian spirit.

The man nodded politely and then returned his gaze to the night.

Brea turned the knob to the back door, but unfortunately, the door was locked. She looked up at the warrior. "Can you open this door?" she asked.

The warrior smiled and shook his head. "I cannot interfere with free will."

"Ahh," said Brea. "OK then, I'll just have to find another way in."

The warrior nodded politely and then once again assumed his watchful position.

Brea headed for the sliding glass door that opened to the family room. Beside it was another warrior. Not quite as tall as the first, but looking just as fearless. This time the spirit didn't look at Brea as she approached; instead, he stood still like a statue.

Brea pulled on the glass door but it too was locked. She looked behind. The coast was clear. Brea decided to knock quietly.

No answer.

Brea became antsy. She couldn't wait any longer! Should she go back to her house? She'd give it another try. She knocked again. "Mom…Dad!" she called in a voice just barely above a whisper.

"What do you want?" asked a frighteningly loud voice in her right ear.

Turning, she was terrified! It was the face of the butler inches from her face! He had found her! Brea backed up against the house. *"Get away from me!"* she yelled.

The Butler stared at her with his hollow, black eyes and laughed. "Finding you was easy," he said in a mocking tone, but he didn't advance. "Did you think you could hide here?"

Suddenly, the ugly old woman and boy appeared at his side too. "Oh, there she is! Look! She's huuuge!" said the old woman with a cackling laugh. "No wonder she didn't want to be found. I'd hide too if I were that *fat*!"

"I'm not fat!" said Brea defensively, but then she saw the good spirit move out of the corner of her eye. He was shaking his head slightly, as if to warn her not to engage in the negative banter.

Brea closed her eyes and shut down her emotions. She had to control her anger. That was obvious.

"Brea, don't look at that goof-ball security guard for help," said the boy. "He can't *save* you from us. You might as well give up."

Brea looked up at the armored guard. With the kindest eyes, she saw him wink at her. There was no fear at all in his face. He was strong and calm. This gave her strength. Now she knew the evil spirits were lying. It wasn't that this warrior couldn't save her, it was that he didn't need to. She wasn't in danger! But, contrary to that truth, the evil spirits wanted her to *think* she was. They wanted her to be afraid of them. It was then she remembered that their strength over her came from her fear, and fear was an enemy to faith. If she got rid of the fear, she'd take back the power of faith! Evil spirits were no match for righteous strength!

Brea looked from hideous spirit to hideous spirit. She saw how miserable they were. She could feel their anger and hatred for her. Suddenly, she realized that *they* were the captive ones. They were captive by their own evil choices, damned to spend eternity in their own anger, but wishing they could be free like her and knowing it wasn't possible.

Brea stood up a little taller. These spirits couldn't touch her here. This was a good house. The people inside were good people. And because she was a good person, she knew she had the power! This was *her* territory.

"Girl, come with us," said the old woman. "Your father-in-law wants to see you."

"Matt wants you," said the boy. "He misses you."

Brea looked at the boy in chains. She knew Matt missed her and she didn't need this liar weaving that truth into his deception for his leverage. She wouldn't go with them for anything in the world! Not even for Matt! Turning again, she pounded on the glass door. "Mom! ...Dad! Open up!"

"Mom...Dad," mimicked the woman in a horrid voice. "You're so pathetic. Left out here all by yourself."

"Poor baby," said the boy. "Don't you know you're a menace to these people? They don't really want you here. That's why the door is locked."

Brea knocked again, ignoring these spirits, staying close to the warrior's side.

The curtain to the door pulled back. It was Brea's mother. The door latch flipped and it opened. Hands reached out for Brea, pulling her into the house.

Brea awoke.

ξξξξξξξ

With a firm jerk, Brea pulled the hydraulic lever that would open a door of the tunnel leading to the outside. Slowly, the hatch opened and cool, fall air poured in.

Brea took a deep breath of the freshness. A feeling of de-ja-vu came over her. She had been here before. Was she dreaming again? Looking around at the outside world, it all seemed exactly like the last time she had seen it. She still couldn't tell whether this was real, or yet another dream.

As Brea entered the evening air, a shiver pulsed through her. Yes, she remembered this moment. There were evil spirits lurking nearby. She could feel them. She halted. Did she want to go through this dream again? It wasn't pleasant the first time. Was there something for her to learn?

Despite her thoughts, her dream progressed without her consent. In the next moment she found herself outside her home. She conceded. Someone else was in charge of this dream. She'd patiently participate.

"Tell him," Brea heard an old woman's voice whisper.

"Throw the rock," said a taunting boy's voice. "Go ahead! It will feel good!"

Brea recognized the same spirits having the same conversation as in her first dream.

"No, he should tell the man off first and then throw the rock," said the old female spirit.

"Shut up, woman! This guy is too chicken-livered to do that! He's the kind that throws the rock and then runs and hides so no one knows he did it," said the boy.

Brea was in her previous position behind the large bush as before. Obviously, there was something she needed to learn this time. She didn't fight the dream.

In front was the same man she had seen before. Again, he held a large, threatening rock with writing on it. She thought this could be Brother Reiser, the man she had heard had been so angry with her father. Again, to Brea, it looked like he was listening to the voices of the two translucent, evil spirits, one a frighteningly ugly old woman, and the other a punk kid. Brea wished she could yell a warning to him, but she knew that not only would that alert the spirits to her presence, but he would think she was crazy. She kept her silence.

"Smash that rock into your bishop's face," said the old woman again, with almost a joyful lilt. "He deserves it. He made you lose your house, didn't he? Now you have to ask for help and look like a spineless fool!"

"This guy *is* a spineless fool," sighed the young man.

"Shut up, boy! I think he's breaking. Work with me here!" said the woman, looking deeply into Brother Reiser's face.

"What are we doing? We're supposed to be looking for that girl," said the boy, in frustration.

"That's OK. We can have fun along the way, can't we?" said the woman, still staring at Brother Reiser, as if she could stare him into action.

Brea braced herself for the appearance of the butler. Despite knowing he couldn't hurt her, he still frightened her the most. Right on cue, the butler appeared, complete with white gloves and coattails.

"Did you find her?" The butler asked the two.

"No, but I know she's around here somewhere," said the boy. "This was her house. If I know anything, I know she's not far from here."

"Is she inside?" asked the Butler.

"I don't know!" said the boy. "The house is layered in protection. I can't get near enough to sense her."

Brea smiled. It sure was. And these ghosts were powerless against the armored, muscular, powerful beings of light that stood guard around her house. Now, seeing this dream the second time, she understood more.

"Why don't you just go in?" taunted the old woman. "You said this would be easy."

"I can't, woman! Stop being stupid!"

"Well, at least I have a plan," said the woman. "This guy gets angry, throws the rock, and then Bo will get angry too, and invite us in."

Brea saw the wisdom in the old woman's plan. Her father did have a temper. She hoped she was wrong, and he couldn't be baited into losing his cool.

"Enough!" said the Butler looking around. "We're wasting time when we should be searching for Brea."

Both the boy and the woman stopped bickering for a moment.

The Butler looked like he was listening for something, then he turned Brea's way.

Brea's muscles tensed. Here came the worst part of her dream!

"I can sense her. She is near."

"Well, you've met her before. You know what you're looking for," said the boy. "I just knew her sister, Carea."

Brea pulled her cloak around her, and set her hood on her head. This time she didn't want to run. She bet it was her running alerted the spirits she was hiding.

Holding her breath, Brea inspected her cloak. Was it covering all of her? Exhaling, she saw that it was. Now what? Being driven by instinct, she wondered if she could hide her spirit energy with her cloak. She didn't know if it would work, but she tried. She watched the butler.

The butler scanned the area and continued to hesitate, as if trying to sense Brea. Finally, he said, "This is a waste of our time."

"Can't sense her?" asked the boy. "I thought you said you could."

"There's too many people around."

Brea was relieved. She had been spooked too easily, earlier. The butler wasn't as good as she had thought. For whatever reason, she was hidden. But then a new thought came to her. The butler had said there were too many people around. What people? Were there other people in front of the house she couldn't see? Carefully Brea moved behind the bush and leaned out so she could see down the street. Yes, there was a group of people coming. Each one had a rock, bat, or some kind of weapon in their hands.

Brea frowned. What were they planning to do? She noticed that all of the people walking her way were those that had stopped coming to church and had accepted a chip. These were the worst kind of enemies, those that used to be friends!

"Yes! We're going to have a party!" said the old woman, bouncing slightly and clapping as she watched the on-coming group. "This is going to be fun. We're going to have our own witch trial!" Then suddenly, she disappeared and re-appeared in the midst of the group. She didn't waste time but began whispering in their ears.

The boy in chains did the same.

"Bo Rogers!" yelled Brother Reiser, coaxed by the whispered words of the butler. "Come out and face the people you've wronged!"

Brea waited for the door to open, but it didn't. Good, her father was keeping his temper. She prayed he would continue.

"Bo! I'll give you three seconds to come out here or we'll come in there and drag you out."

The door opened and Brea's mother's voice said, "Go home, Tom. Don't cause problems. You know that my husband had nothing to do with your situation."

"Yes, he did, Corrynne. My wife's dead because of him. Others will die, too, if he's allowed to continue to lead us astray. Now stand aside. This has nothing to do with you. Bo Rogers! Come out! Stop hiding behind your wife!"

Brea couldn't believe that this was happening! Brother Reiser's wife dies? How? Why would they blame her father?

Brea couldn't hold herself back any more. She burst from the bush, pulling back her hood and said, "Brother Reiser! Stop!"

"Brea!" called Corrynne. "Get back!"

"No, Mom!" yelled Brea. "There are evil spirits out here! You guys can't see them but they're here! They're whispering in everyone's ears!"

"There she is!" exclaimed the butler with a condemning finger. "Get her! Shut her up!"

Within a second, the boy, woman, and butler, were binding her with their powers. Their presence fell upon her and for a moment she couldn't tell the difference between them and herself. Each of their personalities was so strong she almost couldn't think independently. Suddenly, she couldn't breathe! It was happening again! The spirits were suffocating her, just like back at the mansion! Falling to her knees and grasping at her throat, she searched her mind frantically for the strength to remember what to do. She looked helplessly at the front of her parent's home where she saw her mother and father bolt towards her from the doorway. Within seconds they were kneeling beside her.

"What's wrong with her?" asked Bo.

"I'm not sure," said Corrynne. "I don't think she's choking—breathe, baby," coaxed Corrynne.

Brea closed her eyes. "In the…" she began, remembering what to say.

"Do we give her mouth to mouth?" asked Bo.

"Not until she loses consciousness," said Corrynne. "Let me try the Heimlich," said her mother.

"No, something else is wrong, Corrynne. It's…"

"…name of…" continued Brea in her mind.

"In the name of Jesus Christ, our master, I command you to depart, servants of Satan!" said Bo, suddenly standing above Brea, with his right hand held up.

With a flash of light the three powerful spirits were ripped off Brea and flung away. They looked similar to spaghetti flying through the air as their arms and legs sprawled and their bodies seemed to elongate from the force of his command.

Brea took in a great breath, as tears fell down her face. "Daddy! You knew!" she managed to say.

Suddenly, she bounced from her bed. It was dark. And the second dream was over.

Brea shook her head as her chest heaved in to breathe. She swallowed and looked around her. She was alone in her home, her house securely locked. ...All was fine—at least she hoped it was.

Notes to "The Fall of Great Nations"

The Fall of Rome

[1] "Those nations who ignore history are doomed to repeat its tragedies" (Cicero, Roman statesman, lawyer, political theorist, and philosopher, 106 BC-43 BC).

[2] "Adversity will surface in some form in every life. How we prepare for it, how we meet it, makes the difference. We can be broken by adversity, or we can become stronger. The final result is up to the individual. Henry Fielding said: 'Adversity is the trial of principle. Without it, a man hardly knows whether he is honest or not.' Realizing that adversity can include suffering, destitution, affliction, calamity, or disaster, how can we best use it as an opportunity for personal growth and development? ...It can be declared accurately and without hesitation that Joseph Smith's noble character and stature were shaped and achieved by constant victories over his afflictions. Jesus, too, developed unique balance mentally, physically, spiritually, and socially as He labored and served under all types of trying circumstances. 'Though he were a Son, yet learned he obedience by the things which he

suffered; and being made perfect, he became the author of eternal salvation unto all them that obey him' (Hebrews 5:8-9). Difficulties can be a valuable tool in our pursuit of perfection. Adversity need have no necessary connection with failure. Proper self-management and self-discipline in all of our trials can bring strength. If we are prepared, we can meet life's challenges victoriously. We become His disciples when we continue faithfully under all circumstances, including suffering and tragedy. C. S. Lewis shared a meaningful observation when he said, 'I have seen great beauty of spirit in some who were great sufferers. I have seen men, for the most part, grow better not worse with advancing years, and I have seen the last illness produce treasures of fortitude and meekness from most unpromising subjects'" (Marvin J. Ashton, *Ye Are My Friends*, pgs. 96, 101).

[3] The premise for this section came from the writings of Edward Gibbon, a famous study, *The Decline and Fall of the Roman Empire* (1776).

[4] "In this day of gathering storm, as the moral deterioration of political power spreads its growing infection, it is essential that every spiritual force be mobilized to defend and preserve the religious base upon which this nation was founded; for it is that base which has been the motivating impulse to our moral and national growth. History fails to record a single precedent in which nations subject to moral decay have not passed into political and economic decline. There had been either a spiritual reawakening to overcome the moral lapse, or a progressive deterioration leading to ultimate national disaster" (General Douglas MacArthur, *A Soldier Speaks,* December 12, 1951, pgs. 285-286).

[5] "Our complacency as a nation is shocking—yes, almost unbelievable! We are a prosperous nation. Our people have high-paying jobs. Our incomes are high. Our standard of living is at an unprecedented level. We do not like to be disturbed as we enjoy our comfortable complacency. We live in the soft present and feel the future is secure. We do not worry about history. We seem oblivious to the causes of the rise and fall of nations. We are blind to the hard fact that nations usually sow the seeds of their own destruction while enjoying unprecedented prosperity. I say to you with all the fervor of my soul: We are sowing the seeds of our own destruction in America and much of the free world today. It is my sober warning to you today that if the trends of the past continue, we will lose that which is as priceless as life itself—our freedom, our liberty, our right to act as free men. It can happen here. It is happening here" (Ezra Taft Benson, *An Enemy Hath Done This*, pg. 90).

[6] "The inhabitants of the earth are ignorant with regard to the design of their being; they are as ignorant in this respect as the wild animals that roam over the plains. ...It is my business to teach mankind how to live, how to honor their present existence, how to treat their bodies so as to live to a good old age on the earth, and have power to do good and not evil all their days, and be ready to enter into the rest prepared for the Saints. ...If you ask them whether they know how to raise potatoes to feed their wives and children, their answer is 'No.' Do you know how to raise grain for your bread? 'No.' Do you know how to raise watermelons? 'No.' Do you know how to raise pigs for your meat? 'No.' Do you know how to raise chickens? 'No.' Do you love to eat them? 'Yes.' Do you know how to raise calves? 'No.' You may give them a cow and calf, and two years will not pass before they have neither cow nor calf. Do you know how to improve your fruit? 'No.' And thus they live without trying to produce for themselves these necessaries and comforts of life. ...The Lord wishes us to know how to provide for ourselves all things necessary for our comfort in bread, fruit, and clothing" (Brigham Young, *Journal of Discourses,* June 8, 1862, Vol. 10, pg. 28).

[7] "With the desire for materialistic security—government imposed or otherwise—usually comes a passive, careless attitude toward the fundamental principles basic to our form of government and way of life. People with this philosophy are easily lulled away into a false sense of security as they cry, 'All is well.' Every young person requires the spur of economic insecurity to force him to do his best. We must have the courage to stand against undue governmental paternalism and the cowardly cry that 'the world owes me a living.' Nobody owes us anything for crops we do not grow, goods we do not produce, or work we do not do! How will it affect the morale and character of the people? That is the acid test which should be applied to every proposal and program. Can any man be politically free who depends upon the state for sustenance? A planned and subsidized economy weakens initiative, discourages industry, destroys character, and demoralizes the people. Emphasis upon materialism always breeds more fears than it cures" (Ezra Taft Benson, Reed A. Benson, *So Shall Ye Reap*, pg. 161-162).

[8] "You Americans are so gullible. No, you won't accept communism outright, but we'll keep feeding you small doses of socialism until you'll finally wake up and find you already have communism. We won't have to fight you. We'll so weaken your economy until you'll fall like over-ripe fruit into our hands" (Nikita, Khrushchev, First Secretary of the Communist Party of the Soviet Union, 1958-1964 as quoted by Ezra Taft Benson while hosting him at the White House in his position as Secretary of Agriculture. *An Enemy Hath Done This*, pg. 320).

[9] "'That government is best which governs least.' So taught the courageous founders of this nation. This simple declaration is diametrically opposed to the all too common philosophy that the government should protect one from the cradle to the grave. The policy of the founding fathers has made our people and our nation strong. The opposite philosophy leads to moral and spiritual decay" (Ezra Taft Benson, Reed A. Benson, *So Shall Ye Reap*, pg. 161).

[10] David O. McKay, Conference Report, April 1966.

[11] Ezra Taft Benson, *An Enemy Hath Done This*, pg. 117.

[12] "There is a just God who presides over the destinies of nation; and who will raise up friends to fight our battles for us. The battle, sir, is not to the strong alone; it is to the vigilant, the active, the brave. ...It is now too late to retire from the contest. There is no retreat, but in submission and slavery! Our chains are forged! Their clanking may be heard. ...Why stand we here idle? ...Is life so dear, or peace so sweet, as to be purchased at the price of chains and slavery? Forbid it, Almighty God! I know not what course others may take; but as for me, give me liberty, or give me death!" (Patrick Henry, March 23 1775 as quoted by Jerreld L. Newquist, *Prophets, Principles and National Survival*, pg. 517)

[13] "And if men come unto me I will show unto them their weakness. I give unto men weakness that they may be humble; and my grace is sufficient for all men that humble themselves before me; for if they humble themselves before me, and have faith in me, then will I make weak things become strong unto them" (Ether 12:27).

[14] "Will the Constitution be destroyed? No: it will be held inviolate by this people; and, as Joseph Smith said, 'The time will come when the destiny of the nation will hang upon a single thread. At that critical juncture, this people will step forth and save it from the threatened destruction.' It will be so" (Brigham Young, *Journal of Discourses*, Vol. 7, pg. 15).

CHAPTER ELEVEN

DESTROYING ANGELS

"Q. What are we to understand by the four angels, spoken of in the 7th chapter and 1st verse of Revelation? A. We are to understand that they are four angels sent forth from God, to whom is given power over the four parts of the earth, to save life and to destroy..." (D&C 77:8).

00:01:27, 16:40:02, Zulu
Monday, November 3rd

Storm

Far Eastern Tundra of Russia
3:20 p.m.

Elder Zebedee pushed his sleigh ahead as he led the tribes traveling to the east. The wind howled as an ugly storm raged around them. Icy rain, mixed with snow, ripped at them like daggers, and would have cut their skin if it wasn't for the long animal coats they wore for protection.

Suddenly, lightning tore through the dark sky and spooked the loose reindeer being herded by the people. The animals bolted and ran in multiple directions.

"Grab 'em!" yelled Braun, looking at Chenille in worry, as he tried to head a few off. "We can't let those deer get away!" Despite his efforts, Braun watched helplessly as most of the herd they depended on for food turned and ran back to more familiar territory. *"Stop them!"* yelled Braun again, this time to the other men, even though he knew they didn't understand English and were already trying their best to corral the animals. With a quick tap of his stick, he urged the single reindeer pulling his sleigh forward till he caught up with John. "Do you see what's happening here?" he yelled over the howling wind.

John turned and calmly watched as men and deer ran in circles trying to salvage what was left. He nodded without a word.

"What do we do? They provide all our food!" asked Braun urgently. "Shouldn't we do something?"

John repositioned himself on his deer. "It will be fine," he answered.

"How?" asked Braun, trying to calm down. "Where will we find more deer?"

"The Lord will provide for us," said John, reflectively. "He is aware."[1]

Braun stared at John, who seemed like he was lost in some other world. He looked out at the barren, snow-covered wilderness that showed neither end nor hint of life. He shook his head in helpless frustration as he allowed his buck to fall back to where he had been traveling before. Looking at Chenille, he couldn't help but worry. What were they going to do? How would he protect her? Then with a mighty prayer, he turned his thoughts to the Lord. He prayed for the strength to believe John and to trust in his calmness. But then the thought came across his mind—of course John could be calm, he didn't have to eat!

Braun shook the judgmental thought from his head. That wasn't fair. He had to trust the apostle; he spoke for Heavenly Father.[2] When hadn't the Lord provided? He couldn't think of a time. There were moments he felt abandoned, only to find he had been mistaken.[3] This was probably one of those times. He would have to be strong.

More lightning ripped through the sky, causing Braun to flinch. Placing an arm around Chenille, he pulled her in tight. She laid her head on his shoulder. Neither spoke as they continued their journey east toward the sea.

Increasing Disasters

Frankfurt, Germany
4:12 p.m.

MD stood over his computer and looked up around his room of digital screens while puffing furiously on his cigar.

Matt sat nearby in an office chair reading a report about the diminishing magnetic force of the earth and the sun's destructive influence on the ozone layer.[4]

"There goes another one," said MD between his teeth.

Matt's eyes automatically shifted to see the reason for his father's sudden anger. Another screen was black. One of MD's favorite links to the United States, a congressman out of San Diego, had been broken. That was never a good sign. A black screen, without any auditory or visual feeds, normally meant the person had died. Half the screens linking MD to his pet moles were now blank.

"What happened?" asked Matt.

MD jammed his cigar into the ashtray and then hit the desk with his open hand. "What's happening?" he yelled. *"How can there be so many disasters in so many places at one time?"*

Matt didn't offer anything. He just shook his head, empathetically.

"Who needs plagues when you've got—" MD held up a hand gesturing to the screens, *"this!"* he exclaimed with obvious fury. "At least with plagues we can control the fatalities with medicine!" MD shook his fist at God. "You're ruining all my hard work! Stop it! I'm in control now! You get out of it!"

Matt couldn't help a smile that crept across his face. His father was acting like a lunatic. It was liberating to see *him* out of control for a change. Maybe the tide was turning.

MD held up reports and let them fall one by one out of his hands, "Heat waves,[5] earthquakes,[6] hurricanes,[7] the ice caps are melting, the water's rising,[8] the land is sinking,[9] and according to my scientists, *the world is wobbling*![10] What next!" MD searched Matt's face for a response.

Matt became very serious and shrugged, shaking his head. "Maybe we need to call in someone—an environmental expert, just to help us plan..."

"Expert?" yelled MD, his face red. "I've got experts coming out my ears! They don't know what's going on! They're *idiots*!"

"OK," said Matt. "Or we can just watch as our screens go out one by one."

Suddenly, three more screens went blank.

"Ahh!" yelled MD, rushing to them and touching each one. "No, no, no, not any more! I need eyes! I need to know what's happening!" MD turned and walked angrily to his automatic door that swished open. He yelled out his door, *"Kyle West!"*

A thin, skittish man with a big nose and black glasses perched on his face, nervously rushed in. "Y-yes, sir?" he asked, with obvious terror on his face.

"You see these screens?"

Kyle looked up at the patchwork of half empty screens. "Yes, sir."

With a chubby hand pointing and the other hand on his hip, MD screamed, "I need numbers! I need people to fill these screens. Get me more feeds. Plug in more chip addresses! Give me resonance!"

"Do you need politicians? Stars? Who would you like, sir?"

Matt let out a quiet laugh as he covered his face with his report, careful not to reveal himself. So, his father had become voyeuristic? ...Interesting.

"I don't care! Just get me people! Get me anybody!"

"It's just that normally you like..."

"Did you hear me?" yelled MD, interrupting Kyle with his anger, casting a look towards Matt who now was maintaining his usual control.

"Yes, sir!" said Kyle. "Do you want us to report these disasters on the video device?"

"To who, Kyle? The people who would have benefited from such a broadcast—are *dead*!"

"I don't know. Just to let people know what's happening?"

"Who needs to know? Those who are safe? Those who have no use for this information? Because that's who would get it! It would be useless!"

"Ahhh," said Kyle, looking like he didn't know what to say next.

"No, no, no, you imbecile! Let me educate you," MD said, pointing at Kyle. "We are not the town gossip! We don't report when children lose their dogs, or any other human interest *hullabaloo*. Our job is simple. Create perceptions to make money. We use the media to make money! We'll report plagues, we'll report wars, because it will drive people to us who will labor and consume, making us money, but what good is reporting things we can't control?" he said, gesturing to the empty screens. *"Nothing!* We'll look weak and gain no benefit from that kind of garbage! It will only *cost* us money, and that would be stupid! I've already *lost* a fortune!"

Kyle looked confused and then nodded quickly. "Yes, sir," he said, and then he rushed out.

MD stomped back to his desk, mumbling to himself, "Stupid disasters took my investments...." In disgust, he stared at the reports that were scattered in front of him. Pushing them around on his desk, he looked as if he were trying to make sense out of them. "There must be a pattern. If we can find a pattern, we can stay ahead of these *acts of God* that I call acts of the *grim reaper*!"

After a few moments of quiet, MD looked from his desk and motioned to his son. "Matt, come over here."

Matt stood, folded his report, and approached the desk.

"I paid for your PhD. Put it to good use! Read these!" he exclaimed, pushing the reports towards his son. "Tell me what's going on. Tell me what they say."

Matt took the stack, straightened it, and then began to put them in order.

The room lightened a little as digital screens came on line.

MD cheered, his mood lightening almost instantaneously. "Yes! That's what I want! My office needs to be full of life!" he exclaimed happily with arms out wide, then in a moment, half went blank again. MD stood in awe. "What the...." Either something huge had just happened, or a connection was faulty. "Ahhhgrrrr!" he yelled in rage, as he stomped around the desk again to yell at Kyle. The automatic door opened "What's going on out there?" MD waited for an answer but no one offered any. *"Answer me!"* he demanded.

"It was a tsunami off the West Coast of the United States, sir," said Kyle, as he meekly approached. "There was a 9.5 earthquake in the Pacific Ocean, off the coast of Oregon, and it hit the whole coast."[11]

"You've got to be kidding me!" said MD with a hand to his forehead.

"No sir."

"First Alaska had an earthquake, then California," exclaimed MD, counting with his fingers in the air, "now you tell me *Oregon* had one?"

"Yes, sir."

"Affecting the whole coast?"

"Yes, sir."

"How are my crews out there?" turning to Matt he said, "I had my best people on the coast. We were making headway. Nearly 80% chip saturation!"

"We're searching for survivors now, sir, but we aren't finding much in the large metropolitan cities west of the Cascades or the Sierra Nevada range.[12]

"What?" he said, with a strangled voice.

"There was already flooding from the ice caps melting, sir.[13] The water has risen four feet in some areas, adding weight to the land, and causing it to sink. This makes the effective flooding to be six feet, sir..."[14]

"Stop!" yelled MD.

"...And then with the tsunami..."[15]

"Stop, I said! I don't want to hear this!" he demanded. "I don't tolerate my investments doing poorly!"

Kyle fell silent.

"Get more screens up! Now!" he yelled, and then went back to his desk and sat down, putting his head in his hands.

Matt scanned the reports MD had given him and sat back down in his chair. He stayed quiet, waiting for his father to decompress.

After a few minutes MD said, "Well?"

Matt looked at his father, who still had his head down. "Are you talking to me?" asked Matt.

MD looked up in anger. "Of course I'm talking to you, who else? The planter?"

Matt patiently nodded. "Just giving you some space."

"I don't want space! I want answers! *Answers! Give me answers!*" MD shouted at the top of his lungs as he pounded his desk.

"Which topic would you like me to explain?" asked Matt. "Global warming? The weakening magnetic field?"

"No! I'm sick to death of hearing about those topics. That's old news, and who knows if that's what's really going on.[16] No, we need to stay ahead of the curve. Tell me about that crust shifting—thing," said MD, pointing and wagging his finger. "I bet that's what's going to give us the most trouble in the future, tell me about that. I need to know the very worst scenario."

"OK," said Matt, as he shuffled the pages.

"My science guy seems to think all the ice melting is going to make the world imbalanced and shift things around," continued MD. "I need to know which parts of his findings are real and which are hooey."

"Alright," said Matt, as he scanned the pages. "This isn't good news though; are you sure you're ready for it?" he asked.

MD made a motion with his hand, indicating to go ahead. "Give me the simplified version, will ya?"

Matt nodded. "This report says that any time the earth becomes unbalanced, either because of land masses forming from volcanism..."

"Volcanism, what's that?" interrupted MD.

"Lava flows," said Matt.

"Oh, volcanoes," said MD nodding, as a few more screens went out. MD shook his head and shielded his face from the screens and said, "Go ahead."

"...Land masses colliding, creating heavy mountain ranges, large ice bodies melting—any of these can cause the earth's crust to shift in order to regain balance."[17]

"Why does the earth have to be balanced?" asked MD.

Matt was surprised by his father's question. "It just does, Dad. As the earth spins, the heaviest part must be right at the equator. This makes sense if you visualize the earth like a spinning top. A top only spins when its center of gravity is the largest and heaviest part, otherwise it would only wobble and fall over. We already know that the earth wobbles when there are tsunamis. The weight of all the water moving together on the earth causes the wobble. [18] It's the same idea. If the earth becomes unbalanced because of a change in the weight distribution of all its parts, it will shift, rotating on its core to create a new center of gravity, and reestablish balance."

"And that's what they think is happening?" asked MD.

"That's what they think *might* happen."

"But isn't the heaviest part of the land already along the equator?" asked MD, his mustache twitching.

"We don't know," said Matt. "We hope so, but if it isn't, with all the ice melting there will be a shift. It's unavoidable."[19]

"So what would happen if a shift occurred?"

"There would be a massive earthquake that would shake every continent at the same time. Rivers would flow in new directions, climates would radically change."[20]

"Give me an example," said MD.

"Well, let's say the crust shifted south. Germany would become tropical and the Amazon would become more seasonal."

MD thought about Matt's words. "Maybe that wouldn't be so bad...but then a global earthquake would cause an incalculable amount of damage in the public sector."

"Yes, it would," said Matt.

"Buildings would fall, roads would crack, plumbing would break..."

"You're right."

"The scientists are only guessing, though, right—this isn't a sure thing?"

Matt nodded. "I guess you can say that, but I'd call it an educated guess, predicting a potential event considering all the factors."

"That's a guess!" said MD. "I'm not going to get all excited over a guess."

"OK," said Matt nodding.

MD stood and watched his screens again. "So is there anything else I need to think about?"

"There is that issue of 99942 Apophis."[21]

"What's that again?"

"It's a 270-meter wide asteroid heading our way."

MD waved his hand. "That won't be an issue."

"It could be," said Matt.

"No, we'd just shoot an asteroid out of the sky. I can handle asteroids."

"NASA used to handle near-earth objects and NASA is out of commission."

"I know that!" said MD, looking like he was getting angry again.

"Alright," said Matt, shrugging as another segment of television screens went blank.

MD, furious, got up from his desk and stomped back out the door. *"Kyle!"*

Matt shook his head. All he wanted to do was stay out of his father's way, and secretly watch Utah. So far it seemed quiet. Good thing. Plans were on schedule....

Disinformation

Provo, Utah
11:02 a.m.

Jax attempted to use his eraser, only to rip a huge hole in his yellow, cheap paper. He hated this *worthless* recycled paper, and he hated his *brainless* school now that they made him sit in a corner meant for non-UN "charity" students. He was part of a group that was given substandard materials, because they didn't have money assigned to them. He was there because his parents hadn't entered the "system."

The teacher was kneeling on the floor looking behind the large video display. He was hooking up the hand-held video player, so the class could see something that had been broadcast from the UN.

"Pay attention, class," said Mr. Gant, the history teacher. "A war is going on all around us. I want you to ask yourself who the warring parties are," he said, as he stood up from kneeling, "because they are among us. Violence is no longer across the ocean, but here, killing good people, who are selfless in their service to those of us who need help."

The teacher pushed a button and a deep voice filled the room. "Between September and November, there have been approximately 120 major terrorist attacks aimed at the UN. Suicide bombers, posing as American economic refugees, executed 61 of the attacks, all of whom belonged to radical extremist religious organizations, who refuse to join the economic system."

There was a gasp in the room as the kids looked at each other in shock.

"That's a *lie*," said Jax under his breath, knowing this report was aimed at him, his family, and others who chose to remain free of the UN's claws.

The announcer continued. "Consequently, more than 436 peace-keeping internationalists were murdered, and thousands more have been badly wounded across America."

A couple of kids looked back at Jax and the other kids in the roped-off section.

"What 'cha looking at?" he asked, defiantly.

"Mr. Rogers."

Jax looked angrily at the teacher.

"There will be no more of that."

The report continued. "The attacks were prompted by intensified religious and political conflicts between the radical Christian groups, and the territorial and governorship agencies over rights to American soil. After unsuccessful attempts by the UN and the head of the organizations to find a solution to the problem, the Christian extremists took up arms, turning to terror tactics, such as suicide bombings to achieve political goals."

Jax stood up abruptly, thrusting his desk aside. "That stuff is not true!" he yelled. "Why do you show it? It only makes people hate each other more!"[22]

The teacher stared at Jax and pushed the stop button on the video. "Mr. Rogers, you are excused to the principal's office."

Jax grabbed his coat off the back of his chair. "Fine! I'd rather go to the Principal's office than stay in this bigoted, lying *prison*!"

The class was silent as everyone held their breath.

Jax thrust the door open hard enough to make it hit the wall with a startling bang as he exited the room.

Lost, Now Found

Provo, Utah
12:12 p.m.

"Does anyone know Leonard Smith?" asked a nearly barefoot woman dressed in shabby, dirty clothes, and carrying a pack.[23] She seemed out of place and in need of the basics of life. There was a little girl at her side, hiding behind her leg.

Corrynne was up on a ladder picking the last of the apples on Mr. Griffin's property. "I'm sorry, I haven't heard of him," she said as she climbed down to speak to the woman. "Does he live around here?"

The woman looked hungrily at an apple that had fallen on the ground. "I'm not sure," she said as if she had forgotten the question.

"Are you hungry?" asked Corrynne.

"Yes," said the woman, not taking her eyes off the fruit. "We haven't eaten for two days."

"Would you like an apple?" asked Corrynne, reaching into a cloth bag tied around her waist.

"I'll just take that one from the ground," said the woman, bending down. "My daughter needs food."

Corrynne cringed. "That's a rotten one. Take these instead," she said holding out beautiful, flawless, yellow apples to both mother and daughter. "You can both have one."

The woman looked overwhelmed as she gently took both pieces of fruit. "You don't know how much this means to us!" she said as she handed one to her daughter and then bit into the second. The woman closed her eyes and took pleasure in the taste for a moment.

"Is it good?" asked Corrynne, enjoying this stranger's gratitude.

The woman nodded slowly and said, "Oh, yes. Thank you! After days of rotten food from dumpsters, this tastes so *great*."

Corrynne wrinkled her nose. "Rotten food? That's—" she stopped, trying to think of the appropriate words. "That's not very healthy."

"When there's no other choice, what does a mother do?" said the woman apologetically, as she took another bite.

Corrynne watched as the little girl ate her apple like it was corn-on-the-cob. She was so hungry! "I have other food you might like. How about homemade bread and soup?"

The woman took on a hopeful look. "You have food? Real food?"

"Yes, of course," said Corrynne, as she transferred the apples in her bag to a large burlap sack on the ground. "Come on," she said, smiling and then heading for her house.

"How do you have food?" asked the woman, following and looking confused. "Did you get it from the relief stations?"

Corrynne shook her head. "Oh, no. It's ours. We stored it."

"You stored it? You mean you bought it?"

"A while ago," said Corrynne, wondering what was so odd.

"That's good," said the woman looking around, as if searching for something. Then she whispered, "The food from the relief stations..." she began, and then she looked around again.

"Yes?" asked Corrynne.

"Is poisoned," she said behind her hand.

"What?"

"There's something in it that makes people feel hungry all the time."

"What are you talking about?" asked Corrynne, fighting off a smile. "Why would they *need* to do that?" she finished, wondering if this woman was joking.

"Because the people at the UN centers are aliens! If you look closely, you'll see it, too!"

"What?" asked Corrynne, breaking out in laughter.

"No really! Don't laugh. If you watch the people who hand out food, you'll see. There's something odd about them. I think they're trying to fatten us up."

"For what purpose?" asked Corrynne, trying to contain her amusement.

"To *eat* us!" the woman said, as if her conclusion was obvious.

"What?" Corrynne asked impulsively, her voice lilting up an octave.

"That's why I like to stay skinny. They don't like the skinny people."

Corrynne folded her arms and studied the woman. She was serious.

"They've taken human form, you know," the woman continued. "You can't tell the difference between them and real people."

"Tell me again why you think this?" asked Corrynne, switching into nurse mode, watching and assessing. It was obvious the woman had some psychological issues and most likely hadn't had her medications in a while.

"Why else would someone give expensive food for free, unless there was a catch?"

Corrynne nodded. "Now, I agree with that."

"If you watch those people at the relief center," explained the woman, as they stepped up the curb to the sidewalk, "you'll notice that they smile too much, and are way too friendly. I think they're trying to lull all of us to sleep. 'Come take my food,' they say. 'Eat, eat!'" she said in an airy, eerie voice, with her hands waving in the air, as if she were trying to put Corrynne under a trance. "And they wear all white. Who wears all white any more? Nurses don't even wear white any more."

Corrynne nodded "I know," she agreed. "You might have a point there."

"I get the chills every time I see a UN worker. There's something wrong with them. I just know it."

"So, you don't have a chip implanted under your skin?"

The woman shook her head as she took another bite of her apple. "No way! That's how they know where to find you," she said, chewing. "Haven't you watched those UFO shows where people have been abducted and then some sort of tracking machine is put in their ear, so the space ships can find them?"

Corrynne shook her head as she climbed her porch stairs. "No, sorry."

"Well, that's how they do it. I won't let those psycho space-people touch me or my daughter."

Corrynne opened her front door. "Come sit at the table. I'll get some food for you." Holding up a finger she said, "Excuse me, my children are playing in the back. Ahh, Louise?" she called down the hall.

"Yes?" answered a voice from the back.

"I'm back."

"OK," Louise answered.

Corrynne looked around and smiled as she closed the door. "The electricity seems to still be working right now, so maybe I can heat up the soup in the microwave."

"That would be wonderful," said the woman looking around Corrynne's house.

"What's your name?" asked Corrynne, heading to the kitchen.

"Caroline," said the woman as she wandered over and looked at Corrynne's couch.

"And your daughter?"

"Her name is Rebecca. She's six."

"We have a couple of children that age in our house right now," said Corrynne, as she pushed the start button on the microwave.

Caroline studied the patchwork material that made up the cushion covers, her daughter glued to her leg. "Did you make these?"

Corrynne was embarrassed. "Oh, don't look at those. We had to throw some rags together the best we could for our couch. The dam broke a while back and ruined all our furniture."

"I—" began the woman, and then she faltered.

"What?" asked Corrynne, as she began to cut some bread. "What were you saying?"

"I can make couch covers. Can I make some for you?" asked Caroline.

Corrynne was surprised. "That would be too hard. It's not necessary."

"I want to do it," said the woman, as she and her daughter sat at the table.

"Caroline, it's fine..."

"But I *want* to do it," said Caroline, her voice urgent. Corrynne took the bowls out of the microwave and studied the face of this new stranger as she placed the soup on the table. She was anxious about something. Corrynne couldn't quite put her finger on it, but she had seen that look before. Not in her house, but at the hospital. "You really like to make things, don't you?"

"Yes, it's what I do," said Caroline. "Do you have a piano?" she asked, looking around.

Corrynne nodded. "Yes."

"Rebecca plays the piano while I sew."

The woman's expression was intense. It looked like she was going to lose control of her emotions if Corrynne wouldn't agree to have her make something for her. "Tell you what. You eat, and then we'll figure out what you can sew. We need seamstresses around here. No one remembers how to sew anything, so I'm sure we can keep you busy."

Caroline nodded and then she and her daughter began to eat voraciously. After her bowl was drained, she held it out again. "Do you mind if I have another round?"

Corrynne shook her head and took the bowl. "Not a problem. I made extra."

"How come you stored food?" asked Caroline abruptly.

"Because we knew this crash was coming," said Corrynne, as she put another bowl of soup into the microwave.

"How did you know? And who's 'we,'" asked the woman.

"Our church."

"Which church is that?"

"The Church of Jesus Christ of Latter-day Saints."

"Oh," said Caroline, looking contemplative.

"We have a prophet[24] and twelve apostles[25] that receive revelation for our church, just as Christ guided the people back in his day.[26] They encouraged us to store food."[27]

"A living who?" asked Caroline, with a confused stare.

"A living prophet. A man who speaks to God and then teaches us."

"You have a prophet who teaches you how to store food?"

Corrynne smiled. This wasn't going to be easy. "He doesn't only tell us to store food. He teaches us about the good in life; everything that's in the scriptures, he teaches."[28]

"Like what?"

"How to get along, how to love each other, how to be safe, and how to repent so we can be free of guilt..."

"Is he like Jesus?" asked Caroline.

"Yes," said Corrynne, nodding. "He speaks for Jesus and acts in his stead."[29]

"Those UN people have a prophet that does all those things. Is he your prophet, too?"

Corrynne bit her lip. This woman was speaking about Imam Mahdi. Angry feelings rose in Corrynne's chest. She shook her head. "That man's an imposter."

"How do you know?" asked Caroline. "Maybe your prophet and that prophet are the same."

"They aren't," said Corrynne. "They're opposites. One leads people to Jesus Christ and eternal life, and one leads people away. That's how you can tell the difference."[30]

Corrynne turned and took the bowl from the microwave and placed it in front of Caroline. Rebecca continued to sip her soup quietly, not getting involved in the adult conversation.

"Well, good," said Caroline. "I hope you're right. I wouldn't want you to get eaten by the aliens. It smells like you make good barley soup."

Corrynne nodded and decided to change the subject. "Where are you from?"

The woman swallowed and said, "Chicago."

"What's happening in Chicago?"

"Chicago is gone."

"What do you mean, 'it's gone'?" asked Corrynne with shock.

Caroline shook her head. "There was some terrible shaking, fires, and then a large tornado. After that, the water started rising. It all happened so suddenly. I think the earthquake made the land sink."

"When did this happen?" asked Corrynne.

"About two weeks ago."

"Where did the water come from?"

"I don't know. It just poured in from everywhere, swallowing everything. I took my little girl and did what I could to survive. I moved to higher ground."[31]

"Are you saying Chicago is under water?"

Caroline nodded. "Everything is under water. There aren't even lakes left. It's all ocean."

Corrynne covered her mouth. "It can't be!" she said.

Caroline nodded, "It is, huh, baby?" she asked Rebecca.

Rebecca nodded. "The water was cold. I was shivering."

"But we warmed up after a while, huh?"

"Yep," said Rebecca.

Corrynne watched the mother and daughter, still not quite believing what she was hearing. Could it be true? "Is all the land gone on the East Coast?"[32] she asked aloud.

"No. If I stood on the bank and looked east, I could see there were islands of land, rising above the water."

"How far away?" asked Corrynne.

"I would need a boat if I wanted to cross."

Corrynne shook her head. "I can't believe it."

"That's why we liked the idea of coming here," said Caroline. "We're safe from the water at this altitude."

"I would hope so!" said Corrynne. "Do you know anything about the West Coast?"

Caroline shook her head. "All I know is what I saw."

"Hmmm," said Corrynne, thinking, wondering if the West Coast was flooding, too. Her family lived on the West Coast.... After a few moments of worrying, she decided there was no way of finding out, and worrying would only make her crazy. She shook the negative thoughts from her head. With a sigh, she returned her attention to Caroline. "Tell me how you arrived in Provo. There's desert all around. You couldn't possibly have walked all this way without drinking water."

"We didn't. We stowed away in a UN bus."

"How?"

"We hid in the luggage compartment. My husband used to drive those kinds of big busses, so we knew how to get in."

"I see," said Corrynne. "So you're afraid of the UN people, but you rode in their bus?"

"Yes, no one else has gas. It was either take the chip or ride in the hull. At least in the hull, I knew my daughter and I would be safe."

"Safe from what?"

"Robbers, looters, and murderers; they run every city I've passed through, taking whatever they want from the sick and the weak."

"Then you'd have to be pretty smart to stay safe, wouldn't you?" asked Corrynne.

"Yes. We're smart, aren't we, honey?" Caroline asked her daughter, as she ran her fingers through her hair, lovingly.

Rebecca smiled and nodded.

Corrynne sat down at the table. "Tell me what it's like in the cities you've seen."

"Why? It's much better here. Why would you want to know what's out there?" asked Caroline.

Corrynne shrugged. There wasn't any reason other than her interest. "I just want to know."

Caroline took a bite of bread, chewed a couple of times, and then with a full mouth, she said, "All the cities are in shambles. There are two laws out there: the UN's law and the law of the wild—the survival of the meanest, strongest, or most brutal. [33] Nothing, or no one is safe. Because of that, there's death everywhere; people, animals, fish—you name it. Wild animals roam the streets and birds pick at the garbage.[34] Everything's rotting and it reeks."

Corrynne watched Caroline speak. She spoke without emotion as if she was reporting that the snow was falling, or that she had gone grocery shopping. It was obvious that this was old news to her.

"So where's your husband. Where's your family?" asked Corrynne.

"My husband left me two years ago for another woman. Before the water took the land, I went to live with my parents on their farm. I couldn't support Rebecca by myself, so my parents helped out. I lived there until a mob of jerks kicked us off our own land."

"Why did they do that?"

"Because there wasn't any UN out there to feed them, and we had food. We couldn't fight them. We lost everything. We had a hundred head of cows, not to mention the other animals we kept."[35]

"I'm sorry," said Corrynne, feeling genuinely sorry for this woman. "What happened to your parents?"

Caroline looked down at the table and then back up. This was the first sign of sadness Corrynne had seen.

"I lost them. We were surviving by moving from empty house to empty house, but we were separated."

"Was that before or after the flood?" asked Corrynne.

"Before. My mom liked the bed in one house, but I liked another house with a great play area for Rebecca. We fought about which way to go, and then they went their way, and I went mine. We were angry. It was stupid. Now, I'll probably never see them again."

Corrynne nodded as she bit her lip. This woman had been through a lot. "Oh, that must have been hard," said Corrynne.

"It is now. They were all I had in the world," said Caroline, beginning to cry.

Corrynne pulled a tissue from the counter Kleenex box and handed it to Caroline. "You've had a hard run of things, haven't you?"

Caroline nodded as she blew her nose loudly.

"Where were the people from the empty houses?" asked Corrynne.

Caroline shrugged. "Gone. I don't know. Probably they died. Empty houses line most streets."[36]

"Do you know why so many people might have died?"

"They got sick from bad water, maybe. Some, I'm sure, were robbed and killed for their things. But to be honest, I don't know," said Caroline as she took her last bite of bread. "It was different in every city. I just know that Rebecca and I could walk into practically any house in any city, and sleep there, as long as no one saw us go in."

"What would happen if someone saw you go into a house?" asked Corrynne.

"Some mob guy would eventually kick us out into the cold, and tell us to get out or die."

"That's nice," said Corrynne, sarcastically.

"That's when we started sneaking into the bottoms of the buses. It was warm there, and no bullies would threaten to beat us."

"I can see how it would be," said Corrynne.

"Did your prophet tell you why any of this is happening?" asked Caroline.

Corrynne studied Caroline. She was asking with a serious tone. It seemed she wanted to know.

Corrynne nodded and took a breath. "Yes."

"Tell me what he said."

"We were told that if this nation becomes evil, loving money rather than people, hating their own family members, defiling the oath of marriage, hating God who founded it, then it would be swept off the land. The government would be broken up until mobs ruled the land."[37]

Caroline's mouth fell open. "You were told that *before* it happened?"

"Yes."

"Because that's what's going on. Mobs *do* rule the land. The government *has* broken up!"[38]

"I believe it," said Corrynne.

"What happens now?" asked Caroline, putting an arm around her little girl.

"We find safety in each other," said Corrynne. "Here, we have trustworthy people. Mobs can't come in here and fight against us, because there's too many of us."[39]

"Really?" asked Caroline with large, hopeful eyes.

"Yes," said Corrynne.

"But where could we stay?" asked Caroline, looking sadly at her child. "We don't have any money."

"Old Man Griffin has many empty rooms in his house, I bet he'd let you two have a room."

"You think?"

Corrynne nodded. "I do. He's a very kind man."

"What would that be like?" asked Caroline to her daughter. "Does he have a piano?"

Corrynne tried to remember the inside of Mr. Griffin's home. She remembered seeing an upright piano in the corner of the living room. "I believe he does."

"Then that would be perfect!" said Caroline, smiling.

"Good," said Corrynne, nodding. "What about Leonard Smith?"

"Who?" asked Caroline.

"The man you were looking for when I met you."

Caroline shook her head, "There's no such person."

Corrynne was confused. "Then why did you ask for him?"

"Because if you ask for food people think you're a beggar. If you ask for a lost family member, most often people feel sorry for you and they feed you. It's an ice breaker, I've learned."

Corrynne smiled and nodded. "It worked on me," she said with raised eyebrows, understanding that to a degree, her kindness had been taken advantage of, but it was OK with her. Hopefully Caroline wouldn't have to manipulate for her meals any longer. Finally, she and her daughter were safe.

Notes to "Angels of Destruction"

Storm

[1] "Are not five sparrows sold for two farthings, and not one of them is forgotten before God? But even the very hairs of your head are all numbered. Fear not therefore: ye are of more value than many sparrows" (Luke 12:6-7).

"Now my brethren, we see that God is mindful of every people, whatsoever land they may be in; yea, he numbereth his people, and his bowels of mercy are over all the earth" (Alma 26:37).

[2] "...Whether by mine own voice or by the voice of my servants, it is the same" (D&C 1:38).

[3] "The Savior teaches that we will have tribulation in the world, but we should 'be of good cheer' because He has 'overcome the world' (John 16:33). His Atonement reaches and is powerful enough not only to pay the price for sin but also to heal every mortal affliction. The Book of Mormon teaches that 'He shall go forth, suffering pains and afflictions and temptations of every kind; and this that the word might be fulfilled which saith he will take upon him the pains and the sicknesses of his people' (Alma 7:11; see also 2 Nephi 9:21). He knows of our anguish, and He is there for us. Like the good Samaritan in His parable, when He finds us wounded at the wayside, He binds up our wounds and cares for us (see Luke 10:34). Brothers and sisters, the healing power of His Atonement is for you, for us, for all" (Dallin H. Oaks, "He Heals the Heavy Laden," *Liahona,* November 2006, pgs. 6–9).

Increasing Disasters

[4] "A new study confirms a long-held theory that large solar storms rain electrically charged particles down on Earth's atmosphere and deplete the upper-level ozone for weeks to months thereafter. Solar flares are explosions on the Sun that happen when energy stored in twisted magnetic fields (usually above sunspots) is suddenly released. When protons like these bombard the upper atmosphere, they break up molecules of gases like nitrogen and water vapor, and once freed, those atoms react with ozone molecules and reduce the layer" (NASA/Goddard Space Flight Center, "Solar Storms Destroy Ozone, Study Reconfirms," *ScienceDaily*. August 2, 2001, available online: http://www.sciencedaily.com/releases/2001/08/010802080620.htm).

"'If magnetic shielding is lower [over time], charged particles from the sun would penetrate deeper [into Earth's atmosphere] and create large holes in the ozone,' says John Tarduno, a scientist at the University of Rochester who studies physical forces on Earth. The ozone layer protects you from invisible energy waves called ultraviolet (UV) rays. Without it, radiation would zap your skin, causing increased cancer rates," (Karen Barrow, "Which Way is North? Beware: Earth's Natural Compass May be Turning Upside Down," *Science World*, March 7, 2005, available online: http://www.findarticles.com/p/articles/mi_m1590/is_11_61/ai_n13248415).

[5] "And men were *scorched with great heat*, and blasphemed the name of God, which hath power over these plagues: and they repented not to give him glory" (Revelation 16:9).

"In Fresno, the morgue is full of victims from a California heat wave. A combination of heat and power outages killed a dozen people in Missouri. And in parts of Europe, temperatures are hotter than in 2003 when a heat wave killed 35,000 people. Get used to it. ...The computer models show that soon, we'll get many more—and hotter—heat waves that will leave the old Dust Bowl records of the 1930s in the dust, said Ken Kunkel, director of the Center for Atmospheric Sciences at the Illinois State Water Survey" ("Scientists: Killer Heat Waves Tied to Global Warming" *Foxnews.com*, August 01, 2006, available online: http://www.foxnews.com/story/0,2933,206371,00.html).

[6] "For after your testimony cometh the *testimony of earthquakes*, that shall cause groanings in the midst of her, and men shall fall upon the ground and shall not be able to stand" (D&C 88:89).

According to the USGS Earthquake Hazards Program website statistics, the volume of earthquakes have been **increasing** consistently since the recording of earthquakes began by our government. However, the website claims these numbers might have increased because reporting of the occurrences have improved, not necessarily because of a true increase in earthquakes. The simple fact that USGS cannot prove or disprove a rate of increase due to suspected inconsistencies in their data collection practices, leads to the possibility that earthquakes are increasing, just as their data indicates. See http://earthquake.usgs.gov for statistics.

[7] "And all they who receive the oracles of God, let them beware how they hold them lest they are accounted as a light thing, and are brought under condemnation thereby, and stumble and fall when the storms descend, and the winds blow, and the rains descend, and beat upon their house" (D&C 90:5).

"About twice as many Atlantic hurricanes form each year on average than a century ago, according to a new statistical analysis of hurricanes and tropical storms in the north Atlantic. The study concludes that warmer sea surface temperatures (SSTs) and altered wind patterns associated with global climate change are fueling much of the increase" (National Center for Atmospheric Research, "Frequency Of Atlantic Hurricanes Doubled Over Last Century, Climate Change Suspected" *ScienceDaily*, August 1, 2007, available online: http://www.sciencedaily.com/releases/2007/07/070730092544.htm).

[8] "And also cometh the testimony of the voice of thunderings, and the voice of lightnings, and the voice of tempests, and the voice of the waves of the sea heaving themselves beyond their bounds" (D&C 88:90).

"The ocean is rising! The ocean is rising! It's a cry reminiscent of Chicken Little, who thought the sky was falling when an acorn hit him on the head. The important difference is the ocean *is* rising. Scientists estimate sea level is roughly four inches higher than it was 100 years ago, and satellite measurements show it going up one to three millimeters a year" (Aaron Sawdey, Matthew O'Keefe & Rainer Bleck, "The Design, Implementation, and Performance of a Parallel Ocean Circulation Model," This research is supported by the Office of Naval Research, the National Science Foundation, the Department of Energy and the U.S. Army. Available online: http://www.psc.edu/science/OKeefe/OKeefe.html).

[9] "Globally, rising seas threaten to submerge low-lying island groups, erode coastlines and force the construction of vast new levees. Some scientists have warned that melting of the vast glaciers of Greenland could cause a 13-foot rise in sea levels in coming centuries" ("China warns its coastal cities of rising seas" *MSNBC*, January 17, 2008, available online: http://www.msnbc.msn.com/id/22705628).

[10] "For not many days hence and the earth shall tremble and reel to and fro as a drunken man" (D&C 88:87).

"To make the Earth wobble, large amounts of mass need to be moved from one place to another so that the Earth is 'off balance,' according to NASA-funded researcher Blewitt, who said the North Pole then adjusts to a new position to compensate. Large amounts of water are displaced seasonally when glaciers and ice sheets melt in spring, for example. The mass shifts back when they refreeze in winter. 'We measured the earth's shape directly,' he said. 'It agrees with the wobble. What our measurements are showing is that everything is consistent—the earth is wobbling while it's changing its shape,' he said. 'The Earth isn't a perfect sphere,' Blewitt noted. 'It bulges at the equator because it's spinning'" (University Of Nevada, Reno, "Geophysicist Discovers Why Earth 'Wobbles,'" *ScienceDaily*, May 20, 2004, available online: http://www.sciencedaily.com/releases/2004/05/040520065656.htm).

[11] The day before this section was written a 5.7 earthquake occurred right off the coast of Oregon. Did you feel it? See the following address for other recent earthquakes:
http://earthquake.usgs.gov/eqcenter/recenteqsww/Quakes/us2008pqa5.php.

The largest earthquake has been a 9.5 in Chile in 1960.

[12] Most of the large cities in America were built in low lying areas near water sources. This potentially leaves them vulnerable to low elevation flooding, especially near the oceans. See elevation maps of the United States.

[13] According to the Environmental Protection Agency, the oceans have risen 6-8 inches in the last 100 years. In the next 90 years, it's predicted that they will rise approximately another 2-4 feet if the environment continues its present behavior. See

http://www.epa.gov/climatechange/effects/coastal/index.html for more discussion.

[14] To understand how the land may sink as the water rises, see NASA's PDF found at http://www.usc.edu/org/cosee-west/glaciers/Issealevelrising.pdf.

[15] The December 26th 2004 earthquake off the Indian Ocean was 9.1 leading to a tsunami up to 100 feet tall. See Wikipedia "2004 Indian Ocean Earthquake" for more details.

[16] The following are examples of how science is torn concerning the planet's warming.

"Simultaneous warming on Earth and Mars suggests that our planet's recent climate changes have a natural—and not a human-induced—cause, according to one scientist's controversial theory. Earth is currently experiencing rapid warming, which the vast majority of climate scientists says is due to humans pumping huge amounts of greenhouse gases into the atmosphere. Mars, too, appears to be enjoying more mild and balmy temperatures. In 2005 data from NASA's Mars Global Surveyor and Odyssey missions revealed that the carbon dioxide 'ice caps' near Mars's south pole had been diminishing for three summers in a row. Habibullo Abdussamatov, head of space research at St. Petersburg's Pulkovo Astronomical Observatory in Russia, says the Mars data is evidence that the current global warming on Earth is being caused by changes in the sun. 'The long-term increase in solar irradiance is heating both Earth and Mars,' he said. Abdussamatov believes that changes in the sun's heat output can account for almost all the climate changes we see on both planets. Mars and Earth, for instance, have experienced periodic ice ages throughout their histories. 'Man-made greenhouse warming has made a small contribution to the warming seen on Earth in recent years, but it cannot compete with the increase in solar irradiance,' Abdussamatov said" (Kate Ravilious, "Mars Melt Hints at Solar, Not Human, Cause for Warming, Scientist Says" *National Geographic News,*February 28, 2007, available online: http://news.nationalgeographic.com/news/2007/02/070228-mars-warming_2.html).

"'The public likes simple answers,' Pielke said. 'But there isn't any simple answer here.' Simplicity is hard to come by because Earth is a giant, complex heat-moving machine. ...The Earth does have natural cycles of cooling and warming-during the past 740,000 years there have been eight cycles with four ice ages. The cycles appear to be tied to slight variations in the tilt of the Earth toward the sun. During the last ice age-which ended about 10,000 years ago-Earth was on average about 4 degrees Fahrenheit cooler, and what is now Manhattan was buried under ice. At some point the Earth will wobble on its axis again, setting the stage for an ice age. There are other phenomena affecting global temperatures over time, such as El Niño, a Pacific Ocean warm-water mass that appears in roughly five-year cycles and changes world weather patterns. And there is the Atlantic thermohaline current, a conveyor belt moving heat north on the surface and then dropping it to the ocean floor and heading back to the equator-a 1,200-year trip. ...Many issues still have to be resolved, said Chris Folland, a researcher at Britain's Hadley Centre for Climate Prediction, but the science continues to point in one direction. 'We've shown that the climate change is a true thing,' he said. We've done that with global averages, since that was easiest 'The American government might not agree,' Folland said. Most American scientists do.'' (Mark Jaffe, "Global Warming?" *Denverpost.com*, December 26, 2006, available online: http://www.denverpost.com/news/ci_4387552).

[17] "The theory, known as true polar wander, postulates that if an object of sufficient weight--such as a supersized volcano--ever formed far from the equator, the force of the planet's rotation would gradually pull the heavy object away from the axis the Earth spins around. If the volcanoes, land and other masses that exist within the spinning Earth ever became sufficiently imbalanced, the planet would tilt and rotate itself until this extra weight was relocated to a point along the equator. ...True polar wander is different from the more familiar idea of 'continental drift,' which is the inchwise movement of individual continents relative to one another across the Earth's surface. Polar wander can tip the entire planet on its side at a rate of perhaps several meters per year, about 10 to 100 times as fast as the continents drift due to plate tectonics. Though the poles themselves would still point in the same direction with respect to the solar system, the process could conceivably shift entire continents from the tropics to the Arctic, or vice versa, within a relatively brief geological time span" ("Planet Earth may have 'tilted' to keep its balance, say scientists" *News at Princeton*, August 25, 2006, available online:

http://www.princeton.edu/main/news/archive/S15/64/72A37/index.xml?section=newsreleases).

[18] Water has massive weight. See end note #10 to understand how a tsunami can cause the earth to wobble as a huge wave of water courses across its face.

[19] This is a literary extrapolation of the data presented above and should be deemed as unproven. In theory, if the ice in the north melts, there will be less weight at one pole to keep the crust and the continents steady as it is presently. The crust would have to shift to adjust for the imbalance.

[20] If the crust of the earth were to shift, it would cause a global earthquake that might cause the "mountains and islands to be moved out of their places".

"And I beheld when he had opened the sixth seal, and, lo, there was a great earthquake; and the sun became black as sackcloth of hair, and the moon became as blood; And the stars of heaven fell unto the earth, even as a fig tree casteth her untimely figs, when she is shaken of a mighty wind. And the heaven departed as a scroll when it is rolled together; and every mountain and island were moved out of their places" (Revelation 6:12-14).

"And there were voices, and thunders, and lightnings; and there was a great earthquake, such as was not since men were upon the earth, so mighty an earthquake, *and* so great" (Revelation 16:18).

[21] This is a factual asteroid that is expected to have a near miss course with earth in 2029 and 2039. There's a 1 in 40,000 chance of collision in 2029 and a 1 in 5-10,000 chance of collision in 2039. NASA is actively working on strategies to adjust its orbit if needed. See http://neo.jpl.nasa.gov/risk/a99942.html for specific information.

Disinformation

[22] "...The same horn made war with the saints, and prevailed against them...And he shall speak *great* words against the most High, and shall wear out the saints of the most High, and think to change times and laws: and they shall be given into his hand until a time and times and the dividing of time" (Daniel 7:21, 25).

Lost, Now Found

[23] "...There will be millions on millions that will come much in the same way, only they will not have hand carts, for they will take their bundles under their arms, and their children on their backs, and under their arms, and flee; and Zion's people will have to send out relief to them, for they will come when the judgments come on the nation" (Heber C. Kimball, *Journal of Discourses,* September 28, 1856, Vol. 4, pg. 106).

"The day will come when the people of the United States will come lugging their bundles under their arms, coming to us for bread to eat" (Heber C. Kimball, *Journal of Discourses*, July 5, 1857, Vol. 5, pg. 10).

[24] "We do have a prophet, a living prophet, who presides in this church and who teaches the will of the Lord. ...Could any people have a greater blessing than to have standing at their head one who receives and teaches the will of God concerning them? ...'Surely the Lord God will do nothing, but he revealeth his secret unto his servants the prophets.' (Amos 3:7) It was so in the days of Amos and in all the years when men of God spake as they were moved upon by the Holy Ghost. (See 2 peter 1:21.) Those ancient prophets not only warned of things to come but, more important, became the revealers of truth to people. It was they who pointed the way men should live if they were to be happy and find peace in their lives" (Gordon B. Hinckley, "'We Thank Thee, O God, for a Prophet'," *Ensign*, September 1991, pg. 2).

[25] "The Bible Dictionary states that Apostle means '"one sent forth." ...The calling of an apostle is to be a special witness of the name of Jesus Christ in all the world, particularly of his divinity and of his bodily resurrection from the dead. ...Twelve men with this high calling constitute an administrative council in the work of the ministry. ...Today twelve men with this same divine calling and ordination constitute the Quorum of the Twelve Apostles in The Church of Jesus Christ of Latter-day Saints' ('Apostle,' 612). An Apostle today continues to be 'one sent forth.' ...[Christ] instructed His called

Twelve to 'go ye therefore, and teach all nations, baptizing them in the name of the Father, and of the Son, and of the Holy Ghost: teaching them to observe all things whatsoever I have commanded you: and, lo, I am with you always, even unto the end of the world' (Matthew 28:19–20)" (L. Tom Perry, "What Is a Quorum?" *Liahona,* November 2004, pgs. 23–26).

[26] "We know not all that lies ahead of us. We live in a world of uncertainty. For some, there will be great accomplishment. For others, disappointment. For some, much of rejoicing and gladness, good health, and gracious living. For others, perhaps sickness and a measure of sorrow. We do not know. But one thing we do know. Like the Polar Star in the heavens, regardless of what the future holds, there stands the Redeemer of the world, the Son of God, certain and sure as the anchor of our immortal lives. He is the rock of our salvation, our strength, our comfort, the very focus of our faith. In sunshine and in shadow we look to Him, and He is there to assure and smile upon us. He is the central focus of our worship. He is the Son of the living God, the Firstborn of the Father, the Only Begotten in the flesh. He is 'risen from the dead, …the first fruits of them that slept' (1 Corinthians 15:20). He is the Lord who shall come again 'to reign on the earth over his people' (D&C 76:63; see also Micah 4:7, Revelation 11:15). None so great has ever walked the earth. None other has made a comparable sacrifice or granted a comparable blessing. He is the Savior and the Redeemer of the world. I believe in Him. I declare His divinity without equivocation or compromise. I love Him. I speak the name of Jesus Christ in reverence and wonder. He is our King, our Lord, our Master, the living Christ, who stands on the right hand of His Father. He lives! He lives, resplendent and wonderful, the living Son of the living God" (Gordon B. Hinckley, "We Testify of Jesus Christ," *Liahona*, Mar 2008, pgs. 4–7).

[27] "We encourage Church members worldwide to prepare for adversity in life by having a basic supply of food and water and some money in savings. We ask that you be wise as you store food and water and build your savings. Do not go to extremes; it is not prudent, for example, to go into debt to establish your food storage all at once. With careful planning, you can, over time, establish a home storage supply and a financial reserve" (The First Presidency, *All Is Safely Gathered In: Family Home Storage,* February 2007, pg. 1).

[28] "As we consider the role of prophets, it is vital to understand that, first, prophets are called of God and He testifies to the world of their calling. ...Second, the role of prophets is to teach of Christ and testify of His divinity and His mission. ...The third characteristic of prophets is that their teachings are recorded and are taught by succeeding prophets and teachers to the inhabitants of the earth. ...The Lord's living prophets today have given an equally compelling testimony...At their very core, the doctrines of The Church of Jesus Christ of Latter-day Saints are intended to convey to the soul of every sincere person who will ask of God in faith a personal testimony of our Lord and Savior and the role of the prophets from the dawn of time to this very moment. I testify that the succession of prophets has continued from Joseph Smith, the first prophet of this dispensation, to Gordon B. Hinckley, the Lord's prophet today. Of that I bear my witness and testimony. In the name of Jesus Christ, amen" (Shirley D. Christensen, "The Clarion Call of Prophets," *Liahona*, Nov 2003, pgs. 32–34).

[29] "What I the Lord have spoken, I have spoken, and I excuse not myself; and though the heavens and the earth pass away, my word shall not pass away, but shall all be fulfilled, whether by mine own voice or by the voice of my servants, it is the same" (D&C 1:38).

[30] "For behold, a bitter fountain cannot bring forth good water; neither can a good fountain bring forth bitter water; wherefore, a man being a servant of the devil cannot follow Christ; and if he follow Christ he cannot be a servant of the devil. ...But whatsoever thing persuadeth men to do evil, and believe not in Christ, and deny him, and serve not God, then ye may know with a perfect knowledge it is of the devil; for after this manner doth the devil work, for he persuadeth no man to do good, no, not one; neither do his angels; neither do they who subject themselves unto him" (Moroni 7:11, 17).

[31] "...The time will come when there will be no safety in carrying on the peaceable pursuits of farming or agriculture. But these will be neglected, and the people will think themselves well off if they can flee from city to city, from town to town and escape with their lives. Thus will the Lord visit the people, if they will not repent. Thus will He pour out His wrath and indignation upon them..." (Orson Pratt, *Journal of Discourses*, December 27, 1868, Vol. 12, pg. 344).

[32] " '...Come home; I will now preach my own sermons to the nations of the earth,' all you now know can scarcely be called a preface to the sermon that will be preached with fire and sword, tempests, earthquakes, hail, rain, thunders and lightnings, and fearful destruction. What matters the destruction of a few railway cars? You will hear of magnificent cities, now idolized by the people, sinking in the earth, entombing the inhabitants. The sea will heave itself beyond its bounds, engulfing mighty cities. Famine will spread over the nations, and nation will rise up against nation, kingdom against kingdom, and states against states, in our own country and in foreign lands" (Brigham Young, *Journal of Discourses*, July 15, 1860, Vol. 8, pg. 123).

[33] "...Then shall there be a fleeing from one city to another, from one State to another, from one part of the continent to another, seeking refuge, from the devastations of bandits and armies..." (Orson Pratt, *Millennial Star*, October 6, 1866, Vol. 28, pgs. 633-634).

[34] "...Then shall their dead be left unburied, and the fowls of heaven shall summer upon them, and the beasts of the earth shall winter upon them. Moreover, the Lord will visit them with the deadly pestilence which shall sweep away many millions by its ravages" (Orson Pratt, *Millennial Star*, October 6, 1866, Vol. 28, pgs. 633-634).

[35] "What then will be the condition of that people, when this great and terrible war shall come? It will be very different from the war between the North and the South. Do you wish me to describe it? I will do so. It will be a war of neighborhood against neighborhood, city against city, county against county, state against state, and they will go forth destroying and being destroyed, and manufacturing, will, in a great measure, cease, for a time, among the American nation. Why? Because in these terrible wars, they will not be privileged to manufacture; there will be too much blood-shed-too much mobocracy-too much going forth in bands and destroying and pillaging the land to suffer people to pursue any local vocation with any degree of safety. What will become of millions of the farmers upon that land? They will leave their farms and they will flee before the ravaging armies from place to place; and thus will they go forth burning and pillaging the whole country; and that great and powerful nation, now consisting of some forty millions of people, will be wasted away, unless they repent" (Orson Pratt, *Journal of Discourses*, March 9, 1879, Vol. 20, pg. 151).

[36] "For instance the great and populous city of New York, that may be considered one of the greatest cities of the world, will in a few years become a mass of ruins. The people will wonder while gazing on the ruins that cost hundreds of millions to build, what has become of its inhabitants. Their houses will be there, but they will be left desolate. So saith the Lord God. That will be only a sample of numerous other towns and cities on the face of this continent" (Orson Pratt, *Journal of Discourses*, December 27, 1868, Vol. 12, pg. 344).

[37] " 'They shall have mobbings to their hearts' content, if they do not redress the wrongs of the Latter-day Saints.' Mobs will not decrease but will increase until the whole government becomes a mob, and eventually it will be State against State, city against city, neighborhood against neighborhood, Methodists against Methodists, and so on" (Brigham Young, *Deseret News,* May 1, 1861, Vol. 9, pg. 2).

[38] "I warn future historians to give credence to my history; for my testimony is true, and the truth of its record will be manifest in the world to come. All the words of the Lord will be fulfilled upon the nations, which are written in this book. The American nation will be broken in pieces like a potter's vessel, and will be cast down to hell if it does not repent-and this, because of murders, whoredoms, wickedness and all manner of abominations, for the Lord has spoken it" (Matthias F. Cowley, Wilford Woodruff, *History of His Life and Labors,* pg. 500).

[39] "There will be here and there a Stake (of Zion) for the gathering of the Saints. Some may have cried peace, but the Saints and the world will have little peace from henceforth. Let this not hinder us from going to the Stakes; for God has told us to flee, not dallying, or we shall be scattered, one here, and another there. There your children shall be blessed, and you in the midst of friends where you may be blessed. The Gospel net gathers of every kind" See D&C 45:65-67" (Joseph Smith, *DHC*, July 2, 1839, Vol. 3, pg. 390).

CHAPTER TWELVE

TIME AND THE DIVIDING OF TIME

"And when the dragon saw that he was cast unto the earth, he persecuted the woman which brought forth the man child" (Revelation 12:13).

00:01:10, 16:48:55, Zulu
Thursday, November 20th

Gun Shot

Provo, Utah
12:12 a.m.

With a firm jerk, Brea pulled the hydraulic lever that would open the grass-covered door of the tunnel leading to the outside. Slowly, the hatch opened, and cool, fall air poured in.

Brea took a deep breath of the freshness, just as recognition filtered through her. She had been here before.

"OK, this is that dream again," she said to herself, recognizing the sights and sounds she was experiencing. "What is the deal? Am I supposed to be learning something?" she asked heaven-ward.

No obvious answer came to her mind. She meditated, searching for knowledge. Finally, after losing patience, she pivoted and attempted to return underground. Maybe she could end the dream and avoid the unpleasantness that she knew would come later if she continued.

The moment Brea's foot touched the floor she was whisked out of her home and across the street. With a sigh, she pulled the hood of her cloak over her head and wrapped the rest around her body. It was obvious she was meant to experience whatever the next moments would bring her, so she'd be patient.

Leaning against the log corner of her parent's home, Brea watched the dream unfold exactly as she remembered it. There were the evil spirits, the mob, and Brother Reiser. Now, she was approaching the moments where either she ran behind the house, or ran out in front of it. Neither of those choices seemed right. Both times the evil spirits found her and either verbally or physically assaulted her. She wondered what should she do *this* time? Maybe she'd just watch and see what would happen if she didn't do anything.

Suddenly, Brother Reiser threw his large stone at her parent's window, shattering it.

Brea could hear the babies crying inside and her mother's voice trying to comfort them.

Brea's heart twisted. Standing and doing nothing was very hard. She was used to solving problems. To avoid the temptation to do something else stupid, she tried to close her eyes to block out what was happening, but to her dismay, even with her eyes closed, she could see. "This is a stupid dream!" she found herself saying in frustration.

"Tom! I've had enough!" yelled a man's voice. It was her father.

Brea couldn't help herself now. She peeked around the corner of the home to see her father pounding down the porch stairs with a shot gun cocked in his hands. He wasn't even finished with the last step when an explosion came from the mob. It pealed through the air and echoed off the surrounding mountains.

Brea jumped with surprise.

Bo collapsed on the stairs of her home.

"No!!!!!" she yelled and ran from the bush. "Why did you come out? You were being protect…"

In the next moment she was bound by evil, as before. Her mother rushed from the house, this time to find both her husband and Brea collapsed in the front of the house, a look of helplessness on her face.

It was too much.

"Ahhhhh!" Brea screamed, as she sat up in bed with sweat pouring off her face. *"Stop it! Stop it! Stop it!"* she yelled with deep, gasping breaths. "I can't stand these dreams!" she said, starting to cry. "Make them stop!" she pleaded into the night.

Starvation

Far East, Russia
4:40 p.m.

Braun cut the last piece of reindeer meat and handed half of it to Chenille.

With tears in her eyes, she took the piece and chewed slowly.

Braun looked at the lean piece and his heart ached. This was their faithful animal that had pulled their sleigh across hundreds of miles of snow, but now because the herds were completely depleted, this animal was their last source of food.

Braun remembered the moment that he had to kill his reindeer. The buck seemed to look at him with knowing, kind eyes. He had nuzzled Braun and then patiently waited for the knife. Because of that, it seemed like he had offered himself willingly so Braun and Chenille could live. With these memories, partaking of his flesh meant something different.

Braun felt nauseous. He couldn't believe it had come to this. John told them that they were still three days from the ocean. Three days? Would they have enough energy to pull the sleigh themselves for three more days?

Looking at Chenille, Braun said, "I think we should simplify our sleigh."

Chenille stared at her hands and nodded. "I was thinking the same thing."

"We should make an uncomplicated, minature sleigh and only take with us a few furs and supplies, enough to help us with shelter at night, and leave the rest for anyone else who might need them. There are more trees around now, so we can use their branches and the furs to protect us from the snow at night."

Chenille nodded again. "Three days isn't that long to live like that. I can do it."

Braun leaned over and kissed Chenille's forehead. "Thank you for being so…so…" He was at a loss for words. Then he knew the perfect word; it was patient. She was the perfect example of Christ-like patience as she endured her afflictions.[1] He was a blessed man to have such a wonderful wife. "...Patient," he finished his sentence. "Thank you for being so patient."

Chenille smiled at Braun and nodded, giving him a kiss on the cheek. "We can sleep in our Choom tonight though, can't we?"

Braun nodded, feeling the food begin to strengthen his body. "Of course. I'll set it up this minute," he said, as he stood to get to work.

"Braun?"

"Yes?" asked Braun, looking down at his beautiful bride, pausing in his work for a moment.

"The Lord *will* provide, won't he?" asked Chenille, with hope in her eyes.

Braun squatted down and put a kind hand on Chenille's cheek. "Of course he will. He has said it, so it will be done."[2]

"Good," said Chenille, as she stood to help Braun. "I just wanted to hear you say those words. Now I'm good."

Braun nodded once as his heart poured out in silent weeping. He prayed to his Heavenly Father that he might see their hunger and have mercy on them.

United

Provo, Utah
3:10 a.m.

Brea was flying in a flowing white nightgown. She soared up through the clouds as if she were lighter than air. It felt so good to fly. She was very happy.

Brea scanned the ground below her. She was flying over her neighborhood. There was Sister Vance's house, and Sister Browne's. There was her parent's log home, but it was dark. Did that mean no one was home? She didn't know, but she'd find out.

Next she flew over Old Man Griffin's little farm. There were tents all over his hay field. Small lamps burned brightly near each one, making a festive design in the night. Brea noticed, as she floated above the little tent city, that there was also a white hue that rested upon them. She recognized that the light was the protection of the Spirit as the people lived in peace.[3] She smiled. The feeling over his farm was so gentle and accepting. She had a desire to be down there among her friends and neighbors.

Coming down out of the sky, she gently landed on the street corner across from her parent's house. The ground was not cold or rough despite her bare feet. It seemed she wasn't in her body in this dream. How odd.

Looking across the street, she noticed Brother Reiser standing in the street with a rock in his hand, just as she had seen over and over again in her other dreams. She also saw the three evil spirits moving about him almost as if they were dancing.

Next, she saw the angry mob approach from down the street. Brea studied Brother Reiser. He was looking around as if he didn't know what to do next. He kept peering over at old man Griffin's place. Brea looked behind her. What was there that he was interested in? Then it dawned on her. Her family *wasn't* home! She bet they were at the farm.

Brea watched the angry group congregate in front of her home. The evil spirits among them appeared and disappeared, flying from person to person, reminding her of flickering fire-flies as they worked to incite the mob to a murderous fervor.[4]

"Bo Rogers is not here," said Brother Reiser to his angry neighbors.

"Maybe he's at Old Man Griffin's house," said a person out of the crowd.

"Let's get him!" yelled another.

"Yes, go get him," said the old female evil spirit, clapping and laughing.

"He can't hide from you," said the boy.

"He can't hide! We'll find him!" said another person in the crowd, obviously influenced by the evil voices.

In anger, the mob moved down the street and around the corner to the Griffin farm.

Then Brea saw a beautiful sight. Two huge guardian warrior spirits brandished their swords at the entrance to Mr. Griffin's hedge leading to the inside of the farm. She noticed there were other white beings this time hovering in the air, each also wearing armor and wielding swords. Their presence pleased her.

Brea watched the neighbors approach but as they did, she noticed the evil spirits disappeared one by one until all three were gone. Obviously, this celestial army was too much for the wicked.

As the mob came closer, it seemed that their resolve weakened, too. Brother Reiser stood a few feet ahead of the mob, alone. "Bring out Bishop Rogers!" he yelled into the darkness, as he stood on the threshold of the little tent city. "You can't hide him!"

From around the tall cement wall appeared a group of about fifty men, accompanied by Dane, who had something flat and circular in his hand and wearing glasses. Each of them was surrounded by the same white hue that emanated from the little city. None of the other men were carrying weapons.

"What do you want?" called a man Brea didn't know.

"I want the bishop. He is responsible for the death of my wife."

"Is he?" asked Dane. "Or are you?"

Brother Reiser swallowed and looked from man to man. Looking back at the mob who were now more subdued, he said, "I asked a simple thing. I asked for a blessing of health and he wouldn't give it to her. She died. There's some accountability required here."

"Accountability is not what's required. Understanding is," said Dane. "The Priesthood only heals those who are not sealed to die.[5] It's no fault of any man that your wife did not live."

"I don't agree," said Brother Reiser.

"It doesn't matter. God decides who to save, not the bishop. Go home, Brother Reiser. You don't want a fight tonight," said Dane. "You won't win. There's far too many of us here."

Brother Reiser sized up the men who stood with Dane and then looked behind him, as if to compare strength. Returning his gaze, he said, "So you're united on this?"[6] he asked the men from the tent city. He glanced once again behind him at the mob that was growing smaller as people began to drift away.

Most of the men who were standing guard against the mob nodded.

"We're united," said Dane. "Now go home."

Finally Brother Reiser nodded as he retreated. "OK, maybe not tonight, but that doesn't mean this is over." Then he turned and walked home.

Brea was astonished. What a different outcome of this dream than the previous ones! What was the difference? The number of people? The circumstance? The absence of the evil spirits? It was obvious that there was power among the people who lived on Old Man Griffin's land in unity and righteousness.[7] It was beautiful.

Brea smiled as she settled into a satisfying, deep sleep. Peace had come to her. Somehow she knew that now, the dreams would stop.

Zulu

Provo, Utah
10:23 a.m.

Corrynne searched through some old files in her bedroom. It was time to purge. Looking at the tabs, she said, "No need for insurance papers—they're all out of business. No need for US stamps—the UN won't honor them. No use for income statements, bank statements, or stock-earning statements—all from another era, serving no purpose now, and only making me depressed...." she said to herself, as she took the whole group of files, and dumped them in the trash. She went back for another load, when her eyes fell on a tab entitled, "Zulu."

Corrynne stared at the writing. It was written in large, black, deliberate handwriting—her handwriting. She had written it that way so she would remember it. At one time she had felt that word was more important than most others. "Zulu," according to Imam Mahdi, had pinpointed the exact moment fire was to rain down from heaven, punishing the United States for their arrogance. But now...now that America had imploded before Zulu 00:00:00 had occurred...

"I'm taking the kids out for a walk," said Louise from the bedroom door, interrupting Corrynne's thoughts.

Startled, Corrynne jumped and looked up from her sitting position on the floor.

"They're bouncing off the walls," finished Louise.

Corrynne smiled and nodded, recovering. "Sounds like a great plan."

"Do you want to come?" asked Louise. "I don't want you to feel left out."

Corrynne shook her head. "I don't feel left out. I want to get some things done this afternoon—unless you need me to come."

Louise shook her head. "No, I have this one covered. Nebraska and Rebecca want to take the twins and play with them at the park. It will be fun."

"Is Caroline going with you?"

"She's busy sewing some curtains for Old Man Griffin in lieu of rent."

"I see," said Corrynne, nodding. "Great idea. Mr. Griffin has a heart of gold."

"Yes, he does," said Louise.

"You sure you don't need help?"

Louise shook her head with a look of pure joy. "Are you kidding? I've been looking forward to the day I can just languish out at a park watching innocent children play for years! Never thought it would happen to me, so just walking out your door, in total freedom, listening to the laughter of innocent children, is a dream come true."

Corrynne laughed. "Well, then, I don't want to smash your dreams! Have at it!"

"Thanks!"

"You're welcome," said Corrynne.

Just before Louise left, she winked, pointed, and said, "Don't work too hard. Take it from me, life's too short."

"Never!" said Corrynne, joking. She waved as Louise left the doorway.

Taking a deep breath, Corrynne returned her attention to the file in her hands. Once again she thumbed through its contents, only this time she stopped when she noticed a piece of paper with a group of numbers written on it, again in her handwriting. She had written them down on the day she had discovered Zulu time. They were 01:03:05, 02:30:20. Next to it she had scrawled 2:30 p.m.

Corrynne looked up and narrowed her eyes as she tried to remember what it had all meant. She recalled the numbers referred to time beginning with the year, month and day for the first set, and then hour, minutes and seconds for the second set. However they did not move forward, they moved backwards. It was a countdown, to...when? Corrynne flipped the pages in her file to review.

She saw a city name that caught her attention. It was Greenwich, England. Corrynne remembered that Greenwich was located at the "zero meridian of the world" and that all other time zones were figured from the time kept in that city, named by a reverse alphabet system.[8] Utah was in the T zone, as she remembered, T for "tango." She scanned the page to double-check her memory. She had been right on every count.

"So..." said Corrynne as she concentrated, "The countdown refers to England's time, thus once the numbers run out, all flipping to zero—it would be midnight in England, not Utah." Corrynne looked up from her file. What was the time difference between England and Utah?

Corrynne thumbed through the pages in her file to see if she had written it down anywhere. She couldn't find it. She frowned as she tried to remember off the top of her head, but her thoughts were all jumbled. She decided instead to figure it out.

Well, if England is at the Z zone and Utah is in the T zone...U, V, W, X, Y, Z, she stated in her mind, counting each letter. There are seven letters between Z and T. That must mean there are seven time zones, or seven hours between England and Utah. If that's true, then—Corrynne looked at her watch. "It's ten in the morning here, so that means it's five p.m. there," She said out loud. "That being true, then, when it's zero time, or midnight in England, it should be...five p.m. here," she said, feeling a bit impressed with herself. "Yes, that's right! A seven hour difference would make it five in the afternoon." she said, remembering now that her mind had been stimulated. "The Zulu date was scheduled to run out at *zero* time on the *zero* day of the year, which would be New Year's Eve, the last day of the year, at *midnight*!"

Corrynne was smiling, but then she wondered at herself. Why was she smiling? The clock running out was not a good thing. Bad things were scheduled to happen then...or were they?

Quickly, Corrynne grabbed a pencil that was lying near her on the floor. She started scribbling the date and time and trying to figure out what Zulu time would be now. "It's November 20th in the zero year. The first two digits would be 00. There's only one month left of this year, so the second set would be 01, and there's 30 days in this month, so the last two digits would be 10 for ten days remaining in the month. 00:01:10," she said, looking at her numbers. "One month and ten days until..."

Corrynne's pencil hovered in the air. Then she started scribbling again, continuing her calculations, but now of time. "It's 10:30 a.m. that would mean it's 5:30 now in England. There are 24 hours in a day, there are only six and a half left today in England. Therefore, the first set of numbers in the time set would be 06, the second set would be 30 and the last set would refer to seconds, which are..." Corrynne looked at her watch and it said 23 seconds. Subtracting 23 from 60 she wrote the final number. "Zulu time, right now, is "06:30:37" said Corrynne, finishing her writing and making a period.

"Hmmm," said Corrynne, as she wondered what all this meant. "So in one month, ten days, six hours, thirty minutes and thirty-seven seconds, something—might happen."

A vision returned to Corrynne of Imam Mahdi. She remembered his angry predictions. He'd call fire down from heaven[9] to destroy society, so it could then be rebuilt. Those with the chips would be protected...then Corrynne realized that that was sort of what was happening now. Fire came out of heaven in the form of digital energy that wiped the banks clean. Their society had been broken down and now was in the process of being rebuilt by the UN. Ironically, or maybe *not so ironically*, those with the chips were being taken care of. She wondered if there was a connection. Was the same script being followed? Was the original plan being fulfilled? Or did it go deeper than that? Maybe the common thread between the two plans wasn't Imam Mahdi like she had thought, but Satan himself?[10] So what if MD jumped the gun in bringing about America's downfall? The end result, Satan's victory, was the same.

Corrynne could feel her heart beating fast as she swallowed. "Fire, blood, destruction, terror…beasts acting together…break down to build up…." It all was occurring now, not in the future, not in a month, but now. The world was being reshaped *now*.

So, then...what was going to happen when Zulu reached zero? Anything? ...She hoped not.

Corrynne closed her eyes as she shook her head. She hoped not....

Fateful Plans

Frankfurt, Germany
6:35 p.m.

"It won't be long," said MD, with a fresh cigar hanging out of his mouth. "As long as the world hangs together, it won't be long." He tied a big bow on a blue box meant for the new infant Daimler scheduled to arrive soon.

"No, it won't," said Matt. He glanced at his father and then returned his gaze to the window and the rolling lawn outside the mansion in Germany. He was being mocked. Always, being mocked...

"Have you been in contact with Brea?" asked MD with a sly smile. He blew a cloud of smoke from his lungs as he looked at Matt out of the corner of his eye.

Matt shook his head. He hadn't—not that he didn't want to talk to the love of his life, but he hadn't figured out how to do it safely. He couldn't do it by voice, and with no hands…

"Have you?" demanded MD, with his beady eyes boring into Matt.

"No, I haven't," said Matt calmly. "But then, you knew that."

MD chuckled. "Yes, I did. I did, I did," he said as he put his cigar down in the ashtray and continued to fuss with the ends of the bow. "And I might say, that makes me very happy." MD let out an uncharacteristic giggle. "You've done well."

MD's strange noise caused Matt to turn and look at his father and the box he was gaining so much pleasure wrapping. This present was for his and Brea's son, but his parents would raise him as his brother, unless….

"It's time to contact the woman," said MD "You need to work out the details of her delivery. Make sure there's no funny business."

"That '*woman*' is my wife," said Matt, the anger for his father's disrespect was instant.

"No, she's not. She's *not* your wife," said MD, eyeing Matt. "You took care of that divorce, correct?"

Matt turned back to the window and shook his head in pent-up anger. "Yes, I did."

"Then, I repeat. She is *not* your wife; in fact she's nothing to you. We used her as a tool to create an heir for me and nothing more." MD waited for a reply from Matt.

Matt refused to give his father the satisfaction he was seeking. He stayed silent and unengaged.

"Do you understand?" asked MD pointedly.

"Yes," said Matt, continuing to stare outside.

"Good. That woman has fulfilled her role and now it's time to collect the infant and be done with her forever. Agreed?" asked MD, picking up his cigar again and defiantly, boldly standing with his belly and chest puffed out.

"Agreed," said Matt. "As long as you stick with your end of the bargain."

"What was that exactly?" asked MD with a hidden smile.

Matt looked at his father with disdain, and shook his head again. "You know what that agreement was."

"Oh yes, that I would let her disappear into oblivion."

"That you would never seek her out or threaten her," said Matt with a cold stare, enough to let his father know he meant what he said, but not enough to get him in trouble. "You'd let her live in peace."

"I'm just playing with you, son," said MD, with a laugh and a pat on the back. "Have a little sense of humor," then with seriousness, he said, "and if you don't, *all deals are off.*"

Matt slowly nodded his head. "I'll try to be more jovial."

"Good," said MD. Picking up the package and putting it under the Christmas tree, he said, "So how have you set up communication?"

"I haven't."

"Does the girl have a cell phone?"

"No," said Matt.

"Does she have a land line?"

"No."

"A computer?"

"No."

"Then what? What's your plan?" asked MD.

"I'll just go to her."

"That could be dangerous," said MD, as he held his cigar between his fingers.

"It's the only option," said Matt. "I'll bring my own son back to Germany."

"My son," corrected MD.

"Your son," said Matt, painfully. "That's the only way I can assure safe passage. But you aren't to follow me. You'll have to turn off the tracking and recording functions in my chip."

MD studied Matt. "You drive a steep bargain...I don't know."

Matt didn't reply but just waited. Again, more toying....

"You know I don't have good self-control," said MD, shaking his head. "The temptation will be too hard to ignore."

"You can do it," said Matt. "Do it or I'll disappear with the child and his mother."

"You can't."

"There's always a way. You know that and you know I know that. Don't try me. I'll know if you trace me."

"Oh, alright," said MD. "You're no fun."

"I'll need one of your radar-invisible company jets."

"Fine."

"I'll also need a body cloak."

"OK."

"And if I find out you so much as peeked at your computer, I'm gone, and so is my child."

"You've got a deal," said MD smiling. "I like how you just laid it on the line. See, this divorce has already been good for you. You're growing a spine!"

"I'll leave New Year's Eve," said Matt, massaging his forearms. He was having phantom pain.

"I'll put it on my calendar," said MD.

Foreclosure

Provo, Utah
3:40 p.m.

Knock, knock, knock.

Nebraska answered.

"Is your Daddy home?" asked the man at the door.

Nebraska shook her head.

"Is your Mommy home?"

Nebraska shook her head.

"Who's home with you?"

Nebraska didn't answer but stared blankly out the door.

"She's not our sister," said Jax. "She just lives in our house."

Bo reached over Nebraska and opened the door wider. Relieved of any responsibility, Nebraska slipped off down the hall. At the door, Bo's three sons, Jax, Ry, and Roc were standing with an official-looking man. "May I help you?" he asked, in an intimidating tone. He could tell he wasn't going to like this conversation.

"Mr. Rogers?"

"Yes?" asked Bo. "What's going on?"

"I'm the Superintendent of the Provo School District. I'm afraid your children cannot attend our schools any longer."

Bo frowned and studied the school official. "What's this about?"

"The fact of the matter is that we cannot financially support children who are not funded by the UN. Since our schools are not run by tax money any longer..."

Bo nodded. He wasn't going to get mad. He had thought this day was coming. His sons were getting into an unusual amount of trouble lately. He had felt intolerance growing for those who hadn't taken the chip. He held out his hand to his sons. "Come in, boys," he said, without arguing.

Jax, Ry, and Roc moved passed Bo and into the house.

"I'm sorry, Mr. Rogers..." began the man, with his hands out to his sides.

Bo nodded and closed the door.

"Take off your coats, boys," said Bo.

"What are we going to do, Dad?" asked Jax, with anger in his eyes.

"Whatever it takes."

"Do you know lies are being told about us on those UN video devices? They say we're terrorists. It's been going on for a while. I think that's why we're being kicked out of school."

Bo shook his head. "It might be. Let's not worry about that now."

"Is it true?" asked Jax, stubbornly. "I told them it wasn't true, but people don't believe me."

"No. It's not," said Bo, slicing the air with his hand. Gathering his patience, Bo continued in a calm tone. "I can't speak for people in other parts of the nation, or for other religions, but I can speak for us here. We're good people. We care only for truth, righteousness, and freedom. We'd never kill innocent people, *ever*."[11]

"I know, but..." said Jax.

There was a pounding at the door. It was so loud it shook the walls and the windows.

"I'll answer it," said Dane, who had just come into the room. "You look like you need a break, Dad."

Bo nodded. "Thanks, Dane," then turning back to Jax he said, "We'll talk more later, but I want you to look inside yourself for the truth. There are a lot of people in this world who do strange things because they *think* they're on the right side. Suicide bombers are some of them. We, as true Christians, do not bomb innocent people, because we know that's wrong under every circumstance."

The banging repeated.

"I'm coming," Dane called, waiting a moment for his father to finish.

"Things in the near future are going to get confusing, son. We were told that there would come a day when bad would seem good and good would seem bad.[12] Well, that day is here. The people who run the UN are manipulating our fears and our perceptions. It's going to get confusing, but our job is to hold fast to the iron rod, so we aren't led astray into the mists of darkness.[13] If you're ever confused, just ask yourself, 'What would Christ do?' You'll never be led astray if you do that."[14]

"OK," said Jax, as he nodded thoughtfully, then left the room.

The heavy rapping started for the third time.

Dane opened the door.

"Is your father home?" Brother Reiser asked.

Bo looked through the opening in the door and saw his neighbor was red-faced and sweating. He had a white piece of paper in his hand, which he promptly shook and unfolded to display.

"What's that?" asked Dane looking closely at the writing.

"It's a foreclosure notice."

Dane looked confused. "A foreclosure notice?"

"Yes! Did your parents receive one of these?" he asked, shaking the note.

Dane shook his head, not knowing quite what to say. "I'm sorry, I don't know. If they did," he said, as he looked back at his father, "I didn't hear about it."

"What's going on here?" asked Bo, coming up behind his son and placing a hand on his shoulder.

"Bishop!" barked Brother Reiser, as he shook the notice. "You've ruined my life! If I hadn't listened to your psycho-babble about computer chips and *death*, I'd still have a house."

Bo frowned. With a hand up he said, "Now hold your horses, Tom. I think you're jumping to conclusions."

"*No—I'm—not.* I have one month to pay up my back payments for my mortgage, or I'm out on the street. *How do you feel about that?*" he asked. There was so much anger in his face, that Bo wouldn't have been surprised if he took a swing at him.

With authority in his voice, Dane commanded. "Stand back and calm down."

"Don't tell me what to do, *pipsqueak*!" yelled Brother Reiser, pushing Dane away from him.

Dane patiently returned to his defensive stance, close enough to protect his father if it came to that.

"I'm mad! I'm losing my house that's worth three-quarters of a mil," said Brother Reiser.

"Calm down," repeated Bo.

"*No!* I'm not going to calm down!"

Dane moved closer in response.

Bo put a gentle hand on his son's chest. "It's OK, Dane," said Bo, noticing the look in his neighbor's eye. This man was close to losing it. That only meant one thing: danger. In an effort to diffuse the situation, he continued, "I'm sure Brother Reiser didn't come here to assault me, did you, Tom?"

"Dad, I wouldn't put it past him. He's pretty angry," Dane said quietly.

"You're dang right I'm angry!" shouted Brother Reiser. "How am I going to pay this mortgage? It's over forty thousand in back payments. Are you going to pay it for me? Huh?" asked Brother Reiser, taking another threatening step towards Bo. *"Huh? Answer me!"*

"Back down!" commanded Dane again, now standing between Bo and Brother Reiser.

"No. I'm not going to pay it for you," said Bo, calmly over Dane's shoulder.

Brother Reiser looked at Bo with disbelief. He looked at his notice and then back again. "Did you say—*no*?"

"Yes, Brother. I said 'no.' The Church doesn't have that kind of money. You're going to have to move out and in with someone else in the ward. I'm sure we can find…"

"I will not lose my house!" screamed Brother Reiser, as he ripped apart the notice and threw it in their faces. Then attempting to shove Dane aside, he tried to put a finger in Bo's chest, but Dane barely shifted and continued to shield his father.

Brother Reiser stepped back and looked Dane up and down.

Dane stood firm.

"It's OK," said Bo in a whisper. "I want to talk to this guy."

Dane cautiously stepped aside.

With a finger still pointed, Brother Reiser said, "I was in the business of racing boats! I have three national championships and ten regional championships. I own six boats and two companies. I'm a multi-millionaire and no one, I mean, *no one* will take away my house!"

In a calm voice, Bo said, "It is not my fault your priorities have been in the wrong places."

"Wrong places?" asked Brother Reiser, his face turning red. "*Wrong places?* I'm a work horse! I'm the goose that lays the golden egg. I bring home the money! What are you talking about?"

Bo nodded, "Yes, but where is all this success? You have nothing to show for it. You didn't store food as the prophet suggested. You didn't lay up money for a rainy day, and now you're in trouble and blaming everyone else for it..."

"You want to know where my money is? It's in stocks, CD's, properties, assets..."

"Yes, but can you eat your stocks, and CDs? Can you drink your championships?"

"You *conceited, power-hungry...*" fumed Brother Reiser, looking like he was going to blow.

"Look, Tom. We've been warned for years all this was coming. You, and only you, are responsible for the state you find yourself in."

Brother Reiser shook his head. "No! That's not true. This is *your fault*!"

Bo shook his head. "Don't push this on me."

"I don't have to push anything. Because I've followed your advice I'm in danger of losing my most valuable asset. I could *sue* you for that."

"Whatever, Tom," said Bo, shaking his head. "It wasn't my advice, it was the Prophet's. The Lord gave council to our Prophet, and he gave it to us."

"Then I don't believe in that God or his prophet! A true prophet would see the future and know we'd lose our houses if we followed such terrible advice!"[15]

"Oh, come on Tom! You made your choices, managed your money as you saw fit, and now you're facing the same challenges as everyone else. The playing field has been leveled and you can't stand it."

"I've heard enough from you, *Bishop*," Brother Reiser spat out mockingly. "You're a *joke*. You don't have any idea what you're doing. All you want is control. You're a little *Hitler*!"

"No," said Bo, feeling anger growing inside him. "Hitler is out there!" he said pointing to the outside. "He's luring you into his trap. Take the bait and see where it gets you!"[16]

"Well, newsflash!" snarled Brother Reiser, "if the UN is Hitler, then Hail Hitler!" he said while saluting.

"You don't mean that," said Bo.

"Yes I do—if they will pay my mortgage, I do. And, Bishop, from now on I'll do just as I please, when I please. It's a free country for heaven's sake! I was a fool to listen to you."

"It's not a free country for long," said Bo. "Especially if you and others like you are willing to give up so much, so easily."[17]

Brother Reiser took hold of the doorknob and said, "Oh, by the way, don't look for me on Sunday. And for that matter, stay away from my property. If I see any ward member approaching my door, they'll get a bullet in their head."

"Nice, Tom. I'll be sure to tell the ward," said Bo, right before the door slammed.

Dane hesitated a moment and then said, "I'm glad that guy is gone. He doesn't deserve the gospel. I say good riddance!"

Bo turned to Dane and said briskly, anger still in his voice, "Everyone deserves the gospel!"[18]

"Not those who aren't willing to pay the price for it!" retorted Dane quickly.

Bo didn't respond. He was too mad.

"You OK, Dad?"

"I will be. I just have to blow off some steam."

"That guy is a jerk. Don't feel bad about him," said Dane.

"It's only the beginning," said Bo, feeling exhausted.

"What do you mean, Dad?"

"Soon, all the people in our ward who refused the UN's help will be receiving those foreclosure letters."

"You sure?" asked Dane.

"Yes, I'm sure. I've already received mine."

Dane looked surprised. "You received a foreclosure notice?"

"Yes."

"But this house doesn't have a mortgage. We built it ourselves from materials from Brother DeVine's company."

"I know. But the land and the house that stood on this property before this one, wasn't paid for."

Dane looked confused. "You mean, they are asking you to pay for a house that doesn't exist anymore?"

"Yes."

"How can they do that?"

"Easy," said Bo, looking at his son. "If you buy a car and it's stolen without insurance, you're still expected to pay the loan off. It's perfectly legal. Money is owed. It doesn't matter that the government put us in forbearance because of the flooding. Now the offshore banks that held the loans want their money."

"But can't you appeal to someone?"

"Who? The government is gone. The UN is keeping order around here now, and they're offering mortgage relief, so in their mind and the bank's mind, if we are stupid enough not to take their offer, that's our fault."

Dane nodded, seeming to understand the seriousness of the situation. "So what are we going to do?"

Bo shrugged. "Since Mom worked a while after the economic crash, we have some money, but since she's not working any more, the money has stopped."

"But can't she get a job again? I hear the hospital's functioning."

"No. The UN is running the place and no one will be employed without a chip."

"So no one can work or go to the hospital for care unless they have a chip?"

"Right," said Bo.

"What a racket! Feels like blackmail."

"It's leverage," said Bo. "They thought we'd starve if we didn't take their help. But we didn't. So now they're kicking us out of our houses."

"Are they trying to *kill* us?"

"Not yet."

"What do you mean?" asked Dane.

"We both know if they wanted to kill us, they'd do it."[19]

"Right," said Dane, thoughtfully. "Just like they did in New York and DC."

"Right. No, they still think there's a chance we'll give in and take the chip. They want us in their economy. We're productive people."

"They're right, you know. Many good people will take the chip," said Dane.

"I know," said Bo, looking out the window towards Tom's house. "But many won't. The Saints will pull together and we'll be fine. You'll see."

"So where are we going to live?" asked Dane.

"Old Man Griffin has offered us space on his land."

"He has?" asked Dane.

"Yes. He's offered everything he's got to us."

"He's generous," said Dane.

"Yes, he is. I wish there were more people like him. Heavenly Father loves him."

"You'd think we'd have people like that in our church."

"We do," said Bo. "There are some wonderful, selfless and giving people among us; it's just that we only notice the selfish ones. We wouldn't have been able to last this long if good, anonymous people hadn't taken other families in our ward under their wing."

"Well, that's good. That gives me more hope," said Dane.

"We'll be just fine. We'll have painful choices and have to live very simply, but it will be fine," said Bo.

"So what do we do next?" asked Dane.

"We have a month left to live here. I say we begin packing and then stay the course."

"OK, Dad," said Dane. "Good luck with the rest of the ward. I hope they don't all come here one by one and let you have it."

"I'm going to go out and visit all of them. I think the trauma of being kicked out of your house deserves a personal visit."

"That's tough," said Dane. "I respect you, Dad. You're in a hard position to try and help so many."

Bo nodded as he twisted his wedding ring on his finger. "Yes, but that's OK. We all do our part in our own way."

"Right," said Dane, as he walked away. "I'll go downstairs and begin packing our food storage."

"Great idea," said Bo, as he walked into the kitchen. "If someone else comes to the door, I'll answer it this time."

"No problem," said Dane, knowing he'd still be on alert, just in case his father needed backup.

Notes to "Time and Dividing of Time"

Starvation

[1] "Be patient in afflictions, for thou shalt have many; but endure them, for, lo, I am with thee, even unto the end of thy days" (D&C 24:8).

[2] "But the Lord knoweth all things from the beginning; wherefore, he prepareth a way to accomplish all his works among the children of men; for behold, he hath all power unto the fulfilling of all his words. And thus it is. Amen" (1 Nephi 9:6).

United

[3] "Peace cannot be found in external things. Peace comes from within. 'There is no peace except by the triumph of principles,' said the wise Emerson. There is no peace when one's conscience is seared or when one is conscious of having committed some untoward act. Peace springs from righteousness in the soul, from upright living" (David O. McKay, *Pathways to Peace*, pg. 209).

[4] "Now the Spirit speaketh expressly, that in the latter times some shall depart from the faith, giving heed to seducing spirits, and doctrines of devils; speaking lies in hypocrisy; having their conscience seared with a hot iron" (1 Timothy 4:1-2).

[5] "And again, it shall come to pass that he that hath faith in me to be healed, and is not appointed unto death, shall be healed" (D&C 42:48).

[6] "The Lord said, Except ye are one, ye are not mine. (See D&C 38:27.) This great unity is the hallmark of the true church of Christ. It is felt among our people throughout the world. As we are one, we are his" (Gordon B. Hinkley "Except Ye Are One," *Ensign*, November 1983, pg. 5).

[7] "We pray that Satan's efforts will be thwarted, that personal lives can be peaceful and calm, that families can be close and concerned with every member, that wards and stakes, branches and districts can form the great body of Christ, meeting every need, soothing every hurt, healing every wound until the whole world, as Nephi pleaded, will 'press forward with a steadfastness in Christ, having a perfect brightness of hope, and a love of God and of all men...This is the way; and there is none other way' (2 Nephi 31:20-21)" (Howard W. Hunter, *That We Might Have Joy*, pg. 51).

Zulu

[8] For further information on time zones see, http://wwp.greenwichmeantime.com/info/timezone.htm.

[9] "And he [the antichrist] doeth great wonders, so that he maketh fire come down from heaven on the earth in the sight of men" (Revelation 13:13).

[10] "Wherefore, O ye Gentiles, it is wisdom in God that these things should be shown unto you, that thereby ye may repent of your sins, and suffer not that these murderous combinations shall get above you, which are built up to get power and gain—and the work, yea, even the work of destruction come upon you, yea, even the sword of the justice of the Eternal God shall fall upon you, to your overthrow and destruction if ye shall suffer these things to be. Wherefore, the Lord commandeth you, when ye shall see these things come among you that ye shall awake to a sense of your awful situation, because of this secret combination which shall be among you; or wo be unto it, because of the blood of them who have been slain; for they cry from the dust for vengeance upon it, and also upon those who built it up. For it cometh to pass that whoso buildeth it up seeketh to overthrow the freedom of all lands, nations, and countries; and it bringeth to pass the destruction of all people, for it is built up by the devil, who is the father of all lies; even that same liar who beguiled our first parents, yea, even that same liar who hath caused man to commit murder from the beginning; who hath hardened the hearts of men that they have murdered the prophets, and stoned them, and cast them out from the beginning" (Ether 8:23-25).

[11] "And now, behold, I speak unto the church. Thou shalt not kill; and he that kills shall not have forgiveness in this world, nor in the world to come" (D&C 42:18).

[12] "Woe unto them that call evil good, and good evil; that put darkness for light, and light for darkness; that put bitter for sweet, and sweet for bitter!" (Isaiah 5:20)

[13] "And it came to pass that there arose a mist of darkness; yea, even an exceedingly great mist of darkness, insomuch that they who had commenced in the path did lose their way, that they wandered off and were lost" (1 Nephi 8:23).

"And the mists of darkness are the temptations of the devil, which blindeth the eyes, and hardeneth the hearts of the children of men, and leadeth them away into broad roads, that they perish and are lost" (1 Nephi 12:17).

[14] "We should measure everything against the teachings of the Savior. Measure whatever anyone else asks you to do, whether it be from your family, loved ones, your cultural heritage, or traditions you have inherited—measure everything against the teachings of the Savior. Where you find a variance from those teachings, set that matter aside and do not pursue it. It will not bring you happiness" (Howard W. Hunter, *Teachings of Howard W. Hunter*, pg. 66).

[15] "You cannot destroy the appointment of a prophet of God, but you can cut the thread which binds you to a prophet of God and sink yourselves to hell" (Brigham Young, as quoted by Harold B. Lee, *Ye are the Light of the World*, Ch. 5).

[16] "O that ye would awake; awake from a deep asleep, yea, even from the sleep of hell, and shake off the awful chains by which ye are bound, which are the chains which bind the children of men, that they are carried away captive down to the eternal gulf of misery and woe" (2 Nephi 1:13).

[17] "If our blood-bought freedom is surrendered, it will be because of Americans. What is more, it will probably not be only the work of subversive Americans. The Benedict Arnolds will not be the only ones to forfeit our freedom. ...If America is destroyed, it may be by Americans who salute the flag, sing the national anthem, march in patriotic parades, cheer Fourth of July speakers-normally 'good' Americans, but Americans who fail to comprehend what is required to keep our country strong and free, Americans who have been lulled away into a false security" (Ezra Taft Benson, *Teachings of Ezra Taft Benson*, pgs. 373-374).

[18] "And [Christ] cometh into the world that he may save all men if they will hearken unto his voice; for behold, he suffereth the pains of all men, yea, the pains of every living creature, both men, women, and children, who belong to the family of Adam" (2 Nephi 9:21).

[19] "And I saw the woman drunken with the blood of the saints, and with the blood of the martyrs of Jesus: and when I saw her, I wondered with great admiration" (Revelation 17:6).

CHAPTER THIRTEEN

CORRUPTION OF POWER

"But if ye will not hear it, my soul shall weep in secret places for your pride; and mine eye shall weep sore, and run down with tears, because the LORD's flock is carried away captive" (Jeremiah 13:17).

00:01:10, 00:38:42, Zulu
Thursday, November 20th

The Power of the Little Horn

Provo, Utah
4:22 p.m.

Corrynne entered the house with the twins in tow. Louise was right behind her holding Nebraska's hand. They had just come from old man Griffin's home. Louise was carrying a load of eggs.

Dane was carrying boxes up from the basement as Ry and Jax came down the stairs bringing things from their rooms.

"Hello all," said Dane, to the women, as he unloaded a heavy box onto another one already in the hall, and then turned around and went back down the stairs.

Corrynne looked confused as she scanned all the neatly stacked boxes lined up against the wall. Releasing the twins' hands to let them walk around, she asked, "What's going on?" She looked briefly at Louise in wonder. "Is someone moving?" she said, joking.

"Rocwell!" Nebraska called, with her hands cupped around her mouth.

Rocwell peeked around the corner of the wall on the second level through the bars of the handrail.

Nebraska saw him and ran up the stairs giggling and pushing through Jax and Ry to get to Roc. "I'm coming! I'm going to get you!"

Rocwell laughed and disappeared quickly. The banging upstairs was evidence he was running to hide.

Louise smiled at Corrynne, who smiled back.

"Hi, Mom," said Jax, laying down the armful of bags he had carried down the stairs and gave his mother a hug.

Corrynne noticed he had a sad look on his face. "What's wrong with you?" she asked.

"We've been kicked out of school," said Jax. "Since no one's paying taxes, we can't go to school anymore."

"What?" asked Corrynne.

"When did this happen?" asked Louise, looking concerned.

"Today," said Ry. "A guy from the school district brought us home."

"Is everyone kicked out of school?" asked Corrynne.

"No," said Ry. "Just us, the Wilcox kids, the Jensen kids, the Coterer kids..."

Corrynne nodded. Now she understood, "Oh, all those who are refusing the UN's help, right?"

Ry nodded. "They said that because you and Dad didn't work for the UN, there's no money for us to go to school anymore."

Corrynne shook her head and said, "No, it's not because we don't work *for* the UN, it's because the UN is controlling all the available jobs and only allowing people who have a computer chip under their skin to have UN credits in return for work. We don't have a choice. The UN isn't allowing us to work. No one will hire us unless we get a chip and join the international workforce."

"Why can't you do that, then?" asked Ry.

Corrynne smiled slightly and then said, "Sweetheart, we've talked about this before. Our freedom is more important than what the UN can give us."

"More important than college?" asked Jax, pointedly. "Because without school, I'll never get into college."

Corrynne looked at Louise with pain evident in her face, and then with a gentle hand on Jax's shoulder she said, "Things in our world have changed. I know I've encouraged you to prepare to go to college almost your whole life, but now I don't know if that will be an option."

"Young man," said Louise, wanting to help, "We certainly hope you can go to college, but if not, know that many of the best men in history have been self-taught. Just because someone denies you schooling, doesn't mean you stop learning. Abraham Lincoln only attended school a few months of his life. Albert Einstein was kicked out of school when he was only a few years older than you, and George Washington's education ended about that time, too."

"We'll teach you," said Corrynne. "Don't you worry. Lots of kids are home-schooled."

"Joseph Smith only had three years of formal education," interjected Brea as she entered the living room, followed by Caroline and her daughter.

"Brea! Caroline!" said Corrynne. "Where did you guys come from?"

"Caroline was teaching me how to sew some fun things for my house," said Brea nodding. "We were using your machine."

"That's so nice of her!" said Corrynne, smiling at Caroline.

Caroline nodded as she self-consciously pulled Rebecca close.

"How did you get over here without being seen?" asked Corrynne.

"I snuck," said Brea, with a laugh. "No one saw me."

"That's not very smart," said Corrynne.

"I know," said Brea. "But I couldn't wait for dark. Caroline had such great ideas. She's very talented. I was anxious to get started."

Corrynne shook her head. "Brea Nicole..."

"I'm fine, Mom. Don't worry. I'm a big girl. I made sure I was totally covered. If MD was looking, he wouldn't see anything he could identify."

Corrynne raised her eyebrows in disagreement.

"OK, OK," said Brea, giving in. "I won't do it again."

Bo entered the living room carrying a heavy box, right as Dane came up the stairs with a box of his own. Both of them unloaded on top of the other stacks and Dane went back downstairs.

Bo scratched his head as he looked at the women gathered in the foyer and spilling over into the living room.

Strykker patted his leg and Bo picked him up.

"Either this place is getting smaller or there's more of us," said Bo. "Jax, Ry, I want you to go downstairs and help Dane box up the food storage. There's a bunch of boxes down there that need to be filled. You guys box, and he'll bring them up."

"But, Dad, we're not done with our room," said Jax.

"We're not moving today," said Bo. "I want you to help with the food storage now to get it out of the way. You can finish your room later."

Jax and Ry moaned and begrudgingly went through the door leading to the downstairs and disappeared.

"Moving?" asked Corrynne, looking at Brea, Louise, and Caroline. "What's this about moving?"

Bo took a breath and said, "Everyone without a job is being served with eviction papers from the banks."

"Eviction papers?" asked Brea.

Striynna reached up her hands, "Bea, up," said her little voice.

Brea picked up her little sister with great effort and pulled her into her arms, holding her on her abdomen.

"How can the banks expect us to pay mortgages with no economy?" asked Corrynne.

Bo shook his head. "The banks know the UN is offering relief and job counseling. I guess they believe that if we're not taking that relief and finding jobs—to at least *attempt* to pay the mortgages, we shouldn't live here. It seems logical. If I was a bank I'd probably do the same."

"Who's going to enforce the eviction notices?" asked Louise.

Bo shook his head. "Maybe the UN police?"

Louise nodded. "I wouldn't put it past MD."

"So what's going to happen, Dad?" asked Brea.

Bo considered Brea's question and said, "Let's all take a seat in the living room. We need to talk."

The women, along with Rebecca, took seats on the two couches in the living room.

"The important thing here is to keep our wits about us," said Bo. "We have options. There's Old Man Griffin's place and his farm. There's also church property, if worse comes to worst. We've built one home; we can do anything we need to, especially if we pull together."

Right then, Dane came up the stairs again. He set his box down with the others and then came over to the couches. "Wits about us for what?" he asked.

"Have a seat, son," said Bo. "This conversation concerns you, too."

Dane smiled. "Don't mind if I do," he said, as he jumped over the back of the couch where Brea sat by herself.

"Dane!" exclaimed Brea, in a scolding tone as she bounced up, catapulted by his weight. "What are you? A monkey?"

"I didn't teach him that," said Corrynne, shaking her head.

The others, except for Bo, laughed, especially Rebecca, who giggled without restraint.

"Sorry," said Dane as he scratched his armpit like a monkey, playing up to Rebecca. "Go ahead," he said to his father, making a monkey face. "Don't mind me."

Bo shook his head in amazement. Pointing, he said, "I sent him away to the military to make him a man, and he still acts this way."

"Dad," said Dane, "I sent myself. No one *sent* me."

"Oh, yes, that's right," said Bo, laughing. "And you're still a monkey."

"Hey!" said Dane defensively.

"Anyway," Bo said, clearing his throat and becoming serious again. "Monkeys aside, considering the eviction notice we've received, and the impossibility for us to avoid being evicted when the time comes, I think we should come up with a plan. We have options that will allow us to approach this situation with strength. As odd as it might sound, we need to look at the coming days and welcome them, knowing that they will lead us to the glorious future God himself has promised us."[1]

"Yes," nodded Louise. "I agree. A positive outlook, no matter what basis it's built on, will be the best tool possible for success. Our future can be anything we make it. In times of trauma, or disaster, it's always those with a positive outlook who tend to succeed."

"That's the power of faith in a master plan,"[2] said Brea.

"I would agree with you," said Louise, nodding.

"What future is that?" asked Caroline, as she brushed Rebecca's cheek with her hand.

Bo hesitated for a moment as he gathered his thoughts, and then said, "God has told us this day would come. The evil powers of the earth..."

"Oh, you mean the UN," said Caroline, interrupting with the best of intentions, interest suddenly filling her eyes.

Bo smiled. "It's not necessarily the UN, but the men behind it."[3]

"You mean the pope?" asked Caroline.

"He has something to do with this, yes, but he doesn't run the UN."

"Then, who's behind the UN?" asked Caroline, looking from person to person around the room.

"It's a man called Matthew Daimler, Senior," said Louise. "He's a very wicked man who has taken control of all the governments of the earth.[4] America, parts of Europe, and Canada were the last places he didn't have power, but now through the UN, he controls us, and if we could see the news, he probably controls those other places, too."[5]

"Are you sure he's not an alien?" asked Caroline. "I can hear myself, and I know that sounds crazy, but I had thought the UN was a covert operation of extra-terrestrials."

Louise smiled but refrained from laughing. "I'm sure he's not an alien. I believe that alien theory is only a rumor."

"Hmmm," said Caroline, looking contemplative.

"In Daniel, in the Old Testament, it tells us clearly how this is all going to play out," said Bo.

"Oh, explain!" said Caroline. Looking to Corrynne, she said, "I love to talk like this! I never could understand the Bible, no matter how hard I tried!"

"We are clearly in a war that will eventually lead up to Armageddon," said Bo. "This war is beginning like other wars, where people prey upon other people. However, in this case, MD, or Matthew Daimler, is pretending to be the friend of the people by giving them everything they need,[6] so he can wrap them in his chains and then destroy them, by ripping away personal freedoms.[7] He is, as the scriptures said, destroying through peace."

"Do the scriptures actually say that?" asked Louise. "I mean, are those the words actually used?"

"Yes," said Bo, looking around the room for a Bible.

"Dad, I know that one," said Dane holding up a finger.

"Well, go ahead then," said Bo, nodding.

"In Daniel 8:25 it says, 'And through his policy also he shall cause craft to prosper in his hand; and he shall magnify himself in his heart, and by peace shall destroy many.'"

"Say that scripture again slowly," said Louise. "I have to understand it."

Dane nodded. "'And through his policy...'"

"Or laws, government, ways of doing things, right?"[8] asked Louise.

"There are some circumstances where it might refer to 'shrewdness'," [9] said Bo.

"OK, go on," said Louise, nodding. "I can see that."

"'He shall cause craft to prosper in his hand.'"

"What does 'craft' refer to here?"

"Deceit, cunning, skillful deception,"[10] said Brea. "Fits, doesn't it?"

"Yes," said Louise, amazed.

"It also could refer to false authority, as in priestcraft, or witchcraft,"[11] said Bo.

"Meaning that MD has set himself up as an authority over the earth for gain and praise, but doesn't really care about the people," said Brea. "It says in the scriptures that he'll stamp the residue and devour the whole earth, breaking it into pieces.[12] Doesn't sound very altruistic, does it?"

"Or couldn't MD do that through the pope, too?"[13] asked Corrynne.

"Sure," said Bo.

"See?" asked Brea. "This is amazing, isn't it? These descriptions fit so well, it's scary."

Louise stared at the floor and shook her head. "I don't know what to say, I'm—*astounded*."

"Do you want me to continue?" asked Dane.

"Yes," said Caroline.

"'And he shall magnify himself in his heart...'"

Louise put out a palm to Brea and laughed. "That's MD to a tee! Wow! Is God smart or what?"

Brea laughed. "Yep, he's pretty smart!"

"Continue," Louise said to Dane.

"'And by peace shall destroy many.'"

Louise hit the armrest of the couch.

"What?" asked Bo.

"That's what all this is about. MD conquered our nation through the back door. He silently pulled out the support blocks until it fell. It looked to the people like it imploded, but we all know differently.[14] Our nation was destroyed by peace and through peace, or the UN's efforts to enroll Americans in the UN international marketplace, it will destroy many more."[15]

"Yep," said Brea, nodding. "Pretty *crafty*."

"Pretty crafty," repeated Louise, thoughtfully. Looking pointedly at Bo, she said, "I cannot believe the scriptures actually say those words!"

"Well, they do," said Bo.

"How do you guys know the man who runs the UN?" asked Caroline.

"...It's a long story," said Louise and Brea, at the same time. Then they looked at each other and laughed.

"Family closet secrets," said Dane, behind his hand. "Don't go there right now."

Caroline lifted her eyebrows and nodded. "OK..." she whispered. Turning back to Bo, she said, "Then continue with the scripture. What else does it say?"

"It says that MD, who is a very powerful man, will make war with the Saints,[16] which is another word for Christians or anyone who refuses to do as MD wants because of a belief in the true teachings of Jesus Christ."[17]

"And that's what's happening now," said Louise.

"Yes," said Corrynne. "He caused the nation to fall, taking away our power and independence, then he offers false humanitarian relief to lure the people to love him. After that, he'll try to strong-arm the Christians to fall in line, by trying to take away everything they have,[18] but when they don't give in, he'll try to destroy them."[19]

Caroline frowned. "That doesn't sound promising. Will he be successful?"[20]

Bo nodded as Strykker reached for the ground. "I imagine in some parts of the world, he will."[21] Bo let Strykker down.

"But not here?" asked Caroline.

"Hundreds of thousands have already died," said Louise.

"Right," said Caroline, "I believe that. I came from out there," she said with a thumb over her shoulder. "I mean, are we safe *here*?"

Bo nodded. "I believe we are, as long as we become a united people,[22] and are obedient to God's laws."[23]

"Do the scriptures say that?"

"Absolutely, they do,"[24] said Bo.

"How does this all end?" asked Caroline. "Because aliens or not, those people at the UN are stronger than us."

"First of all, we don't have to be stronger than the UN or MD. We have a greater power on our side. God is on our side. He will fight our battles;[25] in fact, his message to the Saints is clear. We are not to fight. We are to be patient in our afflictions and examples of peace.[26] The Lord has gone on to say that if we do fight, we'll end up losing our lives."[27]

"Because the foe is too powerful,"[28] said Louise, nodding.

"Right. The foe is way too powerful," said Bo. "The best thing to do, is to lay low."

"I agree," said Louise. "Just disappear—and without a tracking chip, that's exactly what we can do. That's exactly what *I* suggest."

"Right," said Bo thoughtfully, recognizing her emphasis, seeming to border on urgency.

"So if we're not going to fight MD, how will he lose?" asked Caroline.

"Christ will come, just as he says he will,"[29] said Dane. "Then at that time, MD and his little puppet, the pope, will be thrown into a lake of fire and brimstone."[30]

"How long until that happens?" asked Caroline, looking from Bo to Dane and back.

Bo shook his head. "I don't know. But the signs of Christ's coming are all around us.[31] It won't be long."[32]

"Will you teach me about those signs?" asked Caroline.

"'And there shall be signs in the sun, and in the moon, and in the stars; and upon the earth distress of nations, with perplexity; the sea and the waves roaring,'" began Dane, quoting scripture out of Luke 21. "'Men's hearts failing them for fear, and for looking after those things which are coming on the earth: for the powers of heaven shall be shaken. And then shall they see the Son of man coming in a cloud with power and great glory. And when these things begin to come to pass, then look up, and lift up your heads; for your redemption draweth nigh.'"[33]

Caroline stared at Dane with her mouth open. Then after a moment, she said, "I just got chills. ...Some of those things are happening already. He's really coming, isn't he?"

Corrynne and Dane nodded as Bo said, "Yes, Caroline, he really is."

The Hunt

Denali Prison Camp, Alaska
2:50 p.m.

A shiver of anticipation pulsed through Carea as she scanned the white, crusted snow that lay perfect and undisturbed in her path. Today was her solo day, a testing time meant to decide her future among the bear clan. For a month she had been in training with the clan's experts, and now, it was time to prove her worth. If she successfully brought back a bear she'd be given a place among the leaders of the prison camp detainees; something that had never been done by a female. Finally she'd have enough clout to talk to Gruff face to face without having to go to Jack first. She couldn't wait.

Carea put her fingers to her lips and whistled. Kobe, Kina, Kayna, Kiko, and Kee, five wolf-like dogs the clan had raised from two different pup litters and trained for the hunt, jumped about her, their ropes threatening to tie in knots from their frolicking. "Woah, kiddos," she said lovingly, patting them firmly, and then holding Kobe steady to keep him from running under his sister's ropes. "You're my good babies, aren't you?" she said kindly, as the dogs licked her face. "Time to get going," she said, her stomach tightening in silent worry—in reality, she knew if anything went wrong, it could be the last day of her life.

Carea pulled a bear skin, still poignant with scent, from inside her coat. She held it out for the dogs.

Kobe sniffed it and then snatched it from Carea's grasp with his teeth. He growled as he shook the skin violently. The other dogs joined in the tussle, looking like they might start to brawl.

"Hey-ya, Kobe, Kina, Kayna!" she yelled as she snapped the ropes that bound the dogs. "Kiko, Kee!" she demanded authoritatively, feeling like she was in the middle of a tongue twister. Who had named these dogs?

"Hey! Get going!" she exclaimed, snapping the ropes again. Carea blew a horn made from the base of antelope antler that was strung around her neck. That was the signal to send the dogs after the bear.

The dogs tugged at the woven bark ropes that bound a rudimentary three-log sled to their bodies. They were anxious and full of energy and the sled slid easily across the hardened snow. Carea stepped onto the sled as it moved past, and then crouched down in the middle. She wedged her elbows between her knees to stabilize the weight of the sled and hung on as she had been taught. Despite her training and the harnesses, she was not the boss here, the dogs were, and they knew it. If they got away from her in the pursuit of bear, she might never find them or the base again.

Since it was November, the bears were settling in their dens to begin hibernation. That made finding bear a thousand times easier than in the summer. Right now they were fat, slow, and sleepy—easy prey for the dogs. If she was lucky, they'd kill the bear before she even got there. But if they didn't, she had a newly-strung bow with flint arrows on her back, and a sharp flint knife sheathed at her waist, to finish the job.

Carea reviewed her plan in her head. She would let the dogs corner the bear, then she would climb into a tree and shoot it in the chest with her arrows. Because of the bear's weight, she'd have to harvest the meat right on the spot. She'd then load the meat, wrapped in skin, onto the sled and bring it back to camp. The plan seemed pretty straight-forward. She could do it. She had been on five hunts before, and as long as she didn't get close to the bear, she knew she could bring it down safely.

Carea scrunched down until the edge of her black fur coat covered her mouth and nose. She blew warm air into the fur to counter the cold wind. As she did this, she imagined the struggle she was rushing towards. The whole thing was ominous. Hunting was her least-favorite activity. She hated taking animals' lives, but she had to keep in mind that all of this was being accomplished for the good of the people. Five camp members would receive coats and fifty could eat tonight, as long as she made it back in time for dinner. The Lord understood their need to survive and had given them animals for the purpose of sustaining their health, especially when other food sources weren't available.

Suddenly, the dogs took an abrupt turn and nearly tipped the sled over. Carea was able to muscle the thing to straighten out, but it was close. She took a deep breath as she tried to calm her rapid heart rate. "Can't tip over," she said to herself. That would be disastrous!

Watching the fervor and strength of the dogs' run, she realized now that they had caught the scent of a bear. They were heading into the woods and near a rock cliff. She hoped the dogs wouldn't move into a thick wooded area, because then she'd have to let them loose and follow them on foot, but despite her hope, that's exactly what happened. Eventually, the sled became wedged between two trees and the dogs tugged dangerously against the ropes, threatening to snap them. Quickly, Carea jumped off the sled, and one by one, pulled on the quick-release knots at the back of each dog and set them free. She had to preserve the ropes for the trek back.

The dogs ran out of her sight, since the trees were thick in this part of the wilderness. Carea pulled the pack off her back and reached in and took out a handful sticks with natural red bark. She had cut them into small segments before her trip. These would mark her way so she could retrace her steps back to her sled. Next, she untied her snow shoes from her pack and laced them on. She had to hurry. The dogs' barking was getting quieter as the distance grew between them.

Carea slung the pack on her back and began trudging through the snow, taking huge steps and following the dog's tracks. Her snow shoes were large and clumsy. She kept catching the snow with her toes or hooking the weaving of the shoes on branches of brush just under the surface. With that, she reminded herself to keep her feet flat and away from branches sticking out of the ground. By correcting her snow shoe technique, she picked up the pace.

After Carea had followed the dogs about a mile the sound of their barking had stopped moving. She bet her dogs had found a bear! "Good dogs," she said, breathing out a cloud of mist. Soon, it would be over.

Pushing on towards the sounds of distant growling and barking, she was led up a steep hill. Her snow shoes cracked as she attempted to climb it. In frustration, she unlaced the shoes and carried them. She'd put them in her pack later. She couldn't afford the time now.

It was getting dark already. Carea didn't like how early the sun disappeared in Alaska. In the dark, it would be harder to shoot accurately. She shook her head as she refused to consider how much harder this could get. No room for doubts. Doubts made people hesitate and a second of hesitation could be deadly.

Quickly, Carea climbed the last ridge to see her dogs barking up a tree. The bear, which was of moderate size, was perched in a large fork, snarling angrily and batting harmlessly at the dogs.

Carea let out an exasperated sigh. This was *not* as she had envisioned this going. The bear was supposed to be *sleeping* in his *lair*, not up in a tree! She had taken way too long in coming, and now with the darkness closing in, things were becoming more complicated by the second.

Throwing down her snowshoes, Carea searched the white ground feverishly for some dry wood that might burn to make a light. There wasn't any, not even a twig. Everything was wet or too green. She turned to the bark of the nearby trees. Grasping, pulling, tugging, she was desperate to find anything that might burn. To her dismay, all the bark on all the trees around her held fast. She reluctantly turned back to her bag. Looking up at the bear, she noticed he was backing out of the tree, she decided crunch time had arrived. She had to resort to her emergency fire fuel—bear fat.

With quick hands, Carea opened her bag and pulled out a bundle. Unwrapping the fat from the skin that protected it, she set the fat aside and used the skin, rolling it into a funnel. With leather strings, she tied the end of the skin around the body of a stick, and then placed the fat inside the funnel, piercing it with the end, like a shish-ka-bob. The skin would conserve the fat so the fire would burn longer.

As the dogs jumped and snapped at the bear's back feet, keeping it, for the moment in the tree, Carea struck a flint, causing a spark to land on some bear hair from yet a different swatch of skin. The hair was excellent tinder. With a couple more strikes, she had an ember that began to smoke. Gently she blew it until it built up to a flame. Carefully, she placed the flame on top of the fat, shielding it from the evening breeze with her hand. Within moments, she had a moderate fire. She watched it for a few seconds, making sure it wouldn't go out, and then she lodged the stick in another small fork opposite the bear in a different tree to her right. "There," she said, feeling satisfied. The lamp glowed brighter, lighting the bear and the dogs, but casting huge shadows on the rocks behind.

With adequate light, Carea felt confident enough to load up her bow. With a strong arm, she aimed and released. The arrow sailed through the air and bounced off the tree trunk just to the left of the bear. The shadows had caused Carea to miscalculate her aim, enticing her to think the bear was wider than he was. "Shoot!" she exclaimed, as she hit her leg with her fist.

The bear climbed higher in the tree in response to the arrow, but moved out on a limb above Carea. This new position was a turn of great luck! The light that was burning bright now, was almost directly below him, lighting his chest with the yellow glow.

Carea pulled another arrow from her back, loaded her bow, pulled back with all her might, and released. The arrow flew true to her aim this time and landed deep in the bear's chest. There was a loud growl and the bear fell out of the tree, landing on the ground only a few feet from Carea. She expected it to die quickly, but instead, it stood and threatened to charge her with an unholy yell. As she retreated, she wondered where the arrow landed. It seemed like a perfect hit! She hated this! Didn't she hit its heart? Why couldn't it be over?

In a moment, the dogs were all over the bear and an angry battle of teeth and claws ensued.

Carea debated what she should do next. Should she try another arrow? With the dogs in the way she was afraid she'd hit one of them instead. In a moment of desperation, she threw off her pack and pulled her large flint knife from its sheath. She wasn't leaving without this bear. Either the dogs would kill it, or she would.

Carea watched as the dogs battled the bear, leaving a bloody trail down the hill as fur shook and teeth flashed, in a mass of fury. There was a yelp as Kiko flew through the air and landed beside Carea on the ground, but she didn't stay down for long. Within a second she was back at the bear's throat.

"That a way Kiko! Get the bear!" she encouraged.

The bear tried to retreat, but the dogs went after him, continuing the deadly contest. The dogs forced the bear back up the hill pushing him close to Carea once again. She tightened her grip around her knife as she crouched in readiness.

The bear charged back down the hill again, only to be attacked from all sides. It was fighting less now. It was tiring. The dogs were getting the best of him. Carea followed cautiously.

As the animals fought, she inched sideways around the back of the bear. Carea noticed that if she aimed carefully from above, she could shoot him in the back without hitting the dogs—but her arrows were still up the hill. She'd have to...

A hundred pounds of flailing dog catapulted through the air and hit Carea square in the chest. She went down with a thud. Pushing Kee off, Carea realized the bear and the dogs had moved their fight on top of her. She scrambled to move out of the way, but her leg was caught! She felt sharp knife-like claws dig into her flesh and she screamed in agony.

Reflexively, Carea turned and plunged her knife deep into the bear's face before he could bite her. The knife entered the skull right above the eye. The bear shook his head once and then fell limp on top of her legs.

The dogs continued their attack in blind fury until it became obvious the bear would not fight back. Slowly, one by one, they stopped their assault and sat back, panting.

Carea burst into tears of relief as she took great heaving breaths. Her legs were pinned under the bear, but she was so thankful that she almost didn't care. What did matter was that she was *alive* and the bear was *dead.*

Notes to "Corruption of Power"

The Power of the Little Horn

[1] "I have just two things to say to any of you who are troubled about the future. I say it lovingly and from my heart. First, we must never, in any age or circumstance, let fear and the father of fear (Satan himself) divert us from our faith and faithful living. There have always been questions about the future. Every young person or every young couple in every era has had to walk by faith into what has always been some uncertainty—starting with Adam and Eve in those first tremulous steps out of the Garden of Eden. But that is all right. This is the plan. It will be okay. Just be faithful. God is in charge. He knows your name and He knows your need. ...God expects you to have enough faith and determination and enough trust in Him to keep moving, keep living, keep rejoicing. In fact, He expects you not simply to face the future (that sounds pretty grim and stoic); He expects you to embrace and shape the future—to love it and rejoice in it and delight in your opportunities" (Jeffrey R. Holland, "Terror, Triumph and a Wedding Feast," September 12, 2004, fireside, BYU).

[2] "What is your outlook on life today? Have you courage to face the future? Are you hopeful, contented, helpful, and optimistic? To whom do you look for your inspiration? Have you reserves of valor behind the front lines of your vision? Does your faith make you unafraid of that 'No Man's Land' across which the general plan of campaign requires you to go? ...Man is that he might have joy—the joy of conquest over self, the joy of achievement, the joy of having fought the good fight, of having kept the faith, the joy of a peace that is earned, the joy of increase, the joy of living that more abundant life exemplified by the Master, the joy that comes from patient continuance in well-doing, the joy of comradeship, the joy of awareness and appreciation. That joy which is the purpose of our being could not have been achieved without the refining fires of life's experience. If man had remained in that untried, innocent state of pre-existent infancy, he would have done no good, for he knew no evil, would have had no joy, for he knew no sorrow. Man is, then, that he might have the joy which comes through understanding and obeying those eternal laws upon which all blessings are predicated" (Hugh B. Brown, *Eternal Quest*, pg. 263).

[3] "...The individual is handicapped by coming face to face with a conspiracy so monstrous he cannot believe it exists. The American mind simply has not come to a realization of the evil which has been

introduced into our midst" (J. Edgar Hoover, *The Elks Magazine*, August 1956, *An Enemy Hath Done This*, pg. 308).

[4] "And I stood upon the sand of the sea, and saw a beast [a political power] rise up out of the sea, having seven heads [referring to the 'seven hills of Rome,' evolving out of Europe and acting as other kings with the same power] and ten horns, [connected and controlling ten powers in the world] and upon his horns ten crowns, [representing ten kings, or presidents of the ten powers] and upon his heads the name of blasphemy. And the beast which I saw was like unto a leopard, and his feet were as *the feet* of a bear, and his mouth as the mouth of a lion: [having characteristics of carnivorous beasts, hungry for bloody conquests, as well as acting as other vicious leaders who held power over the world] and the dragon [Satan] gave him his power, and his seat, and great authority" (Revelation 13:1-2).

[5] The beast will obtain political control over the world: "...And they worshipped the beast, saying, Who is like unto the beast? Who is able to make war with him?" (Revelation 13:4)

[6] "There was a time when Americans roared like lions for liberty; now they bleat like sheep for security" (Norman Vincent Peale, as quoted by Ezra Taft Benson, *An Enemy Hath Done This*, pg. 312).

[7] "...So [in America] one constitutional right after another [is] yielded without any real contest, our backs getting nearer to the wall with each retreat...And do not think that all these usurpations, intimidations, and impositions are being done to us through inadvertence our mistake; the whole course is deliberately planned and carried out; it's purpose is to destroy the Constitution and our constitutional government; then to bring chaos, out of which the new Statism with its slavery, is to arise, with a cruel, relentless, selfish, ambitious crew in the saddle, riding hard with whip and spur, a red shrouded band of night riders for despotism...If we do not vigorously fight for our liberties, we shall go clear through to the end of the road and become another Russia, or worse" (J. Reuben Clark, Jr., *Church News*, September 25, 1949).

[8] "A course of action adopted and pursued by a government, ruler, political party, action or procedure conforming to or considered with reference to prudence or expediency" (Dictionary.com, "policy," http://dictionary.reference.com/browse/policy).

"And he shall speak great words against the most High, and shall wear out the saints of the most High, and think to change times and laws" (Daniel 7: 25).

[9] "sagacity; shrewdness" (Dictionary.com, "policy," http://dictionary.reference.com/browse/policy).

[10] "Skill in evasion or deception; guile" (Dictionary.com, "craft" http://dictionary.reference.com/browse/craft).

In the topical guide craftiness is synonymous to deceit, guile, and subtleness. See http://scriptures.lds.org/en/tg/c/238.

[11] "Priestcraft--Men preaching and setting themselves up for a light to the world that they may get gain and praise of the world; they do not seek the welfare of Zion" (Guide to the Scriptures, "Priestcraft," http://scriptures.lds.org/en/gs/p/55).

[12] "The fourth beast, which was diverse from all the others, exceeding dreadful, whose teeth *were of* iron, and his nails *of* brass; *which* devoured, brake in pieces, and stamped the residue with his feet. ...Thus he said, The fourth beast shall be the fourth kingdom upon earth, which shall be diverse from all kingdoms, and shall devour the whole earth, and shall tread it down, and break it in pieces" (Daniel 7:19, 23).

[13] "And I beheld another beast coming up out of the earth; [Antichrist] and he had two horns like a lamb, [appears gentle] and he spake as a dragon [the words of Satan]. And he exerciseth all the power of the first beast before him, and causeth the earth and them which dwell therein [nations of the earth] to worship the first beast, [or honor, obey] whose deadly wound was healed [the world thought the head was dead but it wasn't]" (Revelation 13:11-12).

[14] "Wherefore, O ye Gentiles, it is wisdom in God that these things should be shown unto you, that thereby ye may repent of your sins, and suffer not that these murderous combinations shall get above you, which are built up to get power and gain—and the work, yea, even the work of destruction come upon you, yea, even the sword of the justice of the Eternal God shall fall upon you, to your overthrow and destruction if ye shall suffer these things to be. Wherefore, the Lord commandeth you, when ye shall see these things come among you that ye shall awake to a sense of your awful situation, because of this secret combination which shall be among you" (Ether 8:23-24).

[15] "And the first went, and poured out his vial upon the earth; and there fell a noisome and grievous sore upon the men which had the mark of the beast, and *upon* them which worshipped his image" (Revelation 16:2).

[16] "I beheld, and the same horn made war with the saints, and prevailed against them" (Daniel 7:21).

"And it was given unto him to make war with the saints, and to overcome them: and power was given him over all kindreds, and tongues, and nations" (Revelation 13:7).

"Wherefore, he maketh war with the saints of God, and encompasseth them round about" (D&C 76:29).

[17] "A name given to believers in Jesus Christ. Although this term is commonly used throughout the world, the Lord has designated true followers of Christ as Saints (Acts 9: 13, 32, 41; 1 Corinthians. 1: 2; D&C 115: 4)" (Guide to the Scriptures, "Saints," http://scriptures.lds.org/en/gs/c/29).

[18] "Purpose of Persecution—Let any people enjoy peace and quiet, unmolested, undisturbed,—never be persecuted for their religion, and they are very likely to neglect their duty, to become cold and indifferent, and lose their faith" (Brigham Young, *Discourses of Brigham Young*, Vol. 7, pg. 52).

[19] "And his power shall be mighty, but not by his own power; and he shall destroy wonderfully, and shall prosper, and practise, and shall destroy the mighty and the holy people" (Daniel 8:25).

[20] "Time is rapidly rolling on, and the prophecies must be fulfilled. The days of tribulation are fast approaching, and the time to test the fidelity of the Saints has come. Rumor with her ten thousand tongues is diffusing her uncertain sounds in almost every ear; but in these times of sore trial, let the Saints be patient and see the salvation of God. Those who cannot endure persecution, and stand in the day of affliction, cannot stand in the day when the Son of God shall burst the veil, and appear in all the glory of his Father, with all the holy angels" (Joseph Smith, *History of the Church*, Vol. 1, pg. 468).

[21] "And he beheld Satan; and he had a great chain in his hand, and it veiled the whole face of the earth with darkness; and he looked up and laughed, and his angels rejoiced" (Moses 7:26).

[22] Unity of the people is mandatory for Zion to be successful in the last days, when turmoil overcomes the earth. There was another time in history in which the Saints were unable to reap the promised blessings held out to them because they were not unified: "[My people] are not united according to the union required by the law of the celestial kingdom; And Zion cannot be built up unless it is by the principles of the law of the celestial kingdom; otherwise I cannot receive her unto myself" (D&C 105:4-5).

If we wish for the blessings of protection and victory over our enemies in the perilous times to come, we, God's people, must become truly one heart and one mind, being knit together in faith.

[23] Another prerequisite for protection in Zion is *obedience* to the laws of God. If we are stubborn, the Lord will allow us to suffer many things until we learn how to obey. "Behold, I say unto you, were it not for the transgressions of my people, speaking concerning the church and not individuals, they might have been redeemed even now. But behold, they have not learned to be obedient to the things which I required at their hands, but are full of all manner of evil, and do not impart of their substance, as becometh saints, to the poor and afflicted among them...And my people must needs be chastened until they learn obedience, if it must needs be, by the things which they suffer" (D&C 105:3-4, 6).

[24] "The Book of Mormon prophet Nephi foresaw the day when the Saints would be scattered in stakes all over the world. He saw the time when the Lord would extend His protection to them when

menaced by storms of destruction that threatened their existence. Nephi prophesied: 'And it came to pass that I, Nephi, beheld the power of the lamb of God that it descended upon the saints of the church of the Lamb and upon the covenant people of the Lord, who were scattered upon all the face of the earth; and they were armed with righteousness and with the power of God in great glory' (1 Nephi 14:14). Through revelation we know that there will be perils, calamities, and persecution in the latter days, but through righteousness the Saints may be spared. The promise of the Lord in the Book of Mormon is sure: 'He will preserve the righteous by his power' (1 Nephi 22:17)" (Ezra Taft Benson, *Come Unto Christ*, pg. 104).

[25] "For behold, I do not require at their hands to fight the battles of Zion; for, as I said in a former commandment, even so will I fulfill—**I will fight your battles**. Behold, the destroyer I have sent forth to destroy and lay waste mine enemies; and not many years hence they shall not be left to pollute mine heritage, and to blaspheme my name upon the lands which I have consecrated for the gathering together of my saints" (D&C 105:14-15).

[26] "And again I say unto you, sue for peace, not only to the people that have smitten you, but also to all people; And lift up an ensign of peace, and make a proclamation of peace unto the ends of the earth; And make proposals for peace unto those who have smitten you, according to the voice of the Spirit which is in you, and all things shall work together for your good. Therefore, be faithful; and behold, and lo, I am with you even unto the end. Even so. Amen" (D&C 105: 38-41).

[27] "He that leadeth into captivity shall go into captivity: he that killeth with the sword must be killed with the sword. Here is the patience and the faith of the saints" (Revelation 13:10).

[28] "...And his power shall be mighty...and he shall destroy wonderfully" (Daniel 8:25).

[29] "And then they shall look for me, and, behold, I will come; and they shall see me in the clouds of heaven, clothed with power and great glory; with all the holy angels; and he that watches not for me shall be cut off" (D&C 45:44).

[30] "And the devil that deceived them was cast into the lake of fire and brimstone, where the beast and the false prophet *are,* and shall be tormented day and night for ever and ever" (Revelation 20:10).

[31] "And it shall come to pass that he that feareth me shall be looking forth for the great day of the Lord to come, even for the signs of the coming of the Son of Man" (D&C 45:39).

[32] "And he spake to them a parable; Behold the fig tree, and all the trees; When they now shoot forth, ye see and know of your own selves that summer is now nigh at hand. So likewise ye, when ye see these things come to pass, know ye that the kingdom of God is nigh at hand. Verily I say unto you, This generation shall not pass away, till all be fulfilled" (Luke 21:29-32).

[33] Luke 21:25-28.

CHAPTER FOURTEEN

EVIL LAWS

"...For, behold, the devil was before Adam, for he rebelled against me, saying, Give me thine honor, which is my power; and also a third part of the hosts of heaven turned he away from me because of their agency" (D&C 29:36).

00:01:10, 00:05:05, Zulu
Thursday, November 20th

Satan's Strategies

Provo, Utah
4:55 p.m.

"Hey, Dane! What are you doing up there?" Jax yelled from the basement. "We've got a lot of boxes filled down here!"

"I'm talking to Dad and Mom! I'll be down when I'm finished," Dane yelled to his brothers. "Sorry," said Dane turning apologetically to the group. "So, what's the plan?" asked Dane. "What comes next?"

"What do you mean?" asked Bo, squinting. It felt like a headache might be coming on.

"Well, OK, we've received an eviction notice along with all of our neighbors. Times are tough, but we're tougher. What comes next?" he asked, rubbing his hands together as if he was anxious to get to work.

Corrynne sat back and cleared her throat. "Umm, Old Man Griffin has offered his land to those in our neighborhood that might need it."

"And do what?" asked Dane, with worry in his voice. "Live in tents? *Is that the plan?* Come on, there must be a better option than that."

Corrynne raised her eyebrows in acknowledgement and said, "People have lived in tents for most of the world's history. We have some pretty nice tents. It's a good short-term solution until something better comes along," she said, while fingering Strykker's soft, golden hair as he stood at her knee. "We can bring our bedding, and furniture. It's only across the street. I'm sure we can make it as nice as we want to."

"I'm not living in a tent," scoffed Dane. "I've done that already in the military, and if you want to know the truth, it wasn't my favorite experience."

"Well, we don't have to worry about this for at least a month," said Bo. "Maybe..."

Suddenly, Brea held up her hand. She had a thoughtful look on her face. "Dad—that might not be true. I think I need to tell you something."

"What?" asked Bo.

Brea searched the room as if she was wondering if this was the setting she should be revealing things.

"Go ahead," said Louise. "Unless you want us to leave." She looked like she was preparing to stand.

Brea shook her head, "No, it's OK. I just have to make a disclaimer."

"What?" asked Corrynne.

Talking to Caroline and Louise, she said, "This might sound strange, but we as Latter-day Saints believe in spiritual abilities called gifts of the Holy Ghost.[1] Through these gifts we are able to do unusual things to build up the kingdom of God."[2]

Louise nodded knowingly. "I've witnessed a little of those abilities personally. This family is very unusual," she said to Caroline.

Brea smiled and said, "Well, anyone can have them. All one must do to obtain a gift is to be worthy of the blessings and seek them,"[3] said Brea.

"Then your family is very—*worthy*," said Louise with a nod, "if I might use your word."

Brea laughed in obvious embarrassment. "I don't know about that, but we try," she said, as she looked to her mother and father briefly, then back to Louise. "But, thank you for that vote of confidence."

"You're welcome," replied Louise.

"Anyway, I would like to forge ahead and tell all of you what's been happening to me. I've been having unusual dreams...."[4]

Bo studied his daughter. "*You've* been having dreams now?"

"Since when?" asked Corrynne, looking at Brea and then back to Bo.

"Just a month or so," said Brea.

"Are these dreams like Braun's?" asked Louise, sitting a little higher.

Bo and Corrynne looked at each other in surprise.

"Like Braun?" asked Bo, questioning Louise.

Louise gave an acquiescent smile. "Yes, like your son, Braun. He's an amazing young man, by the way. I loved our discussions in the short time we knew each other. You must be wonderful parents to have such exceptional children."

Corrynne covered her mouth in astonishment. Up to this point, Louise had kept up her façade, but now she was letting them in without reservation. Tears sprung to Corrynne's eyes and spilled over immediately.

Louise reached over and empathetically squeezed Corrynne's hand. "I'm sorry to make you cry. Please forgive me. You don't deserve to be sad."

Corrynne shook her head, her look speaking volumes of understanding about her son. She sought to minimize the effect of her tears. "No, it's OK. I just missed him all of a sudden. I'll be fine. I enjoyed what you said. It made me happy," she said, wiping her eyes and smiling.

"Good," said Louise, nodding. "And I want you to know that I value each of you, too. I'm finding that I'm actually grateful for this time, despite what has happened. My life has been enriched because of the Rogers family."

"Thank you," said Corrynne, as she wiped away another tear.

Turning to Brea, Louise asked calmly, "Did you dream about the future?"

Brea smiled politely. "No, not really—I think my dreams were more warnings than proclamations of the future."

"Wait, there's people in this family that can *tell the future*?" asked Caroline, intrigued and looking from person to person.

Corrynne shook her head. "No, it's not like that," she said. "I assure you, it's nothing mystical. Spiritual gifts are generally vague in their manifestation, but once in a while, the Spirit causes a very poignant experience in one's life."

Caroline listened thoughtfully. "That's very interesting. And your dreams were like that? *Poignant*, I mean?"

Brea nodded. "It seemed the messages were very important and they applied to us, as a family and a community."

"Tell us then," said Bo.

"OK," said Brea, taking a breath and hugging Striynna, who had fallen asleep in her arms. "Well, first of all, I guess I should tell you guys something else," started Brea, as she stroked the fingers of Striynna's little hand. "As you know, I can sense things. I know if someone's good or bad[5] and sometimes I know what certain people are thinking."[6]

"I have that gift, too," said Corrynne. "I think you got that from me."

Brea nodded. "Well, that particular gift has grown. Now, I can sense spirits.[7] Sometimes I can even see them."[8]

Corrynne looked perplexed. "What are you talking about?"

"I can see spirits. Good and bad," said Brea, again.

"Dead people?" asked Bo, a little shocked.

Brea shook her head. "I don't think I've ever seen any dead people, yet, but…then I guess I wouldn't know. What's the difference? Spirits are spirits, right? Evil spirits[9] or good disembodied spirits,[10] there are times I can see or sense them, depending on the circumstance."

Bo looked at Corrynne to assess her reaction to this news.

Corrynne raised her eyebrows in obvious confusion. It seemed she was still processing the information.

Turning to Brea, Dane asked, "Let me get this right. You sense spirits, alive or dead, in the body or out."

"I guess so," said Brea.

"When did you realize this?" asked Corrynne.

"Not until I went to visit Matt's family. In his house, I began to sense evil spirits there. It was very frightening."

"Were there many evil spirits in Matt's home?" asked Corrynne, with reserved interest. "I would think with MD there, it might be."

"Absolutely," said Brea. "It was a nexus for evil."[11]

"That's terrible!" said Corrynne.

"So, you're saying the house was haunted?" asked Dane.

"For sure! It was totally possessed!" said Brea, with wide eyes. "No haunted about it. Evil has control of that house, and the people inside."

"Who's Matt?" asked Caroline, interrupting the flow of the conversation.

"The father of my twins," said Brea.

Caroline looked at Brea's abdomen momentarily and said, "You're going to have twins?"

"Yes," said Brea, patting her abdomen lovingly, "at the end of next month."

"Is that why you moved back home, because your in-laws' home was haunted?" asked Caroline.

Brea shook her head. "That was only part of it."

"Oh," said Caroline, nodding.

"I can't believe this," said Corrynne, as Bo pursed his lips in dismay. "We had no idea."

"I would hide in my room most of the time, because for some reason, the evil spirits wouldn't come into my room. I felt safe there," continued Brea.

"It's because you're good," said Bo. "If you have the armor spirituality gives you, evil knows there's no contest."[12]

"Maybe," said Brea. "I think Matt must be better at arming himself than I am.[13] When he was home, the evil spirits stayed away. When he was gone, they would tease me like it was a game until I learned the words to say to send them away."[14]

"That's basic spiritual survival knowledge," said Bo. "Especially for you, since you can see evil personages. I would imagine they could really make your life miserable."

"I agree," said Brea, nodding. "They did make my life miserable."

"Did these spirits know you could see them?" asked Dane.

"They didn't at first, but then they figured it out."

"These spirits," said Caroline. "Are you saying they're people?"

Brea nodded. "Disembodied people."[15]

"Disembodied?" asked Caroline.

Dane laughed. "Your alien theory is sounding saner all the time isn't it?"

Caroline shook her head. "I just didn't know all this stuff. I'm really learning a lot."[16]

"Religion deals with the seen *and* unseen,"[17] Explained Bo. "We have the physical world that we can touch, see, smell, and manipulate, but then the scriptures tell us that there's another world out there, one that is riddled with evil forces[18] fighting against us, that are beyond our physical senses.[19] Brea obviously has broken that barrier between our world and theirs. It's a gift I hadn't even thought about."[20]

"To have that ability would be such an interesting experience," said Louise. "I'm a little envious."

Brea shook her head. "Don't be. It's overwhelming. Be thankful you can't see spirits. It's kind of spooky at times."

"Hmmm," said Bo.

"This is all so strange," said Corrynne.

"Anyway, back to my original topic, the reason I'm telling you any of this is because I met an evil spirit in Matt's home..."

"You met him?" asked Caroline, looking like she was concentrating on Brea's words. "So that means you can talk to these disembodied people?"

Brea nodded. "Just like I'm talking to you."

"This is amazing," said Louise, shaking her head.

"Who was this spirit?" asked Bo.

"He was the most powerful of all the evil spirits I saw. He was their leader. But, at first, I was confused about who he really was, because he looked like the butler."

"What do you mean?" asked Dane.

"I mean, he looked identical to the real butler in MD's home, so at first I thought they were the same person, but as I saw them more often, I realized that there were two butlers. There was the physical man, who served as the butler to MD—he was a benign, normal old man, but then there was this evil spirit that chose to look like the butler."

"How do you know that it *wasn't* the butler?" asked Dane. "Maybe it was the butler, in the *library* with a *knife*," he said, making a joke alluding to the game Clue he and Brea played as kids.

Brea gave him an irritated look. "Dane, this is serious. Don't make jokes."

"Sorry," said Dane, still smiling to himself. "I thought it was an appropriate point."

"He brings up a good question," said Caroline. "How *did* you know that the spirit and the person weren't the same?"

Brea thought for a moment and said, "I just knew. They felt totally different to me. The butler was kind, simple-minded, and caring, where the spirit who looked like the butler was evil, intensely intelligent, and angry.[21] Plus if the evil ghost-like person was really the butler's spirit, the butler would have died, or at least been unconscious when his spirit wasn't in his body, don't you think?"

"And he wasn't?" asked Dane.

"No," said Brea. Turning to her mother, she asked, "What do you think? Don't you think that makes sense? A person's spirit can't separate and the body continue to wonder around the house, can it?"

Bo interjected. "No, a person can't separate from his body and still live. That's the definition of death."[22]

Corrynne, who had a thoughtful look, shook her head. "However, there are instances where people can have a serious illness or injury and have near-death experiences, where their spirits leave their body for a short time. I've had patients that have awakened to tell me about them."[23]

"Yes, but no one can do housework, or putter in the garden without their spirit," said Brea. "Right?"

"Right," said Corrynne, nodding. "My patients have always been in a coma when their spirits have left."

"I think my spirit left my body when I was in the hospital," said Dane thoughtfully.

"It did?" asked Brea, looking surprised.

Dane nodded, looking like he was searching deep in his memory. "Yes, I think so—no, I'm *sure* it did."

"Do you remember any of it?" asked Corrynne.

"Sometimes," said Dane, looking happy. "I see sunshine...blowing hair...and sparkling water..."

"What?" asked Brea, covering a laugh with her hand. "Blowing hair? Sparkling water? Are you serious?"

"What's so funny about that?" asked Dane. "That's what I remember."

"Well, if you're serious, nothing," said Brea, forcing her face straight. "It just sounded funny coming from you. I thought you were joking."

"Do you remember anything else?" asked Corrynne.

Dane shrugged. "Well, now I don't want to tell anyone," he said, giving his sister a sour look. "I might get laughed at."

"I'm sorry, Dane," said Brea, still snickering. "I won't laugh anymore."

"Yeah, whatever," said Dane. "You're still laughing."

"Tell me later, OK?" said Corrynne, giving her son a wink. "I'm very interested."

"Sure," said Dane, still looking warily at Brea. "Go on with your *own* story," he said to her.

"Yes, tell us more about this butler," said Caroline. "Tell us why you think that bad spirit looked like the butler."

"This is my theory," began Brea. "The spirit, ours and those that are evil, have different laws by which they function. I'm the first one to say I don't know what they are. But there is something I do know; evil spirits can appear any way they wish,[24] and I suspect that some choose to appear a certain way for identification purposes. For example, if the butler look-a-like spirit changed the way he appeared to me, I might think he was a different spirit each time. I wouldn't know who he was."

"And that spirit wanted you to know who he was?"

"Yes," said Brea, nodding. "I believe so. Part of his power over me came from me being afraid of him.[25] If I were to guess, I would say that this particular evil spirit inhabited the butler's body when he needed a body,[26] and then chose to look like him when he didn't. The point is, without straying too much further off my original topic, was that both the butler and the evil spirit had a strong affinity for Matt's father. Both of them served MD similarly."

"One in the spiritual realm and one in the physical realm," said Louise nodding and tapping her chin.

"Yes," said Brea. "That's what I think, anyway."

"Did MD know about the powerful, evil spirit?" asked Bo.

"Of course!" said Brea. "I saw them talking together."

"You did?" asked Corrynne.

"Yes, Mother. I can see those things."

"So MD can see spirits too?" asked Bo.

"Of course," said Brea. "They're working together.[27] Evil has its own set of gifts.[28] Satan and his hosts are very powerful, spiritual beings. Evil power is real, just as righteous power is real."[29]

"Brea's right," said Bo. "One of the ways the world will be tricked into following evil is through miracles brought about through great evil power."[30]

"Hmmm," said Corrynne. "I guess you're right."

"That fits the pattern," said Louise. "MD is *pure* evil. I wouldn't put it past him to use the occult for his governing purposes."[31]

"Or for any purpose," said Brea.

Struggle

Denali Prison Camp, Alaska
3:10 p.m.

After a few moments of recovery, Carea pushed the dogs away. They were licking her mercilessly. She strained to pull her legs free of the bear's weight, but they were wedged tight. It took her a couple of tries and all her effort but finally, she managed to pull them clear.

Carea assessed her wound. Her punctured and peeled skin lay back on top of itself in three places. She could see clearly that the wounds were inflicted by the bear's claw. Looking closer, she thought she could see her leg muscle. She wiggled her toes, and sure enough, the muscle moved. It shocked her at first, but then as she watched, she realized this was a good sign. At least the internal structures of her leg were intact. She was very lucky.

Carea closed her eyes tight as she tried to think of what to do. There was probably dirt, wood and dirty dog hair deep in the wound. That could cause an infection that she knew could kill her later. Carea pinched her leg to get the wound to bleed and rolled to the right as the blood dripped from her leg, onto the snow.

Vapor rose from the pool of blood, looking golden in the dying lantern light. A puddle formed quickly and ran down the hill, filling in the spaces around the dead bear's head. The dogs sniffed the bear and the new blood, lapping it up, quickly.

"Stop it," Carea said, kicking their heads gently with her other foot. There was something wrong with her dogs licking up *her* blood. "Stop it!" she said again, but none of her dogs listened. She shook her head. It was no use. Might as well talk to a stone.

After a while, and a good amount of blood loss, Carea hoped the wound was cleaner. She had milked her leg, trying to expel the dirt and debris. Now the blood ran dirt free. It was time for a bandage.

Struggling to stand, Carea balanced herself and hopped on one foot over to her pack and snowshoes that she had flung on the ground. She opened the top of the bag and rummaged around inside looking for some bandage material. Her hand found what it was looking for, and she pulled out orange fabric. It was a large square swatch of the prison jumper she was wearing when she first arrived at the camp. With her knife, she nicked the edges and then ripped the material in strips.

Sitting again, she studied the wound. The edges of the skin weren't too jagged, and luckily all three pieces were still attached at one end. Gently she coaxed the skin flaps back into their places. They fit relatively well. That would be better for healing. Then she applied the folded bandage to hold the skin stationary and keep out the dirt. Next, she took the other strips and wrapped them around her leg, keeping the edges flat and overlapping. The bleeding had nearly stopped now, so there was no need for a tourniquet. Applying the last strip, she gently but securely, tied it in place with a square knot. She knew, as she inspected her work, that if the bear had dug any deeper, he would have hit an artery, and the situation might have been very different. She closed her eyes in thankfulness that she was still alive.

Carea opened her eyes and scanned the body-length of the bear. It was huge. She estimated it to be a little more than three times her size, putting it at about 320 pounds. It was an impressive catch. It would feed many. That made her happy.

Carea stood and tried out her wounded leg. It stung as she put weight on it, but it was bearable.

Since it was dark, and the fat-fueled lantern Carea had made earlier, had burned out, she knew she had no choice but to start a fire to have light to work by. Searching the near-by trees again, she found a half-dead fir tree she hadn't seen before. Methodically, she removed the driest twigs off the pine and the remaining dried needles. There were larger dead branches too, that broke away easily. This, and more bear fur would get a good fire going.

Brushing the snow from two large rocks stuck out of the ground, Carea crisscrossed the wood between them. Building an elevated fire would keep the wood off the wet ground and let the air circulate to give adequate oxygen to feed the flames. Then, with her flint, she sparked more fur. It caught fire right away. It was tricky to get the wood to ignite, but after trying for a while, it worked, and a fire began to grow. The warmth and light was satisfying. Instantly Carea felt successful as she piled wood onto the stack until she had a bright, hot fire.

"Just what the doctor ordered," Carea said happily to her dogs, who licked their lips expectantly. They knew what came next.

Carea limped down to the bear. He was laying the wrong way. She needed to roll him onto his back so she could skin him properly. With a push, she attempted to move the bear on her own, but he was too heavy, especially with her injured leg. She took a step back and thought about her task. She studied her dogs. They still had their harnesses on. Maybe she could use the dogs to help roll the bear over. She set to work attaching the dogs to the bear. Soon they were tied to the bear's right legs with more bark rope she'd had in her pack.

"Come on!" she coaxed, and she blew her antelope horn. The dogs barked and pulled as she pushed. Quickly, the bear rolled. "Woah!" she called, as she pulled back sharply on their harnesses.

The dogs stopped pulling and looked back at her.

"Come on," she coaxed, "I've got some meat for you." She said, taking out her knife again.

The dogs understood what she said, and they sauntered back, panting happily, wagging their tails.

Carea made an incision in the bear's pelt right under the center of the jaw and then stuck the fingers of her left hand into the hole, lifting the skin away from the underlying muscle. Then, being careful, she inserted the knife and made a clean incision down the chest, lifting with her fingers and cutting with her knife. She continued in this manner until she had cut along the appropriate body lines to remove the skin. After assuring all the cuts were good, she started at the right leg and rolled the pelt back off the muscle. There, she sliced some meat for the dogs. They had been very patient and they deserved the first cut.

"Here Kiko, Kee, Kayna," she said, as she threw meat onto the snow. "Kobe, Kina, here you go too," as she sliced some more meat and tossed it.

The dogs hungrily tussled to claim their pieces.

"There's enough for all of you," she said, as she cut more for good measure. "Play nice."

As Carea watched the dogs feast, she decided to cut some for herself, too. Her stomach was growling reminding her she hadn't eaten for awhile.

After she had cut a generous helping, Carea limped to the fire and roasted the meat on the end of a skewer. As she watched it cook she marveled. She had learned so much about survival and the strength of the human spirit in such a short time! It seemed like yesterday that she was at school, worrying about what she was going to wear, who she was going to date, or what play to try out for. Those thoughts were so unimportant and foolish to her now.

Carea looked at her beat-up hands. They were the hands of strength. How could she have been so unaware of her potential? Her mind had been blind. Never, in a million years would she have thought she could come up against an angry bear and live! It was a miracle! She liked what she had become.

Carea's mind returned to the day she was taken into custody. She remembered the prison and the guard. She remembered being put in isolation. She had been so angry and lost then. But now, all that pain had led her to greater knowledge and understanding. She could stand back and say that there was purpose to her suffering. There were lessons that she was forced to learn here, that she would never have learned otherwise. Right then, a poignant thought came to her. She had proven to herself what Heavenly Father had known all along. She was a powerful child of God with potential far beyond her own understanding. Carea fell on her knees in prayer. It was time to be thankful.

Notes to "Evil Laws"

Satan's Strategies

[1] "We believe in the gift of tongues, prophecy, revelation, visions, healing, interpretation of tongues and so forth" (Article of Faith 7).

[2] "...All these gifts come from God, for the benefit of the children of God" (D&C 46:26).

[3] "...Seek ye earnestly the best gifts, always remembering for what they are given; For verily I say unto you, they are given for the benefit of those who love me and keep all my commandments, and him that seeketh so to do; that all may be benefited that seek or that ask of me... And again, verily I say unto you, I would that ye should always remember, and always retain in your minds what those gifts are, that are given unto the church. For all have not every gift given unto them; for there are many gifts, and to every man is given a gift by the Spirit of God. To some is given one, and to some is given another, that all may be profited thereby" (D&C 46:8-12).

[4] "And it shall come to pass in the last days, saith God, I will pour out of my Spirit upon all flesh: and your sons and your daughters shall prophesy, and your young men shall see visions, and your old men shall dream dreams" (Acts 2:17).

[5] "Then shall ye return, and discern between the righteous and the wicked, between him that serveth God and him that serveth him not" (Malachi 3:18).

[6] "For the word of God is quick, and powerful...and is a discerner of the thoughts and intents of the heart" (Hebrews 4:12).

[7] "...And to others the discerning of spirits" (D&C 46:23).

[8] There are instances where people are able to see evil spirits. See the following:

Heber C. Kimball, Joseph Fielding Smith, Willard Richards and Orson Hyde, were shown a vision simultaneously of the world of evil spirits. "...A vision was opened to our minds, and we could distinctly see the evil spirits, who foamed and gnashed their teeth at us. We gazed upon them about an hour and a half (by Willard's watch). We were not looking towards the window, but towards the wall. Space appeared before us, and we saw the devils coming in legions, with their leaders, who came within a few feet of us. They came towards us like armies rushing to battle. They appeared to be men of full stature, possessing every form and feature of men in the flesh, who were angry and desperate; and I shall never forget the vindictive malignity depicted on their countenances as they looked me in the eye; and any attempt to paint the scene which then presented itself, or portray their malice and enmity, would be vain. I perspired exceedingly, my clothes becoming as wet as if I had been taken out of the river. I felt excessive pain, and was in the greatest distress for sometime. I cannot even look back on the scene without feelings of horror; yet by it I learned the power of the adversary, his enmity against the servants of God, and got some understanding of the invisible world. We distinctly heard these spirits talk and express their wrath and hellish designs against us. However, the Lord delivered us from them, and blessed us exceedingly that day" (Joseph Fielding Smith, *Church History and Modern Revelation*, Vol. 3, pg. 99).

[9] "The spirits of all men, as soon as they depart from this mortal body, whether they are good or evil are taken home to that God who gave them life, where there is a separation, a partial judgment, and the spirits of those who are righteous are received into a state of happiness which is called Paradise, a state of rest, a state of peace, where they expand in wisdom, where they have respite from all their troubles, and where care and sorrow do not annoy. The wicked, on the contrary, have no part nor portion in the Spirit of the Lord, and they are cast into outer darkness, being led captive, because of their own iniquity, by the evil one. And in this space between death and the resurrection of the body, the two classes of souls remain, in happiness or in misery, until the time which is appointed of God that the dead shall come forth and be reunited, both soul and body, and be brought to stand before God, and be judged according to their works. This is the final judgment" (Joseph F. Smith, *Improvement Era,* June, 1904, Vol. 7 pgs. 621-622).

[10] "Can you see spirits in this room? No. Suppose the Lord should touch your eyes that you might see, could you then see the spirits? Yes, as plainly as you now see bodies, as did the servant of Elijah. If the Lord would permit it, and it was His will that it should be done, you could see the spirits that have departed from this world as plainly as you now see with natural eyes" (Brigham Young, *Journal of Discourses*, June 22, 1856, Vol. 3, pg. 368).

[11] "I have no doubt that many of my brethren and sisters have sensibly felt in various places and at various times evil influences around them. Brother Joseph Smith gave an explanation of this. There are places in the Mississippi Valley where the influence or the presence of invisible spirits are very perceptibly felt. He said that numbers had been slain there in war and that there were evil influences or spirits which affect the spirits of those who have tabernacles on the earth. I myself have felt those influences in other places besides the continent of America; I have felt them on the old battle grounds on the Sandwich Islands" (George Q.Cannon, Jerreld L. Newquist, *Gospel Truth,* pg. 54).

[12] "...Be strong in the Lord, and in the power of his might. Put on the whole armour of God, that ye may be able to stand against the wiles of the devil. For we wrestle not against flesh and blood, but against principalities, against the rulers of the darkness of this world, against spiritual wickedness in high places. Wherefore take unto you the whole armour of God, that ye may be able to withstand in the evil day, and having done all, to stand" (Ephesians 6:10-13).

[13] "The Apostle Paul demonstrates his great ability as an inspired teacher as he pictures each of us as a warrior being clothed with the essential armor to protect the four parts of the human body which apparently Satan and his hosts, by their vigilant spy system, have found to be the most vulnerable parts through which the enemies of righteousness might make their 'landing,' as it were, and invade the human soul. Here are his inspired teachings: 'Stand therefore, having your loins girt about with truth, and having on the breastplate of righteousness; And your feet shod with the preparation of the gospel of peace. And take the helmet of salvation...' (Ephesians 6:14-15, 17). Did you note carefully the four main parts of your bodies to be guarded: 1. A girdle about your loins. 2. A breastplate over your heart. 3. Your feet shod. 4. A helmet on your head. These instructions take on full significance when it is

remembered the loins are those portions of the body between the lower ribs and the hips in which are located the vital generative organs, and also that in the scriptures and other inspired writings the loins symbolize virtue or moral purity and vital strength. The heart suggests our daily conduct in life, for as the Master taught: '...Out of the abundance of the heart the mouth speaketh. A good man...bringeth forth good things: and an evil man...bringeth forth evil things' (Matthew 12:34-35). The feet typify the course you chart in the journey of life. The head, of course, represents your intellect" (Harold B. Lee, *Stand Ye in Holy Places*, pgs. 330-331).

[14] "...But Paul, being grieved, turned and said to the spirit, I command thee in the name of Jesus Christ to come out of her. And he came out the same hour" (Acts 16:18).

[15] "There are myriads of disembodied evil spirits—those who have long ago laid down their bodies here and in the regions round about, among and around us; and they are trying to make us and our children sick, and are trying to destroy us and to tempt us to evil. They will try every possible means they are masters of to draw us aside from the path of righteousness" (Brigham Young, *Discourses of Brigham Young*, Vol. 6, pg. 73-74).

[16] "One great evil is, that men are ignorant of the nature of spirits; their power, laws, government, intelligence, etc., and imagine that when there is anything like power, revelation, or vision manifested, that it must be of God" (Joseph Smith, *Teachings of the Prophet Joseph Smith*, pg. 202-203).

[17] "Satan commands a mighty force comprising one-third of all God's spirit children who were cast out with him—tangible and real although not always discernible by sight, and under whose masterful direction there goes forward constantly propaganda of lying and deceit. One of the most potent of his lies is described by a prophet: And behold, others he flattereth away, and telleth them there is no hell; and he saith unto them: I am no devil, for there is none—and thus he whispereth in their ears, until he grasps them with his awful chains, from whence there is no deliverance (2 Nephi 28:22)" (Harold B. Lee, *Stand Ye in Holy Places*, pg. 329).

[18] "Wherefore, because that Satan rebelled against me, and sought to destroy the agency of man, which I, the Lord God, had given him, and also, that I should give unto him mine own power...I caused that he should be cast down; And he became Satan, yea, even the devil, the father of all lies, to deceive and to blind men, and to lead them captive at his will, even as many as would not hearken unto my voice" (Moses 4:3-4).

[19] "...Fear not them which kill the body, but are not able to kill the soul; but rather fear him which is able to destroy both soul and body in hell" (Matthew 10:28).

[20] "Discerning of spirits: What this means may be illustrated by relating a remarkable experience which the Prophet records. On the 9th of November, 1835, a man came to his home and introduced himself as a Jewish minister whose name was Joshua. The Prophet entertained him hospitably, as he always did both strangers and friends who visited him. One day Mr. Joshua said that he was a lineal descendant of Matthias, and a re-incarnation of this Apostle. The Prophet writes: 'I told him that his doctrine was of the Devil, that he was in reality in possession of a wicked and depraved spirit, although he professed to be the spirit of truth itself. He said also that he possessed the Spirit of Christ. He tarried until Wednesday, 11th, when, after breakfast, I told him that my God told me that his god was the Devil, and I could not keep him any longer' (History of the Church, Vol. 2 pg. 307). Thus the Prophet Joseph had the gift to discern spirits" (Janne M. Sjodahl, Hyrum M. Smith, *Doctrine and Covenants Commentary*, pgs. 275-276).

[21] "Try the spirits. The Apostle John has written these words, 'Beloved, believe not every spirit, but try the spirits whether they are of God' (1 John 4:1). This counsel applies to Saints in these days as it did in those unto whom the Apostle John wrote. It is right that Latter-day Saints should try every spirit which manifests itself or seeks to obtrude itself among them, not by seeking after it, but when it makes its appearance to see and understand by its fruits whether it be of God or not. It is necessary that we who live in these days should be careful not to be deceived. ...The Latter-day Saints should be careful not to entertain spirits which are not of God—spirits of delusion, spirits which lead men into darkness and error and which, if they follow, will lead them to destruction" (George Q. Cannon, Jerreld L. Newquist, *Gospel Truth*, pg. 499).

[22] "Death is a separation of the spirit from the physical body. The physical death is usually described in the scriptures as 'temporal death,' since it is temporary and will eventually be overcome through the resurrection. As Paul wrote anciently: 'As in Adam all die, even so in Christ shall all be made alive' (1 Corinthians 15:22)" (Daniel H. Ludlow, *Companion to Your Study of the Doctrine and Covenants, Volume 2*, pg. 64).

[23] The near death experience (NDE) is a factual phenomenon among mortals, described in detail by Alma the Younger when he was struck nigh unto death. "And it came to pass that I fell to the earth; and it was for the space of three days and three nights that I could not open my mouth, neither had I the use of my limbs..." (See Alma 36 for the complete account.)

Modern research into these experiences demonstrate many common patterns. "...Contemporary near-death research casts light on several episodes in the Book of Mormon. Alma's conversion while 'nigh unto death' fits a common pattern of experience. Modern researchers have noticed distinctive after-effects among NDErs. In the Book of Mormon, both Alma and the resurrected Christ demonstrate these aftereffects" (Kevin Christensen, *FARMS Journal of Book of Mormon Studies, Volume 2, number 1,* Spring 1993, pg. 1).

There are times where the spirit can leave the body to have spiritual experiences. During these times, the body cannot move or act independently, although it can still biologically survive until the spirit returns.

[24] "It is not every revelation that is of God, for Satan has the power to transform himself into an angel of light; he can give visions and revelations as well as spiritual manifestations and table-rappings" (John Taylor, *Millennial Star*, March 1857, pg. 197).

[25] "...the ancient truth [is] that fear is the devil's first and chief weapon. Make a man or a nation afraid, and his strength like that of Samson shorn of his locks, is gone. He is no longer useful in the work of the world. He becomes a tool of the unholy forces which seek to destroy mankind. ...Fear never fails to lead a man or a group of people to weakness and to ultimate failure. The fears of man are legion. They float to the surface from submerged corners in our consciousness. They are often the products of our imagination" (John A. Widtsoe, *Conference Report*, October 1950, pg. 184).

[26] "The spirits in the eternal world are like the spirits in this world. When those have come into this world and received tabernacles, then died and again have risen and received glorified bodies, they will have an ascendancy over the spirits who have received no bodies, or kept not their first estate, like the devil. The punishment of the devil was that he should not have a habitation like men. The devil's retaliation is, he comes into this world, binds up men's bodies, and occupies them himself. When the authorities come along, they eject him from a stolen habitation" (Joseph Smith, *History of The Church of Jesus Christ of Latter-day Saints,* Vol. 5, pg. 403).

"There must be circumstances of depression and sin and physical weakness that within the restrictions of divine control, permit evil spirits to enter human bodies. We do know their curse is to be denied tabernacles, and we surmise that the desire for such tenancy is so great that they, when permitted, even enter the bodies of beasts" (Bruce R. McConkie, *The Mortal Messiah*, Vol. 2, pg. 282).

[27] "And behold, it is he who is the author of all sin. And behold, he doth carry on his works of darkness and secret murder, and doth hand down their plots, and their oaths, and their covenants, and their plans of awful wickedness, from generation to generation according as he can get hold upon the hearts of the children of men" (Helaman 6:30).

[28] "Evil spirits or devils, who follow Lucifer in his task of afflicting and tormenting and destroying mortals, do seem to be assigned specific powers or missions. And interestingly, this seems to be done in the manner of an organized assault, just as Christ's missionary force is an organized assault against these same powers of darkness" (Blaine Yorgason, *Spiritual Progression in the Last Days*, pg. 214-215). See Alma 30:42, D&C 123:7-8, Mark 5:1-13 for examples.

[29] "...'Peace shall be taken from the earth, and the devil shall have power over his own dominion,' we are also assured that 'the Lord shall have power over his saints, and shall reign in their midst' (D&C 1:35-36)" (Ezra Taft Benson, *Conference Report*, October 1974).

[30] "And [the Antichrist, through Satan's power] deceiveth them that dwell on the earth by the means of those miracles which he had power to do in the sight of the beast; saying to them that dwell on the earth, that they should make an image to the beast, which had the wound by a sword, and did live" (Revelation 13:14).

[31] "For behind the concrete forces of revolution...beyond that invisible secret circle which perhaps directs them all, is there not yet another force, still more potent, that must be taken into account? In looking back over the centuries at the dark episodes that have marked the history of the human race from its earliest origins—strange and horrible cults, waves of witchcraft, blasphemies, and desecrations—how is it possible to ignore the existence of an Occult Power at work in the world? Individuals, sects, or races bred with the desire of world domination, have provided the fighting forces of destruction, but behind them are the veritable powers of darkness in eternal conflict with the powers of light" (Nesta H. Webster, as quoted by Ezra Taft Benson, *An Enemy Hath Done This*, pg. 331).

CHAPTER FIFTEEN

FLEE UNTO ZION

"And the LORD will create upon every dwelling place of mount Zion, and upon her assemblies, a cloud and smoke by day, and the shining of a flaming fire by night: for upon all the glory shall be a defense" (Isaiah 4:5).

00:01:09, 23:25:56, Zulu
Thursday, November 20th

Thy Will Be Done

Provo, Utah
5:35 p.m.

"Like I said, dreams are not normally something I have," said Brea, "but lately, I've been dreaming that the butler, the evil spirit who lived in Matt's home, visited *this* house."

"Our house?" asked Corrynne, looking surprised.

Brea nodded. "He was accompanied by two other spirits, an old woman, and a boy who wore chains and leather."

Bo frowned. The memory of the ugly old woman who used to terrorize him coming home from work burst into his mind. "Tell me what that old woman looked like."

"She was hunched over with strings of gray hair that hung from her head…"

"And one frosty white eye?" asked Bo, a sweat breaking out on his forehead.

Brea tried to think. "I think so. I didn't see her up close, but I think I did notice she had one eye that looked blind to me."

Bo looked nervously at Corrynne. "And you're saying this woman was outside our house, too?"

Brea nodded. "Yes."

Bo shook his head. "That's not good."

"Why?" asked Brea, looking at her father. "Do you know her? Have you seen her too?"

"If it's the same woman, yes, I saw her when she had a body—or was using someone's body" said Bo, seeming confused. "This is getting complicated."

"I know," said Brea, smiling.

"Anyway, she used to follow me from work and yell all sorts of inflammatory things at me."

"What?" said Brea, almost laughing. "What sort of things?"

"She told me I would grovel before her master and thousands of others before I would die."

Brea blinked, looking a little surprised. "That's awful!"

"She said many other things I would prefer not to remember, but the point here is that she scared me more than any other evil element I've ever experienced, and I'm not easily frightened."

"I'm sorry, Dad," said Brea.

"I just hope your dream was symbolic and not literal. I don't want her anywhere near my home any time soon."

Brea thought a moment and then said, "Dad, I don't know if my dream is literal or figurative. Let me tell you all of it, and you decide."

"Good idea," said Bo.

"The quick version then. I had a few dreams," said Brea. "Each one was different. However, they all represented the same day and time. I was shown the consequences of different choices we might make."

"We, as in, our family?" asked Corrynne, as she bent down to give Strykker a kiss.

"Specifically, Dad and I."

"OK, go on," said Corrynne as Strykker moved away from her, patting each person's knee as he came to them.

"I came out of the door of my house and I heard someone talking over near this house. It was the boy and the old woman. They were nearly yelling into Brother Reiser's ear."

"Brother Reiser?" asked Bo, caught off guard. "He was in your dream?"

Brea nodded. "Yes."

"What were those spirits saying to him?" asked Bo.

"They were trying to get him to throw a rock through the front window. They were egging him on.[1] Their plan was to make you so angry that you'd come out of the house and retaliate with violence, so that others would have an excuse to shoot you dead."[2]

"What?" exclaimed Corrynne.

"What?" asked Bo, beside himself in surprise. "Brother Reiser kills me?" asked Bo, seeing how Brea's scenario could really happen.

"No, I didn't say that. I said that was the plan. I was shown three different outcomes to that plan."

"Oh, this is so interesting!" said Caroline, smiling at Louise.

"In the first dream, I was hiding behind the bushes around the side of the house and listening to their conversations, when the spirit I knew appeared out of thin air. He had been sent from MD to find me."

Corrynne shook her head. "See, Brea? Do not go out of your place during the day!"

"Mom, this wasn't during the day, it was at night. Anyway, I'm never safe from spirits, day or night! They are out any time."

Corrynne shook her head in frustration.

"Why would that particular spirit be looking for you?" asked Louise.

"Because MD promised Matt that if he divorced me he wouldn't try and find me through conventional means."

"Ahh, so he'd send his invisible henchman," said Louise.

"Yes," said Brea. "Anyway, I ran when I saw him. I tried to get into our house through the back door in the garage. I instinctively knew I'd be protected from those evil beings inside the house with you guys, but all the doors were locked."

"So I guess we shouldn't lock the doors," said Bo, smiling.

"Did the spirits find you?" asked Caroline.

"Yes, but that's not the most important point here. The most important point was the white hue of protection I discovered enveloping your home. Not only that, but you also had huge warrior spirits dressed in gold armor guarding the doors of the house."[3]

"Our home was spiritually protected from evil?" asked Corrynne. "I love that!"

Brea nodded. "This home is good. It's a house of prayer and prayer keeps us safe from evil.[4] The evil spirits had no choice but to stay outside and hope someone would come out."

"Oh, that's so nice to hear!" said Corrynne, with a laugh. "At least there's something we're doing right! I love it that we have spiritual protectors!"

"They reminded me of seven foot tall Nephite warriors."

"I wish I could see them!" said Corrynne, with light in her eyes.

"What's a Nephite?" asked Caroline.

"It's a type of warrior that used to live in America a little before and after the time of Christ," said Louise.

Corrynne and Dane looked at Bo and Brea with surprise.

"How did you know that?" asked Dane.

"I've been reading," said Louise, with a wink. In a whisper, she said, "You left a Book of Mormon out and I picked it up."

"I've never heard of them," said Caroline, shaking her head.

"I think they were related to the Native Americans," said Louise, looking at Bo for confirmation.

Bo nodded, "I'm sure there's some genetic similarity," said Bo. "There was more than one group of people that came to this land anciently.[5] We only have the records of a couple in the Book of Mormon. Eventually, most were annihilated in war."[6]

"Oh," said Louise, nodding.

"Can I have a copy of that book?" asked Caroline.

"I'll get you one," said Dane.

"So what happened with the evil spirits in your dream?" asked Corrynne.

"They couldn't touch me as long as I was near the house or one of the warrior spirits."

"Was it the house itself and the warrior spirits that kept you safe, or was it just your goodness that kept them at bay?" asked Bo.

Brea shook her head. "I wasn't sure. That's where symbolism probably comes in."

"I agree," said Bo. "Because places are not holy by themselves, it's the people present within them, and their obedience to God's laws that make a place holy, and serves as a protection against evil.[7] A church is just blocks of rock and planks of wood, until those inside make it an edifice of worship by their righteousness."

"Maybe that's what was being communicated. When I join with my family in their righteous household, or with God's angels, I'm safe."[8]

"Did you ever get in the house?" asked Caroline.

"Yes. Mom, you opened the sliding back door and I was taken in."

"Good," said Corrynne. "I like that ending."

"The next dream started the same way. I was coming out of the tunnel of my home and again I was placed behind the bush at the side of your house. I heard the same conversation between the evil spirits, only this time, I didn't run when the butler appeared. I decided to see what would happen if I stayed."

"Did he find you?"

"No," said Brea. "At least not at first. This time, a mob of angry people joined Brother Reiser."

"Who were they?" asked Bo, feeling worried.

"They were people that used to be in the Church, but had since joined the UN and turned against the Saints."[9]

"How did you know that?"

"I don't know, but that's who they were," said Brea. "I'm sure of it."

"So they were disgruntled ward members?"

"Yes," said Brea, nodding. "Every one of them had a gun or a club and all of them were very angry at you, Dad."

"Great," said Bo. "I'm dead, aren't I?"

Brea looked at her father for a moment and said, "Well, actually in this dream you did die."

Bo took in a deep breath and sighed as he shook his head.

"But hear me out. If the dreams are telling me what I think they are, then I don't think you have to."

"Continue," said Corrynne. "How did Dad die?"

"Because the evil spirits didn't come after me, they put all their energy into making the mob angry, by going to each person and speaking in their ears."[10]

"What good would that do?" asked Caroline. "We can't hear those people."

Brea thought a moment. "You know, I don't know, but in my dream, their whispering sure affected people."[11]

"I think it's telepathy," said Dane. "Spirits can give thoughts to us.[12] We have the ability to get rid of those thoughts, but we can also accept those thoughts and let them affect our choices."[13]

"Right," said Brea. "That's what was happening. Those evil spirits were inspiring anger in the mob. They were really enjoying what they were doing, too. At one point, it looked like they were dancing between all the people in some evil fervor."

"What a frightening image," said Louise.

"What happened next?" asked Caroline.

"Brother Reiser threw the rock through the front window and it scared the babies. Dad got angry, just as they wanted you to…"[14]

"And he went outside with his gun," said Corrynne, finishing for Brea.

Brea nodded. "Yes, and then he was shot by someone in the crowd before he even left the porch steps. I couldn't tell who."

Corrynne shook her head and looked at the floor. "Guns are bad news, Bo."

Bo shook his head. "No they're not. I have a responsibility to protect my family.[15] I just need to have better judgment when I do."

Louise smiled and nodded. "How do you still have a gun?" she asked. "I thought they were all taken when the State of Emergency was declared."

Bo looked at Louise with a guilty face. "I didn't register mine. I got it at a gun show."

"Ahh," said Louise, as she shrugged. "I was just wondering." Then she leaned forward and said, "I'm glad it wasn't. We need it. No one knows what we're going to face. I hope you have more."

Bo nodded in relief. "I do."

"My husband just needs anger management," said Corrynne.

"Hey, I'm getting better."

Corrynne nodded. "You are getting better, but I think if a mob came to our door and the safety of our family was being threatened, you'd resort to violence even after hearing the outcome of Brea's dreams, and you know it."

"Of course I would. It's my job to protect my family. As Brigham Young has said, 'It is far better to die in a good cause than to live in a bad one.' [16] I'm not afraid to die. I'm not a coward."

"Bo!" said Corrynne. "Don't talk like that. No one has to die. Protecting the family by violence might be necessary sometimes, but listen to your daughter. Don't be a hot head and start a fight alone!" [17]

"Hey, if violence is how I do my duty as a father, then that's how I do it,"[18] said Bo, defensively. "But, even *I* wouldn't go outside with one gun where there were many against me. That would be suicide."

"It was suicide," said Brea.

That statement punched Bo in the stomach and he was left astounded, not knowing what else to say.

"Anyway, after that," continued Brea, "I rushed out from my hiding place to Dad, but the evil spirits saw me and attacked me."

"Attacked you?" asked Caroline. "How does someone without a body attack someone who does?"

"I'm not sure how it works, but spirits have some way to manipulate matter, including the body. For me, they bound my body so I had no power over it. I couldn't even breathe, and I collapsed."[19]

Corrynne ran her fingers through her hair nervously. "Let's make sure that scenario never happens."

"I could have commanded them to leave in the name of Christ.[20] I know that works because I had to do it in the Daimler mansion, but I didn't have a chance. My dream ended," said Brea.

"So there's a way to fight off evil spirits?" asked Caroline.

"Yes," said Corrynne. "Being good generally keeps their temptations in check, but commanding them in the name of Jesus Christ to leave you alone works the best."

"Why?"

"There's a hierarchy between spirits," said Bo, "where evil spirits must obey the authority of Christ, even though they are evil."[21]

"And God has more power than Satan,"[22] said Dane. "God can throw evil into the bottomless pit at any time,[23] just like he tossed Satan out of heaven,[24] he just doesn't yet, because we still have more testing to go through."

"Those evil spirits only exist here on earth because the Lord allows them to," said Brea.

"Why does he allow them to?" asked Caroline.

"Because this life is a test,"[25] said Louise, smiling at Bo and Corrynne. "Isn't that right?"

"Right," said Bo, remembering their earlier conversation about that topic.

"I imagine having an adversary makes learning good from evil quicker than not having one,"[26] said Louise. "And if that's one of the purposes of this life, we need to learn as quickly as possible, because life is short. Opposition does that for us."[27]

Dane began to clap. "Bravo, Professor. Bravo."

Louise smiled and nodded. "As you can tell, I've been thinking about this issue a lot."

"Were there any more dreams?" Caroline asked Brea.

"Yes, actually, there was one more," said Brea. "This time I was flying through the air like the wind, don't ask me what that meant. I hope that doesn't mean I'll die and become a spirit, but anyway, that wasn't the focus of the dream."

Corrynne looked worriedly at Bo and then back to Brea.

"What was the focus?" asked Bo, now thoroughly interested.

"I saw Brother Reiser outside the house with the same rock, just like the first two times. I saw the evil spirits, jumping around trying to cause trouble, but the house was completely dark."

"As if it was empty?" asked Corrynne.

"Right," said Brea. "No one was home."

"Where were we?" asked Corrynne.

"We were living on Old Man Griffin's property—in a tent."

"I told you!" said Corrynne.

Brea smiled and said, "Lots of people were camped on his property. It was a tent city surrounded by the same protective spirit that protected this house. The whole encampment was blanketed in a soft, radiant white."

"Were the warriors there too?" asked Dane.

"Yes. They guarded the entrance to the hay field where everyone was living.[28] As I flew over I could feel peace and thankfulness emanating from the little encampment."

"What happened to Brother Reiser?" asked Bo.

"Brother Reiser didn't know what to do since we weren't home. The mob came and joined him like before. After realizing we were probably living at the Griffin place, they tromped over there and demanded Dad be delivered to them."

"What happened after that?" asked Caroline.

"A huge group of men, including you, Dane, told the mob to go home. Dane, you had some strange circular weapon in your hand."

Dane smiled and looked over at Louise, who looked surprised.

"Sounds about right," said Dane.

"And did they?" asked Corrynne.

"Yes, actually, an interesting thing happened. As the mob moved closer to the farm, the evil spirits disappeared. With the spirits and their whisperings gone, the mob lost their steam. Finally, all of them decided to just disband and go home."[29]

"So it was over?" asked Bo.

Brea shook her head. "No, they were still intent on fighting another day, but that night no one died."

Corrynne looked at Bo. "So, I guess the choice is clear. We should go earlier rather than later to Mr. Griffin's home."

"We are to flee to Zion, or live among those who are of one heart and one mind, if we don't want to fight against our neighbor,"[30] said Dane.

"Does it say that in your scriptures too?" asked Caroline.

"Yes, it does," said Dane, with a smile.

"Did you ever find out why that mob was so angry?" asked Bo.

Brea hesitated, trying to remember the details. "I got the impression there were many reasons. You were blamed for practically everything, but the big one was that Brother Reiser's wife died of a heart attack. The people with him believed you should have saved her."

"Saved her?" asked Bo. "I'm not a doctor."

"I know," said Brea, "Actually it had something to do with blessings. You gave a blessing, but it didn't work—I don't know," said Brea shaking her head.

Bo shook his head, "Great," he said, wondering how he was going to avoid this one. He was the bishop! People asked him to give blessings all the time. He didn't know what to do.

"So the division's beginning, isn't it, Bo?" asked Corrynne. "The tares are being divided from the wheat."[31]

"Being readied for harvest," said Bo, nodding. "It's interesting how things play out. I wish all our ward members would just put aside their pride and unify, but it's obvious from Brea's dream that there's going to be some of our friends and neighbors who are willing to kill out of anger."

"I think I'll start packing," said Corrynne. "It seems obvious we're moving on." Turning to Dane, she said, "Think about how to make our tent comfy, will you?"

"Got it," said Dane in a resigned voice as he hopped over the back of the couch. "I kind of like this sofa," he said under his breath.

"I'll go talk to Mr. Griffin," said Bo as he stood from his chair. Right as Corrynne passed by him, he caught her wrist, and pulled her into his arms. "Oh, by the way, thanks for being so willing to live with a man who's still working on his weaknesses."

Corrynne smiled and kissed Bo on the cheek. "Live with him, *I love him*!" she said, winking at Caroline and Louise, who were smiling at the fond display.

"So do I," said Brea as she laid Striynna down on the couch.

Bo felt an overwhelming love for his family. Looking at Brea he said, "Thanks."

Brea nodded. "You got it. And remember, you can come and sleep at my tropical hideaway any time, because I'm not coming over to sleep in your tent."

Coronation

Denali Prison Camp, Alaska
10:20 p.m.

"Hay-ya!" yelled Carea, as she snapped the reigns of her dogs. "Hay-yahh," she called again, as she urged the dogs on.

The night was bitterly cold. The moon was bright, full and white, giving them more than enough light to travel by.

"Come'on, let's get home!" she called, as the frozen air whipped her face, stinging her eyes.

The dogs, running swiftly, had brought her close to camp. She could see it off in the distance, and that's why she wore the bear head firmly upon her own, and allowed the heavy pelt to flow powerfully behind her. It had become a tradition for the warrior suing for leadership, to wear the conquered beast into camp, to prove their victory.

Carea blew her antelope horn loud and long. ...She repeated the sound.

Off in the distance two horns answered her. Now they knew she was coming.

Lights went on in the camp as lamps were lit.

Carea's eyes teared. She felt like bawling like a baby. As she watched the camp prepare for her return, all the stress of the hunt began to bubble to the surface. She had done it! She had killed a bear, harvested it, and brought it home to feed her clan. Her solo hunt had been successful. She'd live to enjoy the fruits of her labor!

Carea wiped the tears from her face as she steadily held the ropes of the dogs with the other. Now she had to put away her tears and be strong again. It was time to face the camp.

Things were going to be different. Carea had sway over the people before the hunt, by virtue of her courage and optimism, but now, because she had proven an unusual bravery, strength, and wisdom as a female hunter, the people would automatically respect her ideas and her teachings. Her influence would exponentially expand. Being the youngest and only female council member of the bear clan, she promised herself to be a good steward over the camp's trust.

The sled glided over the border of the camp and was welcomed with cheers and chanting. The crowd enveloped her, pressing in tightly as hands were extended to her. She touched many of them. Everyone was so happy! Carea was overwhelmed by their adulation. She thought she might burst! Was this really happening? She wanted to slow time so she could enjoy every moment!

Next, the sled was overtaken by large, scary-looking men with tattoos, who lifted her upon their shoulders letting the bear skin dangle to the ground. Carea steadied the head on top of hers and she smiled to herself. So many things had changed. These people were no longer strangers or frightening enemies, they had become her people, and she found she loved them.

"White Bear! White Bear! White Bear!" the crowd chanted. Carea had been given her name of leadership.

"White Bear! White Bear! White Bear!" they continued clapping and chanting.

Carea was taken to a rock staircase to take her seat among the council members. She was set down, feet first, gently on the first stone step. She turned and waved at all her friends. She saw Bones cheering wildly over on the border of the crowd surrounded by her cabin buddies. Carea pointed, to acknowledge them and they cheered even louder.

Then Carea turned to walk up the stairs, limping only slightly.

Jack met her halfway, with his own bear head and pelt upon his head. With a hand, he led Carea up the stairs and to her stone throne that was set among six others.

At the top, Carea pulled her pelt behind her and sat on the center stone chair, as the crowd continued to cheer. She looked out on the camp. Good things were happening. Today, instead of starving and fighting, the people were working together to assure food for all, water in every cup and warm skins to fight the winter. There had been many changes for the better, and now she could work to assure even more would come.

November 23rd

Miracle of the Whale

Bering Sea, Russia
1:10 p.m.

Despite the winter month, the snow was melting. The temperature was unseasonably warm near the sea. Chenille and Braun walked in muddy slush, dragging their sleigh through muck. They were so hungry and weak, but through sheer will, they forced themselves forward with staggering steps. Supposedly there were people and food ahead. They had to walk, just a little more.

Finally they came over a ridge to gaze on the glacier-riddled sea. It was a beautiful, awe-inspiring sight, but still, there was something terribly, terribly wrong. Where were the people? Where were the other tribes? Despite the stories they had heard of a group of over a million people camping on the cliffs above the water, there wasn't one soul to be seen.

"Where's everyone?" asked Chenille, looking like she was near collapse. "Did they cross without us?" She asked, her voice breathy. It sounded like she was about to cry any moment.

Braun shook his head. "I don't know. I was wondering the same thing." Looking for John, he saw him. He was ahead, standing at the cliff's edge overlooking the sea. "Let's go talk to John and find out," Braun said, his weariness deepening from his disappointment. Grasping Chenille's hand, together they managed to pick up their pace. It was just a little ways more.

When they were within earshot, Chenille called out, "Elder Zebedee!"

John looked over his shoulder. He was smiling. Then he turned back to whatever he was looking at. With a hand he motioned to Braun and Chenille to join him, to see what he saw.

Braun and Chenille looked at each other with hope.

"Did you see his smile?" Chenille asked.

"Yep," answered Braun, beginning to smile too.

"What's he looking at?"

"Your guess is as good as mine," said Braun, as new energy filled his muscles. "But if he's smiling, it must be good news."

The couple approached the cliff's edge.

Braun expected to see a long land bridge linking Russia to Alaska, but to his disappointment there was nothing in the water but large, flat glaciers threatening to bash into each other with the growing wind and waves of the sea.

"Where's the land bridge?" asked Braun feeling intense discouragement.

"Don't worry. It's there, you just can't see it. But look, my friend, a little closer. Look at the beach!" said John.

Braun and Chenille both gazed down below them at the strip of rocky sand that bordered the beach. There on its shores were many stranded whales and sea turtles.

"Why are those animals on the beach?" asked Chenille, looking disturbed. "Are they sick?"

"No, they're just disoriented. They are stranded on the sand and they will die."

"That's terrible!" exclaimed Chenille.

"No! That's *wonderful*!" exclaimed Braun.

"Yes! The Lord has provided for us!" said John, with a laugh. "Now everyone can not only eat, but dry extra food for the rest of our journey. At last, our people can be strengthened!"

"There's enough animals on this shore to feed all of us, plus anyone else who happens to come this way!" said Braun.

"They are the quail[32] and manna[33] from heaven that fed the children of Israel!" said John.

"Aren't we the children of Israel?" asked Chenille.

"Yes, we are, Chenille," said John, with a smile. "We are the children of Abraham, Isaac, and Jacob. And their God is our God. We are led as they were led, and by power, we'll obtain the good land."[34]

Suddenly, Chenille broke down and started to cry.

"What's wrong?" asked Braun looking into Chenille's face. "Are those happy or sad tears?"

"I'm just overwhelmed," she said, as she wiped the tears from her face. "Those animals are giving their lives for us! I wish I could thank them…but…"

"Don't think like that," said Braun. "Thinking like that will only make you depressed."

John kindly turned to Chenille. With a gentle hand on her arm, he said, "Your heart is tender for the Lord's creations, this is good.[35] But, see these are the last times when the sun will become hot,[36] the earth will become sick[37] and the sea creatures will lose their way.[38] Eventually, all the creatures in the sea will die. At least these creatures will die for a purpose."

"All of the creatures in the sea will die?" asked Chenille.

"Yes, all of them,"[39] said John. "The earth will be purged of all unrepentant life through the woes and judgments that are coming.[40] Then it will be renewed and become as the Garden of Eden where lush life will live alongside man in peace."[41]

"The sea animals aren't unrepentant," said Chenille. "They can't even sin."

"That's true," said John. "But for this purpose were they placed on the earth, to sustain man.[42] They will receive their own glory for their sacrifices."[43]

"What about us? Are we unrepentant? Are we making this journey only to die another day?" Chenille's eyes were searching Braun's.

"Chenille, people die for all sorts of reasons, not only because of unrighteousness. There are many natural causes of death..."

"I know that," snapped Chenille. "I'm just wondering if my hopes for the future have been futile after all we've been through."

John nodded to Braun. "Tell Chenille the future of the righteous. Tell her what she has to look forward to. Give her hope."

With that prompting, Braun's mind was catapulted through space and time. He saw Chenille. She was happy. She and Braun were surrounded by beautiful children, strong young boys and beautiful girls with long, golden hair. He had so much love for them as they played around him and his sweet wife. He noticed as he took in the beauty of the moment that there was immeasurable peace in his heart and satisfaction in his soul.[44] Then his mind broadened to see that they lived in a great city, with sparkling clean buildings, manicured lawns, and fruitful gardens.[45] In the middle of the city was a grand temple with twelve other temples surrounding it.[46] They all sparkled as if jewels littered the walls. The spires of the main temple rose over the city and peace thrived among the inhabitants. He took his view inward. He felt strong and very healthy, as if he had never felt hunger or thirst ever before. Instantly he knew that he was changed somehow, unable to suffer the problems of mortality, yet he knew he was still mortal.[47]

Suddenly, Braun's mind changed to another place. It must have been another place on earth. He noticed great darkness and the signs of relentless heat.[48] Men were languishing, propped against walls and in the cavities of rocks.[49] They gnashed their teeth as they suffered from burns, great sores[50] and diseases.[51] Braun looked down at his own hands and body. His body remained strong. There was no hint of sickness or deformity. He wasn't like them. Next, he noticed that not only was he not sick like the men on the ground, the heat didn't affect him. That was strange. If this part of the world was as hot as it seemed, wouldn't it affect him, too?[52]

...Without warning, he was brought back to the present. He gasped with the pain of his physical body. The cold and hunger was excruciating once again.

"What's wrong, Braun?" asked Chenille, with worry. "Are you OK?"

Braun nodded and weakly brought Chenille's hand up to his lips and kissed it. "I'm good." He found he was breathless and tapped for energy, even more than before.

"Did you just have a vision?" she asked. "You looked lost in your thoughts."

Braun nodded. "I did." With a weak smile and in a voice barely above a whisper, he said, "It was beautiful. You and I had children and we were safe. We were healthy and strong. There wasn't a power on earth that could hurt us."

"When? ...How?" asked Chenille shaking her head.

With a great feeling of gratefulness growing in his heart, he said, "By and by, my love. We'll make it through all of this. It will be like a dream that passes in the night."

Tears came to Chenille's eyes as she fell into the weak embrace of Braun's arms. She didn't have energy to speak another word.

With a soft hand, Braun stroked Chenille's hair as he spoke into her ear. "Each day will bring us closer to that moment. I promise. We'll make it, and it will be beautiful!"

Notes to "Flee unto Zion"

Thy Will Be Done

[1] "...The spirit that the Lord puts into a tabernacle of flesh, is under the dictation of the Lord Almighty; but the spirit and body are united in order that the spirit may have a tabernacle, and be exalted; and the spirit is influenced by the body, and the body by the spirit. In the first place the spirit is pure, and under the special control and influence of the Lord, but the body is of the earth, and is subject to the power of the Devil, and is under the mighty influence of that fallen nature that is of the earth. If the spirit yields to the body, the Devil then has power to overcome the body and spirit of that man, and he loses both. Recollect, brethren and sisters, every one of you, that when evil is suggested to you, when it arises in your hearts, it is through the temporal organization. When you are tempted, buffeted, and step out of the way inadvertently; when you are overtaken in a fault, or commit an overt act unthinkingly; when you are full of evil passion, and wish to yield to it, then stop and let the spirit, which God has put into your tabernacles, take the lead. If you do that, I will promise that you will overcome all evil, and obtain eternal lives. But many, very many, let the spirit yield to the body, and are overcome and destroyed" (Brigham Young, *Discourses of Brigham Young*, Vol. 2, pg. 255).

[2] "The Devil delights in the work of destruction—to burn and lay waste and destroy the whole earth. He delights to convulse and throw into confusion the affairs of men, politically, religiously and morally, introducing war with its long train of dreadful consequences. It is evil which causeth all these miseries and all deformity to come upon the inhabitants of the earth" (Brigham Young, *Discourses of Brigham young*, Vol. 11, pg. 240).

[3] "There are many instances in which angels have saved men from perilous circumstances. Faithful people have repeatedly been guarded and watched over. Whole groups have been preserved, such as when the angel of the Lord's presence saved Israel (see Isaiah 7-9; D&C 133:53)" (Oscar W. McConkie, *Angels*, pg. 44).

[4] "Prayer is an armor of protection against temptation and I promise you that if you will teach your children to pray, fervently and full of faith, many of your problems are solved before they begin" (Spencer W. Kimball, *Teachings of Spencer W. Kimball*, pg. 117).

[5] "...Four thousand years ago a small colony, under the leadership of the Brother of Jared, came to this hemisphere from Asia, from the very region of the original home of mankind after the flood. These colonists flourished here for perhaps eighteen or nineteen centuries, during which time they branched out in every direction, built cities and established 'kingdoms.' This accounts for the Aryan, or Asiatic, characteristics of the Indian languages and religious ideas. The Book of Mormon tells us that about 600 B.C., two companies of colonists from Jerusalem, one later known as Mulekites, and the other as Nephites and Lamanites, came over and settled, the first in a northern country and the second in a southern. It also tells us that, about 200 B.C., the Mulekites united with a portion of the Nephites, and the two became one people. This accounts for the strong Semitic element in the languages and the culture of the Indians" (George Reynolds, Janne M. Sjodahl, *Commentary on the Book of Mormon, Volume 4, Theories and Facts,* pg. 385).

[6] "The Book of Mormon, further, relates that the Jaredites were decimated by savage warfare, accompanied by famine and pestilence, and that they were harassed by murdering and plundering bands of outlaws. Under these conditions their civilization, naturally, suffered, and the people degenerated. The Book of Mormon describes, also, how the Nephites and Lamanites, through internal strife and bloodshed, suffered a similar fate. In that book we read that the Nephites were driven from place to place and, consequently, were scattered in all directions. Some of them must have amalgamated with such remnants of Jaredites as may have been found in out-of-the-way places, while the main body retreated and was, finally, crushed at Cumorah, about A.D. 385. War and bloodshed continued among the Lamanites. All records had been destroyed, or hidden, to escape destruction"

(George Reynolds, Janne M. Sjodahl, *Commentary on the Book of Mormon, Volume 4, Theories and Facts,* pg. 385).

[7] "The nearer we approach God, the better we endeavor to keep his commandments, the more we will search to know his will as it has been revealed, the less likely it will be for us to be led astray by every wind of doctrine, by these false spirits that lie in wait to deceive, and by the spirits of men, as the Lord has stated in the revelations which I have read to you. We will be protected, and we will have the power to understand, to segregate truth from error, we will walk in the light and we will not be deceived" (Joseph Fielding Smith, *Take Heed to Yourselves,* pg. 105).

[8] "As one studies the commandments of God, it seems crystal clear that the all-important thing is not where we live, but whether or not our hearts are pure" (Harold B. Lee, *Stand Ye in Holy Places,* pg. 24).

[9] "If you want to see the principle of devilism to perfection, hunt among those who have once enjoyed the faith of the holy Gospel and then forsaken their religion. We have the best and the worst. Why the worst? Because the Devil prompts men and women of the meanest and lowest grade to embrace the Gospel and get a foothold in the Kingdom of God to destroy it" (Brigham Young, *Discourses of Brigham Young*, Vol. 7, pg. 145).

[10] And the mists of darkness are the temptations of the devil, which blindeth the eyes, and hardeneth the hearts of the children of men, and leadeth them away into broad roads, that they perish and are lost" (1 Nephi 12:17).

[11] "May I state two simple but fundamental truths. First: Satan with all his cunning cannot overthrow you if you strive with all your might to keep the commandments of the Lord. And second: With the first breaking of one of these commandments, you have taken your first step into the devil's territory" (Harold B. Lee, Teachings of Harold B. Lee, pg. 39).

[12] "We should be on guard always to resist Satan's advances. He will appear to us in a person of a friend or a relative in whom we have confidence. He has power to place thoughts in our minds and to whisper to us in unspoken impressions to entice us to satisfy our appetites or desires and in various other ways he plays upon our weaknesses and desires" (Joseph Fielding Smith, *Answers to Gospel Questions*, Vol. 3, pg. 81).

[13] "And why should I yield to sin, because of my flesh? Yea, why should I give way to temptations, that the evil one have place in my heart to destroy my peace and afflict my soul?" (2 Nephi 4:27)

[14] "There are many spirits who have gone abroad in the world, and men are overcome by false spirits, and led astray from the path of truth. They will begin by doing some evil thing out of sight, and say, 'O, it is nothing, it is a mere trifle, and the Lord is merciful and forgiveth sin.' The sins which are considered trifles lay the foundation for greater evils, and expose men to be tempted, and buffeted by Satan, and they will be overcome little by little, until by and by they are overtaken in a fault which is more aggravating in the sight of justice, which lays the foundation for another trial more severe, and to be buffeted more by the Devil, for they lay themselves more liable to his power" (Brigham Young, *Discourses of Brigham Young*, Vol. 2, pg. 121).

[15] "By divine design, fathers are to preside over their families in love and righteousness and are responsible to provide the necessities of life and protection for their families" ("The Family: A Proclamation to the World," *Ensign,* November 1995, pg. 102).

[16] *Discourses of Brigham Young*, Vol. 11, pg. 134.

[17] "He that leadeth into captivity shall go into captivity: he that killeth with the sword must be killed with the sword. Here is the patience and the faith of the saints" (Revelation 13:10).

[18] "And again, the Lord has said that: Ye shall defend your families even unto bloodshed. Therefore for this cause were the Nephites contending with the Lamanites, to defend themselves, and their families, and their lands, their country, and their rights, and their religion" (Alma 43:47).

[19] Evil spirits have the ability to bind our bodies. See the following accounts:

"One night I was awakened out of my sleep by my wife making a noise as though she was nearly choking to death. I inquired the cause, and she replied that she had dreamed that a personage came and seized her by the throat and was choking her. I immediately lit a candle and saw that her eyes were sunken and her nose pinched in as though she was in the last stage of the cholera. I laid hands upon her and rebuked the evil spirit in the name of Jesus, and by the power of the holy Priesthood commanded it to depart. In a moment afterwards I heard some half a dozen children in different parts of the Bozier house crying as if in great distress. The cattle also began to bellow, the horses neighed, the dogs barked, the hogs squealed, the hens cackled and roosters crowed, and everything around seemed in great commotion. In a few minutes afterwards I was sent for to lay hands upon Sister Patten, the widow of David W. Patten, who was living in the room adjoining mine, and who was seized in a similar manner to my wife" (Heber C. Kimball, *Journal of Heber C. Kimball*, June 3, 1839, pg. 79).

Joseph Smith's account:

"I was seized upon by some power which entirely overcame me, and had such an astonishing influence over me as to bind my tongue so that I could not speak. Thick darkness gathered around me, and it seemed to me for a time as if I were doomed to sudden destruction" (Joseph Smith History 1:15).

[20] "Wilderness wanderers may or may not see the devil; we may or may not hear his voice or witness the manifestations of his presence. Yet like Moses and Joseph, we will be required to overcome our fear of him and confront him. Otherwise we will surely experience at least somewhat the bitterness of hell, for our fear is part of what gives Satan his power over us. We must also reach the point where we can face him directly, bear witness of our allegiance to Christ and His Father, spurn completely his temptations, and finally, in the name of Christ, command him to depart" (Joseph Smith, *Discourses of the Prophet Joseph Smith*, pg. 116).

[21] "It would seem also, that wicked spirits have their bounds, limits, and laws by which they are governed or controlled, and know their future destiny; hence, those that were in the maniac said to our Savior, "Art thou come to torment us before the time..." (Joseph Smith, *Discourses of the Prophet Joseph Smith*, pg. 116).

[22] "But again, who is Satan? He is a being of God's own make, under his control, subject to his will, cast out of heaven for rebellion; and when his services can be dispensed with, an angel will cast him into the bottomless pit. Can he fight against and overcome God? Verily, No. Can he alter the designs of God? Verily, No Satan may rage, but the Lord can confine him within proper limits. He may instigate rebellion against God, but the Lord can bind him in chains" (John Taylor, *The Government of God*, pp. 80-81).

[23] "And I saw an angel come down from heaven, having the key of the bottomless pit and a great chain in his hand. And he laid hold on the dragon, that old serpent, which is the Devil, and Satan, and bound him a thousand years, And cast him into the bottomless pit, and shut him up, and set a seal upon him, that he should deceive the nations no more, till the thousand years should be fulfilled: and after that he must be loosed a little season" (Revelation 20:1-3).

[24] "And the great dragon was cast out, that old serpent, called the Devil, and Satan, which deceiveth the whole world: he was cast out into the earth, and his angels were cast out with him" (Revelation 12:9).

[25] "Very frequently I have this question asked of me: 'When Lucifer, or the devil, was cast out of heaven, why did a Lord permit him to come to this earth to tempt and torment mankind? Why did he not punish him by sending him to some other, but isolated place with his angels?' My answer has been that the Father permitted Lucifer to come here so that he could tempt us and test our faith. It is a divine decree, and [to] me that is evidently essential, that we have this mortal probation, we are in it to be tested and proved to see if we can keep the commandments in the face of temptation or trial" (Joseph Fielding Smith, *Conference Report*, October 1966).

[26] "Who is Satan? A being powerful, energetic, deceptive, insinuating; and yet necessary to develop the evil, as there are bitters, to make us appreciate the sweet; darkness, to make us appreciate the light;

evil and sorrows, that we may appreciate the good; error that we may be enabled to appreciate truth; misery, in order that we may appreciate happiness" John Taylor, *The Government of God*, pg. 80).

[27] "And it must needs be that the devil should tempt the children of men, or they could not be agents unto themselves; for if they never should have bitter they could not know the sweet" (D&C 29:39).

[28] "In truth, the Lord does 'encamp about' the righteous (see Zechariah 9:8). One of the functions of angels is to protect and guard us" (Oscar W. McConkie, *Angels*, pg. 44).

[29] "I am persuaded that if we are to 'conquer Satan and...escape the hands of the servants of Satan who do uphold his work' (D&C 10: 5), we must understand and recognize the situation as it is. This is no time for us to bury our heads in the sand, to equivocate or panic. The difficulties of our times have not caught us unawares. A hundred and forty years ago the Lord clearly revealed the tenor of our times. We know that as the second coming of the Savior approaches, the tempo of Satan's campaign for the souls of men is being, and will continue to be, accelerated. We know that the experiences of the intervening years will try men's souls. We are fortified for the ordeal, however, by our knowledge that God lives; and his 'eternal purposes...shall roll on, until all his promises shall be fulfilled' (Mormon 8:22). We know that, to qualify us to prevail against Satan and his wicked hosts, the gospel of Jesus Christ has been restored in these latter days. We know that the Spirit of Christ and the power of his priesthood is an ample shield to the power of Satan. We know that there is available to each of us the gift of the Holy Ghost—the power of revelation—which embraces the gift of discernment by which we may unerringly detect the devil and the counterfeits he is so successfully foistering upon this gullible generation. Our course is clear and certain. It is to strictly obey the commandments of the Lord as they are recorded in the scriptures and given by the living prophets" (Marion G. Romney, *Look to God and Live*, pg. 145).

[30] "And it shall come to pass among the wicked, that every man that will not take his sword against his neighbor must needs flee unto Zion for safety" (D&C 45:68).

[31] "Therefore, let the wheat and the tares grow together until the harvest is fully ripe; then ye shall first gather out the wheat from among the tares, and after the gathering of the wheat, behold and lo, the tares are bound in bundles, and the field remaineth to be burned" (D&C 86:7).

Miracle of the Whale

[32] "And there went forth a wind from the Lord, and brought quails from the sea, and let them fall by the camp" (Numbers 11:31).

[33] "And when the children of Israel saw it, they said one to another, It is manna: for they wist not what it was. And Moses said unto them, This is the bread which the Lord hath given you to eat" (Exodus 16:15).

[34] "Behold, I say unto you, the redemption of Zion must needs come by power; Therefore, I will raise up unto my people a man, who shall lead them like as Moses led the children of Israel. For ye are the children of Israel, and of the seed of Abraham, and ye must needs be bled out of bondage by power, and with a stretched-out arm. And as your fathers were led at the first, even so shall the redemption of Zion be. Therefore, let not your hearts faint, for I say not unto you as I said unto your fathers: Mine angel shall go up before you, but not my presence. But I say unto you: Mine angels shall go up before you, and also my presence, and in time ye shall possess the goodly land" (D&C 103:15-20).

[35] "For every creature of God is good, and nothing to be refused, if it be received with thanksgiving" (1 Timothy 4:4).

[36] "And the fourth angel poured out his vial upon the sun; and power was given unto him to scorch men with fire" (Revelation 16:8).

[37] "And it came to pass that Enoch looked upon the earth; and he heard a voice from the bowels thereof, saying: Wo, wo is me, the mother of men; I am pained, I am weary, because of the wickedness of my children. When shall I crest, and be cleansed from the filthiness which is gone forth out of me? When will my Creator sanctify me, that I may rest, and righteousness for a season abide upon my face?" (Moses 7:48).

[38] Stranding of the whales is a factual occurrence that may be linked to increased solar activity and the decrease in the earth's magnetic field.

"In the final decades of the last century, an increasing number of strandings of male sperm whales (*Physeter macrocephalus*) around the North Sea led to an increase in public interest. ...We compared the documented sperm whale strandings in the period from 1712 to 2003 with solar activity, especially with sun spot number periodicity and found that 90% of 97 sperm whale stranding events around the North Sea took place when the smoothed sun spot period length was below the mean value of 11 years, while only 10% happened during periods of longer sun spot cycles. The relation becomes even more pronounced (94% to 6%, n = 70) if a smaller time window from November to March is used (which seems to be the main southward migration period of male sperm whales). Adequate chi-square tests of the data give a significance of 1% error probability that sperm whale strandings can depend on solar activity. As an alternative explanation, we suggest that variations of the earth's magnetic field, due to variable energy fluxes from the sun to the earth, may cause a temporary disorientation of migrating animals" (Klaus Heinrich Vanselow, and Klaus Ricklefs, "Are solar activity and sperm whale *Physeter macrocephalus* strandings around the North Sea related?" *Journal of Sea Research,* December 8, 2003, available online: http://www.sciencedirect.com/science/journal/13851101).

[39] "And the second angel poured out his vial upon the sea; and it became as the blood of a dead *man:* and every living soul died in the sea" (Revelation 16:3).

[40] "The mountains quake at him, and the hills melt, and the earth is burned at his presence, yea, the world, and all that dwell therein" (Nahum 1:5).

[41] "For the Lord shall comfort Zion, he will comfort all her waste places; and he will make her wilderness like Eden, and her desert like the garden of the Lord. Joy and gladness shall be found therein, thanksgiving and the voice of melody" (2 Nephi 8:3).

[42] "And whoso forbiddeth to abstain from meats, that man should not eat the same, is not ordained of God; For, behold, the beasts of the field and the fowls of the air, and that which cometh of the earth, is ordained for the use of man for food and for raiment, and that he might have in abundance" (D&C 49:18-19).

[43] "Question: 'Do animals have spirits? If so, will they obtain the resurrection, and if so, where will they go?' Answer: The simple answer is that animals do have spirits and that through the redemption made by our Savior they will come forth in the resurrection to enjoy the blessing of immortal life" (Joseph Fielding Smith, *Answers to Gospel Questions*, Volume 2, pg. 48).

[44] "And the ransomed of the Lord shall return, and come to Zion with songs and everlasting joy upon their heads: they shall obtain joy and gladness, and sorrow and sighing shall flee away" (Isaiah 35:10).

[45] "In June 1833, according to the description, [the city of New Jerusalem] contains measurements representing one mile square. All the squares in the plot were to be ten acres square. The lots were laid off alternately in the squares, one running from south to north to the line through the center of the square; the next, the lots running from east to west to the center of the line. Each lot was four perches in front, and twenty back, making one half of an acre each. In one square the houses would face one street while on the next they face the opposite street. All the lots were to be of equal size. Certain squares in the center were set apart for public buildings, store-houses, temples, Churches, schools, etc. The Prophet estimated that this plan would permit space for twenty thousand people. South of the plat provision was to be made for barns, stables, etc., so that they would not be scattered throughout the entire city. Beyond were to be farms for the agriculturist. As the city grew other squares could be laid off as needed, 'and so fill up the world in these last days, and let every man live in the city for this is the city of Zion.' All the streets were of one width, being eight perches wide. There were to be eight perches between the main temple and the street, thus placing the temple in the center of the square. Each lot was to contain one house with a small yard in front to be planted as a grove, the back of the lot, for gardens. All the houses were to be of brick or stone" (Joseph Fielding Smith, *Church History and Modern Revelation, Volume 2*, pg. 174).

[46] "There are to be twelve temples in [New Jerusalem]. The idea is quite general that there is to be but one grand temple, but there are to be temples for various purposes. ... The purpose for which these

twelve temples were to be built, the nature of the work of them, is not explained, except as it may be surmised from the descriptions. The great work, however, in the central, commanding temple was without question to be for all the ordinances for the living and the dead such as we have in our temples today" (Joseph Fielding Smith, *Church History and Modern Revelation, Volume 2*, pgs. 174-175).

[47] "When Christ comes the saints who are on the earth will be quickened and caught up to meet him. This does not mean that those who are living in mortality at that time will be changed and pass through the resurrection, for mortals must remain on the earth until after the thousand years are ended. A change, nevertheless, will come over all who remain on the earth; they will be quickened so that they will not be subject unto death until they are old. Men shall die when they are one hundred years of age, and the change shall be made suddenly to the immortal state. Graves will not be made during this thousand years, and Satan shall have no power to tempt any man. Children shall grow up 'as calves of the stall' unto righteousness, that is, without sin or the temptations which are so prevalent today. Even the animal kingdom shall experience a great change, for the enmity of beasts shall disappear, as we have already stated, 'and they shall not hurt nor destroy in all my holy mountain: for the earth shall be full of the knowledge of the Lord, as the waters cover the sea' (Isaiah 11:9)" (Joseph Fielding Smith, *Way to Perfection*, pgs. 298-299).

[48] "And the fourth angel poured out his vial upon the sun; and power was given unto him to scorch men with fire. And men were scorched with great heat, and blasphemed the name of God, which hath power over these plagues: and they repented not to give him glory" (Revelation16:8-9).

[49] "And the kings of the earth, and the great men, and the rich men, and the chief captains, and the mighty men, and every bondman, and every free man, hid themselves in the dens and in the rocks of the mountains" (Revelation 16:15).

[50] "And the first went, and poured out his vial upon the earth; and there fell a noisome and grievous sore upon the men which had the mark of the beast, and *upon* them which worshipped his image" (Revelation 16:2).

[51] "And the fifth angel poured out his vial upon the seat of the beast; and his kingdom was full of darkness; and they gnawed their tongues for pain And blasphemed the God of heaven because of their pains and their sores, and repented not of their deeds" (Revelation 16:10-11).

[52] "And he that liveth in righteousness shall be changed in the twinkling of an eye, and the earth shall pass away so as by fire" (D&C 43:32).

CHAPTER SIXTEEN

VOICES IN THE DARKNESS

"...The still small voice, which whispereth through and pierceth all" (D&C 85:6).

00:00:29, 19:15:11, Zulu
Tuesday, December 2nd

Waiting

Bering Sea, Russia
12:45 p.m.

Fires burned hot on the beach bordering the Bering Straight. Braun, Chenille, and the tribal people feasted daily on the never-ending supply of fresh whale and turtle that appeared miraculously every night to nourish them. Their bounty continued to be as great as their joy was full.

It was John's routine to feast with the people, too, as he moved from fire to fire. He would talk to each in their various tongues and dialects. Braun watched him with admiration from where he sat near the tiny fire he shared with Chenille. He wondered how many languages John knew, and what it would be like to be these people's leader? He thought it must be edifying to see prophecy unfold after waiting so long.

Licking her fingers and gazing out to the dark sea from the beach, Chenille asked, "So, when are we going to see that land bridge we've heard so much about?"

Braun shrugged. "John says it's already there. I don't see it, but I know he's right. There was a great earthquake that lifted the land to the surface somewhere. Maybe it's down the coast a bit."

Chenille looked up and down the coast. "Do you see any land out there?"

"Nope," said Braun. "But I'm sure if we asked, John would tell us where it is."

Chenille took another piece of whale meat and looked for John. Finding him a couple fires over, she said, "He seems to be enjoying himself. I don't want to bother him."

"Just wait till he comes over here. He's making his rounds," said Braun.

"Sounds like a good plan," said Chenille, as she licked her fingers and picked out another piece of meat. "You'd think I'd get tired of this stuff, but I'm finding that I'm not." Looking up at Braun, she asked, "Don't you think that's strange? Back home, I couldn't eat the same thing twice, *ever*."

Braun looked over at Chenille's meat. "What do you have there?"

"Whale—just like you."

"Hmmm," said Braun. "You seem to be enjoying yours better than I am. You must have a different part than I do," he said, exploring Chenille's portion with his eyes. "Do you mind if I have a bite?"

"Sure. Go ahead," she said, holding it out for him.

Braun picked out a piece of meat, tilted his head back, and dropped it in his mouth. After a couple chews he said, "Mmmm, you're right. Your food is much better than mine. I don't know quite why that is, but…"

"Riiiiight," said Chenille, looking at Braun with a sideways glance. "You're making fun of me now."

"No, seriously, your food is fantastic! May I have another bite?"

"Whatever," said Chenille, smiling as she held her food out again.

Braun moved near Chenille, leaned down for another bite, but instead of taking the offering, Braun planted a surprise kiss on her mouth.

"Hey!" said Chenille wiping her mouth. "That was gross. You have a greasy mouth."

"Oh, I didn't get any. Let me try again," said Braun, as he went in another time.

Chenille squealed happily, laughing as if she was being poked in the ribs. "Braun! Stop it! You're slobbering all over me!"

Suddenly, Braun felt like he was being watched. He straightened to see John behind him.

"Elder Zebedee!" said Chenille, in obvious embarrassment, as she stood and wiped her face clean.

"We—ahh—ahh," stammered Braun, turning red.

John held up his hands, "No explanations. I came to see how you two were faring, but I can already tell. Love is the universal language that needs no interpreter."

"Come have a seat with us," requested Chenille as she sat again. "Our whale dinner is especially sweet. We were just talking about that."

John took a seat but held up a hand. "Thank you, but my belly has been filled beyond its natural stretching point. I just came to talk with you about the plans that lay before us."

"Great!" said Chenille as she and Braun connected confirming gazes.

Braun took his previous rock seat.

"I know it's the question of every soul on this beach," said John, looking over the congregation that was growing as new tribes joined them from their journeys. At the moment the gathering stretched the length of at least three football fields and the depth of at least two.

Pointing out to the Bering Sea, John stated, "The land below the water out there is at least a thousand miles long in length. It runs between the two countries, America and Russia."

Chenille gasped. "It's 1000 miles to the other side?"

John smiled and shook his head. "No, it's only 55 miles across the water."

"Whew!" said Chenille. "I didn't *think* it was a thousand miles to the other side."

"Now that we don't have reindeer to pull our sleds, it will probably take us four days to cross on foot," added John.

"So what's 1000 miles long, again?" asked Chenille. "I'm sorry, I missed that."

"If I understand right," started Braun, "there's a land mass that's buried under the water. From north to south, between Russia and America, it's 1000 miles long."[2]

"Right," said John, nodding.

Understanding crossed Chenille's face. "Oh, I'm sorry. Yes, of course. The *land* beneath the water is 1000 miles long. For some reason, in my mind I imagined the land to just be a thin little strip linking each side. I didn't ever expect a whole land mass," she said, looking back and forth between Braun and John. "So you're saying we won't be able to fall off it into the ocean when we cross, right?" asked Chenille, trying to be cute.

"That's exactly what I'm saying," said John. "There will be more than enough room for us all to cross over together."

"Is that what happened before we arrived? Did the others cross already?" asked Braun.

John nodded. "Some of our people are caught on the two islands that lie midway, but the rest have successfully crossed and wait for us on the other side."

"How did they make it across the water?" asked Braun.

"There wasn't water when they crossed. A couple of months ago the earthquake caused the land to rise,[3] but the sun has been growing hot and warmed the atmosphere. The glaciers have melted, making the seas rise. Now the land is about four feet under water again."

"So then, what are we going to do?" asked Chenille. "It's too cold to wade across. Are we going to build boats?"

"No. There's not enough wood around here. We're going to wait," said John.

"Wait for what?" asked Braun.

"The winter is bound to become colder. We'll set up a settlement here on the beach, eat food from the sea, drink melted snow, build tents from the whale skin and wait till the water freezes."

"Ahhh," said Braun, nodding. "Four feet of water won't take long to freeze."

"No. Despite the warm bouts of weather, there's already ice floating in the water. It won't be long."

Chenille closed her eyes and pressed her hands together. "And then..." opening her eyes, with an ecstatic smile, she completed her thought, "I can't believe it! You know what thought I had, Braun?"

"What?"

"We are only *55* miles away from—*America*! We have come thousands of miles and now only 55 measly miles stand between our country and us. Do you know how long it's been since I've stood on American soil? Between my internships in Europe and Russia and now traveling through Siberia, it's been way too long."

"I know the feeling," said Braun.

"We're four days away from flushing toilets, electricity, and central heat," continued Chenille. "Four days away from Hershey's chocolate, McDonalds double cheeseburgers and Cold Stone ice cream! Oh, I can't *wait*."

"I doubt there'll be a McDonalds nearby on the other side," said Braun. "We'll have to travel through quite a bit of wilderness before we get to any towns big enough to have restaurants."

Chenille pursed her lips into a pout. "A girl can dream, can't she?"

"I'll leave you two to yourselves," said John, standing to leave. "I suggest you build a small tent out of the whale bones and skin. Walrus or seal skin works, too, as a water-proof covering, if you can find any."

Braun looked at Chenille and then back. "I don't know how to catch those."

"Then stick to the whales."

"Will there be enough whales to make tents for everyone?"

"Oh, yes," said John smiling.

The Secretary's Declaration

Frankfurt, Germany
08:21 a.m.

Matt watched as his father primped Vladimir Lityny, the new Russian Secretary General, for his first international media address. Vladimir had just been nominated by an overwhelming majority of the delegates at the UN. Thus in a day he had gone from being the President of the European Union to the Secretary General of the United Nations.

Matt had known for quite a while that President Lityny was another puppet of his father's, but even though he had known it, it was quite a different thing to watch the sickening interaction between them. MD doted on the Secretary, who was in his late fifties himself, showing him attention as if he were a son, brushing off his shoulders and straightening his jacket, all the while giving him pointers on his speech.

Secretary Lityny, with his aristocratic pointed nose, stark blue eyes, and cut features, listened to MD with complete respect. He would nod every so often and look down at the notes MD had supplied for him a few weeks earlier. The speech was memorized, but the notes were at his fingertips as a reminder—just to keep him on track. MD demanded it.

The time was nearing. Two minutes to go.

The camera and sound men were stationed in their designated spots. The director was in his chair and the lights were bright. The hair and make-up staff fussed over the Secretary one last time. MD backed up and folded his arms. He had a great smile on his face.

Thirty seconds.

Secretary General Lityny fussed with his notes, placing one on his left and the rest of the stack in the center. He was careful to line the edges up perfectly, checking and rechecking the frivolous detail. The Secretary's speech would be delivered in Russian, out of respect for his own country, but then translated immediately to all other languages.

"Three, two, one—you're on," said the cameraman in Russian.

"Good evening to you, my friends," began Secretary General Lityny. "As your new Secretary General of the UN, I have some grievous news to disclose. For the last month, the UN has come under a series of attacks from the very people we are attempting to serve. In a series of deliberate and deadly terrorist acts, lives were suddenly ended by evil, despicable acts of terror, brought about by the radical, extremist anti-Christians that run rampant in the United States. The victims of these attacks were the selfless UN volunteers, who were providing food, warmth, and necessary monetary support to those of the devastated areas of that nation. These are people who deny the true and living Christ that has come to us to establish paradise among us. Instead, they use their efforts to kill and maim those of us who obediently and humbly worship him."

Matt looked away. All of this was a lie. No such thing was happening. All of this, the speech, the taping, was a part of his father's plan. It had to seem real, so that MD would have a reason to wipe out the "vermin" when a public cry rose up.

"I, being a true follower of religion in all of its forms, stared at the video footage given to me with disbelief, as fires burned and our people suffered. Terrible sadness and a quiet, unyielding holy anger has replaced patience and charity. These acts of mass murder were intended to frighten the world and the United Nations into chaos. But they have failed; we are strong, and we will fight."

Pictures played across the screen, supposedly the footage Vladimir had been referring to, depicting explosions and people suffering, while white-robed people labored over them in a pretended effort to heal them. It was all a ruse. It was staged. The explosions had come from other events and the actors were paid. Matt shook his head in disgust.

"Today, I tell you, we will no longer stand for such human tragedy among our members! A great people have been moved to defend themselves. Terrorist attacks can destroy individual people, but it can't touch the foundation of our faith. War has been declared and those who fight against us will be destroyed. *The anti-Christians will fall!*"[4]

There was a roar of applause, as if Secretary Lityny was speaking to a live audience.

"Who are these anti-Christians—those who refuse our God? They are those who call themselves, ironically, 'Christian.' They have stolen our Savior's name in order to trick the righteous of our people. Tolerance for these deceivers cannot go on.

"Who are these anti-Christians? These are they who controlled the American people in its glory days. These are they who enslaved them with their banks and their interest rates and their policies. These are they who undermined the rest of the world with words such as 'democracy,' 'majority,' 'conscience of the world,' 'world peace,' and 'constitutional rights.' These are they who sought to make the world like them, destroying all the uniqueness of other nations around them through their deviant ways.

"I say there is no safety, no salvation, until the bearer of this atrocity, the anti-Christians who call themselves Christians, are rendered powerless to harm another human on the planet!"

Another round of applause filled the room. Secretary Lityny nodded in gracious humility. He had been practicing this speech for a while.

With his hands balled in fists he continued. "We must call to account the November criminals. It cannot be that a thousand UN peacekeepers, killed in service, should fall in vain. We will not stand for traitors. No, we do not pardon, we demand—vengeance!"

Again, applause.

"To facilitate this hallowed war, we will demand all anti-Christians to give up every legal right as citizens in the International Society. They are to be exposed and hand over all the money they have hoarded, or created through trickery in stock exchanges, or through other shady transactions, have gained their wealth at the expense of the international people."

"The anti-Christians are to give up their houses. The housing scarcity must be relieved through energetic action; houses must be granted to those who deserve them. They must be given to faithful, international citizens! I say extremes must be fought by extremes!"[5]

Again the applause came in like a wave, this time with whistles and yells mixed in.

With hands held out wide, Secretary Lityny appealed. "I speak to you, the united nations of the world. Please, let us stand shoulder to shoulder as we fight for peace and security. Let us stand together to win the war against terrorism.

"Tonight, I ask for your prayers for all those who grieve, for all whose sense of safety and security has been threatened. And I pray they will be comforted by a power greater than any of us.

"Thank you. Good night, and God bless the United Nations."[6]

Video footage would be put in later, depicting a standing ovation.

Matt shook his head. This speech would be played repeatedly all over the world in every home that had entered the world economic system. Soon, a world war would break out. There would be millions of righteous people who would be killed because the people would believe these words. Resolve grew inside Matt. He couldn't wait any longer. His father had to be stopped! And now was the time. He turned and left the studio.

For the Love of Mankind

Provo, Utah
1:10 a.m.

Corrynne coughed. She adjusted her mask over her face. She could feel her fever burning.

"Here's a nitroglycerin pill," she said to a man who was having chest pains. He lifted his tongue and she put the pill under it with her gloved hand. "Just let it dissolve. Nitro should help you feel better, if this pain is coming from your heart. It dilates the blood vessels that feed your heart, giving it more oxygen."

The man nodded.

Corrynne looked up at the monitor. This patient's vital signs were stable but there were slight changes in his EKG, the recordings of the electrical conduction through his heart.

"Corrynne, Dr. Smith is here to take that patient to the Cath Lab," said the secretary through a wireless communicator on a tether hung around Corrynne's neck.

"He's ready," she said.

"I'll send the techs in to get him."

"Thanks," said Corrynne. Turning to the patient, she said, "Mr. Cross, the doctor will be taking you into the Cath Lab. In there, he'll thread a little device through your femoral vein and shoot some dye that will allow him to look at your heart. If he finds some blockages in your cardiac arteries, that device can open them up. You're going to be fine," she said, with a gentle touch on his shoulder, as medical technicians walked in.

"Thank you, my dear. I hope you get over your cold," the patient said empathetically.

Corrynne smiled. "I will. These things come on and then they go."

"Good thing you work in the Emergency Room," said the man as he patted her hand. "You should ask the good doctors for something."

"I will," said Corrynne, as she watched the techs wheel him away.

After the patient was gone, she collected the extra syringes, needles, saline and nitroglycerin off the patient's tray, and put them in her pocket. Next, she pulled the sheets off the bed and threw away the trash.

Walking down the hall to get some sheets for the bed, she swallowed. Her throat was on fire. She wiped her forehead with her forearm. She had lied to her patient. Her sickness wasn't getting better. She hoped it wasn't a strep pneumonia bug. That would be bad.

In the nursing lounge, there was a large plastic box labeled, "Supplies for the homeless." it was filling up pretty fast. It was strange to think of herself as homeless, but that's what she was. Her colleagues were donating to her and her community. They were being very kind. In another time, these supplies might be going to a third-world country. Today, it would go to people just up the street.

Corrynne pushed the supplies around to take an informal inventory. There was gauze, tape, gloves, and half-punctured packages of medications that couldn't be given to the patients. She could use it all.

"Hey, Corrynne," said Dr. Smith, as he poked his head into the lounge. "You don't look well. Why don't you go home?"

"Oh, I will," said Corrynne pulling her mask down. "I'm fine."

The doctor looked at her sideways. He had been hiding a temperature probe behind his back. He whipped it out and quickly touched it to her forehead, and then looked at the reading. "You are 103 degrees. If you weren't so against it, I'd admit you. We should do a chest film."

Corrynne shook her head. She was afraid of what they'd find. She couldn't be admitted. She couldn't afford any of her loved ones to know she had a biochip. "No, seriously, I'm getting better. I'm improving every day," she said, as she tried to smile convincingly.

"Do you need another prescription? Are you out?"

Corrynne's eyes lit up. "Oh yes, that would be wonderful. Thank you, doctor."

Doctor Smith tapped on the screen of his hand-held computer with his stylet. "I'm giving you a decongestant, antibiotic, and extra-strength ibuprofen." He walked over to the counter across the hall and pulled a paper out of the printer. Taking a step back, he handed it to Corrynne and said, "I want you to take these medications and take a few days off. Doctor's orders."

"OK," said Corrynne.

"This schedule you're keeping is going to kill you," he said, with a scolding tone and a stern look.

Corrynne nodded and took the prescription. She looked at it with amazement. He had ordered bulk of everything. She was overcome with happiness. He knew how much she needed supplies and he also knew that if he didn't give her extra, she'd sacrifice herself and give it to someone else.

"Thank you!" she breathed, thanking the doctor as well as her Heavenly Father. Despite her disobedience to his request not to get a chip, she could feel he understood her intentions and still loved her. That was a beautiful feeling. She hoped some day he'd forgive her, too.

ξξξξξξξ

After strapping the plastic box full of supplies and her filled prescriptions to her bike, Corrynne got on and peddled in the direction of home. She was shivering so hard, she almost couldn't ride. She couldn't imagine another feeling being more torturous. Still, she forged on, fighting against herself.

It was after one in the morning. Corrynne's shift normally went from ten at night to two in the morning. It was an odd time to work, but it served her purposes. The Emergency Room was the only place that allowed such short shifts. She was just grateful she could get them. The extra international credits provided things she and others in the ward had forgotten to store, like scissors, tape, rope, tarps, coal for cooking, and seeds for planting. She was beginning to build up a little nest egg and that made her happy. Normally she'd stop at the 24-hour grocery store on her way home, but today she was too sick.

During her long rides home, she had a lot of time to think. She thought about the sacrifices she was making. They were worth whatever price she was paying. People, lives—were worth sacrificing for. Still, guilt riddled her insides every moment of every day. She wondered if she was working so hard to punish herself to pay for her sins. She didn't know. All she knew was, considering all the other choices she had been faced with, these were hers, and if something bad happened to her because of that choice, no one would suffer except her.

Her thoughts turned to her husband. Poor Bo. She knew he suspected what she was doing, but he kept his nose out of her business—probably on purpose. It was easier for everyone that way. Every night she'd go to bed when he did and quietly sneak out after he started snoring; then after her short shift, she'd slip back into bed long before he got up. Sometimes he'd wake up in the night and ask her where she had been, and she'd just answer, "out," or, "couldn't sleep," or "took a walk," all of which answers were technically true...*but not.* Despite the consistency of her vacancy in bed, Bo never pressed her. Corrynne was thankful. She didn't want trouble. She was only doing what she thought best. Sometimes in life there were hard decisions and this was one of them.

Corrynne turned onto the main road and nearly ran into a parade of people that extended the length of her vision. They had large wagon-like structures made with car parts. There were a few animals pulling some of the vehicles, while others were being pushed and pulled by people.

Corrynne rolled up next to them, wondering who they were. "Hello," she said, nearly out of breath. She had to stop peddling and give her aching body a rest. She got off her seat and pushed the bike along-side the group.

"Hi," said a young man about nineteen.

"Where are you guys going so early in the morning?" she asked. "You look like you've come from somewhere far away."

"Our group is trying to find a man named Griffin. He has some land we can camp on for a short time before we move on again. We knew we were close and didn't want to stop traveling till we got there."

"All of you?" asked Corrynne looking at the long line of people.

The boy shook his head. "Out in the country we can all stay together, but here in the city, we have to divide up and stay in different places."

"Because there's too many of you?" asked Corrynne.

"Right. There's about 20 families that will split off to stay at the Griffin property and the rest will keep traveling and go to a different place. We all have our assignments."

"How do you know where to go?" asked Corrynne.

"There's a network set up by the church, telling us where we can gather safely."

"How do you communicate?" asked Corrynne.

"By radio. It's all done by radio. No, wait—sometimes it's done by currier."

"Like the pony express?" asked Corrynne.

"Yes, just like that."

"Well, I live on Griffin's land," she said, nodding as her teeth chattered.

"You do?" he asked, suddenly brightening.

"Yes, it's just a ways up the hill and down a little. I'm going there right now."

"Hey!" the boy called to the others in his group. "We're almost there! This lady's from the Griffin property!"

There were cheers throughout the surrounding crowd.

"Who are you?" asked Corrynne. "I'm assuming you're LDS."

"Yep. We're Mormons from California."

"How many in your group?" asked Corrynne.

The boy shook his head. "I don't know. There's miles and miles of us."

"Wow," said Corrynne. "That's a lot."

"Yep."

"Why are you coming here?"

"Didn't you hear?" asked the boy.

Corrynne shook her head. "Hear what?"

"We were warned by the Prophet by ham radio to leave our homes and cities.[7] We were the lucky ones."

"What do you mean, 'the lucky ones'?" asked Corrynne.

"We listened. We left in time. Anyone who didn't leave when they were told, have died—drowned in the water."

"What happened?" asked Corrynne feeling almost breathless with the news.

"The water rose ten feet, taking over the cities."

"Why?"

"I don't know. I heard from some other people we hooked up with, that at the beginning of November, huge storms ravaged the area. We had a couple earthquakes that caused some of the land to sink at the same time, creating tsunamis. It's been unbelievable."[8]

Corrynne shook her head. "That's amazing..."

"It's tragic," said the boy.

Corrynne nodded, not knowing quite what else to say. She changed the subject. "You've traveled quite a ways, then. I can't imagine traveling from California on foot."

"It's been an experience. We're exhausted," said the boy. "It's taken us months."

"Wow," said Corrynne, shaking her head.

"I'm Tray," he said, holding out a hand.

"Hi, Tray, I'm Corrynne. I have a son about your age," she said, shaking his hand.

"You do? That's cool. Any daughters?"

Corrynne smiled. Carea looked about his age. A lump formed in her throat. "I did..."

"Oh, I'm sorry," said Tray. "Did she die?"

Corrynne shook her head. "I don't think so, but I don't know. She was taken away by the government. She's in a prison camp in Alaska."

"That's too far away," he said.

"Don't remind me," said Corrynne.

"Do you mind me asking you a question?" asked Tray.

"No, go ahead."

"Do you have food?"

Corrynne looked at him and then at the ground, and then nodded. "We have some." She didn't know if they'd have enough for all 20 extra families that were moving in.

"Because we do. We have a lot," said the boy. "We have way more than we need and it's heavy. We were hoping to give our extra to people who were strapped and lighten our load."

Corrynne's heart swelled. Here was a moment that time stood still. God was aware. He was watching and he was helping.

"Thank you," said Corrynne holding back the tears. Twice in a morning! Help had come twice in one morning. "My husband is the bishop; won't he be surprised when he wakes up and finds you! Welcome to Utah!"

"Thanks," said Tray. "We already feel welcomed."

"Great!" said Corrynne as she mounted her bike. "See you there."

"Right," said Tray as he held up a hand to say good-bye.

Secret Communication

Frankfurt, Germany
11:05 p.m.

It was nearing the middle of the night. Matt had already locked up his prosthetic hands, but he couldn't go to sleep yet. There was something else he had to do.

Matt had two nightstands in his room. The right one had a small portable television and on the left one, a standard clock radio. He walked around the bed and bumped the flat button on the television with his forearm to turn it on. A fuzzy reception glowed in the dark of the room. It was perfect. Matt turned and retrieved a thick, black blanket from his bed and tossed it over the screen to block out the light it put off in the room. He wanted the room absolutely dark, leaving only the white noise of the static from the non-broadcast channel. It would drown any extra noises out. His dad would expect that anyway; Matt had been sleeping this way for a couple months.

Matt walked around to the other side of the bed. The clock radio was actually a ham radio with an internal antenna and a built-in noise-activated microphone. He had had it built from the finest technology, and made it look exactly like a radio that his parents had given him when he was young. The clock radio had sat in this room for years, so having the clock on the nightstand was very normal. If his father looked at the video feed coming from the chip in his head and saw the radio, he wouldn't suspect he could call out on the thing. It was one of two radios he had made a few years back, in the off-chance his father might suspect his true goals and try and cut him off from the world. Now it was his only lifeline out of this prison-mansion, and the only thing his father wasn't tracking or recording.

Matt felt the face of the radio in the dark. He had every detail memorized. With the ulnar edge of his right forearm stump, he pushed the large automatic scanning button. He counted to himself. One, two, three, four, five...he was counting the scanning intervals to find the one he wanted. Six, seven, eight, nine. There, nine. Now he was on the right channel. Right time, right channel. Stray Bullet, his right-hand man, would hear him in England. He would then interpret the messages and then pass them on throughout the underground network.

A BYU mug sat next to Matt's radio with what seemed to be harmless, thin, red and white straws. He leaned over and with his teeth picked one out of the batch. He needed the straw to be thin so that it would create a high enough pitch without it being a whistle. With this pitch, Stray Bullet's computers in England would separate his pattern out from the television background interference and interpret his words as marching orders to overthrow his father. Today, he was sending very important information, and he had to get it right. Maybe he'd do it twice.

Matt lay down on his bed, facing his radio. He pointed the straw at the hidden microphone on the radio, but then stopped. Was there any detail he was missing? There could be no mistakes. Everything had to be perfect. He looked around his pitch-black room. He imagined looking at the video screens in his father's office. If the ID number on his chip was called up, MD would see darkness, even if Matt's eyes were open. He listened to himself breathing. He tested the straw by blowing through it. The sound was absorbed by the television interference. Perfect. Now, he'd begin. Stray Bullet would be waiting.

Matt adjusted his pillow and thought about what he wanted to say. He'd blow out through the straw for a dash, and breathe in, through the straw for a dot. He'd communicate through Morse Code. "oo," he inhaled for a single dot to make the letter E. Waiting a short amount of time, he then exhaled, "eeee, eeee" twice to make an M. Pause again, to separate the letters as if they were words. "oo, eeee, eeee, oo" he continued, to make a P. Pause. He had just spelled EMP. Now it was time for the next word. "eeee, oo, oo, oo" for B. "eeee, eeee, eeee" for O, "eeee, eeee" for M, and "eeee, oo, oo, oo" for B. Bomb, there. Matt paused. He had spelled EMP bomb.

Stray Bullet would understand his message to mean that it was time set their plans in motion. It was time to prepare for a large electromagnetic explosion in America. A pulse like that would knock out all the implanted chips of all the people in America and set the country free.

Present

Provo, Utah
3:40 p.m.

Brea looked at her computer. She had Internet now. Matt had set her up with a satellite connection when he had worked out the details for her home. She kept checking her international e-mail, hoping he would send her something, but there weren't any messages. This really bothered her. What did it mean? Was he OK? The last time she had talked to him, he said he'd be in touch, but he didn't say how and he didn't say when. It had been months since they had talked.

In the back of her mind, worry grew. Brea knew that Matt ultimately planned to undermine his father. She also knew that if MD caught him, there was a good chance she'd never talk to her husband again. She squeezed her eyes shut. She couldn't think like that. No, just because she hadn't heard from him didn't mean he was dead. He was probably just being cautious. They had to make her father-in-law believe their marriage was truly over.

A ringing noise came from somewhere down the hall. Brea looked over her shoulder in confusion. She didn't have anything that rang like that. Without a phone, or a beeper, what could make such a noise? Her microwave wasn't on. Brea stood to investigate when the ringing came again.

Brea followed the sound. It drew her down the hall, through the tunnel and to the hydraulic door that led to the outside. Suddenly, she stopped. She sensed someone walking away from her home! Brea touched the wall to try and sense who was out there. There was someone walking away, but she didn't recognize who it was. It wasn't anyone of her family. Could he be a delivery person?

Delivery person? Brea frowned. That was ridiculous. No one would be delivering anything to a patch of ground...unless...maybe it *was* a delivery person and Matt had made her home with a secret doorbell! ...OK, now she was being dumb, but—she'd check outside anyway—just in case. Brea moved up the stairs, afraid to hope; she didn't want to be disappointed if it wasn't true.

Touching the door, Brea closed her eyes so she could sense outside, just to make sure no one was above her. No one was. Slowly, Brea opened the hatch and poked her head out. She was hoping—even though it was illogical—that Matt had sent her something. He could arrange it. He could arrange anything!

Just then, she saw it! It *was* a package! Brea's heart thumped hard in her chest as she carefully tiptoed up enough stairs so she could reach about two feet out of her doorway to where it lay in the tall grass. She caught a corner of the box and pulled it in. The box was plainly wrapped in brown packaging. Her first impulse was to rip it open right there.

Abruptly she froze. A frightening thought hit her mind hard. MD could have sent this package! He had just as many resources as Matt. She looked around the area right outside her door. Was he watching her now? Was the package just a trick to get the rabbit to come out of her hole? After all, it was in the middle of the day. Brea quickly set the box back into the grass and retreated into her home, closing the door after her.

ξξξξξξξ

Brea had been sitting on the bottom stair inside her door for fifteen minutes now, tortured by the thought that there was a package just outside. It was so close. She could easily open the door just enough to bring it in again. Maybe she had been too hasty. She should at least look at the box to see who it was from!

Brea quietly crept back up the stairs and pulled the lever that would open the door slightly. Her curiosity had won out. She had to look at the box.

From the slit in the door, she could see that there were tiny letters written neatly on one side. They were very, very small. Brea moved closer to the opening to read them. "Peter, Peter, Pumpkin Eater," she read out loud. "Ahh!" she exclaimed. This package *was* from Matt! She threw open the hatch and brought it in, slamming the door shut once again.

She giggled happily as she hugged and smelled the box. She could still smell Matt's cologne. It was faint, but it was there. She looked at the message again, this time to read the whole thing. "Peter, Peter, Pumpkin Eater, had a wife and couldn't keep her. Put her in a pumpkin shell, and there he kept her very well."

Brea burst into tears as she laughed hysterically, tears falling down her cheeks. Yes, that stupid rhyme was about her. It came from a conversation they had before they were married. Matt had made a long standing joke, saying, he'd keep her safely in a pumpkin shell, just like Peter, Peter pumpkin eater, did. Now his joke had come true. He was keeping her in a shell. Reality was much stranger than fiction!

Joy exploded inside Brea as she ripped the box open. She pulled back the packing paper and found a simple, white clock inside. It was an older model with AM and FM channels. Brea looked at it with awe. What was Matt sending her an old radio for? She searched the box for a note. On the bottom of the box she found one! It was in Matt's writing. It said, "Place this clock next to the computer to remember me."

"Hmmmm," said Brea, in a whisper. There was something special about this clock, wasn't there? She quickly rushed down the stairs, leaving all the garbage, and went to her computer. She placed the clock next to the computer. It looked cute. It was kind of retro. It gave her ideas about decorating the room in black and white just to match.

Suddenly the radio came to life. Strange sounds came out of it. Most of it sounded like static. Then the internet light began to flash on her computer. A dialog box appeared on the screen that said, "An unknown entity is trying to access your computer," then it gave her the choice to accept or reject it.

Brea hesitated. But then she smiled and pushed "accept."

A program was downloaded automatically. It went through multiple screens quickly, and download bars zipped across her computer. Then, it was quiet as it returned to her desktop.

Brea was disappointed. All that for nothing? ...But wait! There was a new icon on her desktop. It said "Morse." Brea clicked on it. A program opened up to a blank screen with a blinking curser....

Blessings

Provo, Utah
5:35 p.m.

"How many more are there to bless, Brother Stow?"[9] asked Bo.

"About twenty," said the kind-hearted, old man. "We're nearly finished."

"OK, where next?" asked Bo.

"Sister Crane."

Bo cringed. "Oh no. How's her little ones?"

"Sister Jensen has them."

"Oh, good," said Bo, shaking his head as they walked toward her tent. "This must be very hard without her husband. He was killed while on duty in the Middle East."

Brother Stow nodded. "I know. That was a tragedy."

In silence, they walked the rest of the way. Bo concentrated, trying to keep the Spirit strong as he gave these blessings of healing.[10] Some illness had gone through the tents and the families. Corrynne even had it. Luckily, people from California had joined them, bringing a load of medical supplies...although they denied any knowledge of them. But it didn't matter. However the supplies arrived, it was a blessing.

"Knock, knock," said Bo at the entrance of Sister Crane's tent. "May we come in?"

"Come in, Bishop," said a weak, female voice from inside.

Bo pulled back the tent flap and ducked in. "We hear you aren't feeling well."

Sister Crane shook her head. "I'm so weak, I can hardly hold my baby, let alone take care of my other children."

"It's OK," said Bo. "I understand Sister Jensen has that one under control."

"Yes, she's a saint," said Sister Crane.

Bo looked at Brother Stow who was standing patiently by his side. Bo suddenly noticed Brother Stow didn't have his cane, or his tremor. He looked strong standing in the closed tent doorway. Right now wasn't the time to discuss these changes, so Bo continued talking to Sister Crane. "Do you mind if Brother Stow helps me give you a blessing?"

"Not at all," said Sister Crane. She coughed roughly and seemed to be having a difficult time breathing.

Bo knelt on the floor of the tent next to Sister Crane's bed. "But first, I need to ask you some questions."

"Go ahead," she said, as Brother Stow also knelt nearby.

"In order for blessings to work for you, I would like to discuss faith,[11] for it is through the power of faith in God, and His will, that you may receive healing."

"I understand," said Sister Crane.

Bo paused and said, "As you know, faith is to hope for things that aren't seen, but true."[12]

Sister Crane nodded.

Bo continued. "The Prophet Joseph Smith taught that faith is a principle of power that motivates our day-to-day activities. Faith is the reason we get up in the morning to pursue a new day. It's the reason we plant seeds to grow food. It's the reason we try to start a fire to obtain its warmth. When we have faith in a true principle, we apply those principles to obtain an end reward."[13]

"It's like setting a goal," said Sister Crane.

"Yes," said Bo, "but in actuality, it's the reason *why* we set the goal, not the goal itself."

"Alright," said Sister Crane.

"Just like starting a fire with two plain-looking sticks, in hopes of a spark, each day we act upon things we hope for, even when we can't see how it will be fulfilled. We have faith that Christ and our Father in Heaven is real.[14] That's why we obey His commandments. We have faith that living together in this city will protect us from the UN and the violent segment of society, because God has told us it will.[15] All those things are actions of faith."

"OK," said Sister Crane, with another cough. Gasping, she said, "I believe that."

"So now, we're going to give you a blessing in hopes of healing. This is something hoped for, but not seen."

"Yes, I know, and I know with the power of faith, I will be better."[16]

Bo looked at Brother Stow and back again. "Do you know that God lives?"

"Yes, I do," said Sister Crane.

"Do you know he's a real person, with a tangible body like yours and mine?"[17]

"Yes, I do."

"Do you know that He can command your body to be well and the cells will obey his will?"[18]

"Yes, that's what I'm hoping."

"Are you worthy, Sister Crane? For without faith there is no obedience.[19] Likewise, where there is true obedience there is faith. As we place our faith in God by becoming His obedient disciples,[20] we receive the blessings we seek."[21]

"Absolutely," said Sister Crane.

"Do you also know that even though I have asked you all those questions, and you have answered in the affirmative, if it is His will that you do not get better, you will die?"[22]

"Yes, I do, but I know He wants me to live to raise my children," said Sister Crane, as she swallowed, obviously still short of breath.

Bo smiled and nodded. "Then you will receive a blessing of healing sealed with oil as you desire."[23]

"Thank you, Bishop."

Outside the tent Corrynne had stood and listened to Bo's conversation with Sister Crane. She wasn't trying to eavesdrop; she had only come to get Bo for dinner.

She thought about his statements about faith. Did *she* have faith? Did she lean too much on the arm of the flesh?[24] When Ry was sick, why didn't she turn first to the Lord, *before* science? Why did she give up her stand and hand over her life so quickly to the biochip, ultimately forfeiting her freedom?

She thought about all the warnings in the scriptures about getting a chip. She thought about the words of the latter-day prophet echoing the scriptures. She knew about the sores and death. She knew firsthand what it had done to her son and daughter, yet she still chose it over the promised blessings from God. What did that say about her? Was she so stupid to think things would be different for her?

Corrynne put her hands over her face in horrible acknowledgement as she continued to think. What was wrong with her? Didn't God offer healing to his people? Didn't she proclaim to believe in that power? Why didn't she even try to ask the Lord to heal her son? She thought about Dane and how a blessing had healed him, *despite her*. She had doubted then, too. What was her problem? ...She knew the answer inside. ...It was because she was afraid.[25] She didn't have faith in healings.[26] She had seen so many people die without the aid of medicine that she couldn't help herself. She was simply afraid.[27]

God's will. She thought about that one, too, for a moment, as she looked off into the distance. Was it God's will that she could manipulate science and physiology to help heal people? She felt empowered when she was practicing the principles of medicine. She could apply certain laws and expect certain outcomes.[28] She could command the body to respond to her wishes through drugs and computers. Was that power an expression of God's will? It certainly must have been otherwise medicine wouldn't work. God allowed her to help mankind. He tolerated her involvement. He also tolerated her pride,[29] most likely as He waited for her to discover humility. It was sad that somewhere she had forgotten where all her empowerment had come from. She had trusted more in her abilities[30] and the abilities of the doctors than in God's power.[31]

Now, if she was being honest with herself, another thing she would admit was that she was afraid that she would lose the advantage medicine had always given her. If she didn't take the chip, she would have been barred from the hospital. The truth was that she didn't want to give up being a nurse. She liked the prestige and empowerment it had given her in her life. She liked feeling strong in times of injury, because she understood how to help a body return to health. What would she be without her tools? She'd be nothing. She'd be just like everyone else. Maybe Ry's illness was only an excuse to accept the chip. Maybe she lied to herself about the whole situation for her own selfish purposes. Maybe deep down, she was a hypocrite.[32]

Corrynne looked down at her hands. With renewed guilt, she realized the antibiotics the doctor had given her at work had been successful. That part wasn't bad, because she believed antibiotics were given to man for the purpose of healing. However, the bad part was that once again, she had turned so readily to science before God. Why was she so weak? Why was everyone else so much stronger spiritually than she was? Again, she knew the answer. It was because her friends and neighbors didn't have the option of medicine any longer. They were trusting God's promises and His will rather than turning to another source of relief. That exercise was helping them grow. They were being sustained by their faith.

Corrynne swallowed as she came face to face with her own deceit and rationalizations. Now she couldn't escape. She had been caught in her own tightly woven web by lying to herself, claiming her choices were proper.[33] *...What now?*

A sudden urgency clawed at her insides, making her feel like she couldn't breathe. Panic exploded into a feeling of dread. What had she done? Had she put everything at risk because of her love of—what...the world? Money? Prestige? Was she really that shallow?[34]

After a few seconds she raised her eyebrows and nodded. She guessed she was, because that's exactly what she had done. Now, it all became clear. The reason why she lacked faith, the *true* reason she lacked faith, was because she was simply *unfaithful* to the principles she knew to be true.[35] Corrynne cringed at that thought. She never, ever thought she'd ever be at this place, but here she was...And *that* was pathetic!

Corrynne walked away from the tent without calling Bo. She needed to be alone.

Love Notes

Provo, Utah
6:00 p.m.

October 27th, 28th 29th...

Brea tried to read the dates of the messages that were spilling onto her computer. They were downloading at lightening speed.

November 6th, 7th, 8th...

The messages kept coming.

December 2nd finally arrived. That was today. "I love you," it said, and then the curser blinked, as if waiting for her to respond.

Brea felt overwhelmed. Were these all messages from Matt? Was this radio some sort of communication device? She put her fingers on the keyboard, not knowing how to return messages but wanting to try.

"Is this Matt?" she typed, mainly to see what would happen next. As soon as she pushed the enter button, a high pitched noise erupted from the computer. It was a series of beeps. The radio, in turn, lit up as if in a receiving mode. After a few moments it grew dim again.

Brea typed something else, "Is this safe?" Again she pushed the enter button, and again the same noises filled the room. The radio's face lit up again, and then after a few moments, it went silent once again.

Brea smiled. If this was what she thought it was—"*Yahoo!*" she screamed as loud as she pleased and then shivered in excitement. Being underground had its advantages, total and complete privacy. No one could hear her celebrate. It was great.

The radio hissed, surprising her, and then another message appeared on her computer.

"Hello. ...It's me."

Brea's mouth dropped. Matt was receiving her message right now!

Brea typed. "R U OK?" then she pressed enter.

After a few minutes the answer came back. "Yes. Can't talk now. Be happy."

Brea felt like she was going to explode out of her skin! She had so many emotions all at once she didn't even know where to start. She laughed as she typed, "I will. Luv U," and hit enter.

What a glorious early Christmas present Matt had sent her! She kissed the little retro radio as it began to stutter and beep.

Notes to "Voices in the Darkness"

Waiting

1 "For the Lord had not hitherto suffered that we should make much fire, as we journeyed in the wilderness; for he said: I will make thy food become sweet" (1 Nephi 17:12).

2 Beringia—An ancient land mass between America and Russia: "It is currently believed that the ocean levels rose and fell several times in the past. During extended cold periods, tremendous volumes of water are deposited on land in the form of ice and snow, which can cause a corresponding drop in sea level. The last 'ice age' occurred around 12-15,000 years ago. During this period the shallow seas now separating Asia from North America near the present day Bering Strait dropped about 300 feet and created a 1,000 mile wide grassland steppe, linking Asia and North America together with the 'Bering Land Bridge.' Across this vast steppe, plants and animals traveled in both directions, and humans entered the Americas" ("What is Beringia," *Beringian Heritage International Park Program*, available online: http://www.nps.gov/akso/beringia/whatisberingia2.htm).

3 "And an highway shall be cast up in the midst of the great deep" (D&C 133:27).

The Secretary's Declaration

4 The Secretary's speech was created from the text of actual speeches given by world leaders. Words were changed and added to match the direction of the storyline. However, the intent of the speeches given were kept consistent to their deliveries.

"Good evening. Today, our fellow citizens, our way of life, our very freedom came under attack in a series of deliberate and deadly terrorist acts. The victims were in airplanes, or in their offices; secretaries, businessmen and women, military and federal workers; moms and dads, friends and neighbors. Thousands of lives were suddenly ended by evil, despicable acts of terror. The pictures of airplanes flying into buildings, fires burning, huge structures collapsing, have filled us with disbelief, terrible sadness, and a quiet, unyielding anger. These acts of mass murder were intended to frighten our nation into chaos and retreat. But they have failed; our country is strong. A great people have been moved to defend a great nation. Terrorist attacks can shake the foundations of our biggest buildings, but they cannot touch the foundation of America. These acts shattered steel, but they cannot dent the steel of American resolve..." (George W. Bush, "Statement by the President in His Address to the Nation," September 11, 2001, http://www.whitehouse.gov/news/releases/2001/09/20010911-16.html).

5 "Internationalization today means only Judaization. We in Germany have come to this: that a sixty-million people sees its destiny to lie at the will of a few dozen Jewish bankers. This was possible only because our civilization had first been Judaized. The undermining of the German conception of personality by catchwords had begun long before. Ideas such as 'Democracy,' 'Majority,' 'Conscience

of the World,' 'World Solidarity,' 'World Peace,' 'Internationality of Art,' etc., disintegrate our race-consciousness, breed cowardice, and so today we are bound to say that the simple Turk is more man than we are. No salvation is possible until the bearer of disunion, the Jew, has been rendered powerless to harm. ...We must call to account the November criminals of 1918. It cannot be that two million Germans should have fallen in vain and that afterwards one should sit down as friends at the same table with traitors. No, we do not pardon, we demand - Vengeance! ...AS FOUNDATION FOR A NEW CURRENCY THE PROPERTY OF THOSE WHO ARE NOT OF OUR BLOOD MUST DO SERVICE. If families who have lived in Germany for a thousand years are now expropriated, we must do the same to the Jewish usurers. ...WE DEMAND IMMEDIATE EXPULSION OF ALL JEWS WHO HAVE ENTERED GERMANY SINCE 1914, and of all those, too, who through trickery on the Stock Exchange or through other shady transactions have gained their wealth. ...The housing scarcity must be relieved through energetic action; houses must be granted to those who deserve them. Eisner said in 1918 that we had no right to demand the return of our prisoners - he was only saying openly what all Jews were thinking. People who so think must feel how life tastes in a concentration camp! ...Extremes must be fought by extremes...." (Baynes, N. *The Speeches of Adolf Hitler, April 1922-August 1939, Excerpts from Munich*, September 18, 1922).

[6] "America and our friends and allies join with all those who want peace and security in the world, and we stand together to win the war against terrorism. Tonight, I ask for your prayers for all those who grieve, for the children whose worlds have been shattered, for all whose sense of safety and security has been threatened. And I pray they will be comforted by a power greater than any of us, spoken through the ages in Psalm 23: 'Even though I walk through the valley of the shadow of death, I fear no evil, for You are with me.' This is a day when all Americans from every walk of life unite in our resolve for justice and peace. America has stood down enemies before, and we will do so this time. None of us will ever forget this day. Yet, we go forward to defend freedom and all that is good and just in our world. Thank you. Good night, and God bless America" (George W. Bush, "Statement by the President in His Address to the Nation," September 11, 2001, available online: http://www.whitehouse.gov/news/releases/2001/09/20010911-16.html).

For the Love of Mankind

[7] "I prophesy, that the man who tarries after he has an opportunity of going, will be afflicted by the devil. Wars are at hand: we must not delay; but are not required to sacrifice. We ought to have the building up of Zion as our greatest object. When wars come, we shall have to flee to Zion. The cry is to make haste. The last revelation says, Ye shall not have time to have gone over the earth, until these things come. It will come as did the cholera, war, fires, and earthquakes; one pestilence after another. Until the Ancient of Days comes, then judgment will be given to the Saints" (Joseph Smith, *DHC*, July 2, 1839, Vol. 3, pgs. 390-391).

[8] "Do you think there is calamity abroad now among the people? ...All we have yet heard and all we have experienced is scarcely a preface to the sermon that is going to be preached. When the testimony of the elders ceases to be given, and the Lord says to them, 'come home; I will now preach my own sermons to the nations of the earth,' all you now know can scarcely be called a preface to the sermon that will be preached with fire and sword, tempests, earthquake, hail, rain, thunders and lightnings, and fearful destruction. What matters the destruction of a few railway cars? You will hear of magnificent cities, now idolized by the people, sinking in the earth, entombing the inhabitants. The sea will heave itself beyond its bounds, engulfing mighty cities. Famine will spread over the nations, and nation will rise up against nation, kingdom against kingdom, and states against states, in our own country and in foreign lands; and they will destroy each other, caring not for the blood and lives of their neighbors, of their families, or for their own lives. They will be like the Jaredites who preceded the Nephites upon this continent, and will destroy each other to the last man, through the anger that the devil will place in their hearts, because they have rejected the words of life and are given over to Satan to do whatever he listeth to do with them. You may think that the little you hear of now is grievous; yet the faithful of God's people will see days that will cause them to close their eyes because of the sorrow that will come upon the wicked nations. The hearts of the faithful will be filled with pain and anguish for them" (Brigham Young, *Journal of Discourses*, Vol. 8, pg. 123).

Blessings

[9] "Among the blessings promised by the risen Savior as signs which should follow the believers in His Gospel, He said, 'They shall lay hands on the sick, and they shall recover' (Mark 16:18) The '...laying on of hands to cure human sickness,' then, was practiced and taught by the Savior of mankind. And it became an established ordinance of the Church under the direction of His Apostles (See James 5:14-15)" (George Q. Cannon, Jerreld L. Newquist, *Gospel Truth*, pg. 421).

[10] "To another faith by the same Spirit; to another the gifts of healing by the same Spirit" (1 Corinthians12:9).

[11] "Faith [is] the first principle in revealed religion, and the foundation of all righteousness. Faith...is the first great governing principle which has power, dominion, and authority over all things; by it they exist, by it they are upheld, by it they are changed, or by it they remain, agreeable to the will of God. Without it there is no power, and without power there could be no creation nor existence!" (Joseph Smith, *Lectures on Faith,* pgs. 1, 22-24).

[12] "Faith is based on truth and is preceded by knowledge. Until a person gains a knowledge of the truth he can have no faith. Alma said, 'Faith is not to have a perfect knowledge of things; therefore if ye have faith ye hope for things which are not seen, which are true' (Alma 32:21; Ether 12:6). Thus faith is a hope in that which is not seen which is true, and accordingly it can enter the heart of man only after he has received the truth" (Bruce R. McConkie, *Mormon Doctrine*, pg. 262).

[13] "What, then, is faith? In the broad, generic, and universal sense of the word, having no particular reference to religion and salvation, the Prophet tells us that faith 'is the moving cause of all action...in all intelligent beings.' All accountable and intelligent beings have faith in this sense. Such is part of life itself. Because this faith dwells in the hearts of all mankind, they sow with the assurance of reaping; they plant with the hope of harvesting; they exert themselves in the pursuit of knowledge, wisdom, and intelligence because they believe they can obtain them. Without this faith, 'both mind and body would be in a state of inactivity, and all their exertions would cease, both physical and mental'" (Bruce R. McConkie, *A New Witness for the Articles of Faith*, pg. 163).

[14] "...For if [man] did not, in the first instance, believe him to be God, that is, the Creator and upholder of all things, he could not center his faith in him for life and salvation, for fear there should be greater than he who would thwart all his plans, and he, like the gods of the heathen, would be unable to fulfill his promises; but seeing he is God over all, from everlasting to everlasting, the Creator and upholder of all things, no such fear can exist in the minds of those who put their trust in him, so that in this respect their faith can be without wavering" (Joseph Smith, *Lectures on Faith*, pg. 19).

[15] "For it is ordained that in Zion, and in her stakes, and in Jerusalem, those places which I have appointed for refuge" (D&C 124:36).

[16] "The need for faith is often underestimated. The ill person and the family often seem to depend wholly on the power of the priesthood and the gift of healing that they hope the administering brethren may have, whereas the greater responsibility is with him who is blessed. There are persons who seem to have the gift to heal...and it is understandable why a sick one might desire a blessing at the hands of a person who seems to have great faith and proven power, and in whom the recipient has confidence, but the major element is the faith of the individual when that person is conscious and accountable. 'Thy faith hath made thee whole' was repeated so often by the Master that it almost became a chorus" (Spencer W. Kimball, *Spencer W. Kimball Speaks Out*, pg. 75).

[17] "But by the knowledge of God is meant not simply that he exists and is a personal being in whose image man is made; not merely that he is a resurrected, glorified, and perfected man who has all power, all might, and all dominion; not the mere fact that he is the Father of spirits and as such lives in the family unit; rather, in addition to all this, by the knowledge of God is meant the very nature and kind of being that he is. The knowledge of God includes an understanding of his character, perfections, and attributes" (Bruce R. McConkie, *A New Witness for the Articles of Faith*, pg. 168).

[18] The body is subject to God's power as is the whole universe: "...If God framed the worlds by faith, that it is by faith that he exercises power over them, and that faith is the principle of power? And if the principle of power, it must be so in man as well as in the Deity?" (Joseph Smith, *Lectures on Faith,* pg. 17).

[19] "Faith is a gift of God; it is the fruitage of righteous living. It does not come to us by our command but is the result of doing the will of our Heavenly Father" (George Albert Smith, *Conference Reports*, October, 1913, pg. 103).

[20] "The expression, 'true believer,' needs qualifying, for many believe who do not obey—I will qualify it by saying, a believer in Jesus Christ, who manifests his faith to God, angels, and his brethren, by his obedience. Not but that there are believers who do not obey, but the only true believers are they who prove their belief by their obedience to the requirements of the Gospel" (Brigham Young, *Discourses of Brigham Young*, Vol. 1, pg. 234).

[21] "And when we obtain any blessing from God, it is by obedience to that law upon which it is predicated" (D&C 130: 21).

[22] "And again, it shall come to pass that he that hath faith in me to be healed, and is not appointed unto death, shall be healed" (D&C 42:48).

[23] "Can man gain faith unto life and salvation without an understanding of the character, perfections, and attributes of God? The answer is, No. Such knowledge 'is the foundation which is laid, through the revelation of the attributes of God, for the exercise of faith in him for life and salvation; and seeing that these are the attributes of the Deity, they are unchangeable—being the same yesterday, to-day, and for ever—which gives to the minds of the Latter-day Saints the same power and authority to exercise faith in God which the Former-day saints had'" (Joseph Smith, as quoted by Bruce R. McConkie, *A New Witness for the Articles of Faith*, pg. 183).

[24] "Cursed is he that putteth his trust in man, or maketh flesh his arm, or shall hearken unto the precepts of men, save their precepts shall be given by the power of the Holy Ghost" (2 Nephi 28:31).

[25] "The moment a man loses the Spirit of God and the spirit of the adversary takes possession of him, he is filled with fear; for 'the sinners in Zion are afraid; fearfulness hath surprised the hypocrites.' ...No honest man or woman need fear; indeed they never fear. What are they afraid of? They have done nothing to cause the spirit of fear to come upon them. It is only when a man does that which is wrong that he receives the spirit of fear" (George Q. Cannon, *Journal of Discourses*, pg. 252).

[26] "The question may be asked, 'Does the laying on of hands cure in every instance, and if not, why not?' The answer is no, and the reason is because faith is necessary to effectual administration, and faith does not always accompany it. James says, 'the prayer of faith shall save the sick.' Jesus always declared that it was faith which caused the healings that attended His ministry. Said He, 'Go thy way: thy faith hath made thee whole' (Luke 17:19)" (George Q. Cannon, Jerreld L. Newquist, *Gospel Truth*, pg. 421).

[27] "Many of us have not faith enough even to send for the Elders of the Church when any one of our family is sick; but the first thought is, 'go for a doctor,' as though the gift of healing had been lost in the Church. How many of you feel as if the gift of healing no longer existed in the Church of Christ but that doctors must be sent for and drugs administered? And this among the Latter-day Saints, a people who profess what we do and to whom such glorious promises have been made!" (George Q. Cannon, Jerreld L. Newquist, *Gospel Truth*, pg. 425).

[28] "There is a law, irrevocably decreed in heaven before the foundations of this world, upon which all blessings are predicated" (D&C 130:20).

[29] "And it came to pass that I saw and bear record, that the great and spacious building was the pride of the world; and it fell, and the fall thereof was exceedingly great" (1 Nephi 11:36).

[30] "Trust in the Lord with all thine heart; and lean not unto thine own understanding" (Proverbs 3:5).

[31] "I believe in works; I believe in nursing, in taking care of the sick and in doing all that is possible for them; but I believe also in the ordinances of the house of God. God has made precious promises to the Latter-day Saints concerning the health of their families, and I tell you, in the presence of the Lord, that if the Latter-day Saints would observe the Word of Wisdom there would be less of this disposition to send for doctors and more faith in the ordinances that the Lord has established" (George Q. Cannon, Jerreld L. Newquist, *Gospel Truth*, pg. 425).

[32] "Behold, verily I say unto you, there are hypocrites among you, who have deceived some, which has given the adversary power" (D&C 50:7).

[33] "And others will he pacify, and lull them away into carnal security, that they will say: All is well in Zion; yea, Zion prospereth, all is well—and thus the devil cheated their souls, and leadeth them away carefully down to hell" (2 Nephi 28:21).

[34] "Flee out of the midst of Babylon, and deliver every man his soul: be not cut off in her iniquity; for this *is* the time of the Lord's vengeance; he will render unto her a recompence" (Jeremiah 51:6).

[35] To be able to exercise faith, the saints must "live as to have an actual knowledge that he is conforming to the mind and will of the Lord. Faith comes to those who know these truths and who keep the commandments. Those who meet this standard gain faith unto life and salvation. Where there is a deficiency, in part or in whole, their faith is either weak or entirely wanting" (Bruce R. McConkie, *A New Witness for the Articles of Faith*, pg. 167).

CHAPTER SEVENTEEN

OVERCOME

"And there was given unto him a mouth speaking great things and blasphemies. ...And he opened his mouth in blasphemy against God, to blaspheme his name, and his tabernacle, and them that dwell in heaven. And it was given unto him to make war with the saints and to overcome them..." (Revelation 13:5-7).

00:00:02, 23:53:08, Zulu
Monday, December 29th

Hand to Hand

Bering Sea, Russia
8:07 a.m.

"Where's John? Have you seen him?" Braun asked a native couple and their children, who were cooking their breakfast not far from his tent.

The man and woman looked confused. They obviously didn't speak English. They each shook their head, indicating they didn't understand.

Braun had been up and down the beach twice searching the horizon of the frozen Bering Sea. He wondered where John could be hiding. Braun was anxious to tell him what he had discovered! Last night he had gone out about 300 yards off the coast, lit a fire on the ice to melt a section, and then dug with a bone spade in the ice. When he had dug down about four feet, he had hit sand! That meant the Straight was frozen solid! If that was true, they could leave! Just knowing that, made Braun itchy to do something to get the show on the road. Time was wasting! America was only 55 miles away!

Braun returned to his tent. He entered with a quick thrust.

"Did you find him?" asked Chenille, as she handed him some whale meat.

Braun shook his head as he made a face. "I don't think I can eat one more bite of that stuff."

"Well, you better; we have quite a bit dried for our trip," said Chenille.

Braun nodded and quickly gulped down Chenille's offering. After swallowing the last bite whole, he said, "OK, I think we should pack up. I'm thinking I can make a sled out of the large bones in our tent. I'll tie them together with whale tendons. You saved them, didn't you?"

Chenille nodded. "Of course. So, answer me. Did you find John?"

Braun shook his head. "No, but we know the plan. Wait till the sea freezes and then cross. It's frozen now. It's time to pack up."

"I'd rather wait for John to tell us," said Chenille.

"Fine. We can wait till John shows up before we leave, but let's start packing now," said Braun, squatting down to pick up things in the tent and bundle them together.

"There's not much to pack. I could be packed in fifteen minutes," said Chenille. "Why don't you do something else to prepare?"

Braun stopped. "Like what?"

Chenille shrugged. "I don't know, go make something."

"I need the tent materials to make a sled. That's the only thing I need to make."

"Why do we need a sled?" asked Chenille.

"Because we have too much to carry. We need all the food and supplies we've prepared."

A horn sounded outside.

Chenille and Braun looked at each other with wide eyes.

"Maybe that's him," said Chenille.

"Maybe," said Braun. "Or it could be just the call for fighting drills."

"Well, either way, you need to go," said Chenille. "Go on and try to be patient. I will too. If I can wait to leave, you can wait."

Braun studied the floor of their tent and rubbed his neck. "Drills would be better if we were really fighting someone. I'm getting tired of pointless spear throwing."

Chenille laughed. "Personally, I'm glad these are just drills. You're too much of a city boy to really be good at hand-to-hand combat."

The horn sounded again with two blasts this time.

"Oh shoot!" said Braun as he found his bone javelin, his rock knife and a tortoise shell shield.

"What?" asked Chenille, watching Braun rush around the tent. "What's wrong?"

"Two blasts. This is real. Someone's out there. I have to go fight."

"What? You're kidding, right?" asked Chenille.

"No. I love you!" said Braun, with a quick peck on Chenille's cheek. "I'll be back—don't know when."

Enemy of the State

Provo, Utah
1:15 p.m.

A broadcasted voice could be heard from somewhere outside. It sounded authoritative and deliberate. "Good evening, ladies and gentlemen," it said.

Corrynne and Louise paused as they finished washing the dishes from lunch.

"Do you hear that?" asked Corrynne.

"Yes," said Louise. "It sounds like it's coming from a speaker."

Immediately, Louise and Corrynne laid the dishes down on a towel and picked the twins up from where they had been playing on the floor of the tent. They pushed through the flap of the tent to see others gathering outside.

"For the last month, the UN has come under a series of attacks from the very people we are attempting to serve..."

Corrynne looked up into the trees. The voice was coming from the emergency disaster notification speakers mounted in the trees.

"In a series of deliberate and deadly terrorist acts, lives were suddenly ended by evil, despicable acts of terror, brought about by the radical, extremist anti-Christians that run rampant in the United States. The victims of these attacks were the selfless UN volunteers who were providing food, warmth, and necessary monetary support to those of the devastated areas of that nation."

"Did you hear that?" asked Corrynne. "Whose voice is that?"

Louise listened carefully.

The speech continued. "These are people who deny the true and living Christ that has come to us to establish paradise among us. They focus their efforts to kill and maim those of us who obediently and humbly worship him."

"That's President Lityny," said Louise. "I'd stake my life on it."

"Who's President Lityny?" asked Corrynne.

"He's the President of the European Union," said Louise, still listening.

"What's he saying?" asked Corrynne.

"I'm not sure," said Louise. "Let's listen."

Corrynne fell silent as others came out of their tents, also heading her way. She knew what they were thinking. They were going to ask her the same questions she was asking Louise. Corrynne put a finger to her lips and met each person's eyes. She needed to stop the questions so she and Louise could listen. She didn't know anything.

"...These acts of mass murder were intended to frighten the world and the United Nations into chaos and retreat. But they have failed; we are strong, and we will fight."

"Who is the UN fighting against?" Corrynne asked Louise.

Louise shook her head and continued to listen.

"...We will no longer stand for such human tragedy among our members! A great people have been moved to defend itself. Terrorist attacks can destroy individual people, but it can't touch the foundation of our faith. War has been declared and those that fight against us will be destroyed. *The anti-Christians will fall!*"

"Who are the anti-Christians?" asked Sister Kemp, in a whisper as she joined Corrynne and Louise, as a roar of applause could be heard from the speaker.

"I don't know," said Corrynne, cocking her head to try and improve her hearing.

"Who are these anti-Christians?" continued President Lityny over the speakers. "They are those who call themselves, ironically, 'Christian.' They have stolen our Christ's name in order to trick the obedient of our people. Tolerance for these deceivers cannot go on," he continued.

"Did he say the Christians were the anti-Christians?" asked Corrynne thoroughly confused. "How can a Christian be an *anti-Christian*?"

"Shhh," said Louise with a hand in the air.

"...These are they who enslaved their people with their banks and their interest rates and their policies. These are they who undermined the rest of the world with words such as 'democracy,' 'majority,' 'conscience of the world,' 'world peace,' and 'constitutional rights.' These are they who sought to make the world like them; destroying all the uniqueness of all other nations around them through their deviant ways."

"He's saying that Americans, because we are known as a 'Christian nation', are a nation of anti-Christians," said Louise, her face blanching white. "He's setting us up for war."

Corrynne's heart dropped. "How can that be?"

"He's changing the definition of Christianity. Because we don't believe the pope to be Christ, we're anti-Christian. We're the enemy."

Corrynne blinked hard. "What? Of who?"

"Of the world."

"That's so stupid! Why would anyone believe him?"

"He's right. We don't believe the pope is Christ."

"I know, but..."

"So in their eyes, we're anti-Christian," said Louise. "He's appealing to the world, not us."

"But he's a liar."

"We know that, but everyone else believes him."

"But why?"

"Because the world believes leaders by virtue of their position," said Louise.

President Lityny continued, "I say, there is no safety, no salvation, until the bearer of this atrocity, the anti-Christian, who calls himself Christian, is rendered powerless to harm another human on the planet!"

"Now what's he saying?" asked Corrynne.

Louise put a hand over her mouth. "He's declaring war, *now*," she said breathlessly. "He's intending to wipe us out."

Corrynne looked at Louise's face to decipher the meaning of her words. Was she serious?

Avalanche

Bering Sea, Russia
8:20 a.m.

Braun rushed out of the tent armed with his spear and shield. He saw the other men doing the same. All of them climbed up the snow-covered hill to the flatter, ice-covered plain. He assumed his position in the defense force.

Looking ahead, Braun attempted to make out who they were fighting. He caught sight of a Russian flag. ...*What?* Thought Braun, almost stopping his run. *The Russians? How did they expect to win against the Russians?*

Braun continued running alongside his troop, but fell back a little as he considered what was about to happen. He didn't want to be in the front, that's for sure!

As they moved closer, Braun saw the Russian army was small. He thought maybe this patrol had come in response to their growing numbers on the coast, just as John had predicted. Surely the Russians would try and stop them from leaving. Dread entered his chest. There was trouble brewing.

Suddenly, surprise shot through Braun as he noticed John. He was running in the front, leading the charge! John carried an extra long spear and ran swift and strong, his long, black hair blowing behind him. Braun was impressed. He was the perfect leader for these people who respected physical strength. God had chosen well.

A ram horn's sound filled the air. That was their signal to stop.

The tribes stopped about a hundred yards away from the Russians and took a defensive pose with their spears raised and their shields high.

Braun pushed his way forward, through the few layers of men that moved in front of him as the formation collapsed. He wanted to see firsthand what was happening here, because make no mistake about it—*something* was going to happen!

John laid his spear down on the snow and calmly walked toward the Russian force. Their captain met him halfway on a snowmobile.

Braun watched as they talked for a few moments. He wondered if they spoke in Russian or one of the tribal dialects. It was a fleeting thought because in the next moment, a gunshot rang out and John flew back five feet, landing on his back in the snow. The captain had shot him point-blank in the stomach!

Braun was shocked! *They shot John! How could they shoot John?* His muscles contracted in desire to defend his leader, but he held himself back for a moment as he and the others waited to see what would happen next.

John lay motionless in the snow.

When the apostle didn't stir, Braun set off in a full run along with his comrades with a loud, angry war whoop. No one was going to treat his leader like an animal!

Abruptly, John sat up putting his hand in the air. *"Stop!"*

Braun obeyed by digging his heels into the snow to stop his momentum, as did the other men around him, but he realized he hadn't heard the apostle's voice with his ears. Instead, the commanding voice had spoke to him loudly in his mind! That was new!

John stood, brushed himself off, and approached the captain. Again, after a moment he was shot in the chest, blasting a large hole in his tan coat and throwing him head-over-heels so that he laid face-first in the snow.

Braun watched in horror. This treatment was insulting! He couldn't stand it. He had to do something! His grip tightened on his spear as he was tempted to charge again.

Predictably, John picked himself up, giving the halt sign to the warriors. A third time he approached the vehicle with his hands out wide as a token of peace.

This time, two military men grabbed the apostle by his arms, twisting them behind his back and led him away—but then—*poof*! He disappeared, vanishing into thin air!

"Yeah!" yelled Braun, laughing in amusement.

The other warriors cheered too.

The captain looked around in surprise, as did the two soldiers who had been holding John.

Braun busted out laughing even harder. The surprised look on their faces as the army searched for John was priceless!

"Strike the earth in rhythm," said John, without voice but clearly to the mind of each man in his own language. "Make the earth shake for your sakes!"

Braun filled with a feeling of power and anticipation, thumped the snow beneath his feet with his spear. All the other warriors joined him. The sound was intimidating.

Braun looked up and saw John! He stood on a small mountain that loomed above the Russian army. He had his hands stretched out over his men.

Thump, thump, thump.

The noise grew, the ground vibrated...

Thump, thump, thump.

The packed snow cracked, creating a great noise like giant bones snapping.

Thump, thump, thump.

The ice on the large hill where John stood cracked and moved, finally breaking away from the earth.

Thump, thump, thump.

Suddenly an avalanche of snow and ice rumbled down the side of the rise, shaking the earth with its advance.

The Russians yelled and ran, but the mass of heavy snow overtook the whole patrol, burying them within a few seconds.

The warriors stopped thumping....

"...Wahoo!" yelled Braun, breaking the astonished silence of the men. He jumped up and batted one fist in the air. "Got 'em!" he yelled.

Celebratory sounds joined his as the men congratulated each other on a battle fought and won by one man, their leader.

Braun continued to laugh and cheer in exhilaration along with the other men. Now he understood why John didn't want his men to fight. What contest would there be between machine guns and bone weapons? None! They'd probably have been wiped out in a few minutes if John hadn't intervened. It would have been a massacre!

Braun closed his eyes and prayed intensely, thanking his Heavenly Father. It was an insightful God who gave them this moment of victory in yet another miracle in their behalf. Oh, the glory of God was immense!

ξξξξξξξ

Braun returned to Chenille to find his tent gone. In its place was a line of whale rib bones with a skin bundle on top. Braun was astonished! "How did you do this so fast?" he asked her, looking around.

"We heard what was happening up there on the hill," said Chenille, smiling. "I knew we couldn't stay around here, waiting for more military troops to come, so I packed the tent."

"That's great!" said Braun, taking Chenille in his arms. "I love a *strong* woman!" he said, as he growled and nibbled on Chenille's neck.

"We're going across," said John, as he walked by briskly. "Start praying for power over the sea."

Braun pulled Chenille up quickly, setting her beside him. "Yes, sir!" he said.

Chenille burst out laughing and quickly covered her mouth.

"What are you laughing about?" asked Braun.

"The look on your face."

"What?" asked Braun. "I just wish he'd stop sneaking up on us," said Braun, loosening up and laughing too.

"Whatever, Braun," said Chenille, almost looking embarrassed.

Braun cleared his throat, "OK, Chenille, we have to get serious. Power over the sea!" he said, clapping. "I'll get right on it! ...What does that mean actually?" he asked, with a crooked smile. "The sea's frozen. All we have to do is walk."

"I don't know," said Chenille. "But we should do whatever John tells us."

Braun raised his eyebrows "Hey! I agree. John knows best. He beat that whole Russian patrol up on the hill!"

"Tell me what happened." said Chenille, sitting on the sled.

Braun shrugged and said, "John told us to pound our spears into the ground, and so we did."

"What did that do?"

"It caused an avalanche and the ice ate the soldiers for lunch!"

"What?" gasped Chenille. "Well, I'm glad our side was OK, especially you," she said, standing and wrapping her arms around Braun's neck.

"We were only kept safe because John stopped us from fighting. They would have gunned us down otherwise."

"No!" said Chenille, hugging Braun, putting her head against his chest. "That's frightening. Good thing then no one was shot."

"John was shot," said Braun.

Chenille looked up at Braun abruptly. "John was shot?"

"Twice." said Braun. "He was thrown about five feet each time. I bet the bullets went clean through him."

Chenille shook her head in amazement. "Then what happened?"

"He just got up and brushed himself off."

Chenille laughed suddenly. "Oh, that's right. He can't die!"

Braun shook his head. "Nope, he can't."

"I would have given anything to see that happen."

"It was kind of funny that they tried to kill the only man who couldn't be killed. He was our secret weapon! Because of him, we caught them off guard. It was fantastic!"

Chenille hugged Braun again. "I'm so glad you came back to me."

"Thank John. He stopped me from doing something I would have regretted."

"Are you saying I married someone who was *hot* under the collar?" asked Chenille, as she nuzzled Braun's cheek.

"No, just *hot,*" said Braun, joking and feeling warm and happy.

"Ahh, I like," said Chenille, nodding, as she kissed the top of Braun's chest.

"I like, too," said Braun, devouring Chenille in a kiss.

Survival

Provo, Utah
1:35 p.m.

Applause caused the speakers in the trees to rattle with vibration.

"...We must call to account the November criminals," continued President Lityny, "It cannot be that a thousand UN peacekeepers, killed in service, should fall in vain. We will not stand for traitors. No, we do not pardon, we demand—*vengeance*!"

"A thousand UN workers? When did all this happen?" asked Corrynne. "No one is attacking the UN!" she said, as more invisible applause supporting the President reverberated through the air.

"At least not here," said Louise.

"To facilitate this hallowed war, we will demand all anti-Christians to give up every legal right as citizens in the International Society. They are to be exposed and hand over all the money they have hoarded, or created through trickery on the Stock Exchange, or through other shady transactions, have gained their wealth at the expense of the international people."

"Is he saying we have to give our money to the UN?"

Louise nodded. "Sounds like it."

"Right," said Corrynne. "As if that will happen. Over my dead body."

"The anti-Christians are to give up their houses," continued the President. "The housing scarcity must be relieved through energetic action; houses must be granted to those who deserve them. They must be given to faithful international citizens! I say extremes must be fought by extremes!"

"What houses?" asked Corrynne. "They've all been taken away already."

"What housing scarcity?" asked Louise. "There's empty houses all over America," said Louise, shaking her head through the loud applause, whistles, and yells piped through the speakers. "There's a house glut!"

"I speak to you, the united nations of the world. Please, let us stand shoulder-to-shoulder as we fight for peace and security. Let us stand together to win the war against terrorism."

"This is crazy!" said Sister Kemp, looking very angry. "Who is this man? How dare he say such things about us? He doesn't know us!"

Louise looked at Sister Kemp and said, "He can say anything he wants. Because of his power, he can make anything true just by saying the words."

"How come?" said Sister Kemp. "That doesn't seem fair."

"It's not fair, but that's the net effect," said Louise. "That's what ultimate authority does for a person."

"Who's given that man ultimate authority?" asked Sister Kemp. "He's not the law here."

"With the UN running things, he definitely has sway," said Louise, looking at Corrynne pointedly without another word.

Corrynne knew exactly what Louise was referring to; MD had done this.

"Thank you. Good night, and God bless the United Nations," finished the EU president.

Bo came rushing through the crowd of people who were standing outside the tents. He had a piece of paper in one hand and a megaphone in his other. "Did you hear that announcement?" he asked breathlessly.

Corrynne nodded. "Louise says the man who made that speech is the president of the European Union. President Lityny, I think she said his name was."

Louise nodded her agreement.

"Now he's the Secretary General of the UN," said Bo. "I just received word from the stake president that identifies him," he said, displaying his paper.

Louise took a deep breath and shook her head in disgust. "I wouldn't doubt it. The Secretary's office was vacant. That would make MD's most obedient puppet, President Lityny, speak for the world rather than only Europe. Smart. I have to hand it to MD."

Bo set a log on its end so that he could stand above the crowd. With the megaphone he started, "Brothers and Sisters, may I have your attention? I just received a notice from the stake president. The prophet was given an ultimatum for us this morning by Secretary Lityny. In turn, the First Presidency sent this message to us by ham radio. As you know, we somehow have been blamed for the deaths of UN personnel. Whether or not it is true, I don't know, but I do know that because of this rumor, our lives are in danger. We are to pack up immediately and go north to church-owned land. It's out of the city limits and away from the UN. We'll have safety there. Repeat: pack up your things. We'll be heading out to the church property north of us. We have three days. If anyone needs help, please let the brethren know."

Bo stepped off the log as people began to talk in surprise among themselves.

Corrynne rubbed Striynna's back and said, "Bo, what's going on here?"

"You heard the speech by Secretary Lityny. You know what I know."

"But three days, Bo?" she asked. "That's impossible."

Bo shook his head. "It's not impossible. We're not taking much."

"No, Bo. We shouldn't just surrender and leave! We should do something!"

"Like what?" asked Bo.

"Like fight," said Corrynne, looking to Louise who was still standing close by and then back to Bo. "You're itchy to use that gun we have, now's your chance."

Bo looked at Corrynne with dismay. "I know this is hard, I'm sorry," he said, putting out an arm to hug Corrynne, but she refused and backed out of his reach.

"Corrynne, be reasonable. What could I do with one measly gun? Remember, you asked me the same question. I'd be killed. I don't think you want that."

"Well, are you sure you understood right? Are you sure we're being blamed for all this? Maybe there's been a misunderstanding."

"Of course, there's been a huge misunderstanding," said Bo. "But there's one thing that is not misunderstood, and that is that Secretary Lityny has declared that he intends to do anything it takes to protect his UN peacekeepers, as well as all the international citizens who live on American soil, from us."

"Who, us? The *violent* Mormons?" she asked sarcastically, with an edge to her voice.

"Yes, in fact the exact words are, let me read them to you," said Bo, finding the quote on the page. "'Any radical anti-Christians who wish to stay independent of the international economic system will be deemed as terrorists.'" Looking up at Corrynne he said, "That's us."

"This can't be happening," Corrynne said, shaking her head.

"In fact, it's worse," said Bo. "Part of the letter I didn't read to everyone says, 'Authorization will be given to kill all such persons who elect to stay within the UN precincts after being given the warning to leave.'"

"That's another extermination order," said Corrynne with wide eyes.

"I'd agree with you," said Bo.

"What makes up a UN precinct?" asked Corrynne.

"Any city where the UN is governing," said Louise. "That's why we can't stay here."

"Right," said Bo.

"And who will carry out these ridiculous threats?" asked Corrynne.

"The UN army," said Louise.

"Can they do that?" asked Corrynne, looking from Louise to Bo.

Louise nodded. "Yes, they can. America is gone and only the UN remains. They can label anyone an enemy of the state, just as we did to the Japanese back in World War II."

"What if we fight?"

"And become the next Auschwitz?" asked Louise. "We'll be exterminated so fast, we won't even know what hit us. The UN army has huge capacity. Be thankful we're being given a warning."

"So what are we going to do, Bo?"

"We're going to go, Corrynne," said Bo, pointedly.

"And leave this place? How will Braun, Conrad, and Carea find us?" asked Corrynne, her eyes filling with tears.

Bo took his wife by the shoulders and said, "They'll find us. God will help them find us."

"What about our home?" asked Corrynne, now so emotional she wasn't thinking right.

"What home, Corrynne? Our tents are our home. Our family is our home. Our friends and our God are our home. We'll take our home with us. We'll never be without our home because home isn't a place, it's an attitude. It's a way of living."[1]

Louise put a comforting hand on Corrynne's shoulder. With kindness in her eyes, she said, "We aren't giving up, Corrynne. We're surviving. We both know who's running the show and we both know he wouldn't hesitate to kill as many people as necessary to take total control of this land. He's begging us to give him a reason. This is a game, pure and simple. The only reason we're alive now is because MD wants to see if he can push us to do what he wants. We're like rats in a maze. We're his amusement."

"What happens when he's not amused any more?"

Louise didn't answer right away. She thought a moment, her gray eyes becoming intense and looking almost silver-white. "We can beat this, Corrynne. We just have to band together. We need to re-discover the true meaning of America!"[2]

"Yeah!" said a couple brothers standing by, who were agreeing and nodding. Others were gathering to hear what was being said, too.

Louise continued, "Right now, we're too small, too divided, and easily conquered. If we can create unity and purpose among those who all believe the same, we can beat MD at his own game. We can outsmart him. All Christians need to band together and become one, because united, we're strong. *...United—we stand!*"[3]

"Divided, we fall!" finished a few from the surrounding group, as if on cue.

Bo smiled. "Yes, united, we stand, and divided, we fall" he said, nodding. "Now that I know you know that saying, there's no excuse not to live it!"

"Amen, Bishop!" yelled someone from the crowd.

Bo nodded. "Thank you," he said, saluting the listening group. Turning his comments back to Corrynne and Louise, he said, "So, first things first; survival must be priority. Once we've secured our safety, then we can strategize. According to this letter, what we have to do are two things. First, hand over all our money, or real estate. That won't be difficult since we don't have either..."

"Bo, what are you talking about?" asked Corrynne, in a hushed voice, shaking her head. She kept her face turned from her friends as a tear fell down her cheek. "We're not actually going to do that, are we?"

"It'll be fine," said Bo, with compassionate eyes. "All this means to us is that we sign over our mortgage so we're not responsible for it any more. It's a relief! I'm grateful to do it."

Corrynne thought about her little nest egg of International Credits she had been secretly hoarding. She had worked so hard and sacrificed so much to obtain it! It was for a rainy day, and now she was to just hand it over? Waste it? A gasp of despair escaped her throat. She buried her face in Striynna's chest. "They're asking too much, Bo."

Bo took Corrynne in his arms and said, "Sweetheart. We don't need money any more. Between all the people here, we have what we need to sustain us. It will be fine. The Lord has prepared us. We're strong."

"Let's face it," said Louise. "This is all a ploy to intimidate the Christians and all those that watch, into economical submission.[4] He's tried bribing us and frightening us, and since those things didn't work, he's blackmailing us into giving in."

"But we're not attached to money or things,[5] so that won't work either," said Bo.

Louise shook her head. "That's right." Turning to Corrynne, she said, "I don't think MD wants to kill us because the reality is, he needs us to participate in his new economy."

"I agree," said Bo. "I think he's bluffing."

"At least for now," said Louise.

"What do you mean?" asked Corrynne.

"When MD realizes taking our money and homes won't work, then he'll get angry and start making good on his threats of wiping out the 'terrorists'."[6]

"That's awful!" said Corrynne.

"That's why we need to leave quietly, as soon as possible. He's not to that point yet and he can't kill us if he can't find us. We need to just disappear. Without a chip, giving up property and anything else associated with our names, translates to safety. He won't be able to track us. We'll be ghosts, a figment of his imagination."

Corrynne's thoughts jumped to the chip in her hand. Nothing to track? That wasn't true! She shook with anxiety. She had a chip! What was she going to do? This was awful! She could lead her family right into destruction!

"But we also have to remember," continued Bo, "that the end result of MD's shenanigans is his own downfall, and that's a scriptural fact, not an opinion."[7]

"Right," said Louise, "So even a better reason to stay out of MD's line of fire. Help is coming," she said, with a wink at Corrynne. "We just have to wait out the storm, so-to-speak, and then inherit the earth," she said, with a smile and her arms out wide.

"Exactly," said Bo. "So let's get to work," he said, taking a pencil from behind his ear and beginning to write on his paper. "I think we'll need to make some wagon-like-carts from car parts, like our guests from California, and pack our things," said Bo, talking to the men in the group who were still listening.

Corrynne watched him speak. He was so calm.[8] How could he be so calm?

"We're to take only what we need to live," continued Bo. "Leave everything else. Pack only food, clothing, supplies, and tools. That should be it."

Corrynne wiped her face with the back of her hand. She couldn't watch Bo anymore. She swallowed hard to keep her anxiety contained.

"The land we'll occupy initially is only twenty miles north of here, so it won't be a long journey. Think of it as an adventure," Bo said, smiling to his neighbors.

With that, she had had enough of his optimism. She exploded, *"Why is God doing this to us?"* exclaimed Corrynne abruptly, unleashing her pent-up emotions.

There was silence.

Corrynne could feel the eyes of all her friends, staring at her. Why did she have to be the bishop's wife?

A Beloved People

Bering Sea, Russia
9:00 a.m.

The tribal people congregated along the coastline, grouped in their tribes. Each was facing the frozen Bering Sea. Each had their belongings packed and loaded on bone sleds.

John stood in front of the gathered group and motioned for the interpreters from each tribe to take their places. He wished for them to translate. He was going to talk to all of them in all the dialects and languages simultaneously.

John held up his scriptures. Everyone understood he wanted them to pull theirs out, too.

The people of the North Pole had just received a shipment of new scriptures from the prophet right before they had started their exodus.[9] When Braun had first seen the massive quantity of books, brought to the north by dog sleds, he had asked John where they had come from. He remembered that John had a satisfied smile, as he said, "The prophet that resides in the everlasting hills[10] has become aware of the tribes and sent gifts meant to help the people in the north know who they are." This memory made Braun smile as he, too, took his scriptures out of his bundle.

"Do we have time for scriptures right now?" whispered Chenille.

"We must. I trust John implicitly," said Braun.

John looked over the tribes with an unmistakable love in his eyes. Then, opening his scriptures, he began. "You are a beloved, longed-for people. After thousands of years in obscurity you have awakened to your true identity.[11] Through prayer and fasting, each of you has come to the knowledge that you are not the lost, wandering, useless people the world believes you to be. No, you now know that you are wondrous and powerful, children of a living God, whose son sacrificed his life so that you might become gods like him."

Claps and whoops broke out among the crowd as each interpreter finished translating.

"Now, as you stand on the brink of your future, I want you to read some passages out of the scriptures, prophesies concerning you. Please turn to the book named Doctrine and Covenants. Turn to the section one-three-three and go to paragraph 26."

John waited until pages and voices hushed before he continued. Once quiet settled across the people, he said, "I want each of you to open your mind. Invite the Spirit of the Holy Ghost to give you visions that you might be able to see the words, but also the reality that lies within them."

Chenille gasped. "What is he talking about?"

Braun smiled. "Just do what he says. Start praying that the Holy Ghost might be able to give you the gift of visions so you might see what John's talking about."

"Can I do that?"

"Of course you can! Remember the scripture, 'seek ye after the best gifts?'[12] That's a commandment."

Chenille shook her head in awe as she closed her eyes and began to pray.

Braun did the same.

"As a people," continued John. "We can seek the Lord's power. The righteousness and Christ-like love that binds us together is stronger than any other force on earth. Together we can experience miracles. Seek those miracles in your life! Apply your faith to God's words. Know that He is real and wants to share His knowledge with you."

Braun continued to concentrate and seek for the Lord's Spirit. He wanted these innocent and kind people to be rewarded for their faith. He wanted them to see a glimpse of what they could become.

Faintly, Braun noticed a change. There was a change in temperature. No longer could he feel the biting cold on his face. Next, it seemed his consciousness was lifted to another level where he could sense each person in the congregation's personality, their thoughts, emotions, and desires. He knew each of them wanted what John held out for them. After days of learning, growing, and sacrifice, he also knew they were ready. It was at this point in time that a vision of the tundra of Russia opened up to them, unfolding like a scroll.

"And they who are in the north countries shall come in remembrance before the Lord," quoted John, in an eloquent and sublimely spiritual voice.

Braun watched in a flicker of a moment as each person remembered the moment they realized the world wasn't as they had thought. He felt each person's experiences as they were liberated into a new expectation of the future. It was beautiful.

"And their prophets shall hear his voice, and shall no longer stay themselves," continued John.

The vision changed to show John and his three companions laboring over them and then leading them to this moment.

"And they shall smite the rocks, and the ice shall flow down at their presence," said John.

The vision turned to the rhythmic thumping of only hours ago, and the avalanche that literally flowed down upon their enemies.

"And an highway shall be cast up in the midst of the great deep."

They each saw the earthquake that had caused the land to rise from the depths of the ocean, and then each of them standing just as they were, in tribes, smiting the earth with their rods. They also saw the Bering Sea crack and the ice divide, flowing, sliding away from the highest point of the underwater land mass, allowing them to pass on dry ground.

"So that's how we'll do it!" whispered Chenille. There was wonder in her voice.

"Their enemies shall become a prey unto them," John continued.

They saw many battles of hand-to-hand combat in another land where there were trees and green foliage all around. In each battle the tribes not only succeeded, but dominated as they passed through.

"And in the barren deserts there shall come forth pools of living water; and the parched ground shall no longer be a thirsty land."

Their journey would take them through ice, forest, and then desert. The ground would yield up its water for them as they passed through.

"And the boundaries of the everlasting hills shall tremble at their presence," continued John.

Braun saw a series of earthquakes causing even the mountains to shake, as if announcing their coming to Utah, to Ephraim, their brothers.

"And they shall bring forth their rich treasures unto the children of Ephraim, my servants. And there shall they fall down and be crowned with glory, even in Zion, by the hands of the servants of the Lord, even the children of Ephraim."

The vision ended with all these tribes, as well as those that had crossed before them, bringing their records to the Lord's people, and then receiving all their endowments of blessings under the hands of God's servants, all dressed in white. The vision was glorious. So many people in this congregation wanted the blessings of eternal life, eternal family relationships, and the ability to reach out, across the veil, to those they loved there, too. [13]

Braun opened his eyes. Chenille still had hers closed, but tears were running down her face. He looked around and the same scene was everywhere. All of them had partaken of the Spirit that day and had had the love of God shine down on them, revealing his will. They had been edified together.

Braun gave Chenille a hug and a small peck on the cheek. He was so happy, his blessings were overflowing.

"Now, my people!" called John. "Focus your faith upon this large expanse of frozen water that lies before you. There once was another time where the children of Israel looked at a sea not unlike this one. With the great faith of Moses, the Lord divided the sea, and his children were allowed to walk on dry ground.[14] Are you the children of God?"

"Yes!" answered all the people together.

"Will you walk on dry ground?"

"Yes!" they answered again.

"You've seen the future; you know the outcome of your actions! Now strike the rock that lies below your feet with faith in that God whose spirit fills you and the ice will flow down before your feet!"

Together the people began rhythmically striking their staffs, javelins, and spears onto the ground where they stood. Each of them prayed mightily, calling upon the promises God had given them.

After a few moments, there was a distant sound of rumbling, as if a jet was flying over; then the rumbling moved under their feet. They continued to smite the earth until there was a roaring noise, as if lions roared from the wilderness behind them. The ice before them cracked, split, and then slid from the ground before them, damming the water from both the Arctic ocean and the Pacific ocean by it's bulk, and leaving dry ground stretching out for miles.

As the rumbling diminished, their thumping stopped, followed by many congratulatory whoops and yells, while others fell to their knees in thankful prayer.

John smiled broadly. Making eye contact with Braun, he nodded. "We go," he said, as he turned and began to walk, as Moses once did with his people. It was a very nostalgic moment and would be into eternity. People would remember this moment as the day that the Lord brought his people out of obscurity and home to Ephraim.

Becoming Zion

Provo, Utah
2:05 p.m.

Corrynne was instantly embarrassed by her outburst, but she decided not to apologize. Instead, she stood her ground, indulging, although not justly, in a secret desire to punish someone for her anger. "I'm sorry, but I'm just saying what everyone else is thinking. Tell us why God is allowing this to happen. I need to understand. I'm sure others need to, also."

Bo took a deep breath. With disappointment and sadness in his eyes, he looked from Corrynne out to the ward members, then back.

Corrynne knew he didn't like being put on the spot, especially by her, but in her opinion, being put on the spot was a part of his job description.

Bo stepped back on the log.

The ward gathered in expectantly.

"My friends, I know all of this seems confusing," began Bo. "I know, because it's confusing to me, but I have to have faith in God's words that he's given to us to prepare us for this day.

"History is repeating itself. The Saints are being singled out for persecution.[15] How long this will last, I don't know, but I do know we will be blessed if we endure it well.[16]

"We are being refined," continued Bo. "These trials are burning us, cleansing us as if in a kiln.[17] The impurities are melting from our soul. Love of riches, love of the world, love of prestige, all of it is melting away. We are being tested. Where do our hearts lie? God is watching how we respond to our trials and waiting for that answer. Can we live without the idols of cars, fancy clothes, and our symbols of greatness?"

Bo looked around, "Can we? If the answer is yes, then that's good, the purification will not be painful for you. If the answer is no, then that great web of materialism has caught you, and you'll have to make many choices that may led you away from the tree of life and eternal happiness."[18]

Bo continued, "Brothers and Sisters, what is happening today is not a mystery. The Lord has told us that he will have a humble people.[19] He has told us about a scourge that would eventually cover the earth[20] and it would begin at his house, to purify us and prepare us[21] to meet him. Through the years we have seen events that have started that process, but now we face it today like never before. How are we going to do?"

Bo looked around at his friends. No one answered his question.

"Tell me, how are we going to do?"

Still no one attempted to answer.

"Well, let me tell you. I have my weaknesses. God knows I'm not perfect and I struggle, but lately, I've been trying to be a better man. Today, after being handed this terrible news, I tried to see the bright side, which is normally my wife's job," said Bo, smiling slightly and eyeing Corrynne.

Corrynne watched unaffected.

Looking back at the ward, Bo said, "I looked at this turn of events and after being tempted to say things that weren't very bishop-like, I decided instead to force those thoughts from my head and say, 'Wow! Look, the scriptures are being fulfilled! That can only mean one thing! Christ's return must be soon!'[22] Then suddenly, I was filled with a new perception. The hair on my arms stood on end as I allowed myself to imagine standing, a couple years, a year, or maybe even six months from now, at the feet of my Savior as he returned to this world. I imagined myself being faithful. I imagined him saying, 'Well done, my good and faithful servant,' and I wept."[23] Right then, Bo broke down. His face turned red as he struggled to go, on as tears ran down his face. After a moment, he wiped his face with his sleeves and continued, "I want that for myself. Whatever I have to go through, whatever I have to give up, it's worth it."[24]

Corrynne pulled a Kleenex from her pocket and handed it to her husband.

Bo nodded a thank you.

Gaining composure, Bo started again. "Let's each develop a new sight. Let's all look at this situation from a different perspective. Instead of perceiving that the UN is taking away everything we have, what if Heavenly Father is *allowing* this to happen because it fulfills his purposes? What if the opposite is happening? What if by the actions of the UN, the righteous are being gathered from persecution—*to safety*?"[25]

Bo looked around. "Wouldn't that make sense? Think about it, the righteous are being gathered like wheat. We are being harvested, leaving the tares standing alone. What happens after the harvest?"

"A burning of the tares,"[26] said Sister Kemp, from the first row of onlookers.

"Yes, a burning of the tares," said Bo. "As soon as the righteous are safely gathered in, which with the arrival of the California Saints, we see is already happening, the world will be given harsh judgments that will come as storms, diseases, pests, famines, and wars. The world will wobble to and fro, as a drunken man, and waves will heave beyond the ocean's bounds. The world will heat up, the plants and the animals will die, fires will burn out of control, and life on this planet will change.[27] And what's going to happen to the true Saints during these perilous times? Nothing. We will not be affected. We will be safe because we've created Zion among us.[28] I repeat, the pure in heart will be unaffected.[29] Don't ask me how that's going to work, because I don't know. I just know that is what the Lord has said, and that it will come to pass.[30]

"You see, the Lord is not punishing us," continued Bo. "He's loving us. He is protecting us and gathering us to each other.[31] Sure, we'll be tried in all things, shaken till the worldliness is thrown from us, but this is done out of love so that we might be prepared to receive the glory he has in store for us.[32] We can't receive anything unless we are worthy.[33] God is going to give his blessings to someone. Hopefully it will be *us* as we *become Zion*.[34] To do that, we have to be willing to bear the trials and the chastisement he chooses to give us. If we can't bear those, then we aren't worthy of his blessings and cannot withstand the last day."[35]

To Corrynne, it looked like Bo was growing taller as he spoke. Energy flowed from him. Everyone felt it, including her. Corrynne's heart began to soften.

"God has told us to flee. So let's do that. He's warned us not to dally, or we'll be scattered, one here and one there. He has promised us that our children will be blessed in Zion. But he has also said that those that lag behind, staying in the world after having a chance to gather with Zion, will be afflicted by the devil.[36]

"Zion should be our greatest goal.[37] There, we are promised something that won't be found anywhere else: peace, patience, love, the satisfaction of friendships, victory through our sacrifices, dominance through our passivity, invincible strength evolving from sacrifice, and freedom from a sovereign might lording over us. Isn't that what we want? Isn't that what we all want?"[38]

People began to nod and glance at each other.

"Therefore, look to God's promises and be glad," quoted Bo. "Let Zion rejoice while all the wicked shall mourn. For behold, and lo, vengeance cometh speedily upon the ungodly as the whirlwind; and who shall escape it? The Lord's scourge shall pass over by night and by day, and the report thereof shall vex all people; yea, it shall not be stayed until the Lord come; for the indignation of the Lord is kindled against their abominations and all their wicked works. Nevertheless, Zion shall escape if she observe to do all things whatsoever I have commanded her.[39]

"Brothers and Sisters, let's become Zion and inherit all the blessings held out for her. Let's not walk, but run to our future that has only joy and victory within it."

The congregation erupted with clapping and hoots of excitement.

Corrynne looked around. Bo had done it. He had pulled off a miracle. There was actual excitement in the eyes of her friends and neighbors, despite their harsh circumstances. Personally, her feelings were still reserved, because of the unspoken burden she bore. She pushed aside the flap of her tent and retreated.

Notes to "Overcome"

Survival

[1] "Parents who provide a home where gospel principles are lived will have, as the Lord has said, 'a house of prayer, a house of fasting, a house of faith, a house of learning, ...a house of order, a house of God' (D&C 88:119). Regardless of how modest or humble that home may be, it will have love, happiness, peace, and joy. Children will grow up in righteousness and truth, and will desire to serve the Lord" (Ezra Taft Benson, *Conference Report*, October 1982).

[2] "In the 1940s while serving as the executive officer of the National Council of Farmer Cooperatives in Washington, D.C., I saw in a Hilton Hotel a placard depicting Uncle Sam, representing America, on his knees in humility and prayer. Beneath the placard was the inscription, 'Not beaten there by the hammer and sickle, but freely, responsibly, confidently. …We need fear nothing or no one save God.' That picture has stayed in my memory ever since: America on her knees in recognition that all our blessings come from God! America on her knees out of a desire to serve the God of this land by keeping His commandments! America on her knees, not driven there in capitulation to some despotic government, but on her knees freely, willingly, gratefully! This is the sovereign remedy to all of our problems and the preservation of our liberties. ...There should be no doubt what our task is today. If we truly cherish the heritage we have received, we must maintain the same virtues and the same character of our stalwart forebears—faith in God, courage, industry, frugality, self-reliance, and integrity. We have the obligation to maintain what those who pledged their lives, their fortunes, and sacred honor gave to future generations. Our opportunity and obligation for doing so is clearly upon us" (Ezra Taft Benson, "Our Priceless Heritage," *Ensign*, Nov 1976, pg. 33).

[3] "The Lord called his people Zion, because they were of one heart and one mind. Do I need to expatiate to this congregation upon the benefits which flow from unity? Need I repeat that ancient axiom: *'United we stand, divided we fall?'* Need I show to you that power dwells in union, in coming together, just as you Latter-day Saints have come together in this dispensation, this dispensation of gathering, of unity, and consequently of power? No, I do not need to argue with you upon this point, to prove to you that power invariably dwells in the midst of a people who are united, who are of one heart and mind. This was the state of the people of Enoch; and this is one of the reasons why they were worthy of the name Zion—'because they were of one heart and one mind.' They all believed alike; they were not torn asunder by various opinions, by conflicting views and notions, by divers interpretations of the things of God; but they had ascended in the scale of intelligence, of spirituality, to that glorious plane where they saw eye to eye, each man with his neighbor, and all saw God alike, so far as they were capable of comprehending Him and His purposes" (Orson F. Whitney, *Collected Discourses 1888-1898, Volume 1*, September 22, 1889).

[4] "And he causeth all, both small and great, rich and poor, free and bond, to receive a mark in their right hand, or in their foreheads: And that no man might buy or sell, save he that had the mark, or the name of the beast, or the number of his name" (Revelation 13:16-17).

[5] "He that trusteth in his riches shall fall: but the righteous shall flourish as a branch" (Proverbs 11:28).

[6] "And in the latter time of their kingdom, when the transgressors are come to the full, a king of fierce countenance, and understanding dark sentences, shall stand up. And his power shall be mighty...and he shall destroy wonderfully, and shall prosper, and practice, and shall destroy the mighty and the holy people" (Daniel 8: 23-24).

[7] "And through his policy also he shall cause craft to prosper in his hand; and he shall magnify himself in his heart, and by peace shall destroy many: he shall also stand up against the Prince of princes; but he shall be broken without hand" (Daniel 8: 25).

[8] "He maketh the storm calm, so that the waves thereof are still" (Proverbs 107:29).

A Beloved People

[9] "And it shall come to pass that the Jews shall have the words of the Nephites, and the Nephites shall have the words of the Jews; and the Nephites and the Jews shall have the words of the lost tribes of Israel; and the lost tribes of Israel shall have the words of the Nephites and the Jews" (2 Nephi 29:13).

[10] "There is no other way [the Ten Tribes] can be gathered. Of course they will be led by their prophets, prophets who are subject to and receive instructions from, and prophets who report their labors to the one man on the earth who holds and exercises all of the keys of the kingdom in their fullness. ...This is the promised day when there shall be one God, one Shepherd, one prophet, one gospel, one church, and one kingdom for all the earth. This is the day when one man shall direct all of the Lord's work in all the earth; the day when he shall bring all Israel into one fold" (Bruce R. McConkie, *The Millennial Messiah*, pg. 217).

[11] "And they who are in the north countries shall come in remembrance before the Lord; and their prophets shall hear his voice, and shall no longer stay themselves" (D&C 133:26).

[12] D&C 46:8.

[13] See D&C 133:26-32 for scripture describing the return of the lost tribes from the north as discussed in the text.

[14] "Therefore, lift up your heads, and rejoice, and put your trust in God, in that God who was the God of Abraham, and Isaac, and Jacob; and also, that God who brought the children of Israel out of the land of Egypt, and caused that they should walk through the Red Sea on dry ground, and fed them with manna that they might not perish in the wilderness; and many more things did he do for them" (Mosiah 7:19).

Becoming Zion

[15] "Blessed are ye, when men shall revile you, and persecute you, and shall say all manner of evil against you falsely, for my sake" (Matthew 5:11).

[16] "Blessed are they which are persecuted for righteousness' sake: for theirs is the kingdom of heaven" (Matthew 5:10).

[17] "And I will turn my hand upon thee, and purely purge away thy dross, and take away all thy tin" (Isaiah 1:25).

[18] "If our heart is right, we also have righteous attitudes and priorities. ...Our priorities determine what we seek in life. 'Wherefore, seek not the things of this world but seek ye first to build up the kingdom of God, and to establish his righteousness' (JST Matthew 6:38), Jesus taught his disciples. As we read in modern revelation: 'Seek not for riches but for wisdom, and behold, the mysteries of God shall be unfolded unto you, and then shall you be made rich. Behold, he that hath eternal life is rich' (D&C 6:7). The qualities we call materialism and spirituality are expressive of priorities and attitudes toward the nature and purpose of life" (Dallin H. Oaks, *Pure in Heart*, pg. 5-6).

[19] "God will have a humble people. Either we can choose to be humble or we can be compelled to be humble. Alma said, 'Blessed are they who humble themselves without being compelled to be humble' (Alma 32:16). ...We must yield 'to the enticings of the Holy Spirit,' put off the prideful 'natural man,' become 'a saint through the atonement of Christ the Lord,' and become 'as a child, submissive, meek, humble' (Mosiah 3:19)" (Ezra Taft Benson, *Conference Report*, April 1989, pgs. 6-7).

[20] "For a desolating scourge shall go forth among the inhabitants of the earth, and shall continue to be poured out from time to time, if they repent not, until the earth is empty, and the inhabitants thereof are consumed away and utterly destroyed by the brightness of my coming" (D&C 5:19).

[21] "Read a revelation that Joseph received of the Lord to Thomas B. Marsh concerning the Twelve; He told them to go forth and preach the Gospel to every nation, kindred, tongue, and people, or cause it to be done; and after your testimony cometh the testimony of earthquakes, of famine, of fire, and of desolation; it shall come upon the world, and it shall begin at my house, saith the Lord, that is, with that portion who rebel against Him in the midst of His house" (Heber C. Kimball, *Journal of Discourses*, Vol. 4, pg. 338).

[22] "And it shall come to pass that he that feareth me shall be looking forth for the great day of the Lord to come, even for the signs of the coming of the Son of Man" (D&C 45:39).

[23] "Well done, thou good and faithful servant: thou hast been faithful over a few things, I will make thee ruler over many things: enter thou into the joy of thy lord" (Matthew 25:21).

[24] "The Saints must be willing to sacrifice all. We have found the treasure in the field, we have found the pearl of great price, and now we have got to give all that we have for it, at one time or another. The Lord has said that He will prove us even unto death, to see whether we will stand by the covenants we have made with Him. Some Latter-day Saints have things in their possession which are so valuable to them that they would prefer death to the loss of those things. We have to deal with facts, not a mere ideal. In one sense, it is a hard thing for us to sell all that we have that we may secure these glories that have been opened to our view; but it will pay us in the end" (Lorenzo Snow, *Teachings of Lorenzo Snow*, pg. 115).

[25] "In this dispensation there is a principle or commandment peculiar to it. What is that? It is the gathering of the people to one place. The gathering of this people is as necessary to be observed by believers, as faith, repentance, baptism, or any other ordinance. It is an essential part of the Gospel of this dispensation, as much so as the necessity of building an ark by Noah for his deliverance, was a part of the Gospel in his dispensation. Then the world was destroyed by a flood, now it is to be destroyed by war, pestilence, famine, earthquakes, storms, and tempests, the sea roiling beyond its bounds, malarious vapors, vermin, disease, and by fire and the lightnings of God's wrath poured out for destruction upon Babylon" (Joseph F. Smith, *Journal of Discourses*, September 30,1877, Vol. 19, pg. 192).

[26] "Therefore, let the wheat and the tares grow together until the harvest is fully ripe; then ye shall first gather out the wheat from among the tares, and after the gathering of the wheat, behold and lo, the tares are bound in bundles, and the field remaineth to be burned" (D&C 86:7).

[27] "For not many days hence and the earth shall tremble and reel to and fro as a drunken man; and the sun shall hide his face, and shall refuse to give light; and the moon shall be bathed in blood; and the stars shall become exceedingly angry, and shall cast themselves down as a fig that falleth from off a fig-tree. And after your testimony cometh wrath and indignation upon the people. For after your testimony cometh the testimony of earthquakes, that shall cause groanings in the midst of her, and men shall fall upon the ground and shall not be able to stand. And also cometh the testimony of the voice of thunderings, and the voice of lightnings, and the voice of tempests, and the voice of the waves of the sea heaving themselves beyond their bounds. And all things shall be in commotion; and surely, men's hearts shall fail them; for fear shall come upon all people" (D&C 88:87-91).

[28] "...The gathering together upon the land of Zion, and upon her stakes, may be for a defense, and for a refuge from the storm, and from wrath when it shall be poured out without mixture upon the whole earth" (D&C 115:6).

[29] "Who shall be able to stand?" Those who have been sealed by the Living God: "This sealing secures and protects the righteous from the great destructions that will be poured out upon the earth's inhabitants, including the desolations that accompany the blowing of the seven trumpets and the pouring out of the seven vials (bowls) in Rev. 8, 9, and 16. Joseph Smith taught that the sealing mentioned here 'signifies sealing the blessing upon their heads, meaning the everlasting covenant, thereby making their calling and election sure'" (Donald W. Parry, Jay A. Parry, *Understanding the Book of Revelation*, pg. 91).

[30] "And I saw another angel ascending from the east, having the seal of the living God: and he cried with a loud voice to the four angels, to whom it was given to hurt the earth and the sea, Saying, hurt not the earth, neither the sea, nor the trees, till we have sealed the servants of our God in their foreheads" (Revelation 7:2-3).

[31] "...Without Zion, and a place of deliverance, we must fall; because the time is near when the sun will be darkened, and the moon turn to blood, and the stars fall from heaven, and the earth reel to and fro. Then, if this is the case, and if we are not sanctified and gathered to the places God has appointed, with all our former professions and our great love for the Bible, we must fall; we cannot stand; we cannot be saved; for God will gather out his Saints from the Gentiles, and then comes desolation and

destructions, and none can escape except the pure in heart who are gathered" (Joseph Smith, *DHC*, April 21, 1834, Vol. 2, pg. 52).

[32] "Zion is not going to be moved out of her place. The Lord will plead with her strong ones, and if she sins he will chastise her until she is purified before the Lord. I do not pretend to tell how much sorrow you or I are going to meet with before the coming of the Son of Man. That will depend upon our conduct" (Wilford Woodruf, *Millennial Star*, 1889, Vol. 51, pg. 547).

[33] "For I the Lord cannot look upon sin with the least degree of allowance" (D&C 1:31).

[34] "Building on the foundations heretofore laid, we are now ready to inquire: Where shall the temporal gathering of Israel be? Where shall scattered Israel assemble in the last days? Are all converts to the kingdom destined to come to western America? Where is Zion? To all of these, and to all like questions, there are answers from the Lord that no man need misunderstand. Be it remembered that Zion is people; Zion is the pure in heart; Zion is the saints of the living God. And be it also remembered that the people called Zion build the places called Zion. Thus wherever the saints build an old or a new Jerusalem, wherever they establish cities of holiness, wherever they create stakes of Zion, there is Zion; and where these things are not, Zion is not" (Bruce R. McConkie, *Millennial Messiah*, pg. 293).

[35] "Wherefore take unto you the whole armour of God, that ye may be able to withstand in the evil day, and having done all, to stand" (Ephesians 6:13).

[36] "There will be here and there a Stake (of Zion) for the gathering of the Saints. Some may have cried peace, but the Saints and the world will have little peace from henceforth. Let this not hinder us from going to the Stakes; for God has told us to flee, not dallying, or we shall be scattered, one here, and another there. There your children shall be blessed, and you in the midst of friends where you may be blessed. The Gospel net gathers of every kind. I prophesy, that the man who tarries after he has an opportunity of going, will be afflicted by the devil. Wars are at hand: we must not delay; but are not required to sacrifice. We ought to have the building up of Zion as our greatest object. When wars come, we shall have to flee to Zion. The cry is to make haste. The last revelation says, Ye shall not have time to have gone over the earth, until these things come. It will come as did the cholera, war, fires, and earthquakes; one pestilence after another. Until the Ancient of Days comes, then judgment will be given to the Saints" (Joseph Smith, *DHC,* July 2, 1839, Vol. 3, pgs. 390-391).

[37] "Therefore, verily, thus saith the Lord, let Zion rejoice, for this is Zion—THE PURE IN HEART" (D&C 97:21).

"They that remain, and are pure in heart, shall return, and come to their inheritances, they and their children, with songs of everlasting joy, to build up the waste places of Zion" (D&C:101:18).

[38] "'Hearken and hear, O ye inhabitants of the earth. Listen, ye elders of my church together, and hear the voice of the Lord; for he calleth upon all men, and he commandeth all men everywhere to repent' (D&C 133:4-16). This, then, is the message of gathering: Come unto Christ; repent and be baptized; receive the gift of the Holy Ghost and become pure, as pure and untainted from the sins of the world as is a newly born babe. Then assemble with the saints that the sanctifying processes may work in your life and you be a fit subject to stand before the King of Zion when he comes to reign in his glory" (Bruce R. McConkie, *Millennial Messiah*, pg. 292).

[39] D&C 97:21-25.

CHAPTER EIGHTEEN

THY WILL, NOT MINE, BE DONE

"Trust in the Lord with all thine heart; and lean not unto thine own understanding. In all thy ways acknowledge him, and he shall direct thy paths" (Proverbs 3:5-6).

00:00:01, 03:47:32, Zulu
Tuesday, December 30th

Fall Out

Provo, Utah
1:13 p.m.

"Where's the bishop?" demanded Tom Reiser, walking briskly with Brothers Carpenter, Thompson, and Simonson between the tents on Mr. Griffin's property.

"Who let you guys in?" asked Brother Jensen, the Elders Quorum president. He was holding a bucket full of fresh milk that he had just pulled from one of Mr. Griffin's cows.

"What do you mean, who let us in? We can walk around here if we want to," said Tom, with a sneer.

"No, this is private property," said Mr. Griffin, who moseyed up behind the four with an axe over his shoulder. There were four other men standing behind him for support. They had obviously seen the angry ward members come into his field and followed them.

Brother Reiser looked at the old man, the group behind him, and the rusty axe. Then he shot a look back at his friends and said, "What are you planning to do with that axe, old man?"

Mr. Griffin shook his head. "I'm planning on cutting out dead wood." He had a menacing look on his face. "Sound good to you?" he asked, eyes squinted. The men behind him nodded with folded arms.

"What's he mean by that?" Simonson asked Thompson.

Brother Thompson shook his head. "I'm afraid to ask."

"What is it that you gentlemen are after?" asked Mr. Griffin.

"Trouble," said Brother Jensen.

The men looked at each other and then Tom said, "We have a beef to settle."

"What kind of beef?"

"The UN has cut us off," said Simonson.

"Our jobs, mortgages, and medical care have been ripped away," said Thompson.

"Why?" asked Mr. Griffin. "I thought you folks went over to the dark side. What's the problem? Your chip wired wrong?"

Brother Jensen smiled at the jibe.

It seemed to make the four upset. "No," began Simonson. "This isn't a laughing matter. We think the bishop sold us out! We think he told the UN we were Mormons."

"Well, aren't you?" asked Mr. Griffin, tightening his jaw.

The men looked at each other and then back. "That has nothing to do with our benefits. If we took the biochip, we should be able to have what we need," said Brother Reiser, "and no jealous bishop is going to stop us from having it."

"Sounds to me like your beef is with the UN, not the bishop," said Griffin. "And even if he did give the UN a list of Mormons, it's the UN's money. They can choose whoever they want to give it to. If you don't like someone else having control over your life, you should probably become real men and pull yourselves up by your bootstraps, roll up your sleeves, and get to work. There is no such thing as a free lunch."

"Shut up, old man," said Tom.

"Come on, you guys, cool down," said Brother Jensen, looking back and forth between the two groups. "Bo doesn't decide anything for the UN, and I promise you he doesn't have enough time or ink to waste it on vengeance lists. He's just minding his own business serving the ward like always."

"Now, get off my property," demanded Mr. Griffin, as he cocked the axe aggressively. "I'll give you three seconds to start heading out. One!"

The men gave Brother Jensen and Mr. Griffin a last angry stare.

"Two!" said Griffin, tightening his grip around the axe.

The men turned with irritation and trudged away.

"Three!" Griffin yelled after the men. "And don't come back without an invitation!"

Family

Provo, Utah
2:00 p.m.

"Corrynne!" shouted Bo. There was urgency in his voice.

Corrynne looked up. She had been packing clothes in blankets, tying the corners to form a neat bundle. "What?"

"Come quick!"

"What is it?" asked Corrynne, alarmed by the tone of Bo's voice.

"Your mother's here. She needs help."

Corrynne frowned, "My mother? What are you talking about?" she asked, as she rushed out of the tent. She shook her head. It couldn't be true; her mother was in Washington. Without gas, that was a world away.

"She's in the back of a pick-up truck right outside the gate," said Bo, running beside Corrynne.

"What's she doing there?" asked Corrynne.

"I don't know," said Bo. "A man asked for you and that's all he said."

Corrynne reached the perimeter of the Griffin property and saw the back of a red truck. It had a canopy over the bed. A man was standing by the tailgate. "Are you Corrynne Rogers?" he asked.

"Yes," said Corrynne.

The man opened the canopy door. "I believe I have some people here for you."

Corrynne bent down and saw many people packed in the back. The overpowering stench of vomit and diarrhea hit her nose. Immediately she knew exactly what she needed to do. Time was of the essence.

"Corrynne?" asked a weak voice.

Corrynne couldn't tell where it came from. "Yes, yes, I'm here. Mother? Is that you?"

"It's Melynda." The voice was coming from the far right corner. "We're sick. Mom passed out. I think she's dehydrated. We all are."

Corrynne looked back. Bo was standing right behind her. "I need help getting these people out of the truck."

Bo turned and whistled, motioning for someone. Suddenly, there were six men unloading the back of the pick-up truck.

"Let's put these people in Mr. Griffin's home. They need to be quarantined and have the warmth of a real shelter for a little while," said Corrynne. "I'll get the medical supplies."

Corrynne turned and rushed to the house. She knew the food storage and the medical supplies hadn't been loaded up for transport yet. Her heart beat heavily in her chest as she imagined all the things she would need to do to help these people survive. She'd need assistance from everyone in the camp. Luckily there were three other women in her ward who had nursing backgrounds. She'd recruit the doctors she knew, too.

With a quick twist of the doorknob, Corrynne had the front door open and rushed into the house and down the stairs. All of their rationed food from the ward members and the supplies they had gathered had been stored here. She quickly found the stash of medical supplies hidden in a brown box. "Saline, IV starts, tubing, antiseptic, Lomotil," she started, thinking what else she should need. "Phenergan," she said, taking one of two vials that were donated from the hospital. They had their seals broken in the protective covering, so ordinarily they would have been thrown away, but she had rescued them before they were discarded. The medication inside the vial was still good since the glass was still intact. It was a bonus find. She wouldn't use it unless she absolutely had to, since she had only two. "Tape, gauze, masks, gloves," she finished, as she packed her box. "Ahhh, what else?" she asked, as she passed her hand over the shelves. "Lots of saline," she said, as she began to throw the liters in the box. Finally, when it was full, she carried the box up the stairs. It was very heavy.

When she walked into the big living room, the scene tugged at her heart. The men who had unloaded the truck, were now in a circle praying over someone who was at least well enough to sit in a chair. "...Amen," they said in unison, as the circle broke apart. As the tight group opened up, Corrynne could see that the person being administered to, was her sister. She had her baby son asleep in her arms.

"What happened?" Corrynne asked, rushing to her sister's side and giving her a brief hug.

"Help Mom first," said Melynda, pointing to the couch beside her.

Corrynne put the box on the floor and knelt beside her mother.

Tears burst from her eyes as she saw the toll of the illness in her mother's unconscious face. She gathered her wits about her and felt for a pulse. It was weak and very rapid. She could tell, just by the character of the pulse and the lack of sweat on her brow, that not only was her blood pressure dangerously low, but the dehydration was severe.

Looking back at the circle of men, she saw that Bo and Dane were watching her, waiting for instructions.

"Bo, please find those in our ward with medical experience. I'll need help here starting all these IV's. Also, send in some others to prepare more saline solution. We're going to run out quickly. I'll need others to just attend to physical needs, such as helping these people clean up and making them comfortable with the blankets we have."

"How do we make saline solution?" asked Bo, looking worried.

"We'll have to boil water and add salt," said Corrynne. "What other choice do we have?"

"Do you know how to do that?" asked Bo.

Corrynne nodded. She thought she did. She had to try. Anything would be better than nothing at this point. "The saline needs to taste like tears. It will be fine."

"That's strange. Why do we have to add salt?" asked Bo. "Won't that be like drinking sea water?"

Corrynne shook her head. "We'll just add a little salt. If we don't, we'll make the blood cells break apart. We don't want to do that."

Bo nodded and went out the door to gather more people to help.

Corrynne turned to Dane and the other men who were remaining. As she put on a mask and gloves, she said, "Please, find out who needs blessings and continue. I'll need all the help I can get." She silently began to pray. She felt her limitations overwhelm her. She was used to a controlled medical environment with a lab and monitors, machines that would calculate blood sugar, blood pressure, and heart rate. Without her tools, she was going to be slow and potentially inaccurate in her care, but she had to try.

Corrynne picked up her mother's limp hand and looked at the veins. Suddenly a flash of memory returned to her. As a child, she would trace those veins at church during the sacrament meeting talks. As a nurse she had always thought her mother had wonderful veins. Nurses thought things like that. Corrynne kissed her mother's hand. She was overwhelmed with emotion. She needed to resuscitate her mother, if only to say good-bye.

Shaking her head, she knew she had to get those thoughts out of her mind. They would cripple her! She cleared her throat and pulled the box of supplies close.

"Is she going to be OK?" asked Melynda, hovering near.

Corrynne nodded. "I hope so. The key is getting fluids into her and her blood pressure up. How are you feeling?"

"Weak."

"Can you drink?" asked Corrynne, trying to distract her emotional thoughts, as she dug through to find IV supplies.

"Yes. I can."

"Have you been throwing up?"

"Yes. Both Nathan and I have."

"Then put on a mask. You are in quarantine."

"For how long?" asked Melynda, as she applied a mask.

"Until you stop. How did you guys get here?" Corrynne asked.

"We pooled our gas by siphoning all our cars."

"Where's Troy and the girls?" asked Corrynne as she hooked up saline and primed some tubing.

"They're coming. We had to go in separate cars."

Corrynne nodded. She was relieved that her sister still had her family intact, but was overburdened with the thought of more sick, especially when they were under the gun to evacuate. Ripping some tape and setting out some gauze, she asked, "Are they sick, too?"

Melynda nodded. "Some are, but not as bad as these people."

"Where's Dad?" asked Corrynne.

Melynda didn't answer immediately.

"Did he die?" asked Corrynne.

"We don't know," said Melynda. "The Prophet had told us to pack up and leave the area, which we did, but I guess we hadn't moved out far enough. There was an earthquake and massive flooding around Puget Sound, which threatened our camp. Things were crazy. Everyone piled into cars to get away from the water. We couldn't bring anything! Dad said he'd follow us, but..."

Corrynne understood and nodded. She couldn't think too deeply about that one right now. She'd assume everything was fine and he was just still driving. "I'm just glad you guys are here. I've been worried about you."

"Me too," said Melynda. "This was the only place I could think of to go."

"It was a good choice. The mountains are far away from the ocean, aren't they?"

"Yes, thank goodness," sighed Melynda.

Corrynne inserted a butterfly needle into her mother's vein and got a flash of blood. That was good. Quickly she attached the IV tubing to the hub of the needle, but the vein immediately blew. The tissue surrounding the vein began to swell up with the fluid instead of flowing nicely through the vein. "Shoot," said Corrynne, as she clamped the saline. "Lost that IV."

"Why?" asked Melynda.

"It just happens sometimes," she said, looking for a bigger, more durable vein. She saw one in the crook of her mother's elbow. With a finger she touched it, testing its elasticity. It felt flat, but she could still feel it. Again she prepped the area and inserted the needle. Another flash filled the tubing. Again, she connected the IV tubing to the hub and flushed. The fluid moved into the vein smoothly. Corrynne was so relieved!

"Is it in?" asked Melynda.

Corrynne sat back. "It's in."

"Good. Now what?"

"I need you to squeeze this bag as hard as you can and shoot this fluid into her veins. When that bottle is almost done, I want you to open another bag and hook it up the way you saw me, and squeeze it. Do that three times and then come get me."

Melynda nodded as she put her sleeping baby between her mother and the back of the couch. "I think I can do that."

"Tell me if she wakes up. That's really important."

Melynda nodded. "OK."

"Meanwhile, I'm going to get some chicken broth made for you. I want you to drink that stuff until you can't anymore."

Melynda nodded again.

Corrynne turned to see who needed her attention next.

"Ahh, Corrynne?" asked Melynda, grasping her hand.

"What?" A pain shot through Corrynne's hand, "Ouch!" she said automatically.

Melynda frowned. "I didn't touch you that hard," she said as she looked closely at Corrynne's hand.

Corrynne pulled her hand away quickly. She knew why she had the pain. The chip was up against a bone. "It's OK," said Corrynne. "I'm just sensitive today."

Melynda looked at Corrynne with shock in her eyes.

Corrynne instantly knew what was going though Melynda's head.

"You have a biochip!" said Melynda, with a gasp.

Corrynne nodded. "I do," she said, knowing it would be useless to deny it. Corrynne pulled out her stern, big sister voice, hoping Melynda would get the hint, and not pursue the topic. "Just be quiet about it and keep squeezing. Mom needs that fluid."

Melynda nodded and did as she was told.

Corrynne rushed away relieved. She was sure she would have to address that topic later. It wasn't something she looked forward to.

Labor

Provo, Utah
3:12 p.m.

"How are you feeling?" the blinking curser asked Brea.

Brea wasn't feeling well. A massive contraction pulled on her abdomen. It was getting painful. The babies had grown quiet. Their time was near.

Brea closed her eyes and breathed through the pain. Finally, when the pain subsided, she wrote, "My contractions are getting more regular. Are you coming?"

There was a pause, and then the writing started. "Yes, I'm coming...I have some things to do first."

Another contraction started. It worried Brea. One had just ended. Was this the beginning of her labor? Because she had never had a baby before, she didn't know what was normal, despite her nursing education. She had an irresistible feeling of panic and anger at the same time. What was so important that Matt wasn't coming now? If he didn't come now, she was worried he would miss the birth of his first children!

Brea looked around helplessly. Where was Jax? He was just here, in her home. "Jax!" she called.

No answer.

Then Brea remembered him saying something about getting a card game from his house. He had been bored sitting around her place.

Brea shook her head. She hoped he hurried. It was Jax's day to stay with her so he could run for her mother if anything happened...suddenly those thoughts flew from her as her abdomen squeezed painfully. She couldn't think during the pains.

"Hee, hee, hee," she panted through the contraction. "Hee, hee, hee. Hee, hee, hee...."

After two minutes or so, the contractions began to ease. "Jax! Where are you!" she cried, not expecting an answer, but yelling in anxiety as her body began to shake. What was she was going to do? If Jax didn't come back in time, she'd have to deliver these babies alone. Could she do that? Brea looked around again to try and solve this problem before another pain came. It was still light outside, so she couldn't go outside to get her mother. Even if she did make it up the stairs, could she walk?

Another pain came quickly, even before she could recover from the previous one. "What's going on?" she whispered, feeling light-headed as pain gripped her like a vice. Her abdomen squeezed, pushing on her back and putting pressure on her lungs. It was becoming harder and harder to breathe. *"How do people do this?"* she yelled as she closed her eyes. Grabbing the armrest, she was forced to concentrate again and breathe in rhythm until the contraction eased.

When she opened her eyes, she saw on her monitor the question, "Are you there?"

Brea bit her lip and sat up in the chair. With shaking hands, she typed, "Yes, I'm here, but I'm hurting...it's starting...." Then she couldn't help herself, she began to cry. She was full of loneliness, mourning, anger, and helplessness. Her family was right outside her door and she couldn't do anything about it. To make matters worse, her husband was on the computer, but a world away!

With a fist, she hit the desk. Then she let her emotions loose and sobbed. For months she had been holding in her anger, pretending everything was fine, but things weren't fine! She was alone! In a time when all the family should be around her, she was alone! Why was her life so horrible?

With anger and bitterness, she wrote, "Yes, I'm here—*but you're not*!" she pushed enter, then immediately felt sorry she had. She didn't want to hurt Matt. She loved him! She missed him! She wanted nothing more than to be in his arms and smell his skin. She wanted him by her side, helping her through this pain. *She wanted her husband!*

"I'm coming..." appeared on the screen, and then the program closed. Matt had signed off.

Brea moved from the chair and into her bedroom. She crawled up on her air hammock and pulled pillows all around her. Another contraction began. Brea yelled out as the contraction took hold of her body against her will. She took a couple of panting breaths and yelled, *"Mother!"* But her effort was in vain; no one could hear her. Despite that, she prayed for help. She prayed for Jax to return soon.

"Father, help me!" she yelled, and then the pain consumed her again.

Heart Attack

Provo, Utah
3:30 p.m.

Brother Reiser pushed through the people pouring into the Griffin property as cars drove up, and more sick people were helped out.

"Where's Bishop Rogers?" he demanded, looking back and forth frantically. "I have to find the bishop!"

"He's over there," said one of the ward members, who was helping a sick man walk toward the mansion.

"Bo! Bo Rogers!"

Bo looked over his shoulder. He saw brother Reiser coming at him like a charging bull.

Bo held up his hands. "Now, Tom, we don't want any trouble."

Tom's eyes were wild. He looked like he hadn't even heard a word Bo said. "You have to come with me! My wife's having a heart attack!"

Bo shook his head as he swallowed. Instantly, the Spirit told him Tom's wife was going to die, no matter what he did. A blessing wouldn't keep her on earth. Brea's dream had been a true one. Bo shook his head. "I'm so sorry, Tom," was all he could manage to say, but he searched for something else. Thinking quickly to try and avoid giving Sister Reiser an empty blessing, he said, "Tom, we're dealing with our own emergency here. Corrynne's ward from Washington just arrived and everyone's very sick. Her own mother..."

"Bo! Did you hear me?" interrupted Brother Reiser. "My wife's *dying*! She needs a blessing! The hospital won't let us in because they say I'm in your ward and my chip's number is invalid. I've been kicked out of the system. You're my only hope."

Bo held out a hand, to stop Tom's pleadings. Nodding and feeling heavy with worry, it was hard to refuse his brother, despite their differences, but there was no way around this situation. Sister Reiser was going to die.

Suddenly, Bo had a burst of inspiration. The only way to diffuse this conflict and avoid the consequences that had played out in Brea's dreams was to refuse to go to Tom's home. He had to let this man deal with his wife's death himself and not be anywhere near. Later, if Tom and the others still decided to come for him for whatever strange reason they could conjure up, the power of the Lord would protect him among the righteous.

"I'm sorry, Brother Reiser," Bo said quietly, to keep their conversation private. "Go and bless your wife. You have the priesthood. Use it. You have the same ability that I do. Pray for inspiration and the Lord will tell you his will. Then give the blessing as the Spirit dictates. Take one of these men with you," he said, pointing at the good men in his ward. "Any of them will help."

Bo turned and stood on his log to make an announcement for Corrynne, "I know I've already announced this, but Brothers and Sisters, we have many people arriving who have nothing. Floods have forced them to come to us without the necessities of life. Sickness has infected many of them. Many might die. Again, we're calling for anyone with any kind of medical background to come to the Griffin house where they're being put in quarantine..."

"Bo! You're the bishop!" interrupted Tom again, making their conversation very obvious and public. "Don't refuse me! I'm in need! Please help me," pleaded Brother Reiser. "That's your responsibility!"

His responsibility? thought Bo, angry that now this was public. He felt manipulated and pushed into giving in, because of the spectacle. Bo snapped. "And what's *your* responsibility, Tom?" he said pointedly, not blunting his meaning. "Surely you know that blessings only come after the trial of your faith and being found worthy."

Brother Reiser's mouth hung open.

Bo turned back to the ward and said, "So, please, everyone who's able-bodied, gather at the Griffin house." Then he stepped down and walked away.

Tom followed closely behind. "Bishop..." he began.

Bo continued to walk without yielding.

"Bishop," said Brother Reiser, in a quieter tone. "Please. I'm begging. I'm sorry, is that what you want me to say? Here, I'll even say you were right. You knew better and I'm the fool. Please, help me."

Bo turned back to see a humbled man. He studied Tom's eyes. Bo closed his and shook his head.

"Please..." said Brother Reiser. "You have the gift of healing. I've seen you heal so many times I can't count them."

"It's not me," said Bo. "I haven't healed a single person. God heals whom he wishes. I am just the instrument."

Brother Reiser nodded. "I know, but God loves you. He trusts you. You're righteous—and I'm not."

Bo had a flash of vision. In a moment he saw that Brother Reiser and his wife secretly had a rocky marriage. Many words had been said that made each have deep regrets. The bottom line was that Brother Reiser was panicking because he needed time to take his anger back. He needed to make things right.

Bo put a strong hand on Brother Reiser's shoulder. With a bold look, he said, "Go to your wife. Hold her. Say all the loving words you've wanted to, but didn't know how. Now's the time to say you're sorry."

Brother Reiser looked at Bo with shock in his eyes. "What are you saying? A blessing won't help her?"

"No, a blessing from my hand won't help her. She's sealed unto death."

Brother Reiser shook his head in disbelief, looking like he was almost choking.

"But a blessing from your hand would comfort her. Go to her, she needs you. She wonders where you are right now."

"Are you being serious or trying to get rid of me?" asked Brother Reiser, his voice shaky. He looked at Bo sideways.

Bo pointed the direction of Tom's house. "*Go!* You don't have long. The time that's left is a gift. Don't waste a second more!"

Brother Reiser's eyebrows raised as the blood drained from his face. Then he turned and ran out of the tent city.

And the Walls Came Tumbling Down

Bering Sea, Alaska
10:40 a.m.

The tribes had been three days traveling between the undulating ice walls. Each night, they camped, sleeping in their tents of seal and whale skins, ate their dried meat, and drank melted ice. Today, they had been traveling almost all day with only about a mile left. The Alaskan terrain loomed large and gorgeous in front of them.

"Do you know we're walking back in time right now?" Braun asked Chenille.

"Back in time, what do you mean?"

"We are living yesterday now. We just crossed the International Date Line. It ran between those two mountains back there that are normally islands when the water is flowing."

"We did?" asked Chenille, looking behind her. "That's so incredible. But thinking like that makes my brain hurt."

A horn blew somewhere behind them. Braun looked with alarm at John, who was walking near them.

"I'll be right back. Keep the people moving forward," John instructed Braun, and then repeated the same message to others in the various tribal languages. Then he disappeared.

"Where did he go?" asked Chenille.

"That sound was a warning. Something must be happening back there," said Braun, picking up the pace and gesturing to the others to do the same. Soon everyone was moving a little faster until they were jogging at a comfortable pace.

Suddenly, John reappeared.

"So what's going on?" Braun asked.

"The Russians are pursuing with large machines. We need to go faster. We need to run."

"How far away are they?" asked Braun, taking Chenille's hand and beginning to run.

"They are one day of our journeying away, but that will only take an hour or so to make up. Soon they will overtake us."

"Aren't they in American waters?" asked Braun to Chenille. "We should be safe now."

Chenille nodded in agreement.

"Why are the Russians still coming after us if we're in America's territory?" asked Braun to John.

"Because the United States does not have an army to stop them," said John.

"They don't?" asked Chenille with surprise. "What happened?"

John looked behind him. "I don't have time to answer now. You'll know everything soon," said John.

"How many Russians are there?" asked Braun.

"There's about thirty or forty machines with six men in each. All of them have weapons. They wish to make us return."

"What's going to happen to us?" asked Chenille.

"We must make it to land." John blew his ram's horn three times and then motioned for the people to pick up the pace.

The elongating group broke into a run. Many of the parents picked up the small children and ran with them on their backs. Others placed them on the sleds to ride across the frozen sand. They were urged forward more by the concern in John's face than anything else.

After a few minutes, it was obvious that people were tiring. Some were beginning to lag behind, stretching the line of people along the rift in the ice.

In the distance, a machine gun fired, warning them to stop.

"Keep running! Keep running! The Lord will help you," encouraged John. "Keep running!" Translations rippled through the line as they encouraged each other, but still there were those who could not keep up with the rest.

"Chenille, you go and wait for me on the beach, it's not far. I'm going to help back there," Braun said, gesturing at the long line of people.

Chenille looked at her husband as if to argue, but then she changed her mind and nodded. She released his hand, took the sled's rope, and continued running.

Braun rushed to the end of the line. He could see the military machines rolling up the sand between the ice walls. They were catching up quicker than he had expected.

"Up on the ice!" yelled John in English and other languages.

Braun helped as many children as he could climb to the top of the ice.

"Everyone up on the ice," Braun echoed, as did others in the group.

One by one, the people in the tribes were able to climb out of the ravine, up to the top of the frozen strait and on towards the beach. Soon, the corridor of ice was empty of people.

Braun looked back. The military was even closer now. He could feel the ground rumbling with their speed.

John was standing on the beach as he sounded the horn, gathering the people to the land's edge.

As Braun traveled the last fifty yards of ice, he watched the people strike the land with their spears and staffs in rhythm. Excitement grew inside him. Another miracle was about to transpire!

The ground shook and the ice began to crack. Braun almost lost his footing as he jumped to the bank, but Chenille caught his hand and steadied him.

Braun heard the raging sounds of tumultuous water. He turned back to see massive amounts of sea water pouring into the ravine through large, gaping cracks. The vehicles, that looked to be about a hundred yards away, sputtered and stalled as the water engulfed them. Large chunks of ice broke loose hitting the sides of the tanks making them spin and grinding them to a halt. Men dove out of their machines onto the ice as the tanks disappeared beneath the currents. The ice was quickly breaking beneath the soldiers' feet. Some became stranded, calling for help on their radios, as others fell into the water and were sucked under. Bullets were fired into the air as the last man went under the water—then there were no mechanical sounds. The only sounds left were the shaking of the earth and the thumping of the sticks.

John lifted his arms in victory as the tribes broke out in adulation of a mighty God who had given them power over their adversaries.

"We're safe!" Braun said in Chenille's ear. Then he abruptly jumped in the air in uncontrolled excitement, yelling "Yes! Hey America, we're back!"

Birth

Provo, Utah
5:45 p.m.

Corrynne hit the combination on the remote that Brea had given her. The hatch in the ground opened. She took a quick look around to make sure no one was watching her, and then she quickly descended the stairs into Brea's home. She had to tell her that her grandmother and aunt had come to their little city. Corrynne knew Brea would be so excited! She had been very close to both of them. She'd want to see them now that it was dark outside.

"Brea!" called Corrynne, down the dark hall after the door had closed again. "Brea! ...Where are you? Jax?"

"Ahhhh!"

The hair on Corrynne's neck rose. That was Brea's voice! Corrynne rushed down the hall. "Brea! What's wrong?"

"Ahhhh! Mom! ...Help me!"

Corrynne ran through the dining room, then the living room, to the hall, and finally the bedroom. "Brea! Where are you? Where's Jax?"

"Mom!" came another cry. *"Mom!"* there was terror in her voice.

Corrynne entered the bedroom to see Brea on the air hammock. Blood streaked the sheets that were crumpled at Brea's feet. "What's happened?"

"Mom!" cried Brea. "My baby!"

Shock hit Corrynne. "Your baby? *Did you have a baby?*"

"Mom! Help me! *Ahhh!*" yelled Brea again. "I'm having the second one," she said, pushing and shaking. "I couldn't call you. I couldn't do anything!"

"It's OK," said Corrynne, frantically rummaging through the sheets, looking for the infant. "I'm here now, baby. It's OK." Then she saw the infant. It was a boy! He was hidden in the mass of sheets. Pulling him out, she said, "You had a boy, Brea!" she said happily until she realized that the baby wasn't breathing and a dark purple-blue.

"Mom! Is he OK?" Brea asked. "He didn't cry!"

Corrynne panicked for a moment. She wasn't a labor and delivery nurse. She didn't know what to do first. No oxygen, no heating lamps, what was she going to do? Corrynne forced herself to think rationally. She had to stop the blood flowing out of the placenta. Quickly, Corrynne crossed the cord on top of itself and shoved the placenta through the hole, tying a simple knot. That would have to do until she could find scissors. Right now, getting the baby to breathe was more important than detaching the cord.

Corrynne held the infant up by its heels and gave it a slap on the bum. She needed to shock him into taking a breath of air.

"Mom! Please help me!" said Brea. "The second baby's coming."

Corrynne assessed Brea. The baby was crowning but not born yet. "You're doing so well, Brea. Keep pushing," she said as she took her pinky and felt in the baby's mouth. There was mucous plugging the airway. She cleared the baby's throat and hit his bum again. He still didn't cry.

"Is the baby OK?" asked Brea as she panted between pushes.

"I'm not sure, Brea. He's not breathing."

"Mom, help him!"

"I'm trying," said Corrynne as she laid the baby on the bed and began to breathe into his mouth and nose. She met resistance to her breath. She couldn't get the lungs to inflate. Again she raised him up by his heels and hit his bum. "Breathe, baby! Breathe!" Corrynne encouraged.

"Mom! I think the next baby is coming!" Brea screamed in pain.

Suddenly, the little boy gasped and whimpered.

"Brea! He's breathing! He's breathing!" said Corrynne, her body shaking violently with adrenalin. She began crying with joy! "Cry, baby!" encouraged Corrynne again. "Cry!" she spanked his bottom again to get that gasp reflex.

The baby boy cried again, harder this time. His lip quivered as he gasped for a third time and let out a robust yell. His skin quickly turned from blue to pink on his face and torso. Now only his arms, legs and feet were blue.

"Brea! This is wonderful!" said Corrynne, as she pulled the baby close to her, but then she realized he was cold. Way too cold.

"Mom!" yelled Brea. "It's coming! My little girl is coming!"

"Hold on, Brea!" said Corrynne. "Let's get this guy warm. The best place for him is on your stomach. It's warm there."

"I can't," said Brea, shaking her head. "I can't do this anymore!"

"Yes, you can," said Corrynne, as she placed the little one gently on Brea's abdomen, face up. "You're strong!"

"I need to push, Mom!" said Brea, as Corrynne unbuttoned Brea's blouse until the infant's perfect face peaked out the top. She placed a blanket over both of them.

"Then push, sweetheart," said Corrynne, as she assessed Brea's progress. The baby's head had been delivered and now was rotating to allow the shoulders to be born. "Push, Brea! Your little girl is almost here! Push hard!"

Brea took a big breath and bore down, letting out a little scream as her second child shot into Corrynne's hands.

The little girl let out a little sigh immediately and then, taking a great gasp, began to cry.

"This one breathed on her own!" said Corrynne in delight. "That's a very good sign!"

Brea started crying as she looked at her second baby and then back down to her little son, who was looking at her with tranquil eyes. "They're beautiful!" she cried.

"Yes, they are," said Corrynne, holding the girl up in the light so she could look at her fine features. "Just perfect little babies. You did well!"

Placing the little girl's body under a blanket to keep her warm, Corrynne searched for a string. She needed to tie off this placenta. She searched the floor for an odd length of string or floss, but Brea's room was impeccably clean. There was nothing she could use anywhere. Then she had an idea. She reached up and ripped the elastic out of her hair, breaking it, and then tied it around the cord, cinching it tight.

Next, Corrynne wrapped the little girl in the blanket and placed her in Brea's arms. "And here's your little girl," said Corrynne, smiling and crying at the same time. "You did it, baby! You did it! You're a Momma!"

The lights flickered twice.

"What's happening, Mom?" asked Brea, as she looked around.

Corrynne shook her head, looking at the lights. "I don't know, sweetheart."

Suddenly, the lights went out.

Pillar of Salt

Jerusalem, Israel
11:20 a.m.

"'Ye are the salt of the earth,'" exclaimed Elder Strauss, with his hands out wide. He was addressing an angry mob of Ultra-Orthadox Jewish men at the Wailing Wall. "'But if the salt has lost his savour, wherewith shall it be salted? It is thenceforth good for nothing but to be cast out and to be trodden under foot of men! These are the words of our Savior concerning those that claim to be God's but have fallen by the way. Ye have fallen by the way. Come back to truth."

"Zol er krenken un gedenken!" yelled a man with gritted teeth, from the center of the Jewish mob.

"What's that, again?" asked Conrad to Elder Bandar, as he took his last step backwards until his back was up against the stones of the wall.

"I think he said, 'Let him suffer and remember,'" said the apostle out the side of his mouth.

"Who was he talking to?" asked Conrad, nervously. "Because it looks like he's talking to me. Why would he be talking to me? Elder Strauss was the one preaching!"

"Stay calm, Elder."

"OK," said Conrad as he inched sideways along the wall of the temple, as he laughed nervously. He was praying a secret door might open, so he could escape. "Yeah, right, stay calm. Let me out of here and I'll stay calm," he muttered under his breath.

A baseball sized stone flew out of the midst of the crowd, hitting the wall beside Conrad. With wide eyes, he stared at the indention the rock made in the wall. "Stay calm, you say? That was a big rock. Elder Bandar, did you see that rock?" he asked looking back at the wild eyes of the men pressing in on them, and then back to the Elder that stood fearlessly to his right.

"Stand strong," said Elder Bandar. "You are a messenger of the Lord."

"Even messengers get scared!" said Conrad as another stone flew at his face. He ducked at the last moment. "What are we going to do when those stones come at us faster?" he asked, looking at the apostle with wide eyes. "I mean, I'm pretty good at dodge ball, but this—this is ridiculous!"

Suddenly, there was a hot flash of light. Conrad ducked and covered his face.

Silence...The mob quieted. Something had happened.

Conrad opened an eye a sliver to see a different scene. The men weren't yelling or waving sticks above their heads, they were staring listlessly at pile of white sand-like material.

"What's that stuff?" asked Conrad, as she stood slowly.

Elder Bandar put a hand around Conrad's shoulder and said, "It's time to go."

Conrad nodded slowly as he was guided out of the clutches of the mob that parted easily, without further contention. He still wasn't sure what had happened. "Did that man turn to dust?" he whispered, now understanding more.

Elder Strauss kept a straight face and said, "He lost his savour."

Conrad's eyes grew wide. *"Holy Cow!"* he exclaimed.

"Keep walking, Elder," encouraged Elder Bandar. "Just keep walking."

To be continued...

Note to the Reader:

Often the question is asked, "How do you know in what order things will happen before the coming of Christ?" The answer is, I don't. I do my best to compare scriptures and make assumptions. For example: When are the lost tribes going to return? That's a tricky question. There are some views that the lost tribes won't return until after Christ has come again due to some of the language in D&C 133. However, I have learned the scriptures don't always discuss things in chronological order. The Lord often jumps back and forth in time between verses in all the standard works, and why not? He isn't bound by our time. So that knowledge always leads me to unending dilemmas. To solve those, I prayerfully look to the scriptures and prophetic statements, and then seek the companionship of the Spirit as I unravel it all.

In light of this process, I have chosen to have the lost tribes return *before* Christ returns, for the following reasons:

In D&C 133: 26-32 and Jacob 5:21, the Lord seems to be describing our present world geography when he describes the place the lost tribes will travel from: a place of ice, poor land, a "north" country, crossing on a highway from the great deep, the deserts yielding their water, the hills shaking, leading them to the tribe of Ephraim. This journey would be described differently if the earth had already burned, been renewed, re-shaped so that all the land masses were back together and had become a paradise, for this will be the state in the Millennium, after Christ's return.

In D&C 133:28, it says that the lost tribes' enemies will be prey to them. This must mean enemies exist. If Christ had already returned, the enemies of the tribes, or those who could not stand at his coming, would have been burned at his coming.

In 3 Nephi 21:23, we learn that the lost tribes, being a remnant of Jacob, will help in the building of New Jerusalem and the temple. Of course, this temple will be built before Christ's return.

Let us not forget that the lost tribes must be present in the New Jerusalem when Christ makes his visit to Adam-Ondi-Ahmen in Missouri. At that time, 12,000 from each of the 12 tribes of Jacob will be selected to become the 144,000 spoken of in Revelation 7. Of course, this also occurs before Christ comes to the world to establish his kingdom.

So am I right? I hope so. I intend my storylines to be as consistent with revealed knowledge as possible, but honestly, in the grand scheme of things, it doesn't matter. The concrete details of Christ's return, the dates, the places, the hows and whens, don't matter as much as the gospel, our spiritual growth and the introspection that leads us to be ready for that day. My books are fiction not only because the characters and their lives are fiction, but also because there are so many unknown relationships of time between one event and another. In order to sculpt a believable story, however, I must, in some cases, make a leap—a literary extrapolation, as I have called it in the past, to fill in the gaps.

So, how do I know what's going to happen in the future? I read and study like you, searching, praying, and feasting upon the word of Christ. My intention is never to predict the future, but to simply apply what has been revealed to aid us all further preparation for the days that will surely come. May we all partake of the truth and live, as promised—*happily ever after*! ☺

MILLENNIAL GLORY VIII

HE

IS

COMING!

Look for it

Christmas,2008!

www.millennialglory.com

AUTHOR
WENDIE L. EDWARDS

Wendie L. Edwards, the author of the "Millennial Glory" series, grew up in Edmonds, Washington. At Brigham Young University she met her husband Ted and they were sealed in the Seattle Temple. She taught early morning Seminary for the Lynnwood Stake in Washington. After five children, Ted and Wendie felt inspired to return to Brigham Young University where Ted received his Master's degree in Tax Accounting and Wendie graduated Cum Laude with a Bachelor's degree in Nursing. Wendie has been an Intensive Care nurse for twelve years and holds a CCRN certification. Ted and Wendie reside in Cedar Hills with their seven sons and two daughters.

EDITOR
KATHRYN PACKER

Kathryn Packer, the editor of The Millennial Glory Series, is a BYU-Hawaii graduate with a B.S. in Information Systems and Computer Science. She is a technical writer and trainer by day and uses her memberships in the Society for Technical Communication and the American Society for Training & Development to keep her updated in current trends. Kathryn spent most of her growing up years on a small farm in Idaho raising sheep and other small animals with her 5 siblings. She currently resides in Bothell, Washington. Her true passions include traveling, music, quilting, reading, and fine art, not necessarily in that order.

STUDENT EDITOR
KATE MARYON

Kate Maryon is a soon-to-be graduate of Brigham Young University and is currently getting her degree as an English major with an emphasis in editing. She grew up in Orem, Utah and is the oldest of three kids. Books are the true love of her life, but she also enjoys music, movies, hiking, and theater. She is truly grateful for the opportunity to help in the production of the Millennial Glory books!